P. Müller and W. Rumpf

Modern World Fact and Fiction

Volume III:
Man and Economy
Man and Humanities
Man and Belief

Kollegstufe/Abitur/Universität

manz
MANZ VERLAG MÜNCHEN

Herausgegeben von Ute Kretschmann

CIP-Kurztitelaufnahme der Deutschen Bibliothek

Modern world – fact and fiction: Kollegstufe, Abitur, Univ. / P. Müller u. W. Rumpf. – München: Manz
NE: Müller, Peter [Hrsg.]
Vol. 3. Man and economy, man and humanities, man and belief. [Schülerbd.]. – 1. Aufl. – 1987.
ISBN 3-7863-0539-0

Manzbuch 539

6 5 4 3 2 1   1991 90 89 88 87
(Die jeweils letzte Zahl bezeichnet die Auflage bzw. das Erscheinungsjahr)

© 1987 by Manz Verlag, München. Nach dem Urheberrechtsgesetz vom 9. September 1965 i. d. F. vom 10. November 1972 ist die Vervielfältigung oder Übertragung urheberrechtlich geschützter Werke, also auch die Texte dieses Buches, nicht gestattet. Dieses Verbot erstreckt sich auch auf die Vervielfältigung für Zwecke der Unterrichtsgestaltung – mit Ausnahme der in den §§ 53, 54 URG ausdrücklich genannten Sonderfälle –, wenn nicht die Einwilligung des Verlages vorher eingeholt wurde. Im Einzelfall muß über die Zahlung einer Gebühr für die Nutzung fremden geistigen Eigentums entschieden werden. Als Vervielfältigungen gelten alle Verfahren einschließlich der Fotokopie, der Übertragung auf Matrizen, der Speicherung auf Bändern, Platten, Transparenten oder anderen Medien.
Umschlagentwurf: Ingeburg Rothemund, München
Gesamtherstellung: Verlag und Druckerei G. J. Manz AG, München/Dillingen
Printed in Germany

ISBN 3-7863-0539-0

TABLE OF CONTENTS

Preface 5

I Man and Economy

1. *Thatcher and Mitterrand Agree on Rail Tunnel . . . . The Times 7
2. Unemployment . . . . Jeremy Seabrook . . 23
3. Unions: a Burnt-Out Case . . . . Time Magazine 39
4. Player Piano . . . . Kurt Vonnegut 48
5. What is 'Capitalism? . . . . Max Weber, Adam Smith, Milton D. Friedman . . 56
6. Time Machine . . . . H. G. Wells 70
7. The Marks Saving Marx . . . . The Times 85
8. Who Protects the Consumer? . . . . . . Milton D. Friedman . . 95
9. The Room . . . . Ray Russel 105
10. How to Persuade the Consumer (Various advertisements) . . . . . Business Week, Discover, South, Time 109
11. Action Now . . . . Franklin D. Roosevelt 117
    (Title changed by the editors)
12. The Dispossessed . . . . Ursula LeGuin 129
13. Dismissal of a Salesman . . . . Arthur Miller 134
    (Title changed by the editors)
14. *Lee Iacocca: The American Dream Personified . . . . Lee Iacocca 150
    (Title changed by the editors)
15. No Matter how Great the Risk . . . . . . Spotlight 167
16. Utopia . . . . Thomas Morus . . . 170
17. The Underdevelopment of US Agriculture. . Frances Moore-Lappé 176
18. *No, Mac, it just wouldn't Work . . . . . . Robert Graves 187

II Man and Humanities

19. Interview with Arnold Wesker . . . . News of the World . . 191
20. Dictatorship of the Will . . . . The Times 197
21. Country of the Kind . . . . D. Knight 202
22. The State of the Language . . . . Philip Howard 208
23. Flowers for Algernon . . . . D. Keyes 222
24. And he Gave you the Ball, eh? . . . . . . Arthur Miller 233
    (Title changed by the authors)
25. Fahrenheit 451 . . . . R. Bradbury 240
26. The American School System: Facts and Problems . . . . College catalogues and other material 247

III Man and Belief

27	The Lure of Doomsday	Time Magazine	255
28	The Answer	F. Brown	263
29	The Star	Arthur Clarke	268
30	The Star of Bethlehem Mystery	David Hughes	273

* Easy Texts

Abbreviations Used:

abbr.	abbreviation	mil.	military
adj.	adjective	n.	noun
Br.	Britain	N.B.	observe carefully (L. nota bene)
cf.	confer, compare, see		
cp.	compare	no.	number
coll.	colloquial	op. cit.	in the work cited (L. opere citato)
ed.	editor		
eds.	editors	p.	page
e.g.	for example (L. exempli gratia)	pp.	pages
esp.	especially	pl.	plural
et al.	and others (L. et alii)	s.b.	somebody
ex.	example	sf	science fiction
exs.	examples	sing.	singular
f.	and the following page	sl.	slang
ff.	and the following pages	s.o.	someone
Fr.	French	s.th.	something
fig.	not used in the literal sense	US	United States
ibid.	in the same place (L. ibidem)	usu.	usually
i.e.	that is (L. id est)	vol.	volume
L.	Latin	vols.	volumes
loc. cit.	in the place cited (L. loco citato)		

The illustration on p. 78 was drawn by the young artist Michael Brückner from Schriesheim.

> LOMAX: D'you ever read science fiction, Best?
> BEST: No, Sir.
> LOMAX: We'd better start . . . to catch up on fact.

From: N. Kneale, *The Quatermass Experiment,* A Play for Television in Six Parts, Penguin Books, Ltd., Harmondsworth, Middlesex, 1959, p. 52.

PREFACE

The three volumes of *Modern World, Fact and Fiction* are primarily intended for use in courses of advanced classes at the Gymnasium, starting with Klasse 11. They contain texts and tasks of graded levels of difficulty. They may, however, also be used for private study or for university courses at an introductory level.

When planning this book we had in mind a fourfold aim:

Firstly, we did not want to cover what in our schools is called "Landeskunde", but we did want to treat a vast array of modern subjects and fields that are relevant and important for our world, including art, biology, economy, education, emancipation, politics, psychology, sociology, technology, and theology.

Secondly, we wanted to throw light upon these subjects by contrasting fact and fiction. Factual texts are balanced by and contrasted with fictional texts, more specifically with science fiction (sf) texts; these permit us to look at our world and its current problems from a more detached standpoint, and thus make them clearer and more comprehensible. As, increasingly, our future itself becomes a problem, it seems appropriate to give such a role to sf texts.

Here, we might mention the fact that main-stream-literature, has, in general, so far shirked treating the problems that beset our world: problems such as overpopulation, computerization, and genetic manipulation. Sf, however, does tackle them, and helps train us in those "exercises of the imagination", of which H. G. Wells wrote, in intellectual experiments, models and analyses. It can thus strengthen both our intellectual flexibility and our insight. Furthermore, we trust that the inclusion of literary texts will, to some extent, delay the onset of outdatedness.

Thirdly, our aim was to include and embrace a great variety of different kinds of texts and registers. Thus, the reader will find short stories, extracts from novels and plays, poems, newspaper and magazine articles, interviews, essays, cartoons, and so on. Together with a wide range of vocabulary we wanted to present the student with a fair cross-section of different styles and speech-levels, different ways of writing and expressing ideas.

Fourthly, this reader has been designed as a workbook. A number of systematic exercises and assignments has been added to help the student cope with the contents of the texts, and with relevant literary, linguistic and grammatical problems. Grammar exercises are included in the teacher's book (from which they may be copied). Exercises in role play, in essay writing and in translation (elsewhere unduly neglected!) further increase the scope of our assignments.

In order to ease the strain on the student working with this reader it has been "spiced" with puns, wordgames and jokes of different kinds, which we trust will provide a measure of "comic relief". These, of course, also provide tips and suggestions for students (and for teachers) to make up their own, and thus to work with English as a foreign language in a playful and creative way!

We express our gratitude to all those friends and colleagues who helped us develop and finish this project. Our very special thanks go to Mr. Hermann Schulz, Studiendirektor in Schriesheim, who provided us with the preposition exercises used in the book, and to Dr John Worthen, Senior Lecturer in English literature at the University College of Swansea, who read and checked the manuscript from the native speaker's point of view.

Weinheim, August 1987   P. Müller

Schriesheim, August 1987   W. Rumpf

I MAN AND ECONOMY

1 THATCHER AND MITTERRAND AGREE ON RAIL TUNNEL

Historic meeting gives force to Napoleonic vision

- The Prime Minister and President Mitterrand gave the go-ahead for a Channel tunnel rail link opening in 1993, with no chance of a road link before 2006.
- British Rail, the railway unions and freight organisations welcomed yesterday's announcement while road traffic and Kent environmental interests condemned it.
- Building of the 32-mile fixed link with two single-track tunnels will be this country's biggest civil engineering project with immense challenges on meeting time and cost targets.

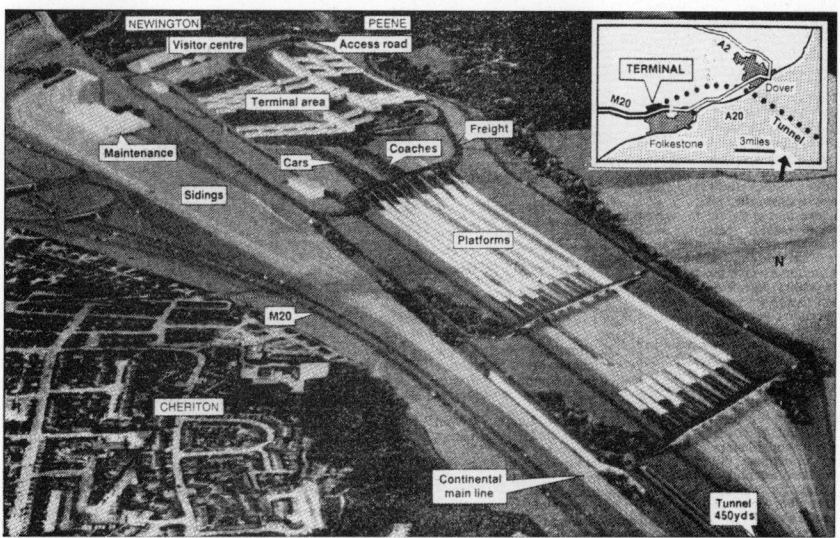

Model of the proposed tunnel access terminal and marshalling area near Cheriton, Kent
Source: *The Times,* Jan. 21, 1986

MPs voice reservations

CHANNEL TUNNEL
The announcement of the proposed Channel tunnel received a mixed reaction from MPs when **Mr Nicholas Ridley,** Secretary of State for Transport, made a statement in the Commons about the Lille decision.
Some MPs saw it as an opportunity for the creation of jobs, particularly Kent. Others saw it as drawing work and jobs away from the north and Scotland. One spoke of widening the north-south divide.
Mr Ridley said the Cabinet was united in the decision to have a twin-bore rail link. He said a White paper would be published shortly and a hybrid Bill introduced allowing interested parties to make representation to MPs and peers. A special committee would be established to consider points of local concern and difficulty.
Mr Ridley said: The Prime Minister and the President of France, meeting earlier today in Lille, announced the decision of the two Governments to take together the necessary steps to facilitate the construction of a fixed link across the Channel by the Channel Tunnel Group . . .
CTG's is a well developed project, relying on well proven technology. It offers a fast and efficient rail shuttle service, for road passengers and freight, with very frequent departures and no booking.
It presents no problems to maritime traffic in the Channel and is not very vulnerable to terrorist attack. Its environmental impact can be reduced to an acceptable level.
The Government concluded that CTG was the best scheme to go forward to the market.
The Government remains very much aware of the arguments that the public would like a drive-through link. In due course the conditions may arise when a drive-through link would be viable.
We have therefore secured an undertaking from the CTG that they will put forward by the year 2000 a proposal for a drive-through link, to be undertaken as soon as its technical feasibility is assured, and economic circumstances and the growth of traffic allow it to be financed without undermining the return on the original link.
At a later stage, the Governments will be free to invite competitive bids for a further link coming into operation not before 2020.
I expect the signature of the Anglo-French treaty to take place in February and the concession agreement between the Governments and the Channel Tunnel Group to be concluded shortly thereafter. The legislation will then be introduced into this House as soon as possible. Construction could begin by summer 1987.
Consultations in Kent have so far focussed on the question of which scheme the government should adopt. We must now concentrate upon making the chosen scheme as acceptable as possible. We will want to minimize the environmental impact, and to consider carefully the employment consequences of this develop-

ment. We will be sympathetic if problems seem likely to arise in east Kent when
the link opens some seven years from now.

We must arrive at satisfactory arrangements with the promoters for the disposal of spoil and on other environmental matters and we will ensure that the necessary road infrastructure is provided. The White Paper will deal with these questions.

The Channel Tunnel is a massive and difficult project. It will be a challenge to our engineers, our technicians and our financial institutions. Equally I believe it will be of great benefit to travellers and exporters alike in giving them cheaper, quicker and more reliable access to the continent of Europe.

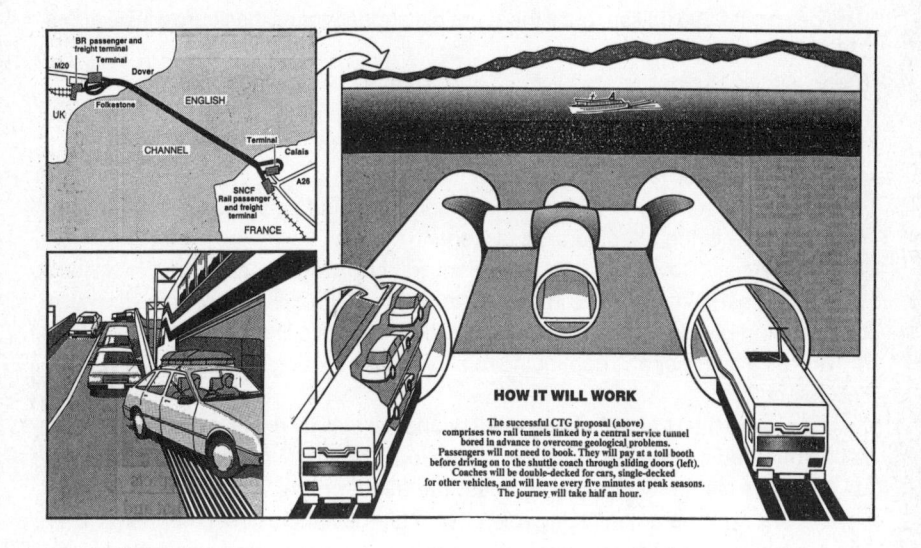

HOW IT WILL WORK

The successful CTG proposal (above) comprises two rail tunnels linked by a central service tunnel bored in advance to overcome geological problems. Passengers will not need to book. They will pay at a toll booth before driving on to the shuttle coach through sliding doors (left). Coaches will be double-decked for cars, single-decked for other vehicles, and will leave every five minutes at peak seasons. The journey will take half an hour.

Mr Robert Hughes, Chief Opposition spokesman on transport, said that in rushing this decision through on such a tight timescale Mr Ridley had broken his promise that he would publish a White Paper on the day the decision was announced.

I suspect (he added) this will not be the last of his broken promises.

What guarantee had Mr Ridley that the British share of construction costs would be spent on British goods and that British labour would be employed on the project? Would Mr Ridley produce an investment plan in conjunction with British Rail so that BR could maximise the opportunities that the link may offer?

Mr Ridley: I am not clear if Mr Hughes is in favour of the link or not. I will publish the White Paper giving the mass of the information required. I hope within a week or soon after that.

Objectors to the scheme would be able to present their case as petitioners before the select committee.

A good deal has been done between British and French railways and between them and the promoters which will bring large-scale orders of rolling stock. I am sure that all those concerned on the British side will do their utmost to provide as many jobs on this side of the Channel as they can.

Mr Stephen Ross (Isle of Wight, L): We welcome the decision. The environmental impact can be cut to suitable level only if British Rail have adequate capital resources to make full use of the whole network. Will Mr Ridley persuade the select committee to hold hearings in Dover or Folkestone or both because local people should be able to make their views heard?

British Rail will require massive investment. If there are conventional speed trains it will be about £290 million, but if there are high speed trains the figure will be about £390 million.

There will be further investment in the shuttle rail equipment which will be undertaken by the CTG itself so there are some large orders. It opens up great new opportunities for the railway system, extending right from the north of our country into the farthest corners of Europe.

He hoped the select committee on the hybrid Bill would be prepared to travel and hear evidence in the affected area of Kent.

Mr Peter Rees (Dover, C): His statement will not allay the deep and legitimate concern in east Kent about the implications of a fixed link, will he recognize the need for close and continuing consultation with local interests likely to be affected?

Will there be a proper and continuing role for the ferries and the ports of Dover and Folkestone?

Can he assure the House that any extra economic activity generated by a fixed link will be retained in east Kent and not drawn to northwest France?

Mr Ridley: I cannot accurately forecast the effect on the ferries and ports but I believe there will be a continuing role even after the link has been opened. Dover has the whole of the longer distance routes as well as the short sea routes.

Growth in traffic is expected to be very great and I am sure the ferries will have a share of that. I am certain that many people would prefer to choose one mode of transport rather than another.

I believe that this huge new artery when opened will take an immense amount of passengers as well as trade between the Continent and this country and will act as a sort of magnet for new development and investment. If the planning policies of local authorities are rightly handled, great opportunities for extra development could take place in the east Kent area.

Mr Donald Stewart (Western Isles, SNP): Some of us will see this proposal as the biggest election bribe in history.

Mr Ridley: There is great benefit to constituents throughout the country. These are not Government funds which could be spent in some other direction. A lot of this money is international money. A lot of it is in capital which only goes to projects which it chooses and cannot be directed elsewhere.

Mr David Howell (Guildford, C), a former Secretary of State for Transport, said the Government had made far the best and most sensible choice.

This is the one scheme (he went on) which ensured that there will be a substantial growth of the traffic still going to the ferry operators. Would he say a word about plans for streamlining Customs and Immigration, particularly the possibility of on-train Customs handling?

Mr Ridley: I welcome his support. With this particular choice the opportunities for continuing ferry operations are very great, although it is difficult to be specific about the precise amount of that.

On Customs and immigration, we are working hard and still hope to find ways of improving the service through the link, but we will have to have both Customs and immigration for many reasons, including the prevention of disease and plant and animals coming through the link. There will have to be some control.

I am keen that there should not be a special arrangement for the through trains through the link which would be competitively disadvantageous to the ferries or other forms of transport.

Sir Julian Ridsdale (Harwich, C): Mr Ridley's optimism about the future of the ferries is not shared by some of the ferry operators.

Mr Ridley: I know some of the ferry operators are more pessimistic than I have been about their prospects. It will be seven or eight years before any link is opened and the massive growth in traffic which should be generated will bring them considerable extra business in the meantime.

Mr Bruce Millan (Glasgow Govan, Lab): This will suck further economic activity into southern England, the last place that needs it. It is just another project that will widen the north-south divide.

Mr Ridley said the order for rolling stock and other manufacturing work would benefit the whole country. Cheapening and quickening of exports and imports would improve competitiveness.

Mr Roland Boyes (Houghton and Washington, Lab) said instead of spending billions digging a hole in the ground the money should be used to encourage building of houses, hospitals and schools.

Abbreviated from *THE TIMES,* January 21, 1986

(~ 1610 words)

Annotations
(The words marked * should be memorized.)

***access** way to a place – – **access road** road giving access – – ***coach** *here:* long-distance, single-decker motor-bus – – **to give force** make actual the realization of sth. – – ***freight** the carriage of goods – – ***maintenance** *here:* workers who keep the tunnel and access roads in good working order – – **siding** short railway track to and from which trains may be shunted; Rangiergleis – – ***single-track** one line only, with traffic in one direction only – – **target** *here:* plan – – ***terminal** end of railway line, bus line, etc. – – **marshalling area** railway area in which goods trains, etc. are assembled – – **twin-bore rail link** railway connection with two tunnels running parallel – – **hybrid bill** ['haɪbrɪd] proposal with several parts put forward to Parliament – – **to make representation to** offer criticism, suggestions concerning a problem to s.b. – – ***to facilitate** make easier – – ***shuttle service** service (of trains, buses, etc.) to and fro between places not far apart – – **vulnerable** liable to be damaged – – **impact** *here:* negative effect – – **drive-through link** road traffic connection – – **in due course** at the time when it is favourable – – **viable** *here:* economically possible – – **to secure an undertaking** *here:* succeed in getting a guarantee – – **feasibility** ability to do s.th. – – **return** *here:* profit on an investment or undertaking – – **bid** offer; tender – – **to focus on** concentrate on – – **sympathetic** verständnisvoll – – **promoters** people or firm who support some project, event, etc. financially and argue for its execution – – **spoil** *here:* earth, unwanted material, etc. thrown or brought up in excavating – – **in conjunction with** together with – – **petitioner** citizen who submits written statement supported by Members of Parliament – – **rolling stock** railway's coaches, wagons, etc. – – **to allay** [ə'leɪ] make (e.g. pain, trouble, etc.) less – – ***bribe** s.th. given, offered or promised to s.b. in order to influence or persuade him in favour of the giver – – **constituents** voters living in a town or district that sends a representative to Parliament – – **to streamline** make more efficient – – ***Customs** Zoll – – **to suck** *here:* channel

WORKSHEET

1. **Language**
1.1 Collect all words and expressions from the two texts that can be grouped under the *superordinates* (= general words that belong to word groups)

	transport and traffic	**parliamentary life**
exs.	rail tunnel	MP's (Members of Parliament)
	Go ahead	

1.2 Examine the text for collocations (here: verb + [preposition] noun combinations) of the expressions gathered in the assignment 1.

	expression	**collocation**
ex.	a rail tunnel	to agree on a rail tunnel
		Go ahead

1.3 Search the text for at least 10 adjective + noun combinations. Then try to replace the adjectives by others of same or similar meaning, or paraphrase them.

	collocation	replacement/paraphrase
ex.	environmental interests	ecological interests; interests that stress/serve the preservation of nature
		Go ahead

1.4 Paraphrase in your own words the following expressions and sentence fragments as far as possible: gave the go-ahead for a channel rail link; meeting time and cost targets; widening the north-south divide (l. 6); best scheme to go forward to the market (l. 20); concession agreement (l. 32); road infrastructure (l. 43); tight timescale (l. 49); large-scale orders (l. 63); on-train Customs handling (l. 108); through train (l. 116).

1.5.1 Our two texts above show a lot of so-called *compounds*, i.e. words which are composed of two or more "elementary words". Below you'll find a list of some possible combinations. Examine the texts for compound words which are in line with the types of compounds given in the list. Then translate the words into German.

	Type	**Example**
Noun	+ Noun	oil refinery
N	+ Verb	bus stop
N	+ Adjective	knee-deep
N	+ Particle	passer-by
N	+ Present Participle	book-keeping
N	+ Past Participle	hand-made
Pr.P.	+ N	washing machine
V	+ N	washday
Pronoun	+ N	she-goat
Par	+ N	on-looker
Par	+ V	intake
Par	+ Pr.P.	out-going
V	+ Par	take-off
V	+ Adj (Adverb)	go-slow
V	+ Adv	get-together
Adj (Adv)	+ Adj	icy-cold
Adj (Adv)	+ N	fast food
Adj (Adv)	+ Pr.P.	easy-going
Adj (Adv)	+ Pa.P.	ill-bred

1.5.2 Produce meaningful compounds (adjectives and nouns!) from the following "elementary" words: fellow, he, early, pick, life, off, man, apple, prince, swim, dish, riser, jacket, shore, pocket, time, colour, watch, table, crown, war, in, up, blind, washer, love, maker, crime, eating, start, self, goat, sauce. Look up what the compounds mean.

2. Contents

2.1 Are you good at solving puzzles? If so, you will have no difficulty in putting together 13 sentences from the sentence fragments listed in the three columns underneath. (Each sentence consists of three fragments!) Twelve sentences refer to the contents of the two texts on pages 7–11. The thirteenth is identical to the caption of one of the three cartoons below. (See *Further Studies*, 3.4.) To make the game more interesting, two of the cartoons are without captions. Thus, you will have to undertake the additional task of matching the solution to the right cartoon. (N.B. the *beginnings* of the sentences have been capitalized but full stops have been left out!)

The *sentence fragments:*

the advantages of the fixed rail link	The meeting of Prime Minister Thatcher and President Mitterrand	Why build a road Channel tunnel as long as
to build a fixed tunnel link between Great Britain and the continent	the latter could not be taken into consideration	because the agreement will put into reality a project
The British Government is convinced	Although the public would have preferred a drive-through link,	The Government decided in favour of the CTG's project
does not hamper maritime traffic and is the least vulnerable to terrorist attack	and answered critical questions	the travelling time will be reduced considerably
Moreover many other jobs	of which Napoleon already dreamed	will be created
is much safer and healthier for the passengers!	Some MPs are worried that	as a rail link
the ferry business will shrink	since it is the cheapest, relies on well-proven technology,	The tunnel decision

there will be a growth in traffic and more jobs for railwaymen	Some advantages are:	in the 20th century
The project will be built	in the construction industry and in feeder plants	due to financial and technical problems
Britain's most challenging civil engineering project	The construction of the tunnel will be	on 20 January 1986 in Lille resulted in an agreement
on 20 Jan. 1986	was discussed in Parliament	and the north-south divide will widen
It was a historic meeting	with two single-track tunnels	Nicholas Ridley, Secretary of State for Transport, explained
can be minimized	going by train	that the environmental impact

2.2 Now arrange the twelve sentences you found in their logical sequence as if you were going to write a summary. (The first starts with the words "The meeting . . .", the last ends with the words ". . . will widen".)

3. **Further Studies**
3.1 The MPs mentioned in our text belong to different parties, the names of which are given in short form. Do you know the full names of the parties in question?
3.2 Three students play the roles of British politicians of different parties who discuss the tunnel rail link. The Conservative supports the project, the other two are against it. A fourth student conducts the discussion. The rest of the class plays the audience, who put carefully worded questions to the "politicians". (You can make up additional pro and con arguments if you think it is helpful. Do not only concentrate on economic and political aspects, but discuss the environmental issues as well. The material below will give you further arguments.)

Britain's link with Europe

LAST JANUARY, Mrs. Thatcher and President Mitterrand met in France to make a final decision. Of the four options proposed, they agreed on the Channel Tunnel Group's (CTG) idea for a twin-track rail tunnel which includes a drive-on/drive-off rail shuttle service. The CTG's proposal is the least expensive and best supported
5 financially. The disadvantage of their plan is that it does not include a direct road link, which most Britons favour, but they have agreed to plan one for the future. The sudden enthusiasm for the Channel link is easily explained: rising unemploy-

ment in both countries and forthcoming elections. The Chunnel would be a dream come true for both Mrs. Thatcher and President Mitterrand. More than 30,000 jobs
10 on either side of the Channel would be created during the five year construction period. There is also the added bonus that the project can be funded privately, by banks and big businesses.
NOT everyone is pleased about a Channel link. Protesters say that the project only provides short-term jobs and Dover will become a ghost town as 40,000 jobs will
15 be lost at ports and ferries. Trade unions are divided depending on whether they represent seamen, whose jobs are at risk, or railway and construction workers, whose job prospects should improve. Yet the main debate seems to be not whether there should be a link, but whether there should be a public inquiry.
In any case, construction work cannot be started immediately. First of all, a report
20 for Parliament must be produced and legislation drawn up. Then an Anglo-French treaty must be signed. So, at the earliest, construction could begin by late 1987. That is, if there are no strikes and neither government walks away from the project.
If the project does go ahead, the Channel link will dramatically change existing travel patterns. Some say it will also sharpen the poor North/rich South divide in Britain.
25 There will also be dramatic changes in the existing rail services between London, Paris and other European capitals. The journey from London to Paris should be cut from over five hours today (using ferries) to about 3 hours 30 minutes.
Journeys with the car will certainly be quicker – 30 minutes by rail shuttle or driving, against 50 minutes by ferry. Ironically, the one question still to be answered is
30 whether journeys will be cheaper.
The threat of a terrorist attack and the risk of rabies spreading across from the Continent are just two of the arguments made against the Channel Tunnel. But not once has the risk of invasion by French troops been mentioned. That, perhaps, is what they call progress.

THE GUARDIAN (ADAPTED)

Vocabulary
(The words marked * should be memorized.)

***LINK** Verbindung – – ***to turn s.th. down** e-e S. zur.weisen, ablehnen – – ***actually** [ˈæktʃuəli] wirklich – – ***site** (Bau)Stelle – – **fierce** heftig – – ***false start** [fɔːls] Fehlstart, -schlag – – **to make a final decision** e-e endgültige Entscheidung treffen – – ***option** [ˈɔpʃən] (Aus)Wahlmöglichkeit – – **twin-track rail tunnel** doppelter Eisenbahntunnel (**twin-track** zweigleisig) – – **rail shuttle service** Beförderung v. Personen, Pkw, Busse u. Lkw durch Züge im Pendelverkehr – – ***to favour** [ˈfeivə] bevorzugen – – ***enthusiasm** [inˈθjuːziæzəm] – – ***to create** schaffen – – **added bonus** Pluspunkt – – **to fund** finanzieren.
NOT . . . To provide sorgen für, bieten – – ***short-term** kurzfristig, befristet – – ***trade union** Gewerkschaft – – ***divided** uneinig; s. w. u.: **divide** Teilung; Gefälle – – ***to be at risk** auf d. Spiel stehen – – **prospect** [ˈ– –] Aussicht – – ***public inquiry** öffentl. Untersuchung.
To draw up legislation [ledʒisˈ – –] e-e Gesetzesgrundlage schaffen – – **to go ahead** durchgeführt werden – – **travel pattern** Reiseverhalten – – **to sharpen** verschärfen, -tiefen – – **ironically** [aiˈ– – – –] – – ***threat** [θret] Gefahr – – **rabies** [ˈreibiːz] Tollwut – – **argument** [ˈɑːgjuˑ–] – – ***to mention** [ˈmenʃən] erwähnen.

16

The impact of the Chunnel on the environment

The Channel link, if it goes ahead, will change the face of East Kent and bring environmental change that no one yet can really imagine.

THE ENVIRONMENTAL IMPACTS ARE OF THREE TYPES:
- Effects on the natural environment and landscape;
5 - the disruption to the people and the land of the building period;
- the effects on the location of jobs and housing and travel patterns.

One big change in landscape will be to the Dover/Folkestone coastline. The attractive, white cliffs will be damaged by the Channel Tunnel. The chalk, mud and stone extracted from the sea bed will have to be dumped somewhere – the Channel
10 Tunnel Group has suggested a site on the coast. The effects of the tunnel on marine ecology are unknown.

There will be massive land development within the county of Kent. There will be a concentration of traffic in south-east Kent, as all roads will lead to the Tunnel. New motorway extensions, roads and railways will have to be built. This will mean the
15 loss of large areas of agricultural land – land which at present provides a home for several rare species of plants, insects and animals.

Towns and villages around the motorways to London will be greatly developed to provide warehouses, factories, firms and housing. Noise, dirt and traffic during the construction phase and afterwards in the villages and towns will be immense.
20 If the Tunnel is built as planned, the villages of Newington and Peene, for example, will be cut in two by a six-lane motorway, the village hall is likely to be bulldozed, a railway will be built on the eastern side, and the rugby field and allotment gardens will be turned into a railway yard for loading the rail shuttle.

Not surprisingly, then, most of the villagers and farmers, and of course the
25 environmentalists are against the Channel Tunnel project. They say there really must be a public inquiry. Perhaps, once again, they will be successful in stopping the building of the Chunnel (in 1974 they stopped its construction), although at present it seems unlikely.

THE GUARDIAN (ADAPTED) *Junior News,* März 1986

IMPACT on ['– –] Auswirkung auf – – **Chunnel** = gebildet aus **Ch(annel)** u. **(T)unnel** – – **environment** [inˈvaiərnmənt –] Umwelt, Umgebung; s. w. u.: **environmental** [invaiərənˈ– –]; **environmentalist** U.schützer – – **link** Verbindung – – **to go ahead** durchgeführt werden – – **disruption** [–ˈrʌpʃən] Störung – – **location** [loukeiʃən] Ortsbestimmung – – **travel pattern** Reiseverhalten – – **to damage** [dæmidʒ] beschädigen – – **chalk** Kreide – – **mud** Schlamm – – **to dump** abladen – – **site** Gelände – – **marine ecology** [məˈriːn iˈkɔlədʒi] Meeresökologie – – **development** Erschließung – – **motorway extension** [iksˈtenʃən] Verlängerung d. Autobahn – – **agricultural** [ægriˈkʌltʃərəl] – – **to provide a home** e-n Lebensraum bieten – – **species** [ˈspiːʃiːz] (pl.) Art(en) – – **warehouse** Lagerhaus – – **phase** [feiz] – – **six-lane** sechsspurig – – **village hall** Gemeindehaus – – **to bulldoze** durch e-n B. einebnen – – **allotment garden** Kleingarten – – **railway yard** Rangier-, Verschiebebahnhof – – **rail shuttle** Pendelzug – – **public inquiry** öffentl. Untersuchung.

3.3 Another three students make speeches about the parties in the United Kingdom. (History, political aims, leading persons, etc.). Two deal with the parties represented in Parliament. The third employs himself with the so-called "Extra-Parliamentary Parties" and the "Northern Irish Parties".
For reference use:
1) H. M. Drucker, *Multy-Party Britain,* The Macmillan Press Ltd, London 1979
2) Anthony Sampson, *The Changing Anatomy of Britain,* Hodder and Stoughton, London 1982
3) *Britain 1981,* HMSO, London 1981

3.4 Have a look at the following three cartoons dealing with the (fixed) link between Britain and the Continent. As you see two of them are left without captions. (See also assignment 2.1.) Make up appropriate captions. (Your teacher may award a good grade for the most interesting suggestions.)

a)

THE WORLD OF KEITH WAITE

"There were plenty of other ideas but that was the quickest solution."

Source: *Daily Mirror,* January 20, 1986

b)

c)

Source: *Time,* January 20, 1986

3.5 After reading the following two texts you'll understand why British Rail has always been the subject of cartoonists. Below you'll find three other cartoons. Match them with the appropriate text. Then fill in the balloon and the gaps in the captions.

A) Queen's train cracks under the strain

The Queen was given a personal view of how fast British Rail gets there yesterday. Her train, the 7.50 am from Kings Lynn to Liverpool Street, broke down eight times and arrived 43 minutes late.

British Rail said: "The delay was due to a locomotive failure which developed south of Cambridge. The engine was changed at Bishop's Stortford when the 8.35 am service from Liverpool Street to Kings Lynn, which was already running late, was terminated and the engine transferred to the Queen's train. The passengers on the 8.35 were transferred to the following train."

The Queen's problems, according to fellow passengers began at breakfast when it was discovered that the door between the breakfast car and the Queen's carriage was locked and that no one had a key.

A breakfast tray was whisked round (= brought hastily) by the platform when the train stopped in Ely, although British Rail refused to confirm that the breakfast was intended for the Queen.

"It is normal security procedure for the door to be locked, but when the breakfast steward wanted to serve someone in the royal party he could not obtain access. The door was opened after the train left Bishop's Stortford".

The train came to its first abrupt halt between Ely and Cambridge. It then made seven more unscheduled stops between Cambridge and Bishop's Stortford.

Because the driver and crew were directing all power to the traction motors, the carriages had no heating. Even so the train could not achieve more than 45 mph and on one section railwaymen walked alongside with flags, waving the train along.

Mr Rodney Collins, chairman of the Fen Line Users Association, who was on the train, said: "In 20 years of daily travelling this was my worst experience. It was a complete shambles (= confusion) and totally disorganized.

"There is not much hope for British Rail when they cannot even turn out a decent engine for the Queen".

Last Thursday, a guest of the Queen, Crown Prince Hassan of Jordan, was on a train which broke down at Broxbourne, Hertfordshire. He arrived more than an hour late for dinner at Sandringham.

From: *The Times,* 5 Febr., 1986

B) When running late can be profitable for all

SIR, – The rail-fare increase is perfectly justifiable, no doubt, but surely the ordinary passenger now, more than ever, has a right to expect good service.

I should like to suggest a way in which this might be achieved, through the use of partial refunds. The idea is that for every minute a train is late, each passenger gets a 5p refund, if travelling second class, and a 10p refund if travelling first class. This would be in the form of British Rail coupons, which could be put towards the price of the next ticket.

Thus, if a train was 20 minutes late, as timed by an independent arbitrator, such as a station clock or, better still, a town hall clock, a second-class passenger would get £1 off his next ticket.

IT MIGHT encourage more people to travel on British Rail, if skilfully advertised. A rider such as, "And remember, if we're late, you get a rebate," added to the usual train adverts, might help to tempt back some of the people who have abandoned trains because of the expense. At least it would stimulate curiosity.
15 It would help to keep people on British Rail; the coupons would be no good except for train travel, thereby encouraging them to buy more tickets to use up their coupons. And it might encourage British Rail to try to maintain a service where at least the trains run on time, if not cheaply.

READER'S LETTER IN *THE GUARDIAN*

Vocabulary
(The words marked * should be memorized.)

*to run late verspätet ankommen, Verspätung haben – – *profitable ['– – – –] vorteilhaft – – *railfare increase ['inkri:s] Erhöhung der Eisenbahn-Fahrpreise – – to be perfectly justifiable ['dʒʌstifaiəbl] völlig berechtigt sein, durchaus gerechtfertigt sein – – *ordinary gewöhnlich.
*To suggest vorschlagen, anregen – – *to achieve [ə'tʃi:v] erreichen – – partial refund(s) ['pɑ:ʃəl 'ri:fʌnd(z)] teilweise Rückerstattung – – British Rail staatl. brit. Eisenbahngesellschaft – – *coupon ['ku:pɔn] Gutschein – – to be put towards verrechnet werden mit – –
*Independent arbitrator ['ɑ:bi – –] unabhängige Schiedsstelle – – town hall Rathaus(-) – – *to get . . . off . . . Preisermäßigung erhalten.
IT MIGHT . . . To encourage a. p. [–'– –] 'jdn. ermuntern, – anreizen – – to be skilfully advertised ['æd– – –] geschickt propagiert werden – – rider Zusatzklausel, -zeile – – *to get a rebate ['ri:–] e-e Preisermäßigung erhalten, e-n Preisnachlaß erhalten – – advert = advertisement ['ædvə:t, əd'və:tis–] Anzeige, Reklame – – to tempt back zur.locken – – *to abandon aufgeben, verzichten auf – – *expense [–'–] Kosten (pl.) – – *to stimulate curiosity ['stimju– kjuəri'– – –] Neugierde erregen – – *to maintain aufrechterhalten – – to run on time pünktlich fahren – – if not cheaply wenn auch nicht billig, – preiswert.

a)

"Are we back to n . . . y or in the midst of chaos caused by unusual w . . . conditions?"

Source: *World & Press,* 1981

b)

Source: *The Times,* Febr. 5, 1986

c)

"IF YOU'RE ALL FOR THE 8·15 FROM GUILDFORD THEN YOU'RE ALL."

DRAWINGS: THE GUARDIAN (2)/PUNCH

Source: *World & Press,* 1981

2 UNEMPLOYMENT

Introducing the Topic

Source: *World and Press,* No 833, 1981

(To answer the following questions read the vocabulary below.)
1. Have a look at the cartoon above. What stunt is Prime Minister Thatcher trying to teach the people standing on the diving-board?
2. What's the man climbing the diving-board going to do, and why?
3. What's the reaction of the people to Mrs Thatcher's commands and the man's approach?

4. The words "unemployment", "dole", "*jobs* slops", and "*monetarist* stunts" show that the cartoon has a special message. Can you explain what it is?

Garland - after - Rembrandt

THE ANATOMY LESSON

Source: Nicholas Garland in *Karikatur in fünf Jahrhunderten – Bild als Waffe*

5. The second cartoon again shows Mrs Thatcher in a similar role. This time she is a professor giving a lesson in anatomy to her "students". What is the intention of her demonstration?
6. Why do the "students" react with surprise and open admiration? (Watch their faces!)
7. Can you explain who these "students" are?
8. On the right a book can be seen. Its open page gives the name "Milton Friedman". Why?
9. Sum up what you have found out about the second cartoon in 3 or 4 sentences.

Vocabulary
(referring to the cartoons)

diving-board flexible board from which to dive into a swimming pool – – **dole** here: weekly payment made under various Insurance Acts in GB (from contributions made by workers, employers and the State) to an unemployed worker; to be on the dole = stempeln gehen – – **Milton Friedman** American professor of Economics and Nobel Prize winner who is the leading proponent of *monetarism,* a neoliberal approach to economy, which aims to direct a country's economy through the provision of the "right" amount of money. It also emphasizes the cutting of government spending so that taxation can be reduced. (For further information on his theories consult Topic 5, text C on pp. 67–69) – – **monetarist** (adj.) referring to monetarism – – **pail** vessel, usu. round and open, of metal or wood, for carrying liquid – – **saw** Säge – – **skeleton** Skelett – – **(a pair of) scissors** Schere – – **slops** dirty waste water from the kitchen which is tipped down the drains – – **jobs slops** unattractive left-over jobs not taken by anybody else – – **stunt** action done to attract attention and involving high risk

Note on the Text

When Jeremy Seabrook's book *Unemployment* was first published in 1982, it was praised by critics as ". . . a book . . . which breaks the mould of British political writing" and compared with George Orwell's *The Road To Wigan Pier* written in the thirties. Indeed, like Orwell Seabrook undertakes to depict the plight of the British working-class, in particular the impact of unemployment on the workers' lives. He is at his best whenever he deals with the daily sorrows and problems of jobless people, whereas his theoretical explanations of capitalism are rather one-sided, dull and bloodless.
Besides *Unemployment* Jeremy Seabrook (1939, Northampton) has written about twenty plays for the stage, television and radio. His most important books are: *The Unprivileged* (100 years of working-class life in a Midland town), *City Close-Up* (about Blackburn, Lancashire), *What Went Wrong?* (working people and the ideals of the Labour movement) and *Mother and Son* (a memoir).
Our extract is taken from the Granada paperback, published in 1983.

On Thursday Mike goes to sign on. There is a line of about fifty people stretching out of the reinforced glass doors of the plain rectangular building. A few children, one or two with dogs, wait outside. The people in the queue do not speak to each other. Movement is slow; a slightly anxious shuffling, as each individual signs at
5 the counter, and then goes on to the desk, which is a sort of glass cage partitioned off from the main counter. The rubberized buff and paleblue floor tiles are covered with crushed cigarette ends and the imprint of muddy boots. You can tell which people in the queue have been out of work the longest: some wear clothes that were in fashion a few years ago – bell-bottomed trousers, parti-coloured imitation-suede
10 jackets, cork-heeled shoes.
Mike says, 'You always get nervous when you go to sign on. There's always the worry that your giro might not be there. You watch them fingering the bundle of giros behind each letter of the alphabet, and you think "What will I do if mine isn't there?" Only once it wasn't. It was terrible. They swore I'd come to the wrong place. You
15 panic, you don't know what you're doing, you can see the wife and kids without any grub. I had to go to Social Security. It was all sorted out, but it scared me.'
Inside the office there are a couple of blue plastic chairs, chained together. There is a notice board with a large poster of the Samaritans, inviting those close to despair to phone them. Mike sees me reading the notice and laughs. 'The reason why most
20 poor buggers'd want to phone them would be because they don't have the five

pence for the bloody phone call.' His laugh has a bitter edge in that silent shuffling crowd.

The post office is about a hundred yards away; and most of those go at once to cash their cheques. A few women are waiting outside. Mike says 'Hello' to one of them, a pale-faced thin woman of perhaps thirty-five, hair once dyed blonde, but darkening again at the roots, wearing an old blazer, torn jeans and plastic sandals. 'Her old man can't be trusted with a week's money in his fist. If she's not standing there when he gets paid, she'll not see a penny of it. They've got three kids.' Some of the children who were waiting outside the Department of Employment office run past, into the tobacconist's, and come out a minute or two later with ice lollies and packets of sweets. "That's their week's money gone," says Mike.

On Friday, Jean is going to a jumble sale at the church. The church is a red-brick building, dim with the soot of vanished industry. The church hall adjoins it, and there is a piece of garden in front with laurel bushes and a holly tree. On a piece of cardboard fixed to the gate post is written 'Jumble Sale, Friday at 6.0'. Jean gets there by quarter past five, and she is by no means among the first. One woman says she has been waiting since three o'clock. She is very knowledgeable about the jumble sales in the area, knowing which ones have good quality stuff and which ones aren't worth waiting for. St Luke's has a good reputation. One woman tells how she once found a five-pound note in a jacket she bought for her husband. 'I took it back.' 'Barmy bugger.' 'No, the Vicar said he knew the woman who gave it, and she put the money in it on purpose. He gave her another fiver for being honest.'

At six o'clock the door opens, people pay their five pence, and rush to the clothing stalls, seizing garments which look good.

'You don't go with anything special in mind' says Jean, 'you just have to make sure you don't get a lot of stuff you don't need. But if I see anything decent for myself or Mike, I'll take it.' There is a hectic quarter of an hour, by which time most of the things worth having will have been taken. Nearly all the customers are women; the husband of many of them are out of work. Jean indicates two who are single parents, one deserted, one unmarried. 'At least we're together', she reflects, 'though sometimes I wonder how much longer if things go on the way they are.' She has a pair of children's jeans for Neil, a bit too long, but they'll turn up, and a dress for Natalie, and a pair of shoes that Natalie will grow into. She has spent 95 pence.

On Friday evening, Mike goes out for a drink to the WMC – a rather gaunt and cheerless room, with snooker, darts, and a space invader machine, which the same group of boys monopolizes for almost two hours. It is a wet night, and coats and umbrellas drip on to the rubber tiles. Most of the men are middle-aged or elderly. Mike comes here in preference to the pub, because the older men are sympathetic. There is a group of younger men out of work who come in only on Fridays and Saturdays. The talk is all of the Yorkshire Ripper, who has appeared in court that week; how many times the police had already interviewed him, how the joker who made the Geordie tape had contributed to the deaths of the last five women. 'He was a fucking animal' says one of the older men, 'and he should be put down like a fucking mad dog. Hanging's too good for him. I don't know about bring back the rope, what he wants is something slow and fucking lingering.' 'Try my missus', says one of the others, and everybody laughs. Mike says, 'Don't take Harry too seriously, he just don't want anybody to know what a kind heart he's got.' Harry denies it. 'Fucking stone, mate,' he says, patting his chest. Later, Mike tells me that Harry and his wife lost their only child when she was seven; that his wife has been in hospital, prematurely senile for ten years, and that Harry goes to see her three times a week. Harry has the role of offering a defining edge to the others. Later he says he thinks Mrs Thatcher is the best thing that's happened to this country for years. 'She put you out of a job.' 'The world don't owe me a fucking living. I don't need her to teach me that, like some of you silly fuckers. Eating seed-corn, that's what we've been doing for years. Eating seed-corn.' The conversation comes back to the Ripper and sex. Harry says 'Sex on the brain, that's the trouble. We never had all this sort of thing years ago. We had better things to think of.' 'Better than sex?' 'It's all got out of hand.' 'Not out of mine it hasn't.' Everybody laughs. 'They'll have a fucking minister for sex next.' There is a sense of release that is quite out of proportion to the modest jokes – it is a way of dealing with all the pent-up frustrations, the long days at home in the week, sleeping in the armchair in the afternoon, inventing things to do in the house that don't cost money, the lack of social contact, which most unemployed people mention as the thing they miss most about work after the money. Mike drinks three pints, and he is visibly more relaxed when he gets home.

On Friday Jean takes Neil and Natalie to see her mother. Alice is fifty-eight, and works full-time in a baker's and confectioner's near the centre of the town that specializes in lunch-time take-away sandwiches. She has been there since her husband died, eighteen years ago, and she always provides good things for tea on Friday; and two or three times a week takes the odd cakes and left-over sandwiches down to Jean. She is generous to the children, and most of their Christmas presents and birthdays toys are provided by her. Nan has a colour tv, which is still a novelty for the children. Jean goes down to see her in mid-afternoon, after she has collected Neil from school. The journey is about a mile. On Friday Mike gets his own tea. Jean is close to her mother, and often has a moan and a weep – a very similar kind of release to that of Mike's. Today, Alice looks at Jean and wonders if she's all right. Jean has been to the doctor's, and takes out a cylinder of Valium, 2 mg, one to be taken three times a day.

She started taking the sleeping tablets because she found herself lying awake all night wondering about her relationship with Mike. She says sometimes she and Mike go for two or three weeks at a time without sex. Jean says she can't bring herself to initiate it.

'Even after all these years, I feel now he's at home all the while, I don't know him as well as I used to. I see more of him, but it's like it's too much effort. You can feel time slipping past, and you know you ought to do something about it, only you don't know what. Sometimes I panic, I think "This is it, I'm on the downwards slope, I'm going to get old, and the kids'll grow up, and then by that time there'll be nothing between me and him, only a lot of years together. Do you know what I mean?' Jean worries because the relationships of so many other people on the estate are all breaking up. 'Half the marriages are on the rocks, they go their separate ways. Not that there's much chance of that, we're forced to be together like bloody convicts.' Alice doesn't try to deny her daughter's feelings. She knows that what she is expressing are her fears – not her real relationship with Mike. She always leaves her mother's before nine o'clock, partly because she feels afraid walking through the streets after dark, and partly because she knows that Mike will be home soon after ten; and she stops at the chip shop on the way for another of their little luxuries. She buys some peas and roe and chips, and puts them in the oven to keep warm; and he brings her a bottle of light ale, and they have supper when the children are in bed.

Saturday afternoon is spent watching sport on the television. Mike's sister sometimes comes in at tea-time: her children, Kerry and Donna, are the same age as Neil and Natalie. Jean and Mike don't have friends. They know a lot of people in the neighbourhood 'to speak to', but they don't visit. Jean says that when people first move, they're in and out of each other's houses for the first weeks, then they fall out, and then your life is all over the estate. Mike's sister and her husband are the only people of their own age they see regularly, and they go out with them at Bank holidays and occasionally weekends; but Roy is working, and since Mike hasn't worked, there has been an awkwardness between them. Roy is generous, but Mike won't accept the outings in the car without paying for some petrol, and it embarrasses him to have Roy buy ice-creams for his children. 'It messes up your relations with everybody,' Mike says. 'You have to budget for the last penny, and you know if you go over that any week, something's got to be sacrificed.' They don't have a newspaper except on Sunday; Jean's mother keeps the *Mirror* for them, but it's nearly always two or three days old by the time they get it.

When she arrives on Sunday afternoon, the children jump up and run to her; she carries an old leather bag; there is bound to be something good in it. She has half a dozen custard tarts, two Florentines. She has brought the last two day's *Daily Mirror*. She makes a great fuss of Natalie, and gives her ten pence. Jean frowns; she doesn't like her mother to give them money. Natalie wants to go to the shop to spend it, but Mike says no. She starts to cry. 'Nana'll go with you in a few minutes, my love.'

Alice looks at Mike. 'I know what you're thinking,' he says to her. 'I never said a word.' 'No, you don't need to.' 'Well, is there anything in the offing?' 'No there isn't. Do you think I'd be bloody sitting here every day if I had any choice?' 'I only asked.'

'You're always only asking. How do you think I spend my sodding time? Do you think I'm on some sort of holiday?"
One of Mike's complaints about Alice is that she doesn't realize how impossible it is to get work at the moment. She's always just heard of somebody who's got a job; Mike thinks she is criticizing him for being feckless. To make matters worse, she tells an anecdote of a pensioner who's just got a part-time job doing up somebody's garden; and Jean says Mike can't even do his own. Mike gets up and storms out. Jean is alarmed now; and she turns on her mother, saying 'Now look what you've done.'

Mike stays out for several hours. In fact, he has been to his sister's, and by the time he comes back Alice has gone. There is a tense silence between him and his wife. She says she is sorry; but for an hour or more, Mike is unrelenting. Later, he yields and says that he knows that Alice is good to the kids but that doesn't give her the right to disapprove, and behave as though she doubted his efforts to get a job. Jean is soothing and they are reconciled, curling up in the same chair together.

On Monday morning, Mike is up out of the house by half-past eight. He says he won't come back until he's got a job.   (~ 2470 words)

Annotations
(The words marked* should be memorized.)

to sign on *here:* register at a Labour Exchange – – **reinforced glass doors** Türen aus Sicherheitsglas – – ***rectangular** viereckig – – ***to shuffle** walk without raising the feet properly – – ***counter** table or flat surface on which goods are shown, customers served, in a shop or bank – – **partitioned off** separated off – – **buff** pale brown – – **rubberized** covered or treated with rubber; gummiert – – ***floor tile** Fußbodenfliese – – **bell-bottomed** made very wide at the bottom of the leg (as worn by some sailors) – – **parti-coloured** differently coloured in different parts – – **suede** ['sweid] kind of leather with a velvet-like surface – – **giro** ['dʒaɪrəʊ] *here:* cheque – – **grub** (sl.) food – – ***to scare** frighten – – **poor bugger** (sl.) armer Schlucker – – **bloody** (sl.) *here:* verdammt – – **edge** *here:* acuteness; Schärfe, Gereiztheit – – **jumble sale** (Br.) sale of old or second-hand articles, usu. for charity – – ***soot** Ruß – – ***to vanish** disappear – – **to adjoin** be next or nearest to – – **holly tree** Stechpalme – – ***cardboard** Karton, Pappe – – **barmy** (Br., coll.) mad, foolish – – **stall** *here:* table used by a trader in a market, on a street, etc. – – **WMC** (short for) Working Men's Club – – **gaunt** ['gɔnt] grim, desolate – – **snooker** game played with 15 red balls and six balls of other colours on a billiard-table – – **Yorkshire Ripper** Peter Sutcliffe, killer from Yorkshire, who sexually assaulted and mutilated a number of women, arrested in 1981 – – ***joker** person who is fond of making jokes – – **Geordie tape** hoax tape recording in a Newcastle ("Geordie") accent, supposedly made by the Yorkshire Ripper, which distracted police attention – – **fucking** (vulg., sl.) word used as intensifier – – **to put down** *here:* kill, do away with; abmurksen – – ***to want** *here:* need, deserve – – **lingering** lasting long, protracted; "... something slow and fucking lingering": dying a slow and painful death – – **missus** ['mɪsɪz] (Br., sl.) *here:* wife – – **to offer a defining edge to s.o.** *here:* provoke others to define their beliefs – – **seed-corn** Saatkorn – – **pent-up** repressed – – **pint** ['paɪnt] appr. half a litre; *here:* a pint of beer – – **odd cakes** extra cakes above the number actually needed; überschüssig, über – – **Nan** (coll.) Grandmother – – **to be on the rocks** *here:* likely to end in divorce or separation – – **convict** person in jail – – **roe** ['rəʊ] a fish delicacy; Rogen – – **ale** beer – – **to fall out** quarrel – – **estate** the housing estate, area of new houses grouped together – – **Bank holidays** holidays on which banks are closed by law, (e.g. Good Friday, Easter Monday, Christmas Day) – – **awkwardness** *here:* (Gefühl der) Verlegenheit, Peinlichkeit – – **to mess up** spoil – – **custard tart** Puddingtörtchen – – **Florentine** a biscuit with nuts, chocolate and dried fruit – – **to be in the offing** in Aussicht sein – – **sodding** (sl.) a vulgar intensifier; cf. fucking – – **feckless** futile, inefficient; untätig, unfähig – – **unrelenting** not changing one's mind about some decided course; unnachgiebig, unerbittlich – – **to yield** give in – – **soothing** making quiet, calm – – **reconciled** being friends again after having quarrelled

WORKSHEET

1. **Language**
   Explain the following words and expressions *in a full sentence:* Social Security (l. 16); Samaritans (l. 18); Department of Employment (l. 29); tobacconist (l. 30); pub (l. 59).
1.2 Insert seven of the following eight words into the sentences below: customers, clothing, desk, giro, jumble sale, to owe, to release, unemployment.
   a) Lynn works as a volunteer on the reception _____ of the local hospital once a week.
   b) Her friend Kath runs a second-hand _____ shop. In the shop, there are racks of dresses, suits, skirts, hats, children's clothes and shoes, which Kath keeps in perfect order even though she has to remind _____ that it's not a _____ when they start rummaging (= search thoroughly) through the neatly packed boxes and the carefully hung rows of coats.
   c) Kath's son is a handicapped boy, who is in a hospital for the severely abnormal. She wants her son home but Dave, the social worker she is talking to, insists that he cannot make the hospital _____ the boy.
   d) Now and then Lynn is called by the _____ review officer for interview. He then asks her what efforts she has made to find work.
   e) So far she has been able to convince him that she is trying hard. If she hadn't her _____ would have been lowered.
1.3 The English language has quite a number of *prepositions* whose correct application is rather difficult for Germans. In the course of this book you'll therefore be confronted with a few of those prepositions which cause most trouble. For instance, ask yourself whether you would have said ". . . has appeared at court" instead of the correct ". . . has appeared **in** court" (l. 61); or "sex in the brain" instead of the correct "sex **on** the brain" (l. 77).

This is a first exercise in prepositions. This time let's deal with "in", "on", "at". Insert the correct preposition in these sentences:
a) I write articles . . . pictures.
b) He nodded his head . . . intervals.
c) He looked at me . . . disbelief.
d) I must be . . . my guard.
e) He was startled . . . her suspicion.
f) He wanted me to be available . . . case I was needed.
g) He had spoken . . . jest.
h) I selected them . . . random.
i) We are . . . war, my friend.
j) She put out her tongue . . . him.
k) He is one of the best fellows . . . earth.
l) No one equaled them . . . knowledge.
m) Why do you insist . . . seeing her?
n) My decision had been based . . . a medical fact.
o) They were few . . . number.

1.4 Our text contains a few grammatical mistakes. Find and correct them. What do you think is the reason for the mistakes?

2. Content and Comment

2.1 The text depicts several events on four days (Thursday through Sunday) in Mike's and Jean's lives on the dole. Retrace them in your own words.
2.2 What does the text tell us about their financial situation?
2.3 In what other way are they affected by Mike's unemployment? Give examples.
2.4 Why are the men apparently more affected by their unemployment than their wives?
2.5 How do you account for the fact that many couples living on the dole are prone to divorce? What about Jean and Mike?
2.6 The text deals with the effects of unemployment on working-class people. Do you think life on the dole is different for university graduates? If so, to what degree?
2.7 Do you know any jobless people? Describe the way they live.
2.8 All over Western Europe there are approximately 12 million unemployed persons (in 1986!). Give some reasons for this social disaster and make suggestions for overcoming the problem. Discuss such proposals.

3. Further Studies

3.1 In his book *Unemployment* Jeremy Seabrook frequently refers to the lack of solidarity among the British working-class of today as compared to that of the **1930's.** How do you account for this phenomenon? Consider the following:

- the economic and social situation in Britain now and then
- the nature of jobs now and then
- the influence of the economic boom in the 1950's and 1960's and the general rise of living standards on the mentality of the working-class
- the changes in the school system and their social effects
- the large number of immigrants from Commonwealth countries

3.2.1 Many young people all over the industrialized West are wondering how to escape unemployment. That, however, means to take a job in a field which has a future. To ease *your* decision we have reprinted informative material from *US News & World Report.* (The statistics refer to the USA but can certainly be applied to Europe as well.)

Your *assignment* is to study and verbalize the information given. (Necessary words cf. p. 33)

A)

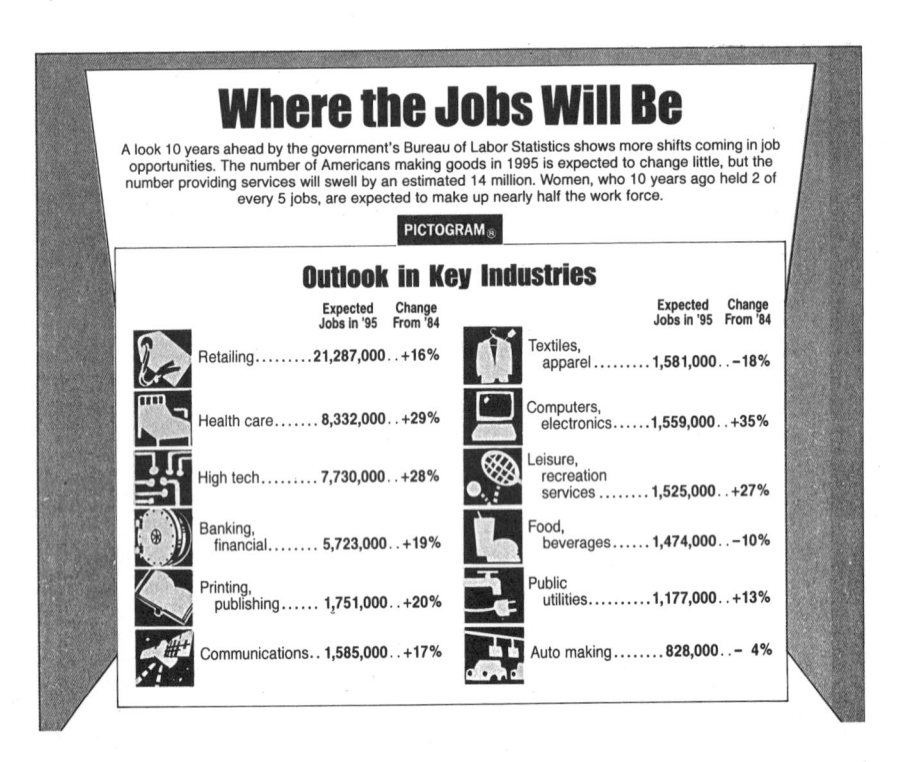

Where the Jobs Will Be

A look 10 years ahead by the government's Bureau of Labor Statistics shows more shifts coming in job opportunities. The number of Americans making goods in 1995 is expected to change little, but the number providing services will swell by an estimated 14 million. Women, who 10 years ago held 2 of every 5 jobs, are expected to make up nearly half the work force.

PICTOGRAM®

Outlook in Key Industries

	Expected Jobs in '95	Change From '84		Expected Jobs in '95	Change From '84
Retailing	21,287,000	+16%	Textiles, apparel	1,581,000	−18%
Health care	8,332,000	+29%	Computers, electronics	1,559,000	+35%
High tech	7,730,000	+28%	Leisure, recreation services	1,525,000	+27%
Banking, financial	5,723,000	+19%	Food, beverages	1,474,000	−10%
Printing, publishing	1,751,000	+20%	Public utilities	1,177,000	+13%
Communications	1,585,000	+17%	Auto making	828,000	−4%

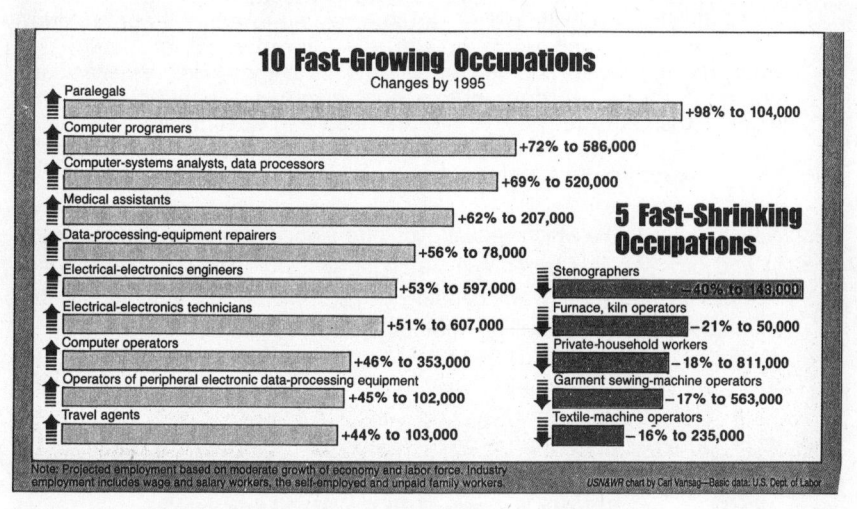

B)

10 Fast-Growing Occupations
Changes by 1995

- Paralegals +98% to 104,000
- Computer programers +72% to 586,000
- Computer-systems analysts, data processors +69% to 520,000
- Medical assistants +62% to 207,000
- Data-processing-equipment repairers +56% to 78,000
- Electrical-electronics engineers +53% to 597,000
- Electrical-electronics technicians +51% to 607,000
- Computer operators +46% to 353,000
- Operators of peripheral electronic data-processing equipment +45% to 102,000
- Travel agents +44% to 103,000

5 Fast-Shrinking Occupations

- Stenographers −40% to 143,000
- Furnace, kiln operators −21% to 50,000
- Private-household workers −18% to 811,000
- Garment sewing-machine operators −17% to 563,000
- Textile-machine operators −16% to 235,000

Note: Projected employment based on moderate growth of economy and labor force. Industry employment includes wage and salary workers, the self-employed and unpaid family workers.

USN&WR chart by Carl Varsaig—Basic data: U.S. Dept. of Labor

Source: U.S. News & World Report, Dec. 23, 1985

Additional vocabulary
(The words marked* should be memorized.)

3.2.3 *__retailing__ selling of goods (usu. in small quantities) to the general public; not for resale – – __apparel__ clothing – – __beverages__ any sort of drinks – – *__public utilities__ public services such as the supply of water, electricity, gas or bus or railways services – – *__occupation__ job – – *__data processor__ here: Datenverarbeiter – – __medical assistant__ Medizinalassistent(in) – – __data-processing-equipment repairer__ Reparateur von Datenverarbeitungsgeräten – – __computer operators__ Bedienungspersonal von elektronischen Rechnern – – __peripheral electronic data processing equipment__ peripheral equipment consists of *input devices, output devices* and *storage devices,* such as card punch, card reader, magnetic disk, magnetic drum, magnetic tape, tape reader, paper tape, etc.; Ein-, Ausgabe- und Speicherteile – – *__travel agent__ Reisebürokaufmann – – __furnace__ Hochofen – – __kiln__ Industrieofen – – __garment sewing-machine__ Nähapparat – – __textile machine__ Webautomat – – *__range__ *here:* variety – – __currently__ at present – – __inventory__ detailed list – – *__comprehensive__ umfassend – – *__item__ *here:* point – – __preliminary__ vorläufig – – __adept at doing s.th.__ skilled in doing s.th. – – __cabinet__ piece of furniture with drawers or shelves – – __forest ranger__ (US) forest guard – – __calculus__ höhere Mathematik – – *__chess__ Schach – – *__bargaining__ *here:* das Feilschen – – __swapping__ (also spelled: swopping) exchanging goods – – *__merchandise__ manufactured goods – – __thrifty__ economical – – *__trait__ characteristic – – *__carpenter__ workman who makes and

33

repairs the wooden parts of buildings – – ***rancher** [rɑntʃə; USræntʃər] person who owns, manages or works, on a large farm – –**investigative** characterized or having a tendency toward investigation, i.e. study, research – – ***self-reliant** selbständig – – **artistic** related to arts – – **appreciation** understanding of and liking for s.th. – – ***librarian** Bibliothekar(in) – – **enterprising** showing courage and willingness to engage in business affairs – – ***goal** object – – ***competitive** Wettbewerb- – – **beautician** cosmetologist; Kosmetiker(in) – – ***to require** need – – ***accountant** here: bookkeeper – – **proof-reader** Korrekturleser – – **occupational theme** Berufsfeld – – **exterminator** Kammerjäger

3.2.2 Now that you know which field and job offers good prospects you may want to find out "Which Career Will Be Right for *You*". The *Strong-Campbell Interest Inventory* below will certainly help you do so. Tell your classmates which career you think will be right for you. Give reasons.

Which Career Will Be Right for You?

Knowing what type of work interests you can help narrow the range of occupations to consider. It also can point you toward careers your interests say you might enjoy, even though currently you may know little about them.

One of the most popular ways to assess career interests is to use the Strong-Campbell Interest Inventory. It offers a comprehensive analysis of an individual's work interests through his or her responses to 325 familiar items. The person's answers are compared with those given by people already working in a wide range of jobs in order to show how well the interests match. Only interests are measured, not abilities.

How It Works For a preliminary indication of where your interests may lie, check which of the following subjects, activities or types of people you like. Do not consider whether you feel adept at doing the activities.

☐ 1. Agriculture
☐ 2. Popular-mechanics magazines
☐ 3. Cabinetmaking
☐ 4. Operating machinery
☐ 5. Being a forest ranger
☐ 6. Calculus
☐ 7. Chemistry
☐ 8. Nature study
☐ 9. Playing chess
☐ 10. Doing research work
☐ 11. Dramatics
☐ 12. Art galleries
☐ 13. Poetry
☐ 14. Magazines about art and music
☐ 15. Musical geniuses
☐ 16. Sociology
☐ 17. Going to religious services
☐ 18. Leading a scout troop
☐ 19. Contributing to charities
☐ 20. Babies
☐ 21. Starting a conversation with a stranger
☐ 22. Bargaining ("swapping")
☐ 23. Buying merchandise for a store
☐ 24. Aggressive people
☐ 25. People who assume leadership
☐ 26. Economics
☐ 27. Making statistical charts
☐ 28. Regular hours for work
☐ 29. Developing business systems
☐ 30. Thrifty people

If You Like–

■ **Items 1 through 5.** You have marked items related to "realistic" traits. *Interests include:* Action rather than thought; concrete problems as opposed to abstract ones; nature; mechanical, construction and repair activities; military activities.
Possible occupations: Carpenter, cartographer, rancher.

■ **Items 6 through 10.** You have marked items related to "artistic" traits. *Interests include:* A great need for self-expression; appreciation of aesthetic qualities.
Possible occupations: Art-museum director, author, reporter, librarian, photographer.

■ **Items 16 through 20.** You have marked items related to "social" traits. *Interests include:* Working with people; sharing responsibilities and being the center of attention;

positions of leadership and power; enjoyment in working with others toward organizational goals and economic success; taking financial and interpersonal risks; participating in competitive activities.
Possible occupations: Beautician, elected public official, life-insurance agent, personnel director, restaurant manager.

■ **Items 26 through 30.** You have marked items related to "conven-

34

marked items related to "investigative" traits. *Interests include:* Scientific activities; gathering information; uncovering new theories; analyzing data; being self-reliant at work.
Possible occupations: Biologist, geographer, mathematician.
■ **Items 11 through 15.** You have marked items related to "investigative" traits. *Interests include:* Scientific activities; gathering information; uncovering new theories; analyzing data; being self-reliant at work.

solving problems by discussing feelings and interaction with others.
Possible occupations: Elementary-school teacher, licensed practical nurse, playground director.
■ **Items 21 through 25.** You have marked items related to "enterprising" traits. *Interests include:* Holding

tional" traits. *Interests include:* Working in large organizations but in subordinate rather than leadership roles; activities that require attention to detail and accuracy.
Possible occupations: Accountant, dental assistant, proofreader, secretary, statistician.

Note: Most people's interests do not fit neatly into just one occupational theme. Answers covering two or three areas produce a host of new career possibilities. For example: Computer programmers typically are people who have interests in the investigative, realistic and conventional areas. Lawyers typically combine interests in the artistic and investigative categories. Exterminators mix interests in the realistic, social and conventional.

Items reproduced by special permission from the distributor, Consulting Psychologists Press, Inc., Palo Alto, Calif., acting for the publisher Stanford University Press, from the Strong-Campbell Interest Inventory form T325 of the Strong Vocational Interest Blank by Edward K. Strong, Jr., and David P. Campbell, copyright 1974, 1981, 1985 by the board of trustees of the Leland Stanford Junior University.

Source: U.S. News & World Report, Dec. 23, 1985

3.3 Writing business letters

One of the directors of *The Channel Tunnel Group LTD,* 316 Dickens Street, London WC2 E 7HR, needed a personal assistant to help him with his huge work-load. So he put the following *help-wanted advertisement* in *The Times* of 26 April 1986.

> ### ARE YOU A GOOD ORGANISER?
>
> Director requires urgently a PA to help organise conferences and exhibitions. Good knowledge of German and French, head for figures, and full secretarial skills essential. Interesting position with some foreign travel.
> Salary according to age and experience.
> To apply, please write full details to Peter K. Kingston, Senior Personnel Officer, *Channel Tunnel Group,* 316 Dickens Street, London WC2 E 7HR.

Within 3 days they received more than a dozen *letters of application,* among them this one:

Letter Head →	Helga L. Dryden 24 Southey Road London SW 1
Date →	April 26, 1986
Inside Address →	Peter K. Kingston Senior Personnel Officer Channel Tunnel Group LTD 316, Dickens Street London WC2 E 7HR
Salutation →	Dear Sir,

Contents	In reply to your advertisement in today's *Times,* I apply for the position of a Personal Assistant. As you can see from the enclosed curriculum vitae, I have had six years experience as a PA with an important firm here in London. However, I would like to change to a company which offers me a better chance to travel abroad and to use my knowledge of foreign languages. As my mother is German, I am fluent in this language. In addition, I have a fair command of French and Spanish, which I acquired during my studies in Paris and Barcelona.
	My present position is subject to one month's notice, after which I am prepared to devote the best of my ability to your company.
	For information about my character I refer you to:
	    Mr. James Higgins, Instructor in English,
	    South West Comprehensive School
	    Tennyson Road
	    London SW 1
	I hope you will be so kind as to grant me the privilege of an interview.

Complimentary Close →	Yours sincerely,
Signature →	Helga L. Dryden
Enclosures →	Encls.: Curriculum Vitae Various certificates

CURRICULUM VITAE
Helga L. Dryden

Personal details:
Date of birth: January 27, 1961
Marital Status: Single
Address: 24, Southey Road, London SW 1
Phone: 01 – 449-6032

Education:
- 1966–1972 South West Primary School, London
- 1972–1978 South West Comprehensive School; GCE "O" Levels in English, Maths, Physics, History, French, German (Grades: B, D, C, B, B, A)
"A" Level in German (Grade: A)
- 1980 Secretarial and shorthand/typing course, London Business Skills, Keats Grove, London E 17

Business Experience:
1981–1986 Personal assistant with EMI Food Company
20 Browning Square
London W1A 1ES

Special Qualifications:
In 1978 I stayed in Paris for a year where I attended classes in „Advanced French" and "Business Administration" at *Le Collège Commercial,* 37 Rue d'Honoré Balzac, Paris.

The following year I lived in Barcelona and enrolled at the local *Collegio Espagnol* for courses in "Spanish for Beginners" and in "Spanish, Intermediate Level".

Certificates are enclosed.

Assignment

a) Imagine you are looking for a job as a language correspondent in English and Spanish. Write a letter of application (+ your Curriculum Vitae) in response to the following help-wanted ad in the *Frankfurter Allgemeine Zeitung* of . . .

**Language correspondent in
German, English, Spanish**

A top class correspondent is required for the German branch of our company situated in Frankfurt/Main. If you can handle with ease English and Spanish correspondence on the basis of German texts or keywords, please send your application and curriculum vitae (in English and Spanish) together with a recent photograph, copies of certificates, quotation of expected salary, and statement of your earliest date of entering to

    Honey & Suckle LTD
    Computer Software

    Mannheimer Straße 30
    7 Frankfurt/Main
    Attention: Mr. Roger Schiller
    Personnel Manager

---

b) Select one of the help-wanted ads in an English newspaper, such as *The Times,* and draft a letter of application.

c) In response to your letter of application for the position of a PA you have been invited to an interview (= Einstellungsgespräch) with the manager of the personnel department. Make up ten questions and answers referring to the reasons for your application, your education, interests, experience, expectations, etc.
Then play the interview. (Use the following vocabulary.)

Additional Vocabulary

*****urgently** dringend – – **PA** Personal Assistant – –*****figure** Zahl – – *****experience** Erfahrung – – **Senior Personnel Officer** Leiter der Personalabteilung – – *****letter of application** Bewerbungsschreiben – – **help-wanted advertisement** Stellenanzeige – – *****curriculum vitae** Lebenslauf – – **subject to one month's notice** kann innerhalb eines Monats gekündigt werden – – *****to refer to** verweisen auf – – *****to grant** gewähren – – *****marital status** Familienstand – – *****GCE** General Certificate of Education; "O"(rdinary) Level: Mittlere-Reife-Niveau; "A"(dvanced) Level: Abiturniveau – – **qualifications** Vorbildung, Eignung – – **to gain** gewinnen – – **knowledge** Kenntnis – – **post** Stellung – – **salary** Gehalt – – **to broaden one's mind** den Horizont erweitern

3 UNIONS: A BURNT-OUT CASE

The British miners' strike ends amid a Continent-wide decline in labor's clout

Introducing the Topic

In Topic 2 we have – among other things – learnt about the lack of solidarity among the British working-class of today (cf. p. 31). This general decline of working-class solidarity is often given as one reason among others for the falling numbers of *union* membership and the declining influence of the *trade unions* on the social and political life of Great Britain. The following statistical material, and the text below adapted from an article in *Time Magazine* of March 18, 1985, mirror this development.

A)

TUC membership: the falling numbers

Union	1979	1982
Transport and General Workers (TGWU)	2,086,000	1,603,000
Engineering workers (AUEN)	1,218,000	1,001,000
General and Municipal (GMWU)	967,000	825,000
Nalgo (= Nat. and Local Government Officers' Association)	753,000	784,000
Public Employees (NUPE)	692,000	702,000
Scientific and Technical (ASTMS)	491,000	410,000
Shopworkers (USDAW)	470,000	417,000
Electricians and plumbers (EETPU)	420,000	380,000
Construction workers (UCATT)	348,000	261,000
Mineworkers (NUM)	259,000	245,000
Teachers (NUT)	249,000	222,000
Civil and Public Services Association	224,000	189,000
Postal workers (UCW)	203,000	198,000
White collar engineering (TASS)	201,000	172,000
Rallwaymen (NUR)	180,000	150,000
Bank workers (BIFU)	132,000	152,000
Boilermakers	130,000	115,000
Society of Civil and Public Servants	109,000	96,000
Iron and steel workers (ISTC)	104,000	95,000
Seamen (NUS)	47,000	25,000
Source: TUC official report	All figures to nearest thousand	

Source: *World & Press*, 1983

1. Have a look at chart A and explain which trade unions have suffered the greatest losses (in absolute and relative figures), and which unions have made most gains in the period between 1979 and 1982.
2. How do you account for the different development of blue-collar and white-collar unions?
3. What effect on the union movement does this development have? Consider this question by referring to chart B. (cf. p. 40).

B)

WHITE-COLLAR UNIONISTS PREFER THE TORIES

POLITICAL ALLEGIANCES OF...
WHITE-COLLAR UNION MEMBERS (3.6 million)

June 1983	Jan/Mar 1984	
27%	36%	LABOUR
38%	39%	CONSERVATIVE
33%	22%	LIBERAL/SDP

BLUE-COLLAR UNION MEMBERS (6.4 million)

June 1983	Jan/Mar 1984	
46%	56%	LABOUR
27%	25%	CONSERVATIVE
26%	16%	LIBERAL/SDP

Source: Mori

Source: *World & Press,* 1984

At 9 a.m. last Tuesday, 2,000 men marched through the black tarmac streets of Grimethorpe (pop. 5,237), a proud coal-mining town in the north of England. Led by the Grimethorpe Colliery Brass Band, in blue blazers with shiny brass buttons, the marchers filed past rows of two-story red brick houses darkened by decades
5 of coal dust. Lining the streets to watch and join the procession were 1,500 of the miners' supporters–wives, mothers and fathers and after a half-day school holiday had been declared, most of the town's children. Though the band boomed out stirring oompah strains and the miners walked with heads held high, an air of sadness marched with them. They had fought the good fight–and lost.
10 Across Britain, in towns much like Grimethorpe, tens of thousands of miners were striding back to work, ending a 51-week strike that ranks among the most bitter, violent and costly labor battles in the country's history. Before it was over, the dispute had resulted in at least 14 deaths (including two suicides and the killing of a taxi driver who was taking a scab to work). 9,808 arrests and countless injuries on the
15 picket lines, as well as an estimated 53 billion in lost output and other economic consequences.
Perhaps the biggest losers were the mine workers and their stubborn, militantly Marxist leader, Arthur Scargill, 47. Despite nearly a year on strike, the miners failed

to achieve anything resembling their key demand, the end of a British government plan to close unprofitable mines. As their members' resolve began to crumble in the face of Prime Minister Margaret Thatcher's continued unwillingness to compromise on the closures, delegates of the National Union of Mineworkers (N.U.M.) two weeks ago voted 98 to 91 to overrule Scargill and end the walkout. Said Johnny Wood, 26, a miner who was among the Grimethorpe marchers: "No one is happy going back on these terms. All we can say is we put up a bloody good fight."

The strike ended as it began, amid dissension and confusion within the union. The miners of Scotland and Kent in southern England voted early last week to continue the walkout until amnesty is granted to the 682 workers around the country who were fired during the dispute for such offenses as vandalism, stealing coal and assaulting police and scabs. In addition, small bands of pickets at several mines persuaded returning workers to stay off the job. But the holdouts were clinging to a lost cause. By week's end the Scottish pitmen had given in, and about 97% of Britain's 186,000 coal miners were back at work. Scargill acknowledged that the strike was formally over but vowed that "our fight will go on".

Scargill's surrender was a stunning setback for British miners, but it was also more than that. It symbolized a new era of turmoil and austerity for organized labor throughout Western Europe. After years of slow economic growth, high unemployment and sweeping industrial change that has closed hundreds of mills and mines forever, unions in France, Italy, West Germany, Belgium and most other West European nations are on the defensive—and perhaps on the wane. Labor leaders are watching helplessly as their membership rolls dwindle and their political clout withers. Accustomed to generous pay increases in the 1960s and 1970s, European workers have had to accept wage hikes in the past few years that barely kept pace with inflation, and in some cases even fell behind.

Nowhere has labor power fallen further and faster than in Britain. In the 1960s union leaders were regular lunch guests at 10 Downing Street, where Prime Minister Harold Wilson and his Labor Party Cabinet sought their advice over beer and sandwiches. Under Wilson's successor, Conservative Edward Heath, the coal miners called a 1974 strike that crippled the economy. To conserve fuel, Heath ordered the entire nation to go on a three-day workweek. When he called general elections as a political test of his stand against the unions, he lost to Wilson, and beer and sandwiches were once again the order of the day. But Wilson's successor as Labor Party leader and Prime Minister, James Callaghan, fell out with the unions during Britain's "winter of discontent" in 1979. In a string of brief but effective strikes, railway workers halted train service, ambulance drivers walked out, and garbage collectors allowed refuse to pile up in London streets. A four-week strike by 80,000 truckers, abetted by dockworkers, reduced foreign trade to a trickle. In the end, unions won pay hikes of as much as 21%.

That militancy backfired: angry and frustrated at the disruptions, voters in 1979 installed Thatcher as Prime Minister. During her campaign, the Iron Lady made it clear that she considered union power a catalyst of inflation and a barrier to productivity. Since 1980, she has pushed through Parliament three laws placing new restrictions on labor actions. Among other things, the legislation sets limits on picketing, requires secret ballots for strike votes and prohibits unions from attacking a company indirectly by pressuring other firms not to do business with it.

The showdown with coal miners began last March after the government-controlled National Coal Board made plans to close as many as 20 of Britain's 174 pits and lay off 20,000 workers. Miners were sharply divided on how to respond, and when Scargill called the strike without taking a vote of the union membership, 26% of the workers stayed on the job. Meanwhile, Scargill was unable to muster the kind of support from other unions that the miners had received in past strikes. Steelworkers continued to accept shipments of coal, and truck drivers hauled it to power stations. Dockworkers called a strike to support the miners but could not hold it together. Having recently suffered through a deep recession, many union members were reluctant to risk jeopardizing their jobs.

In addition, as Britain has developed its North Sea oil and gas fields, the country has become less dependent on coal as an energy source. The government also stockpiled ample coal supplies in anticipation of a strike. With no end to the stoppage in sight, miners this year began drifting back to work in large numbers. The breaking point came two weeks ago, when the returning pitworkers reached 50% of the industry's work force, prompting the N.U.M. executive committee to call the meeting of delegates that ended the strike.

The battle over coal highlighted the breakdown of unity within the British labor movement. The Labor Party splintered in 1981 when most of the leading moderates seceded to form the Social Democratic Party. Many of Labor's rank and file no longer support the party leaders, some of whom have espoused radical leftist positions such as unilateral nuclear disarmament and withdrawal from the European Community. In fact, more than 30% of union members voted for Thatcher and her fellow Tories in the 1983 elections.

Just as alarming to British labor leaders is the sharp decline in union membership. Since 1979, the number of workers represented by the Trades Union Congress, an umbrella labor organization, has dropped 20%, to about 9.6 million. Many of those union members fell from the rolls because their jobs simply disappeared during the recession. Britain's unemployment rate has doubled from 6.3% in 1980 to 12.6% as of January, 1985.

Most ominous for unions is the changing nature of many of the available jobs. Like other developed nations, Britain is undergoing a fundamental transformation in its economic mix. Old-line industries such as steel and coal are shrinking, while

100 high-technology fields like computers and telecommunications expand. As mines and factories shut down, job growth is becoming concentrated among service workers, from secretaries to financial planners to laboratory technicians. Labor leaders find these predominantly young white-collar workers hard to recruit and unreceptive to the gospel of union solidarity and militancy. Says John Edmonds,
105 an official of the General, Municipal, Boilermakers and Allied Trades Union: "We're dealing with better-educated people doing more diverse jobs, people who aren't impressed by battle metaphors and all that macho stuff." (~ 1350 words)

Annotations
(The words marked * should be memorized.)

*TUC (short for Trades Union Congress) association of British trade unions – –
*Tories Conservatives – – **white collar unionists** members of unions which represent workers who do non-manual work – – **allegiance** support, loyalty – – **blue-collar union** union whose members do manual work – – **labor** (US) working people – – **clout** (coll.) *here:* strength; Schlagkraft – – **tarmac** stone and tar road surface – – **to file** march in a line one behind the other – – **to boom out** make loud sounds; dröhnen – – **strains** music – – **air** *here:* melody, tune – – **to stride** (strode, stridden) walk with long steps – – **scab** (coll.) workman who refuses to join a strike, or who takes a striker's place – – **picket** worker stationed at the gates of a factory, dockyard, etc. during a strike, to try to persuade others not to go to work – – **holdouts** those holding out, i.e. not returning to work – – ***output** production – – ***to resemble** be similar, close to – – **resolve** Entschlossenheit, Festigkeit – – ***walkout** strike – – ***terms** conditions – – ***offence** crime, breaking of a rule – – **to assault** attack – – **pitman** miner – – ***to vow** [vaʊ] promise, declare solemnly – – ***surrender** giving up, yielding – – **stunning** (coll.) shocking – – **turmoil** trouble – – ***austerity** Härte, Not – – **mill** factory – – **to be on the wane** im Niedergang begriffen sein – – **membership rolls** lists of names of members; *here:* number of members – – **to dwindle** become less or smaller by degrees – – ***to wither** fade – – **hike** *here:* increase, rise – – **to fall out with s.o.** quarrel with s.o. – – ***refuse** ['refjus] waste – – **to abet** (legal) help s.o. (in doing wrong) – – **disruption** throwing into disorder; Störung der (öffentlichen) Ordnung; Unruhe – – **catalyst** *here:* cause – – ***secret ballot** geheime Wahl – – ***pit** *here:* coal mine – – **Scargill** leader of NUM in the 1980's – – **to muster** gather together – – **to haul** transport – – ***reluctant** slow – – **to jeopardize** put in danger – – **ample** large – – **in anticipation of** expecting – – **to highlight** give emphasis to – – ***moderate** *here:* politician who is not radical – – **rank and file** die Basis, das Fußvolk einer Partei – – **to espouse** [ɪ'spaʊz] give one's support to – – ***unilateral** einseitig – – **umbrella organization** Dachorganisation – – ***gospel** Glaubensbekenntnis

Assignments
1. **Answer** the following questions on the **contents:**
    a) What was the reason for the miners' march through Grimethorpe?
    b) Why had the miners gone on strike?
    c) Why did their strike end in defeat?

d) What conclusion about organised labour does the writer of the article draw from the strikers' defeat and what other arguments does he provide for his theory?
e) Do you agree with his thesis?

2. **Discuss:**
In the 19th and the first half of the 20th century, Trade Unions fought for better working conditions and higher living standards. Nowadays they block improvements in working conditions and increases in productivity because of their hostile attitude towards technological progress (cf. high-tech), and are therefore running the risk of making themselves unnecessary.

3. **Vocabulary practice**
   a) Give synonyms or paraphrase the following words and expressions from the text:
   miner (l. 6); strike (l. 11); key demand (l. 19); unprofitable (l. 20); vandalism (l. 30); garbage collectors (l. 56); to stockpile (l. 79); productivity (l. 63); recession (l. 75); economic mix (l. 99)
   b) Collect together all the words and expressions from the text that belong to these word groups:

Jobs	**Labour conflicts**
ex. miner	strike

   Continue!

   c) Try and find the words given in the wordprobe puzzle below. They may appear horizontally, diagonally, forward and backward. Look up the words you don't know in your English-English dictionary.
   Discover the war-cry of the British Trade Unions hidden in the grid.

   The words:
   - absenteeism
   - associate
   - closed shop
   - convener
   - council
   - craftsman
   - demarcation
   - go slow
   - labour
   - member
   - negotiate
   - overmanning
   - pay
   - shop steward
   - skill
   - strike
   - TUC
   - union
   - wage differential
   - workers

The Trade Union Game

```
     1  2  3  4  5  6  7  8  9  10 11 12 13 14 15 16 17 18
 1   A  B  S  S  R  E  K  R  O  W  A  B  A  Y  E  H  T  T
 2   S  U  N  I  T  E  D  C  U  T  B  W  I  L  L  I  K  S
 3   H  R  E  V  E  N  B  E  B  E  S  N  L  C  D  Z  E  D
 4   O  E  E  S  O  L  C  F  G  D  E  T  A  E  F  E  D  N
 5   P  V  M  L  I  T  S  L  N  G  N  M  B  I  N  G  E  N
 6   S  E  E  S  R  E  K  R  O  W  T  N  O  I  N  U  M  N
 7   T  T  M  R  L  A  I  T  S  S  E  M  U  T  L  K  A  A
 8   E  A  B  N  M  C  I  A  R  M  E  D  E  D  I  C  R  M
 9   W  I  E  L  Y  A  P  E  Y  W  I  D  S  I  C  O  C  S
10   A  C  R  W  T  R  N  C  O  N  S  S  S  O  N  U  A  P
11   R  O  S  E  S  E  I  N  T  U  M  L  H  H  U  N  T  F
12   D  S  F  G  V  S  T  R  I  K  E  O  P  S  O  P  I  A
13   E  S  T  N  I  T  O  G  E  N  E  G  A  W  C  P  O  R
14   C  H  O  P  S  T  E  W  A  R  G  O  S  L  O  W  N  C
15   E  C  L  A  I  T  N  E  R  E  F  F  I  D  E  G  A  W
```

Solution: _____

d) Insert the following words into the text below. Each word is to be used only once.

agreements	management	pay dispute	salary
benefits	members	picketing	shutdown
demands	negotiations	plants	staff
fellow	operate	populars	stoppage
hired	overpaid	proprietors	striking
lay off	owners	quality news-papers	struck
			unions

Revolution on Fleet Street

Eddy Shah and Rupert Murdoch transform the face of the British press

Murdoch, by contrast, has attacked the recalcitrant (1) _____ head on. Over the course of a January weekend, he fired nearly 6,000 (2) _____ printers and moved his four papers – the *Times*, the *Sunday Times*, the *Sun*, and *News of the World* – from the environs of Fleet Street to a $140 million computerized plant
5 in the docklands area of Wapping, in East London. The boxlike building resembles

an armed camp, swept by surveillance cameras and searchlights and ringed by 10-ft.-high fences backed by thick coils of concertina wire. Despite daily (3) _____ by the strikers and occasional battles between thousands of protesters and hundreds of policemen, Murdoch has pledged to stand firm. "I feel like a man who has been on a life sentence and has just been freed," said Murdoch. "I feel wonderful."

For more than two centuries, Fleet Street has been the center of the British newspaper world. But for the past five decades, Fleet Street has also been synonymous with autocratic unions whose members (4) _____ the Linotype machines, produce the finished pages and run the presses. The unions have exercised a paralyzing grip on Fleet Street, dictating who is (5) _____, shutting down presses at will and, in effect, keeping the (6) _____ hostage. Now, because of Shah and Murdoch, the once formidable power of the unions is fast crumbling, swept away by a wave of highly efficient computer-based technology. The two men have opened the way for the country's 13 other major national daily and Sunday papers to break their union shackles and join the high-tech revolution. Most of those papers are now planning to move to modern (7) _____ scattered around London. Soon Fleet Street will no longer be the home of Britain's major newspapers.

The moving plans are already well under way. Robert Maxwell, the mercurial, Czech-born publisher of the left-of-center *Daily Mirror* (circ. 3 million), plans to follow Murdoch to the East London docklands by 1987. He has already persuaded the unions to allow him to (8) _____ one-third of his company's 6,000 workers in exchange for severance (9) _____. The conservative *Daily Telegraph* (circ. 1.2 million) hopes to have its new headquarters in East London ready by fall. The liberal, thoughtful *Guardian* (circ. 487,000) is building a new plant next to the *Telegraph's*. And the breezy, Tory-leaning *Daily Mail* (circ. 1.8 million) should move into offices on the south bank of the Thames by 1988.

It no longer seems to be a question of whether the print unions will allow these moves to take place. Such is the revolution that has overtaken the industry that they will probably be forced to reach (10) _____ with newspaper (11) _____ on reduced staffs and labor-saving technology – or risk seeing their (12) _____ shut out of the new plants. It is a bitter defeat for the unions, which over the years had won control over the newspapers' production from proprietors who considered it easier to grant union (13) _____ than risk a (14) _____.

Over the past four decades, three royal commissions have concluded that poor (15) _____ is partly responsible for Fleet Street's plight but that the unions bear most of the blame for the newspapers' chronic money troubles: on gross revenues of nearly $2 billion last year, Britain's 17 major national papers earned only $34 million in profits, nearly all accounted for by Murdoch's racy *Sun,* the country's largest daily (circ. 4.1 million). The archaic practices of the unions had come to be accepted with a cynical weariness in all of the national newsrooms, from the (16) _____ _____ such as the *Financial Times,* widely considered the country's best national daily, and the *Guardian,* to the screechy (17) _____ some of which, like the *Sun,* serve up offerings of bare breasts along with the news.

Tales of abuse are plentiful. Feather-bedding (= absenteeism) is so widespread that on one occasion, when Murdoch visited one of his now abandoned plants, he found only 60 workers on hand, whereas 500 were supposed to be on the job. Payroll padding (= unnecessary inflation of the number of employees; overmanning) is common, and many printers work only part time but are paid a full week's wages. Senior men can earn up to $40,000 a year, about three times the average British worker's (18) _____. Another practice that has come to haunt Fleet Street is the "blow," a term used for what was supposed to be a short break for men working in the pressrooms. Over the years, these breaks have grown longer and longer, so that printers now save them up and even combine them into paid days off. The staffing levels would never be tolerated at a U.S. newspaper. At Murdoch's San Antonio *Express-News,* for example, four printers operate each press; it took 18 workers to run each press at the *Times's* old plant.

Aside from the National Union of Journalists, Fleet Street has four production unions: the N.G.A., SOGAT, the EETPU and the Amalgamated Union of Engineering Workers. These unions divide their members at each paper into dozens of so-called chapels, each consisting of anywhere between one and 500 workers. Each group guards its turf, and any challenge to that authority by the proprietor, another union or even another chapel can result in a work (19) _____. Countless strikes have been called over the years for myriad reasons. The *Financial Times* stopped printing for ten weeks in 1983 over a $20-a-week (20) _____ _____ with 24 machine managers. When the *Times* reorganized its library personnel in early 1984, SOGAT leaders contested the action and shut down the *Times* and the *Sunday Times* for seven days, causing a loss of $2.8 million. On several occasions, workers have threatened to strike unless the papers withdrew editorials critical of union practices; in some cases, the papers appeared with a blank space in place of the offending words. In all, Fleet Street papers lost nearly 96 million copies in union disputes last year.

Murdoch's showdown with the unions began developing in 1980, when the foundations were laid for the Wapping plant. The following year he opened (21) _____ with the unions about introducing computer technology and making (22) _____ reductions. Among other things, he insisted on a legally binding contract, a novelty for the print unions, which by tradition are bound to agreements only by "trust and honor". The unions not only balked at a legal contract but continued to resist the new technology.

Union negotiations resumed in late 1985, but little progress was made between Murdoch and Brenda Dean, the head of SOGAT, the largest print union. In mid-January Murdoch, without advance notice, inaugurated the Wapping plant by producing a special *Sunday Times* section. Seeing this as a calculated taunt (= mockery) the printers (23) _____ Murdoch's Fleet Street newspapers, fully expecting to bring the proprietor to his knees, as they had so many other publishers in the past.

This time, they failed. Murdoch promptly fired the 6,000 striking workers and within 24 hours moved his papers to Wapping. He persuaded all but 14 of his 700 journalists to join him by offering them free private medical insurance and average raises of $2.800 a year. He hired an Australian-owned trucking firm to deliver the papers. When the strikers tried to discourage (24) _____ union members from distributing copies, the courts, in line with the new labor legislation, fined the print unions $70.000 and seized the assets of SOGAT.

Murdoch's confrontation with the unions has won him wide support. Thatcher has praised him in the House of Commons, while opinion polls show little support for Dean and her followers. Unlike Britain's coal miners, who attracted considerable sympathy during a violence-ridden, twelve-month strike that ended last year, the printers are perceived by the public as (25) _____ and underworked. "Fleet

Street is one of the great bastions of Luddism"[1]), declares a senior government official. "The print unions, which have rejected every attempt to adapt to the future, are now washed up on a very lonely shore."

---
[1]) The beliefs or practices of the **Luddites,** i.e. of a group of early 19th century English workmen engaged in attempting to prevent the use of labour-saving machinery by destroying it.

Adapted from: *Time,* March 17, 1986

4. **Further Study**
Two students prepare a speech, each about the history of the British Trade Unions. One deals with the union movement between 1800 and 1914, the other with the period from 1914 to present time.
For reference use:
- *The Encyclopaedia Britannica*
- Henry Pelling, *A History of British Trade Unionism,* Pelican 1971
- Anthony Sampson, *The Changing Anatomy of Britain,* Coronet Books 1983, Part One, chapters 4 and 5

4 PLAYER PIANO

Note on the Text

The American author Kurt Vonnegut jr. (1922–), who has always tried to avoid being labelled a sf-writer, is widely recognised for his sf and mainstream work, which includes titles like *Player Piano* (1952), *The Sirens of Titan* (1959), *God Bless You Mr Rosewater* (1965), *Slaughterhouse Five* (1969) and others.
Player Piano was his first sf novel. Heavy with irony, verging on black humour, it depicts a dystopian society, an America after World War III, fully reconstructed, nightmarishly automated and computerized after a Second Industrial Revolution. Materialistic well-being, an ever-rising standard of living is ensured and enforced, production and distribution of goods provided by machines that create vast unemployment, except for a small managerial class which runs the country with the help of a gigantic computer. The unemployed are recruited either into the Army or into the Reconstruction and Reclamation Corps (the "Reeks and Wrecks"), whose job is to do small repairs like filling holes in streets.
Player Piano features all the characteristics of a dystopia such as a totalitarian society, especially integrated women, a dissenting hero, rebellion etc.
In the end, masses of jobless people destroy the machines, but then reconstruct them immediately.

Our text has been taken from: Kurt Vonnegut jr., *Player Piano,* Dell Publishing Co. inc., 1 Dag Hammarskjold Plaza, New York, 1980, pp. 27–29, 158–162 passim.

Doctor Haggard from the United States Department of State and Doctor Ned Dodge, a manager, guide and show the Shah of Bradphur around New York.

I

The limousine came to a halt by the end of the bridge, where a large work crew was filling a small chuckhole. The crew had opened a lane for an old Plymouth with a broken headlight, which was coming through from the north side of the river. The limousine waited for the Plymouth to get through, and then proceeded.

5 The Shah turned to stare at the group through the back window, and then spoke at length.

Doctor Halyard smiled and nodded appreciatively, and awaited a translation.

"The Shah," said Khashdrahr, "he would like, please, to know who owns these slaves we see all the way up from New York City."

10 "Not slaves," said Halyard, chuckling patronizingly. "Citizens, employed by government. They have same rights as other citizens – free speech, freedom of worship, the right to vote. Before the war, they worked in the Ilium Works, controlling machines, but now machines control themselves much better."

"Aha!" said the Shah, after Khashdrahr had translated.

15 "Less waste, much better products, cheaper products with automatic control."

"Aha!"

"And any man who cannot support himself by doing a job better than a machine is employed by the government, either in the Army or the Reconstruction and Reclamation Corps."

20 "Aha! *Khabu bonanza-pak?*"

"Eh?"

"He says, 'Where does the money come from to pay them?'" said Khashdrahr.

"Oh. From taxes on the machines, and taxes on personal incomes. Then the Army and the Reconstruction and Reclamation Corps people put their money back into

25 the system for more products for better living."

"Aha!"

Doctor Halyard, a dutiful man with a bad conscience about the size of his expense accounts, went on explaining America, though he knew very little was getting through. He told the Shah that advances had been most profound in purely industrial

30 communities, where the bulk of the population – as in Ilium – had made its living tending machines in one way or another. In New York City, for instance, there were many skills difficult or uneconomical to mechanize, and the advances hadn't liberated as high a percentage of people from production.

"Kuppo!" said the Shah, shaking his head.

35 Khashdrahr blushed, and translated uneasily, apologetically. "Shah says, 'Communism.'"

"No *Kuppo!*" said Halyard vehemently. "The government does not own the machines. They simply tax that part of industry's income that once went into labor,

49

and redistribute it. Industry is privately owned and managed, and co-ordinated – to prevent the waste of competition – by a committee of leaders from private industry, not politicians. By eliminating human error through machinery, and needless competition through organization, we've raised the standard of living of the average man immensely."

Khashdrahr stopped translating and frowned perplexedly. "Please, this *average man,* there is no equivalent in our language, I'm afraid."

"You know," said Halyard, "the ordinary man, like, well, anybody – those men working back on the bridge, the man in that old car we passed. The little man, not brilliant but good-hearted, plain, ordinary, everyday kind of person."

Khashdrahr translated.

"Aha," said the Shah, nodding, *"Takaru."*

"What did he say?"

"Takaru," said Khashdrahr. "Slave."

"No Takaru," said Halyard, speaking directly to the Shah. "Ci-ti-zen."

"Ahhhhh," said the Shah. *"Ci-ti-zen."* He grinned happily. *"Takaru – citizen. Citizen – Takaru."*

"No *Takaru!"* said Halyard.

Khashdrahr shrugged. "In the Shah's land are only the Elite and the *Takaru."*

Halyard's ulcer gave him a twinge, the ulcer that had grown in size and authority over the years of his career as an interpreter of America to provincial and ignorant notables from the backwaters of civilization.

. . .

II

Dodge turned his back and grinned hospitably at the Shah. "Two bedroms, living room with dining alcove, bath, and kitchen," he said. "This is the M-17 house. Radiant heating in the floor. The furniture was designed after an exhaustive national survey of furniture likes and dislikes. The house, the furniture, and the lot are sold as a package. Simplified planning and production all the way round."

"Lakki-ti, Takaru?" piped the Shah, looking at Edgar closely for the first time.

"What's he say?"

"He wants to know if you like it here," said Khashdrahr.

"Sure – I guess. It's all right. I suppose, Yeah."

"It's nice," said Wanda.

"Now, if you'll follow me into the kitchen," said Doctor Dodge, leaving Wanda and Edgar behind, "you'll see the radar range. Cooks by high frequency, and cooks the inside of whatever's being cooked as fast as the outside. Cooks anything in a matter of seconds, with perfect control. Make bread without a crust, if you want to."

"What is the matter with crust on bread?" asked Khashdrahr politely.

"And this is the ultrasonic dishwasher and clotheswasher," said Dodge. "Hi-frequency sound passing through the water strips dirt and grease off anything in a matter of seconds. Dip in, take out, bingo!"

"And then what does the woman do?" asked Khashdrahr.

"Then she puts the clothes or dishes in this drier, which dries them out in a matter of seconds, and – here's a nifty trick, I think – gives the clothes a spanking-clean outdoors odor, like they were dried in the sun, see, with this little ozone lamp in here."

"And then what?" asked Khashdrahr.

"She feeds the clothes through this ironer, which can do what was an hour's ironing before the war in three minutes. Bing!"

"And then what does she do?" asked Khashdrahr.

"And then she's done."

"And then what?"

Doctor Dodge reddened perceptibly. "Is this a joke?"

"No," said Khashdrahr. "The Shah would like to know what it is that the woman *Takaru* –"

"What's a *Takaru*?" said Wanda suspiciously.

"Citizen," said Halyard.

"Yes," said Khashdrahr, smiling at her oddly, "citizen. The Shah would like to know why she has to do everything so quickly – this in a matter of seconds, that in a matter of seconds. What is it she is in such a hurry to get at? What is it she has to do, that she mustn't waste any time on these things?"

"Live!" said Doctor Dodge expansively. "Live! Get a little fun out of life." He laughed, and clapped Khashdrahr on the back, as though to jar him into feeling some of the jollity in this average American man's home.

The effect on Khashdrahr and the Shah was a poor one. "I see," said the interpreter coldly. He turned to Wanda. "And how is it you live and get so much fun out of life?"

Wanda blushed and looked down at the floor, and worried the carpet with her toe. "Oh, television," she murmured. "Watch that a lot, don't we, Ed? And I spend a lot of time with the kids, little Delores and young Edgar, Jr. You know. Things."

"Where are the children now?" asked Khashdrahr.

"Over at the neighbors' place, the Glocks, watching television, I expect."

"Would you like to see the ultrasonic washer work?" said Doctor Dodge. "Right before your eyes, bing! Takes off egg, lipstick, bloodstains –"

"The transducer's shot again," said Edgar, "so the washer's out of commission. Wanda's been doing the washing in a tub for a month now, waiting for a new transducer."

"Oh, I don't mind," said Wanda. "Really I like doin' 'em that way. It's kind of a relief. A body needs a change. I don't mind. Gives me something to do."

Halyard ended the silence that followed her statement with a brisk suggestion that they leave these good people alone and have a look at the central recreation pavilion down the street.

"If we hurry," said Doctor Dodge, "we'll probably catch the leathercraft class still in session."

The Shah patted the radar stove, the laundry console, and peered for a moment at the television screen, which showed five persons seated around a conference table, arguing earnestly. *"Brahouna!"* he chuckled.

Khashdrahr nodded. *"Brahouna!* Live!"

As the party left, Halyard was explaining that the house and contents and car were all paid for by regular deductions from Edgar's R & RC pay check, along with premiums on his combination health, life, and old age security insurance, and that the furnishings and equipment were replaced from time to time with newer models as Edgar – or the payroll machines, rather – completed payments on the old ones.

"He has a *complete* security package," said Halyard. "His standard of living is constantly rising, and he and the country at large are protected from the old economic ups and downs by the orderly, predictable consumer habits the payroll machines give him. Used to be he'd buy on impulse, illogically, and industry would go nutty trying to figure out what he was going to buy next. Why, I remember when I was a little boy, we had a crazy neighbor who blew all his money on an electric organ, while he still had an old-fashioned icebox and kerosene stove in his kitchen!"

Edgar closed the door and leaned against it, against the door of his M-17 castle. Wanda sank to the couch. "The place looked nice, I think," she said. She said it whenever a visitor – Amy Glock, Gladys Pelrine, the Shah of Bratphur, anybody – left.

"Yep," said Edgar. And he felt evil and damned as he looked at Wanda, good, good soul, who'd never done anything to offend him, whose love for him was as big as all outdoors. He fingered the three ten-dollar bills in his pocket, his take-home pay – cigarette money, recreation money, small luxury money the machines let him have. This tiny atom ot the economy under his control he was going to spend, not on himself or Wanda or the kids, but on Marion. Edgar's troubled heart had gone out to the crazy man in Halyard's story, the guy who'd bought himself an electric organ. Expensive, impractical, strictly personal – above and beyond the goddamned package.

But deceit was another thing. "Wanda," said Edgar, "I'm no good."

She knew what he was talking about, all right. She wasn't in the least surprised. "Yes, you are, Edgar," she said lamely. "You're a fine man. I understand." . . .

Chimes range, the clockwork clicked, and the range's humming stopped. "Call the children before everything gets cold," she said.

"They're coming," Edgar tried to hug her again, and she let him this time. "Listen," he said passionately, "it's the world, Wan – me and the world. I'm no good to anybody, not in *this* world. Nothing but a Reek and Wreck, and that's all my kids'll be, and a guy's got to have kicks or he doesn't want to live – and the only kicks left for a dumb bastard like me are the bad ones. I'm no good, Wan, no good!"

"It's me that's no good to anybody," said Wanda wearily. "Nobody needs me. You or even little old Delores could run the house and all, it's so easy. And now I'm too

fat for anybody but the kids to love me. My mother got fat, and my grandmother got fat, and guess it's in the blood; but somebody needed them, they were still some good. But you don't need me, Ed, and you can't help it if you don't love me any more. Just the way men are, and you can't help it if you're the way God made you." She
165 looked at him lovingly, pityingly. "Poor man." (~ 1870 words)

Annotations

chuckhole Schlagloch – – **lane** Fahrspur, -rinne – – **at length** schließlich – – **appreciatively** [ə'priːʃiətivli] anerkennend, dankbar – – **to chuckle** leise (in sich hinein) lachen, kichern – – **to patronize** hier: gönnerhaft behandeln, von oben herab behandeln – – **reclamation** hier: Wiedergewinnung, Rückgewinnung, Regeneration – – **dutiful** gehorsam, pflichtbewußt – – **to tend** bedienen – – **to blush** erröten – – **apologetically** [əpɔləˈdʒetikl] entschuldigend, bedauernd – – **vehement** heftig – – **to frown** [au] die Stirn runzeln – – **ulcer** [ˈʌlsə] Geschwür – – **twinge** zuckender Schmerz – – **notable** bedeutende Persönlichkeit – – **backwater** "tiefste Provinz", "rückständiges Nest" – – **dining alcove** Eßecke – – **radiant heating in the floor** Fußbodenzentralheizung – – **range** Herd – – **grease** Fett – – **to dip** tauchen, stecken – – **nifty** schlau – – **spanking clean** absolut sauber – – **odor** Duft – – **perceptible** wahrnehmbar, deutlich – – **suspicious** argwöhnisch, mißtrauisch – – **odd** eigenartig, sonderbar – – **expansive** mitteilsam – – **to jar** stoßen, schlagen – – **jollity** Fröhlichkeit, Ausgelassenheit – – **to wrong** hier: bearbeiten – – **transducer** Umsetzer – – **out of commission** außer Betrieb – – **tub** Wanne – – **brisk** forsch – – **deduction** Abzug – – **to go nutty** verrückt werden – – **organ** Orgel – – **kerosene** Kerosin – – **deceit** Betrug, Täuschung – – **chime** Glockenspiel, Geläut, Läuten – – **kicks** Spaß – – **dumb** [dʌm] doof, blöd(e).

WORKSHEET

Language

1. As the German translations have been given for the new vocabulary you will be able to find paraphrases, definitions or synonyms for the new words. Go ahead!

   Hidden words

   1 austerity, 2 autarky, 3 automation, 4 boom, 5 bonus, 6 claim, 7 co-rule, 8 decline, 9 demand, 10 earn, 11 free enterprise, 12 income, 13 lockout, 14 market, 15 money, 16 parttime job, 17 picket, 18 planned economy, 19 post, 20 recovery, 21 shift, 22 skill, 23 slump, 24 stagnation, 25 strike, 26 supply, 27 wages, 28 closed shop

2. Word finding game. Find the hidden words. The remaining letters will reveal two sentences!

```
P  B  P  O  H  S  D  E  S  O  L  C  T  Y  H
I  O  E  M  C  L  A  I  M  B  O  O  M  P  E
C  N  A  A  U  T  O  M  A  T  I  O  N  A  R
K  U  K  E  T  E  T  A  S  N  N  S  R  R  S
E  S  E  A  T  N  T  R  U  O  R  N  A  T  U
T  H  Y  M  S  I  T  K  C  I  E  D  T  T  P
T  I  K  H  O  L  E  E  P  T  A  Y  Y  I  P
U  F  R  W  P  C  D  T  A  A  E  S  Y  M  L
O  T  A  E  E  E  N  S  S  N  P  E  R  E  Y
K  P  T  I  N  D  R  I  O  G  A  G  E  J  S
C  M  U  N  L  I  S  M  T  A  U  A  V  O  K
O  U  A  U  S  T  E  R  I  T  Y  W  O  B  I
L  L  E  K  I  R  T  S  R  S  N  I  C  N  L
P  S  E  L  U  R  O  C  D  N  A  M  E  D  L
E  S  I  R  P  R  E  T  N  E  E  E  R  F  G
```

Text Analysis

1. Retell the first part of the story using the following words to make one sentence for each group:
   a limousine, work, crew, hole
   b Shah, slaves, Dr Halyard, citizens
   c war, machines, automatic control
   d less, better, cheaper, but more . . .
   e Army, Reconstruction and Reclamation Corps
   f money, taxes

    g   advances, industrial communities, difficult skills
    h   Shah: communism, Halyard: private ownership
    i   coordination, competition, standard of living
    k   ulcer, interpreter, backwater of civilization.
2. List all the modern appliances mentioned in the second part.
3. List the items of social progress.
4. Have a look at the title of the novel! Find out what it means and interpret it!
5. Make five wh-questions on each part of the text and put them to your fellow students!
6. Is it justified to call the workers 'slaves'?
7. What relation can you make out between the two excerpts?

Discussion and Comment

1. Why does K. Vonnegut make use of the old utopian method of a guide and a visitor?
2. Can you explain the abbreviation "Reeks and Wrecks"? And what does it imply?
3. Is the Shah right to call that sort of country "communist"? What does the guide answer?
4. You could say that the text shows typically American features and also un-American ones. Can you distinguish them?
5. How is the problem of unemployment solved in the text? Does it sound convincing?
6. What would you say is the underlying problem raised by the text? Discuss it!
7. Relish the following story!

Paradise Lost

A man complained that he could never get caught up. Every day for 20 years he looked at his desk piled high with unfinished matters, letters unanswered, bills to be paid, appointments accumulated, problems that should have been settled two weeks ago. When he walked out of the house to get away from the clutter, there was the grass that needed to be cut, hedges that should have been trimmed last spring. If he could only get caught up, just once, if only for 20 minutes!

Then he slept and had a dream. He was in a large room with a beautiful mahogany desk before him, clean, bright and shiny. On it there were no appointments – nothing. Through the window he could see the lawn and hedges neatly trimmed, everything in place. It was a great relief. He had caught up at last – thank the Lord! – and peace was his.

Or was it? All around the edges of his paradise there nibbled a little question: What do I do now? The postman came down the street whistling, and he hailed him. The postman had no letters for him; he was just out for a walk. "Please tell me," the man said, "what place this is."

"Why, don't you know?" replied the postman cheerily. "This is Hell."

From: Reader's Digest, US ed., 8/75

5 WHAT IS CAPITALISM?

Introduction

We have learnt in *Topic* 4 that the Shah, visiting America, calls the American economic system *Communist.* You will also remember why this is so: in the America of the future, competition between the companies, i. e. an important part of the free market system, and unemployment have been abolished by Government interference. The Shah's statement, however, is strongly rejected by Dr Halyard who points out that the firms and machines are privately owned, i. e. society's means of production are owned by a minority of individuals. Karl Marx, the father of Communism, regards the private ownership of capital equipment as the decisive feature of *Capitalism.* Obviously, the economy of the America depicted in Vonnegut's sf shows characteristics of both economic systems.
But there is more to Capitalism and Communism than that: the two not only differ in economic terms, they also mean different political and ethical systems. Throughout the first part of this book you will therefore be confronted with texts which will give you an idea of the philosophical backgrounds of the two systems, their leading theoreticians, main features, important institutions, and their impact on society, particularly on people's daily lives.
The texts (A–C) presented below deal with various aspects of Capitalism, but there are also some comments on Communism in text C.
Max Weber (1864–1920), a well-known German sociologist, sees Capitalism as a product of religious (Puritan) principles and ideas; *Adam Smith* (1723–1790), one of the most famous British economists and the first to propose a theory of Capitalism, follows with texts considering such important aspects as the division of labour, the price of commodities, and the effect of self-interest on the national economy. *Milton Friedman* (1912–), Nobel laureate economist and main spokesperson for *monetarism,* an economic theory which has influenced the economic decisions of governments in most Western industrialized states since the late 1970's, challenges the belief that capitalism creates inequalities.

A) Asceticism and the Spirit of Capitalism

For everyone without exception God's Providence has prepared a calling, which he should profess and in which he should labour. And this calling is not, as it was for the Lutheran, a fate to which he must submit and which he must make the best of, but God's commandment to the individual to work for the divine glory.
5 The Puritan ethic also holds that a man's life in his calling is an exercise in ascetic virtue, a proof of his state of grace through his conscientiousness, which is expressed in the care and method with which he pursues his calling. What God demands is not labour in itself, but rational labour in a calling. In the Puritan concept of the calling the emphasis is always placed on this methodical character of worldly
10 asceticism, not, as with Luther, on the acceptance of the lot which God has irretrievably assigned to man.
Hence the question whether anyone may combine several callings is answered in the affirmative, if it is useful for the common good or one's own, and not injurious to anyone, and if it does not lead to unfaithfulness in one of the callings. Even a

15 change of calling is by no means regarded as objectionable, if it is not thoughtless and is made for the purpose of pursuing a calling more pleasing to God, which means, on general principles, one more useful.

It is true that the usefulness of a calling, and thus its favour in the sight of God, is measured primarily in moral terms, and thus in terms of the importance of the goods
20 produced in it for the community. But a further, and, above all, in practice the most important, criterion is found in private profitableness. For if God, whose hand the Puritan sees in all the occurrences of life, shows one of His elect a chance of profit, he must do it with a purpose. Hence the faithful Christian must follow the call by taking advantage of the opportunity. "If God show you a way in which you may
25 lawfully get more than in another *way (without wrong to your soul or to any other), if you refuse this, and choose the less gainful way, you cross one of the ends of your calling, and you refuse to be God's steward, and to accept His gifts and use them for Him when He requireth it: you may labour to be rich for God, though not for the flesh and sin."
30 Wealth is thus bad ethically only in so far as it is a temptation to idleness and sinful enjoyment of life, and its acquisition is bad only when it is with the purpose of later living merrily and without care. But as a performance of duty in a calling it is not only morally permissible, but actually enjoined. The parable of the servant who was rejected because he did not increase the talent which was entrusted to him seemed
35 to say so directly. To wish to be poor was, it was often argued, the same as wishing to be unhealthy; it is objectionable as a glorification of works and derogatory to the glory of God. Especially begging, on the part of one able to work, is not only the sin of slothfulness, but a violation of the duty of brotherly love according to the Apostle's own word. (~ 560 ws)

From: Max Weber "Asceticism and the Spirit of Capitalism", in *The Protestant Ethic and the Spirit of Capitalism,* Translated by Talcot Parsons, Charles Scribner's Sons, New York 1958, p. 155 ff.

Annotations

(The words marked * should be memorized.)

Providence God's care for human beings and all he has created – – ***calling** occupation, profession or trade; Beruf, Berufung – – **to profess** (formal) have as one's occupation or business – – ***to labour** work; try hard – – ***fate** power looked upon as controlling all events in a way that cannot be resisted; destiny; Schicksal – – ***to submit** put (oneself) under the control of another – – ***commandment** *here:* divine order, esp. one of the ten laws given by God to Moses – – **divine** of, from or like God – – **ascetic** [ə'setik] selfdenying, austere, leading a life of severe self-discipline – – **virtue** (any particular kind of) goodness or excellence – – **grace** *here:* God's mercy and favour towards mankind; influence and result of this; Gnade – – **conscientiousness** quality or state of being guided by one's sense of duty – – ***to pursue** [–'–] go on with; work at – – **irretrievable** that cannot be put or set right; ein für allemal – – ***to assign** give (to s. o.) for use or enjoyment, or as a share or part in a distribution, e. g. of work or duty; Aufgaben verteilen – – **hence** for this

"My Protestant work ethic made me a bundle, but my Puritanical guilt complex won't let me enjoy it."
(**bundle** [sl] a lot of money)

Source: *The New Yorker Magazine,* Inc., 1973

reason – – **in the affirmative** positively, "yes" – – **injurious** (to) (formal) causing injury; hurtful; nachteilig für, schädlich für – – **unfaithfulness** Treulosigkeit, Untreue – – **usefulness** quality of producing good results – – ***criterion** (pl. criteria) [krɑiˈtiəriən] Kriterium – – **profitableness** quality of bringing profit – – **elect** persons specially chosen or considered to be the best – – ***purpose** plan, intention; Absicht, Zweck – – **gainful** profitable – – ***end** *here:* goal, aim – – **steward** *here:* Verwalter – – **flesh** *here:* negative traits in human nature, such as greed etc. – – **temptation** Verführung (in moralischer Hinsicht); (in sexueller Hinsicht: *seduction*) – – ***idleness** laziness – – **acquisition** the action of gaining by skill or ability, by one's own efforts or behaviour; Erwerb(ung) – – **performance of duty** Pflichterfüllung – – **to enjoin** command, urge, prescribe – – ***to entrust** s. th. (to) anvertrauen – – **derogatory** [diˈrɔgətəri] tending to damage or take away s. o. 's reputation, credit – – ***to beg** make a living by asking for money (in the streets, etc.) – – **slothfulness** laziness – – **violation** action contrary to (what one's conscience tells one to do); instance of acting towards (a sacred place, etc) without proper respect; instance of breaking (an oath, a treaty, etc.)

Assignments

1. **Content and Comment**
   Deal with the following questions by using your own words as far as possible.
1.1 What does the text tell us about the Puritan ideas of work and calling?
1.2 To what degree did this concept help develop a positive attitude to wealth?
1.3 In what way alone, however, is wealth to be used?
1.4 Explain why the cartoon above describes very well the possible psychological consequences of such an attitude to wealth?
1.5 What might be the negative implications for the poor, of this concept of wealth?

2. **Playing with words**

In line 1 of our text the word "God" is used. This word is one of many which result in sensible words when read backwards. Thus, "god" becomes "dog" and "nap" becomes "pan". The German language, too, contains numerous words which make sense when read backwards, such as "Regen". The German dictionary calls these words *Palindrome* (cf. Wahrig, *Deutsches Wörterbuch,* column 2653). The English, however, have reserved the expression *palindromes* for words, verses, or sentences (as "Abba", "Live Evil", "Able was I ere I saw Elba") "that read the *same* backwards or forwards" (cf. Webster's *Third New International Dictionary,* page 1625). This means that the words used in the *headline* of the following article are **not** *palindromes* in the English meaning of the term.

God And Dog

Think about this problem: One morning, exactly at sunrise, the monk Otto began to climb a tall mountain. The narrow path, no more than a foot or two wide, spiralled around the mountain to a wonderful temple at the summit. Otto climbed the path at different speeds, stopping many times along the way to rest. He reached the
5 temple shortly before sunset. After . . . several days of fasting and meditation he began his journey back along the same path, starting at sunrise and again walking at different speeds with many pauses along the way. Otto's average descending speed was naturally faster than his average climbing speed.
Is there any point along the path that Otto will occupy on both trips at precisely the
10 same time of day?
The answer, which we will come to later, is surprisingly simple.
Consider for a moment the name Otto, or Bob; or the words mum, dad, deed, noon, radar, rotator . . . What do all these words have in common? They are all "palindromes". The dictionary defines a palindrome as a word or sentence that
15 reads the same backwards as forwards.
Webster's 3rd New International Dictionary lists the word "Kinnikinnik" which besides being an Indian smoking mixture made of bark and leaves, is also the longest single-word palindrome.
The number of palindromic words is clearly limited, but palindromic sentences are
20 a different matter. Over the years, intelligent men and women have spent many sleepless nights in search of the perfect palindromic sentence. Here are the results of some of their efforts:
"Madam, I'm Adam" (amusing to think of Eve's partner showing such good English manners);
25 "A man, a plan, a canal, Panama!" (dedicated to the man who made a deep impression on Central America);
"Sex at noon taxes!" (hardly surprising if one stays up all night pursuing palindromes);
"Ein Neger mit Gazelle zagt im Regen nie" (just to prove that English doesn't have
30 a monopoly on such things).
The American singer Stevie Wonder made an LP record in 1968 with the title: "Eivets Rednow". More recently in 1983 a Black Sabbath LP was titled "Live Evil". And the Swedish pop group Abba has the distinction of a palindromic name *and* hit-song title: "S.O.S.".

35 Palindromes are not easy to invent. The earliest traceable palindrome in English was devised by John Taylor in 1614, when he wrote: "This line is the same backward, as it is forward, and I will give any man five shillings apiece for as many as they can make in English: Lewd did I live, & evil did I dwel."
Since Taylor's time many longer palindromes have been written. A talented
40 contemporary palindromist is John Pool, who is reputed to be the first man in the history of literature to write one thousand palindromes in English. Here are a few of his longer creations:
    Norma, I am Ron!
    Panda here had nap
45   no lemon, no melon
    Ted, a canoe on a cadet
    sin? if Dennis sinned, finis!
    Otto, lotto?
Which reminds me of our friend at the top of the page.
50 In a certain way the monk Otto experienced a "palindromic journey". Like a sentence which reads identically forwards and backwards, his two trips up and down the mountain were along the same path.
And just as in a palindrome the letters "meet themselves" somewhere in the middle; so Otto would meet himself if he were to imagine his "Doppelgänger" coming down
55 the mountain towards him.
The answer therefore is that there must be a point along the path that Otto will occupy on both trips at precisely the same time of day.

Vocabulary

bark – Rinde
contemporary [kən'temprəri] – zeitgenössisch
to dedicate s. th. to s. b. – jdm. etwas widmen
descending speed – Abstiegsgeschwindigkeit
to devise – (sich) ausdenken
to dwell – leben, wohnen
lewd [luːd] – unanständig
monk – Mönch
monopoly [mə'nɔpəli] – Monopol
reputed, he is reputed to be – man sagt, daß er . . . ist
to sin – sündigen, sich versündigen, verstoßen gegen
summit – Gipfel
to tax – strapazieren, anstrengen
traceable ['treisəbl] – auffindbar, nachweisbar

From: *Spotlight,* March 1986

2.1 Find other English words of type "god" – "dog" (at least 10).

2.2 On top of this rhomb is a vowel which forms the first letter of the word (type "god" – "dog"!) to be put in the squares of the second step. The word on the next step (3) begins with the last letter of the preceding word (2). Go on like this filling all squares with the fitting words (type "god" – "dog"!). The vowel on top of the rhomb and the consonant on the bottom also result in a word.

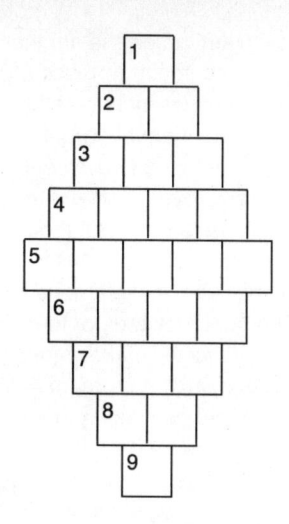

The words explained:
1. vowel; 2. preposition; 3. negation; 4. device for controlling the flow of liquid or gas from a pipe, barrel, etc. (plural!) 5. long narrow piece of leather or other flexible material (often with a buckle) to fasten things together or to keep s. th. (e. g. a wrist watch) in place. 6. something less than the whole 7. piece of advice on how to do s. th. 8. abbreviation of *public relations*. 9. consonant.

2.3 Read the words you found backwards and explain their meaning in English.

B)
Of the Division of Labour

The effects of the division of labour, in the general business of society, will be more easily understood by considering in what manner it operates in some particular manufactures.

To take an example, therefore, from a very trifling manufacture; but one in which
5 the division of labour has been very often taken notice of, the trade of the pin-maker; a workman not educated to this business (which the division of labour has rendered a distinct trade), nor acquainted with the use of the machinery employed in it (to the invention of which the same division of labour has probably given occasion), could scarce, perhaps, with his utmost industry, make one pin in a day, and certainly
10 could not make twenty. But in the way in which this business is now carried on, not only the whole work is a peculiar trade, but it is divided into a number of branches, of which the greater part are likewise peculiar trades. One man draws out the wire, another straights it, a third cuts it, a fourth points it, a fifth grinds it at the top for receiving the head; to make the head requires three distinct operations; to put it

15 on is a peculiar business, to whiten the pins is another; it is even a trade by itself to put them into the paper; and the important business of making a pin is, in this manner, divided into about eighteen distinct operations, which, in some manufactories, are all performed by distinct hands, though in others the same man will sometimes perform two or three of them. I have seen a small manufactory of this
20 kind where ten men only were employed, and where some ot them consequently performed two or three distinct operations. But though they were very poor, and therefore but indifferently accommodated with the necessary machinery, they could, when they exerted themselves, make among them about twelve pounds of pins in a day. There are in a pound upwards of four thousand pins of a middling
25 size. Those ten persons, therefore, could make among them upwards of forty-eight thousand pins in a day. Each person, therefore, making a tenth part of forty-eight thousand pins, might be considered as making four thousand eight hundred pins in a day. But it they had all wrought separately and independently, and without any of them having been educated to this peculiar business, they could certainly not
30 each of them have made twenty, perhaps not one pin in a day; that is, certainly, not the two hundred and fortieth, perhaps not the four thousand eight hundredth part of what they are at present capable of performing, in consequence of a proper division and combination of their different operations. (~ 460 ws)

Of the Principle Which Gives Occasion to the Division of Labour

This division of labour, from which so many advantages are derived, is not originally the effect of any human wisdom, which foresees and intends that general opulence to which it gives occasion. It is the necessary, though very slow and gradual consequence of a certain propensity in human nature which has in view no such
5 extensive utility: the propensity to truck, barter, and exchange one thing for another. This propensity is common to all men, and to be found in no other race of animals, which seem to know neither this nor any other species of contracts.
In civilized society man stands at all times in need of the co-operation and assistance of great multitudes.
10 In almost every other race of animals each individual, when it is grown up to maturity, is entirely independent, and in its natural state has occasion for the assistance of no other living creature. But man has almost constant occasion for the help of his brethren, and it is in vain for him to expect it from their benevolence only. He will be more likely to prevail if he can interest their self-love in his favour, and show them
15 that it is for their own advantage to do for him what he requires of them. Whoever offers to another a bargain of any kind, proposes to do this. Give me that which I want, and you shall have this which you want, is the meaning of every such offer; and it is in this manner that we obtain from one another the far greater part of those good offices which we stand in need of. It is not from the benevolence of the butcher,
20 the brewer, or the baker that we expect our dinner, but from their regard to their

own interest. We address ourselves, not to their humanity but to their self-love, and never talk to them of our own necessities but of their advantages. Nobody but a beggar chooses to depend chiefly upon the benevolence of his fellow-citizens.

25 As it is by treaty, by barter, and by purchase that we obtain from one another the greater part of those mutual good offices which we stand in need of, so it is this same trucking disposition which originally gives occasion to the division of labour. In a tribe of hunters or shepherds a particular person makes bows and arrows, for example, with more readiness and dexterity than any other. He frequently exchanges them for cattle or for venison with his companions; and he finds at last
30 that he can in this manner get more cattle and venison than if he himself went to the field to catch them. From a regard to his own interest, therefore, the making of bows and arrows grows to be his chief business, and he becomes a sort of armourer.

(~ 485 ws)

The Price of Commodities

When the price of any commodity is neither more nor less than what is sufficient to pay the rent of the land, the wages of the labour, and the profits of the stock employed in raising, preparing, and bringing it to market, according to their natural rates, the commodity is then sold for what may be called its *natural* price . . .
5 The actual price at which any commodity is commonly sold is called its *market* price. It may either be above, or below, or exactly the same with its natural price.

The market price of every particular commodity is regulated by the proportion between the *quantity* which is actually brought to market, and the *demand* of those who are willing to pay the natural price of the commodity, or the whole value of the
10 rent, labour, and profit, which must be paid in order to bring it thither. Such people may be called the effectual demanders, and their demand the effectual demand; since it may be sufficient to effectuate the bringing of the commodity to market. It is different from the absolute demand. A very poor man may be said in some sense to have a demand for a coach and six; he might like to have it; but his demand is
15 not an effectual demand, as the commodity can never be brought to market in order to satisfy it.

When the quantity of any commodity which is brought to market falls short of the effectual demand, all those who are willing to pay the whole value of the rent, wages, and profit, which must be paid in order to bring it thither, cannot be supplied with
20 the quantity which they want. Rather than want it altogether, some of them will be willing to give more. A competition will immediately begin among them, and the market price will rise more or less above the natural price, according as either the greatness of the deficiency, or the wealth and wanton luxury of the competitors, happen to animate more or less the eagerness of the competition. Among
25 competitors of equal wealth and luxury the same deficiency will generally occasion a more or less eager competition, according as the acquisition of the commodity

happens to be of more or less importance to them. Hence the exorbitant price of the necessaries of life during the blockade of a town or in a famine.

When the quantity brought to market exceeds the effectual demand, it cannot be all sold to those who are willing to pay the whole value of the rent, wages, and profit, which must be paid in order to bring it thither. Some part must be sold to those who are willing to pay less, and the low price which they give for it must reduce the price of the whole. The market price will sink more or less below the natural price, according as the greatness of the excess increases more or less the competition of the sellers, or according as it happens to be more or less important to them to get immediately rid of the commodity. The same excess in the importation of perishable, will occasion a much greater competition than in that of durable commodities; in the importation of oranges, for example, than in that of old iron.

When the quantity brought to market is just sufficient to supply the effectual demand, and no more, the market price naturally comes to be either exactly, or as nearly as can be judged of, the same with the natural price. The whole quantity upon hand can be disposed of for this price, and cannot be disposed of for more. The competition of the different dealers obliges them all to accept of this price, but does not oblige them to accept of less.

The quantity of every commodity brought to market naturally suits itself to the effectual demand. It is the interest of all those who employ their land, labour, or stock, in bringing any commodity to market, that the quantity never should exceed the effectual demand; and it is the interest of all other people that it never should fall short of that demand.   (~ 715 ws)

Self-Interest, the "Invisible Hand"

As every individual, therefore, endeavors as much as he can both to employ his capital in the support of domestic industry, and so to direct that industry that its produce may be of the greatest value, every individual necessarily labours to render the annual revenue of the society as great as he can. He generally, indeed, neither intends to promote the public interest, nor knows how much he is promoting it . . . he intends only his own security . . . he intends only his own gain, and he is in this, as in many other cases, *led on by an invisible hand* [Italics added] to promote an end which was no part of his intention. Nor is it always the worse for the society that it was no part of it. By pursuing his own interest, he frequently promotes that of the society more effectually than he really intends to promote it. I have never known much good done by those who affected to trade for the public good.
(~ 175 ws)

Abbreviated from: Adam Smith, *The Wealth of Nations,* Penguin Books Ltd, 1983.

Annotations

(Of the Division of Labour):
*manufacture the making or production of goods and materials; (pl) manufactured goods and articles – – **trifling** unimportant – – ***trade** Handel, Gewerbe, Beruf, Handwerk – – **pinmaker** Nadelmacher – – **to give occasion to** be the cause of – – ***scarce** [skɛəs] rare – – **industry** here: effort – – ***likewise** ebenso – – **branch** here: Fachgebiet – – **to grind** (ground, ground) schleifen, wetzen – – **operation** here: Arbeitsschritt – – **manufactory** (arch.) Betrieb; modern English: factory – – **to perform** do – – **distinct** different – – **indifferent** here: of low quality, poor – – **accommodated** here: equipped – – **to exert o. s.** make an effort; sich anstrengen – – **middling** middle – – **wrought** (arch.) worked
(Of the Principle Which Gives Occasion to the Division of Labour): ***to derive** have as a starting-point, source or origin – – **opulence** (formal) wealth, abundance – – **propensity** (to/towards) natural tendency – – **utility** quality of being useful – – **to truck** (arch.) exchange – – **to barter** (with s. o. for sth.) exchange, swop – – **multitude** great number (of people) – – ***maturity** state of being full grown – – **benevolence** [–'– – –] wish to do good; activity in doing good – – **to endeavour** [in'devə] try, attempt – – **brethren** (arch.) brothers – – **to prevail** here: be successful, succeed – – ***bargain** agreement to buy, sell or exchange sth., made after discussion; sth. obtained as the result of such an agreement – – ***obtain** get – – **offices** here: services – – ***purchase** ['pɜtʃəs] buying – – ***mutual** wechselseitig – – **dexterity** skill – – **venison** deer meat; Wildbret – – **armourer** manufacturer or repairer of arms and armour (= Panzerung)
(The Price of Commodities): ***commodity** thing, esp. an article of trade – – ***rent** regular payment for the use of land, a building, a room or rooms, machinery, etc. – – ***stock** here: Kapital – – **it** = commodity – – **rates** here: value; Wert – – ***proportion** Verhältnis – – ***demand** here: Nachfrage – – **to want** wish; lack – – **effectual** bringing about the result required; **effectual demand** durch vorhandenes Bargeld gedeckte Nachfrage – – **to effectuate** bring about, accomplish – – **coach and six** Sechsspänner – – **deficiency** [di'fiʃənsi] the state of being short of what is correct or needed; Mangel, Manko – – **wanton** luxurious; üppig – – **to occasion** be the cause of – – **necessaries** ['nesəsrɪz] things necessary (for living) – – **famine** extreme scarcity (esp. of food) in a region – – ***to exceed** be greater than – – ***excess** abundance; Übermaß, Überschuß – – ***to get rid of** become free of; here: sell – – **importation** act of importing (goods) – – **perishable** (esp. of food) quickly or easily going bad – – **durable** likely to last for a long time – – ***to dispose of** get rid of – – **to accept of sth.** (arch.) to accept sth. – – ***to suit o. s.** (to) adjust o. s. (to); sich anpassen an
(Self-Interest, The "Invisible Hand"): ***invisible** that cannot be seen – – **to affect** here: aim at; modern usage: pretend to have an influence on – – ***to trade** buy and sell

Assignments

1. **Content and Comment**

   1.1 Complete the following sentence fragments. Try and use your own words.
   1. Division of labour means . . .
   2. The advantage of the division of labour lies in the fact that . . .

3. Although division of labour also operates in Communist countries it is typical of Capitalism because . . .
4. The disadvantages of dividing work into more and more individual operations are that 1. . . ., 2. . . . and 3. . . .
5. According to Adam Smith, the original reason for the division of labour was . . .
6. In the text *Self-Interest, the "Invisible Hand"* Smith claims that the self-interest of individuals in a society has . . . though the individual . . .
7. In my opinion this idea is wrong/right, in so far as . . .
8. Smith explains that there are two types of price: 1. the . . . and 2. the . . .
9. The . . . price is sufficient to cover . . .
10. The . . . price depends on the . . . of supply and demand.
11. The . . . price rises if . . . because . . .
12. The . . . price declines if . . .
13. The fall of the . . . price also depends on whether the goods are . . .

2. **Language**
2.1 In this exercise you are presented with a series of pairs of words which look or sound similar but which mean different things. Below each pair there is a list of five possible meanings. For instance, in line 8 of "The Price of Commodities" the word "brought" is used, which looks and sounds similar to "bought". What are the equivalent words or phrases among the five possibilities supplied?

Example: A *brought*   B *bought*
1. sold 2. conveyed by carrying 3. took 4. purchased 5. removed
Answer: A2; B4

(1) A *adverse*   B *averse*
1. disinclined 2. awkward 3. reverse 4. hostile 5. perverse

(2) A *affect*   B *effect*
1. damage 2. bring about 3. result in 4. pretend to 5. fault

(3) A *allusion*   B *illusion*
1. conspiracy 2. reference 3. delusion 4. footnote 5. adherence

(4) A *ascetic*   B *aesthetic*
1. sharp 2. appreciative of the beautiful 3. dandified 4. rendering senseless 5. austere

(5) A *beneficent*   B *beneficial*
1. blessed 2. advantageous 3. ecclesiastical 4. kind 5. magnificent

(6) A *casual*   B *causal*
1. resultant 2. acting as a cause 3. given to adopting causes 4. unmethodical 5. highly toxic

(7) A *complement*   B *compliment*
1. full number 2. expression of distaste 3. implement 4. remainder 5. expression of praise

(8) A *definite*   B *definitive*
1. final 2. uncertain 3. conditional 4. certain 5. comprehensive
(9) A *deferential*   B *differential*
1. distinctive 2. indifferent 3. logical 4. respectful 5. hesitant
(10) A *dependent*   B *dependant*
1. childish 2. suspended 3. trusting 4. one who relies upon another 5. reliant

2.2 Insert the appropriate word from exercise 1.1 in the following sentences:
1. Her feelings were still _____ to any man save one.
2. It is the _____ book on the ghost or near-ghost towns of the Old West.
3. _____ clauses are introduced by connectives.
4. Moist, cool summers are not _____ to such crops as maize.
5. Alexander Pope's works are full of historical _____ (Pl.).
6. He _____ (Past) not to hear me.
7. Heat rays shimmering on the road produced the _____ of pools of water.
8. Each candidate was introduced with the usual _____ (Pl.).
9. The University of Maryland, European Division, provides evening classes for the American soldiers and their _____ (Pl.).
10. Most people are not _____ to a glass of wine or two.

C)
Capitalism and Equality

Everywhere in the world there are gross inequities of income and wealth. They offend most of us. Few can fail to be moved by the contrast between the luxury enjoyed by some and the grinding poverty suffered by others.

In the past century a myth has grown up that free market capitalism – equality of
5 opportunity as we have interpreted that term – increases such inequalities, that it is a system under which the rich exploit the poor.

Nothing could be further from the truth. Wherever the free market has been permitted to operate, wherever anything approaching equality of opportunity has existed, the ordinary man has been able to attain levels of living never dreamed
10 of before. Nowhere is the gap between rich and poor wider, nowhere are the rich richer and the poor poorer, than in those societies that do not permit the free market to operate. That is true of feudal societies like medieval Europe, India before independence, and much of modern South America, where inherited status determines position. It is equally true of centrally planned societies, like Russia or
15 China or India since independence, where access to government determines position. It is true even where central planning was introduced, as in all three of these countries, in the name of equality.

Russia is a country of two nations: a small privileged upper class of bureaucrats,

Communist party officials, technicians; and a great mass of people living little better than their great-grandparents did. The upper class has access to special shops, schools, and luxuries of all kind; the masses are condemned to enjoy little more than the basic necessities. We remember asking a tourist guide in Moscow the cost of a large automobile that we saw and being told, "Oh, those aren't for sale; they're only for the Politburo." Several recent books by American journalists document in great detail the contrast between the privileged life of the upper classes and the poverty of the masses.

Industrial progress, mechanical improvement, all of the great wonders of the modern era have meant relatively little to the wealthy. The rich in Ancient Greece would have benefited hardly at all from modern plumbing: running servants replaced running water. Television and radio – the patricians of Rome could enjoy the leading musicians and actors in their home, could have the leading artists as domestic retainers. Ready-to-wear clothing, supermarkets – all these and many other modern developments would have added little to their life. They would have welcomed the improvements in transportation and in medicine, but for the rest, the great achievements of Western capitalism have redounded primarily to the benefit of the ordinary person. These achievements have made available to the masses conveniences and amenities that were previously the exclusive prerogative of the rich and powerful.

In 1848 John Stuart Mill wrote: "Hitherto it is questionable if all the mechanical inventions yet made have lightened the day's toil of any human being. They have enabled a greater population to live the same life of drudgery and imprisonment, and an increased number of manufacturers and others to make fortunes. They have increased the comforts of the middle classes. But they have not yet begun to effect those great changes in human destiny, which it is in their nature and in their futurity to accomplish."

No one could say that today. You can travel from one end of the industrialized world to the other and almost the only people you will find engaging in backbreaking toil are people who are doing it for sport. To find people whose day's toil has not been lightened by mechanical invention, you must go to the noncapitalist world: to Russia, China, India or Bangladesh, parts of Yugoslavia; or to the more backward capitalist countries – in Africa, the Mideast, South America; and until recently, Spain or Italy.

A society that puts equality – in the sense of equality of outcome – ahead of freedom will end up with neither equality nor freedom. The use of force to achieve equality will destroy freedom, and the force, introduced for good purposes, will end up in the hands of people who use it to promote their own interests.

On the other hand, a society that puts freedom first will, as a happy by-product, end up with both greater freedom and greater equality. Though a by-product of freedom, greater equality is not an accident. A free society releases the energies and abilities of people to pursue their own objectives. It prevents some people from arbitrarily suppressing others. It does not prevent some people from achieving positions of

privilege, but so long as freedom is maintained, it prevents those positions of privilege from becoming institutionalized; they are subject to continued attack by other able, ambitious people. Freedom means diversity but also mobility. It preserves the opportunity for today's disadvantaged to become tomorrow's
65 privileged and, in the process, enables almost everyone, from top to bottom, to enjoy a fuller and richer life. (~ 830 ws)

Abbreviated from: Milton Friedman and Rose Friedman, *Free To Choose,* Pelican Books 1980, pp. 179–182.

Annotations

(The words marked * should be memorized)

(Capitalism and Equality): **inequity** (instance of) injustice or unfairness – – ***to exploit** use selfishly, or for one's own profit – – **to attain** succeed in doing or getting; reach – – ***gap** break or opening; unfilled space – – ***medieval** [medi'ivl] of the Middle Ages (about AD 1000–1500) – – ***to inherit** receive property, etc. as heir; erben – – **access** way to a place; opportunity or means of reaching, using or approaching; Zugang – – ***to benefit** (from) receive advantages, profit; help from – – ***plumbing** [plʌmiŋ] the work of a plumber, i. e. of a workman who fits and repairs pipes; Klempner-, Installateurarbeit – – **retainer** *here:* servant – – **to redound** [ri'daund] (formal) contribute greatly in the end; promote – – ***available** verfügbar – – ***convenience** freedom from difficulty or work; Annehmlichkeit, Bequemlichkeit – – **amenity** thing, circumstance, surrounding, that makes life easy or pleasant – – **prerogative** special right or privilege, esp. of a ruler – – **hitherto** until now – – **to lighten** *here:* make easier, make less heavy; reduce the weight of – – ***toil** hard work – – **drudgery** hard and monotonous work – – ***imprisonment** Einengung, Eingekerkertsein, Freiheitsentzug – – **futurity** the future, future events – – ***outcome** result – – **accident** *here:* chance, fortune; Zufall – – ***to release** set free – – **objective** aim – – **subject** (to) liable to experience; ausgesetzt, unterworfen – – **arbitrary** willkürlich – – ***ambitious** ehrgeizig – – **diversity** variety – – **to preserve** keep from loss

Assignment

The following sentences have been split into fragments. The corresponding fragments have been intermingled. Study the text carefully; then put it aside and combine the corresponding fragments from memory.

Whereever the free market has been permitted to operate, whereever anything approaching equality of opportunity has existed . . .

These achievements have made available to the masses . . .

. . . that free market capitalism (. . .) increases (. . .) inequalities, that it is a system under which the rich exploit the poor.

The upper class has access to special shops, schools, and luxuries of all kind; . . .

Nowhere is the gap between rich and

. . . have meant relatively little to the

poor wider, nowhere are the rich richer and the poor poorer, . . .	wealthy.
Russia is a country of two nations: . . .	. . . and almost the only people you will find engaging in backbreaking toil are people who are doing it for sport.
. . . the masses are condemned to enjoy little more than the basic necessities	A society that puts equality (. . .) ahead of freedom . . .
Industrial progress, mechanical improvement, all of the great wonders of the modern era . . .	. . . has not been lightened by mechanical invention, you must go to the non-capitalist world.
. . . conveniences and amenities that were previously the exclusive prerogative of the rich and the powerful.	. . . a small privileged upper class of bureaucrats, Communist party officials, technician; and a great mass of people living little better than their great-grandparents did.
You can travel from one end of the industrialized world to the other . . .	. . . but so long as freedom is maintained, it prevents those positions of privilege from becoming institutionalized.
. . . will end up with neither equality or freedom.	. . . the ordinary man has been able to attain levels of living never dreamed of before.
To find people whose day's toil . . .	. . . than in those societies that do not permit the free market to operate.
It (a free society) does not prevent some people from achieving positions of privilege, . . .	In the past century a myth has grown up . . .

6 THE TIME MACHINE

Note on the Text

H. G. Wells (1866–1946) has been called one of the two creators of modern sf (the other being Jules Verne). Many of his novels and short stories, revealing an abundance of imagination and inventiveness, have become classics. He was the "great originator of science fictional ideas", many of which have staked out the thematic field of sf and belong to sf's standard repertoire; for example: time travel, alien invasion, invisibility, cosmic catastrophies, the reshaping of beasts as men. The sf-critic B. W. Aldiss called him the "Shakespeare of science fiction". *The Time Machine* (1895), Wells's first of over one hundred books, is generally appreciated as very nearly his most perfect piece of fiction, a splendid blending of originality, scientific extrapolation, social criticism, metaphoric storytelling and symbolic meaning.

The novel depicts an evolutionary future for life on Earth. The human species has subdivided into the gentle, degenerate Eloi and the savage Morlocks, both of which ultimately become extinct, as life and the Earth die.
The time traveller at first only meets the angel-like Eloi, who live aboveground in idyllic surroundings; he thinks that mankind has built a communist society. Afterwards he sees the second species, the dark and predatory Morlocks, who live below ground and only appear at night.
Gradually, the time traveller discovers the horrible relationship that exists between the two species.

The following extract is taken from: H. G. Wells, *Selected Short Stories,* Penguin Books Ltd.; Harmondsworth, Middlesex, 1960, p. 40 ff.

I must confess that my satisfaction with my first theories of an automatic civilization and a decadent humanity did not long endure. Yet I could think of no other. Let me put my difficulties. The several big palaces I had explored were mere living places, great dining-halls and sleeping apartments. I could find no machinery, no appliances
5 of any kind. Yet these people were clothed in pleasant fabrics that must at times need renewal, and their sandals, though undecorated, were fairly complex specimens of metal-work. Somehow such things must be made. And the little people displayed no vestige of a creative tendency. There were no shops, no workshops, no signs of importation among them. They spent all their time in playing gently, in
10 bathing in the river, in making love in a half-playful fashion, in eating fruit and sleeping. I could not see how things were kept going. . . .
A little later, the Time Traveller sees a different kind of creature:
My impression of it is, of course, imperfect; but I know it was a dull white, and had strange large greyish-red eyes; also that there was flaxen hair on its head and down
15 its back. But, as I say, it went too fast for me to see distinctly. I cannot even say whether it ran on all-fours, or only with its forearms held very low. After an instant's pause I followed it into the second heap of ruins. I could not find it at first; but, after a time in profound obscurity, I came upon one of those round well-like openings of which I have told you, half closed by a fallen pillar. A sudden thought came to
20 me. Could this Thing have vanished down the shaft? I lit a match, and, looking down, I saw a small, white, moving creature, with large bright eyes which regarded me steadfastly as it retreated. It made me shudder. It was so like a human spider! . . .
I do not know how long I sat peering down that well. It was not for some time that I could succeed in persuading myself that the thing I had seen was human. But,
25 gradually, the truth dawned on me: that Man had not remained one species, but had differentiated into two distinct animals: that my graceful children of the Upper-world were not the sole descendants of our generation, but that this bleached, obscene, nocturnal Thing, which had flashed before me, was also heir to all the ages. . . .
30 And very vaguely there came a suggestion towards the solution of the economic problem that had puzzled me.

Here was the new view. Plainly, this second species of Man was subterranean. There were three circumstances in particular which made me think that its rare emergence above ground was the outcome of a long-continued underground habit. In the first place, there was the bleached look common in most animals that live largely in the dark – the white fish of the Kentucky caves, for instance. Then, those large eyes, with that capacity for reflecting light, are common features of nocturnal things – witness the owl and the cat. And last of all, that evident confusion in the sunshine, that hasty yet fumbling and awkward flight towards dark shadow, and that peculiar carriage of the head while in the light – all reinforced the theory of an extreme sensitiveness of the retina.

Beneath my feet, then, the earth must be tunnelled enormously, and these tunnellings were the habitat of the new race. The presence of ventilating-shafts and wells along the hill slopes – everywhere, in fact, except along the river valley – showed how universal were its ramifications. What so natural then, as to assume that it was in this artificial Under-world that such work as was necessary to the comfort of the daylight race was done? The notion was so plausible that I at once accepted it, and went on to assume the how of this splitting of the human species. I dare say you will anticipate the shape of my theory; though, for myself, I very soon felt that it fell far short of the truth.

At first, proceeding from the problems of our own age, it seemed as clear as daylight to me that the gradual widening of the present merely temporary and social difference between the Capitalist and the Labourer was the key to the whole position. No doubt it will seem grotesque enough to you – and wildly incredible! – and yet even now there are existing circumstances to point that way. There is a tendency to utilize underground space for the less ornamental purposes of civilization; there is the Metropolitan Railway in London, for instance, there are new electric railways, there are subways, there are underground workrooms and restaurants, and they increase and multiply. Evidently, I thought, this tendency had increased till Industry had gradually lost its birthright in the sky. I mean that it had gone deeper and deeper into larger and ever larger underground factories, spending a still-increasing amount of its time therein, till, in the end –! Even now, does not an East-end worker live in such artificial conditions as practically to be cut off from the natural surface ot the earth?

Again, the exclusive tendency of richer people – due, no doubt, to the increasing refinement of their education, and the widening gulf between them and the rude violence of the poor – is already leading to the closing, in their interest, of considerable portions of the surface of the land. About London, for instance, perhaps half the prettier country is shut in against intrusion. And this same widening gulf – which is due to the length and expense of the higher educational process and the increased facilities for and temptations towards refined habits on the part of the rich – will make that exchange between class and class, that promotion by intermarriage which at present retards the splitting of our species along lines of social stratification, less and less frequent. So, in the end, above ground you must have the Haves, pursuing pleasure and comfort, and beauty, and below ground the Havenots, the Workers getting continually adapted to the conditions of their labour. Once they were there, they would, no doubt, have to pay rent, and not a little of it, for the ventilation of their caverns; and if they refused, they would starve or be suffocated for arrears. Such of them as were so constituted as to be miserable and rebellious would die; and, in the end, the balance being permanent, the survivors would become as well adapted to the conditions of underground life, and as happy in their way, as the Upper-world people were to theirs. As it seemed to me, the refined beauty and the etiolated pallor followed naturally enough.

The great triumph of Humanity I had dreamed of took a different shape in my mind. It had been no such triumph of moral education and general cooperation as I had imagined. Instead, I saw a real aristocracy, armed with a perfected science and working to a logical conclusion, the industrial system of today. Its triumph had not been simply a triumph over Nature, but a triumph over Nature and the fellow-man. This, I must warn you, was my theory at the time. I had no convenient cicerone in the pattern of the Utopian books. My explanation may be absolutely wrong. I still think it is the most plausible one. But even on this supposition the balanced civilization that was at last attained must have long since passed its zenith, and was now far fallen into decay. The too-perfect security of the Upper-worlders had led them to a slow movement of degeneration, to a general dwindling in size, strength, and intelligence. That I could see clearly enough already. What had happened to the Under-grounders I did not yet suspect; but from what I had seen of the Morlocks – that, by the by, was the name by which these creatures were called – I could imagine that the modification of the human type was even far more profound than among the 'Eloi', the beautiful race that I already knew. . . .

Clearly, at some time in the Long-Ago of human decay the Morlocks' food had run short. Possibly they had lived on rats and suchlike vermin. Even now man is far less discriminating and exclusive in his food than he was – far less than any monkey. His prejudice against human flesh is no deep-seated instinct. And so these inhuman sons of men –! I tried to look at the thing in a scientific spirit. After all, they were less human and more remote than our cannibal ancestors of three or four thousand yeans ago. And the intelligence that would have made this state of things a torment had gone. Why should I trouble myself? These Eloi were mere fatted cattle, which the ant-like Morlocks preserved and preyed upon – probably saw to the breeding of. And there was Weena dancing at my side!

Then I tried to preserve myself from the horror that was coming upon me, by regarding it as a rigorous punishment of human selfishness. Man had been content to live in ease and delight upon the labours of his fellow man, had taken Necessity as his watchword and excuse, and in the fullnes of time Necessity had come home to him.

(~ 1550 words)

Annotations

(The words marked * should be memorized)

Appliance [ə'plaiəns] instrument or apparatus – – **vestige** ['vestidʒ] (trace or sign)– – **flaxen** pale yellow – – ***well** shaft, usually lined with brick or stone, for obtaining water from an underground source – – ***pillar** upright column of stone – – ***to bleach** make or become white (by chemical action or sunlight) – – **nocturnal** of or in the night – – ***awkward** clumsy, having little skill – – **carriage** manner of holding the head or body – – **habitat** natural place of growth, home – – **ramification** subdivision of something complex, like a network (Verzweigung) – – **to utilize** make use of – – **refinement** refine: cause to become more cultured – – **gulf** deep hollow, chasm, abyss – – ***facilities** circumstances which make it easy to do things (Gelegenheit, Möglichkeit, Einrichtung, Anlage) – – **to retard** check, hinder – – **stratification** (Schichtung) – – **Haves** those who have, possess – – **arrears** money that is owing and that ought to have been paid – – **to etiolate** ['iːtioleit] to bleach – – **pallor** paleness – – **cicerone** guide who describes to sightseers places and objects of interest – – **vermin** wild animals harmful to plants, birds and other animals (Ungeziefer) – – **to prey on** hunt.

WORKSHEET

1. **Language**
   Looking at English vocabulary in general the English language comprises a larger number of words than any other language. It has the richest vocabulary: over 200.000 words, apart from combinations and derivations, are in constant use. This fact is accounted for by the history of the English language, which has mingled elements of many different languages; the following, among others, have contributed to English:
   Celtic, Roman Latin, Anglo-Saxon, Scandinavian, Normanic, humanistic Latin, Greek, Dutch, Italian, German, Indian, American Indian, Russian, Spanish, Turkish, Eskimo, Chinese, Arabic, Persian. (In all, English has borrowed from more than fifty languages; it is, to a higher degree than any other language, a mixed language.)
   1.1 Try and find out when, why, and under what circumstances English adopted words from foreign languages.
   1.2 Try and assign the following groups of words to the above-mentioned languages: whisky, Thames, bin – corridor, bank, sonnet, umbrella – kindergarten, wanderlust, ostpolitik, – cargo, stampede – coffee, kiosk – grave, solid, position – yacht, deck – pundit, bungalow – mill, church – wife, father, house – skunk, racoon – chess, tiger – silk, tea – law, sky, skin – government, parliament, crown – igloo, kayak – chaos, climax, skeleton – steppe, samovar – zenith, zero.
   1.3 The richness of the English language lies mainly in the vast number of synonyms. (cf. the many corresponding tasks in this book!). In many cases,

where German has only one word, English provides two, three or even more, sometimes, but not always differentiating their meanings, e. g.:

German:	English:
Freiheit	freedom, liberty
Wagen	car, cart, carriage, chariot, wagon
vergrößern	magnify, enlarge, increase, raise, aggrandize, expand
(nach)denken	think, reflect, ponder, cogitate, consider, deliberate, contemplate, meditate, muse, ruminate
groß	big, great, large, tall

1.4 Considering the total (theoretic) vocabulary, Romanic words greatly predominate; considering the actual (practical and spoken) vocabulary this relation shifts. Try and explain this shift!

1.5 Find ten words of Romanic and ten of Anglo-Saxon origin.

1.6 It Pays to Enrich Your Word Power.

English has borrowed freely from other languages. In this list of foreign adoptions now in common use, check the word or phrase you believe is *nearest in meaning* to the key word. (Your dictionary will help you!)

1. **pogrom** – A: sorting process. B: massacre. C: search. D: unruly crowd.
2. **aficionado** – A: playboy. B: official. C: close friend. D: ardent fan.
3. **sarong** – A: loose skirt. B: headband. C: swimsuit. D: shawl.
4. **vendetta** – A: malicious destruction. B: public market. C: blood feud. D: fierce competition.
5. **mesa** – A: river gorge. B: plain. C: mountain range. D: plateau.
6. **regatta** – A: fanfare. B: boat race. C: finery. D: pageant.
7. **siesta** – A: summer rain. B: harvest. C: nap. D: festival.
8. **hegira** – A: custom. B: flight. C: grain sorghum. D: burden.
9. **simpatico** – A: congenial. B: straightforward. C: artless. D: gregarious.
10. **tycoon** – A: violent storm. B: powerful businessman. C: ruthless person. D: primitive shelter.
11. **wanderlust** – A: sadness. B: passion. C: desire to travel. D: daydreaming.
12. **blasé** – A: cultured. B: aloof. C: excited. D: bored.
13. **safari** – A: hunting expedition. B: desert. C: multicolored robe. D: jungle.
14. **cabana** – A: a small inn. B: Mexican scarf. C: secret scheme. D: bathhouse.
15. **kudos** – A: Oriental sport. B: penalty, C: praise. D: African antelope.
16. **imbroglio** – A: complicated situation. B: stone engraving. C: sly intrigue. D: confusion of sounds or voices.
17. **sari** – A: religious teacher. B: Hindu garment. C: spice. D: small boat.
18. **mañana** – A: tomorrow. B: immediately. C: yesterday. D: soon.

19. **kiosk** – A: temple. B: balcony. C: small booth. D: canopy.
20. **bonanza** – A: largess, B: goodwill. C: blessing. D: windfall.

(rating: 20–19 correct: excellent 18–16 correct: good 15–14 correct: fair)

1.7 It Pays to Enrich Your Word Power

Would you have expected to find so many German words in the English language? Note the way the German pronunciation is given!

More people speak German as their mother tongue than any other language in the European Economic Community. Inevitably, some German words have found their way into English, as this selection shows. Tick the word or phrase you believe is *nearest in meaning* to the key word.

(1) **ersatz** (air' zats) – A: origin. B: improvement. C: substitute. D. invention.

(2) **wanderlust** (wŏn der lust, van' der loost) – A: amazement. B: disorientation. C: promiscuity. D: yearning for travel.

(3) **snorkel** (snor' k'l) – A: periscope. B: breathing-tube. C: diving-suit. D: cylinder.

(4) **leitmotiv** (lyte' moh teef) – A: editorial. B: password. C: recurring theme. D: slogan.

(5) **fräulein** (froy' lyne) – A: unmarried woman. B: daughter. C: housewife. D: widow.

(6) **schadenfreude** (shah' den froy de) – A: depression. B: malicious delight. C: pessimistic speech. D: shady deal.

(7) **abseil** (ab' sale, ab' zyle) – A: to sail. B: reduce prices. C: descend by rope. D. advertise.

(8) **Gestapo** (gĕ stah' poh) – A: bodyguards. B: secret police. C: paratroopers. D: prison officers.

(9) **hinterland** (hin' ter land) – A: background. B: building site. C: environment. D: area behind coast.

(10) **edelweiss** (ay' d'l vyss) – A: patriotic song. B: girl's name. C: alpine plant. D: snowflake.

(11) **blitz** – A: inspiration. B: intensive attack. C: retaliation. D: thunder.

(12) **kaput** (kap oot') – A: broken. B: wasted. C: of poor quality. D: weak.

(13) **poltergeist** (pol' ter guyst) – A: exorcism. B: haunted house. C: medium. D: noisy ghost.

(14) **alpenstock** (al' pen stok) – A: guide. B: climbing-stick. C: mountaineer. D: food rations.

(15) **führer** (few' rer) – A: leader. B: fugitive. C: teacher. D: predecessor.

(16) **glockenspiel** (glok' en speel, glok' en shpeel) – A: ball game. B: musical chimes. C: type of dance. D: cuckoo clock.

(17) **putsch** (pootsh) – A: purge. B: censorship. C: advance. D: revolutionary attempt.

(18) **sauerkraut** (sour krowt) – A: strong beer. B: spiced sausage. C: thick sauce. D: pickled cabbage.
(19) **schmaltz** (shmawlts) – A: sweet perfume. B: iron ore. C: sentimentality. D: malt liquor.
(20) **doppelgänger** (dop' el geng er) – A: double. B: criminal. C: spy. D: smuggler.

(both from: Reader's Digest, US edition)

1.8 Man of Letters

In a Letter to *The Economist,* M. J. Shields, of Jarrow, England, points out that George Bernard Shaw, among others, urged spelling reform, suggesting that one letter be altered or deleted each year, thus giving the populace time to absorb the change. Shields writes:

For example, in Year I that useless letter "c" would be dropped to be replased by either "k" or "s," and likewise "x" would no longer be part of the alphabet. The only kase in which "c" would be retained would be the "ch" formation, which will be dealt with later. Year 2 might well reform "w" spelling, so that "which" and "one" would take the same konsonant, wile Year 3 might well abolish "y" replasing it with "i," and lear 4 might fiks the "g-j" anomali wonse and for all. Jenerally, then, the improvement would kontinue iear bai iear, with lear 5 doing awai with useless double konsonants, and lears 6–12 or so modifaiing vowlz and the rimeining voist and unvoist konsonants. Bai ler 15 or sou, it wud fainali bi posibl tu meik ius ov thi ridandant letez "c," "y" and "x" – bai now jast a memori in the maindz ov ould doderez – tu riplais "ch," "sh" and "th" rispektivli.

Fainali, xen, aafte sam 20 iers ov orxogrefkl riform, wi wud hev a lojikl, kohirnt speling in ius xrewawt xe Ingliy-spiking werld. Hawewe, sins xe Wely, xe Airiy, and xe Skots du not spik Ingliy, xei wud hev to hev a speling siutd tu xer oun lengwij. Xei kud, hawewe, orlweiz lern Ingliy az a sekond lengwij et skuul! – lorz feixfuli, M. J. Yilz.

From: Reader's Digest, US ed.
Rewrite the letter in the "old-fashioned" way!

2. Text Analysis

2.1 Gather together all the text's information about the Eloi and the Morlocks. What are the contrasts?
2.2 Describe the three "steps of revelation" by which the timetraveller gradually learns the whole truth about this future world.
2.3 Verbalize the "idea as hero" of this story.

3. Comment and Discussion

3.1 Why did Wells's extrapolation not come true?
3.2 Wells was influenced by Darwin and Marx. Can you make out their ideas in this extract?
3.3 What notion of progress is shown in *The Time Machine?*
3.4 What "message" might Wells have wanted to deliver through *The Time Machine?*

78

4. **For Your Information**
Give the main ideas in your own words!

4.1 **Communism**
The word communism, a term of ancient origin, originally meant a system of society in which property was owned by the community and all citizens shared in the enjoyment of the common wealth, more or less according to their need. Many small communist communities have existed at one time or another, most of them on a religious basis, generally under the inspiration of a literal interpretation of Scripture. The "utopian" socialists of the 19th century also founded communities, though they replaced the religious emphasis with a rational and philanthropic idealism. Best known among them were Robert Owen, who founded New Harmony in Indiana (1825), and Charles Fourier, whose disciples organized other settlements in the United States such as Brook Farm (1841–47). In 1848 the word communism acquired a new meaning when it was used as identical with socialism by Karl Marx and Friedrich Engels in their famous *Communist Manifesto* (see also socialism; Marxism). They, and later their followers, used the term to mean a late stage of socialism in which goods would become so abundant that they would be distributed on the basis of need rather than of endeavour. The Bolshevik wing of the Russian Social-Democratic Workers' Party, which took power in Russia in 1917, adopted the name All-Russian Communist Party in 1918, and some of its allied parties in other countries also adopted the term Communist. Consequently the Soviet state and other states governed by Soviet-type parties are commonly referred to as "Communist" and their official doctrines are called "Communism," although in none of these countries has a communist society yet been established. The word communism is also applied to the doctrines of Communist parties operating within states where they are not in power.

From: *Encyclopaedia Britannica,* 1020

4.2 **Socialism**
Socialism refers to both a set of doctrines and the political movements that aspire to put these doctrines into practice. Although doctrinal aspects loomed largest in the early history of socialism, in its later history the movements have predominated over doctrine, so much so that there is no precise canon on which the various adherents of contemporary socialist movements agree. The most that can be said is that socialism is, in the words of C. A. R. Crosland, a British socialist, "a set of values, or aspirations, which socialists wish to see embodied in the organization of society."

Although it is possible to trace adumbrations of modern socialist ideas as far back as Plato's *Republic,* Thomas More's *Utopia,* and the profuse Utopian literature of the 18th-century Enlightenment, realistically, modern socialism had its roots in the reflections of various writers who opposed the social and economic relations and dislocations that the Industrial Revolution brought in its wake. They directed their critical shafts against what they conceived to be the injustice, the inequalities, the suffering brought about by the capitalist mode of production and the free and uncontrolled market on which it rested. To the acquisitive individualism of their age they opposed a vision of a new community of producers bound to each other through fraternal solidarity. They conceived of a future in which the masses would wrest control of the means of production and the levers of government from the capitalists.

Although the great majority of men calling themselves socialists in the 19th and 20th centuries have shared this vision, they have disagreed about its more specific ideas. Some of them have argued that only the complete nationalization of the means of production would suffice to implement their aims. Others have proposed selective nationalization of key industries, with controlled private ownership of the remainder. Some socialists insist that only strong centralized state direction and a command economy will suffice. Others advocate a "market socialism" in which the market economy would be directed and guided by socialist planners.

Socialists have also disagreed as to the best way of running the good society. Some envisage direction by the government. Others advocate as much dispersion and decentralization as possible through the delegation of decision-making authority to public boards, quasi-public trusts, municipalities, or self-governing communities of producers. Some advocate worker's control; others would rely on governmental planning boards. Although all socialists want to bring about a more equal distribution of national income, some hope for an absolute equality of income, whereas others aim only at ensuring an adequate income for all, while allowing different occupations to be paid at different rates. "To each according to his need" has been a frequent battle cry of socialists, but many of them would in fact settle for a society in which each would be paid in accordance with his contribution to the commonwealth, provided that society would first assure all citizens minimum levels of housing, clothing, and nourishment as well as free access to essential services such as education, health, transportation, and recreation.

Socialists also proclaim the need for more equal political rights for all citizens, and for a levelling of status differences. They disagree, however, on whether difference of status ought to be eradicated entirely, or whether, in practice, some inequality in decision-making powers might not be permitted to persist in a socialist commonwealth.

From: *Encyclopaedia Britannica,* 965

4.3.1 Marxism

Class struggle. Two basic classes around which other less important classes are grouped, oppose each other in the capitalist system: the owners of the means of production, or bourgeoisie, and the workers, or proletariat. With the development of capitalism, the class struggle takes an acute form. "The bourgeoisie produces its own grave-diggers. The fall of the bourgeoisie and the victory of the proletariat are equally inevitable" *(The Communist Manifesto).* For the bourgois relations of production are the last contradictory form of the process of social production, contradictory not in the sense of an individual contradiction, but of a contradiction that is born of the conditions of social existence of individuals; however, the forces of production which develop in the midst of bourgeois society create at the same time the material conditions for resolving this contradiction. With this social development the prehistory of human society ends.

When man has become aware of his loss, of his alienation, as a universal nonhuman situation, it will be possible for him to proceed to a radical transformation of his situation by a revolution. This revolution will be the prelude to the establishment of Communism and the reign of liberty reconquered. "In the place of the old bourgeois society with its classes and its class antagonisms, there will be an association in which the free development of each is the condition for the free development of all."

Marx inherited the ideas of class and class struggle from Utopian Socialism and the theories of Saint-Simon. These had been given substance by the writings of French historians such as Adolphe Thiers and François Guizot on the French Revolution of 1789. But unlike the French historians, Marx made class struggle the central fact of social evolution. "The history of all hitherto existing human society is the history of class struggles."

But for Marx there are two views of revolution. One is that of a final conflagration, "a *violent* suppression of the old conditions of production," which occurs when the opposition between bourgeoisie and proletariat has been carried to its extreme point. This conception is set forth in a manner inspired by the Hegelian dialectic of the master and the slave. in *The Holy Family*. The other conception is that of a permanent revolution involving a provisional coalition between the proletariat and the petty bourgeoisie rebelling against a capitalism that is only superficially united. Once a majority has been won to the coalition, an unofficial proletarian authority constitutes itself alongside the revolutionary bourgeois authority. Its mission is the political and revolutionary education ot the proletariat, gradually assuring the transfer of legal power from the revolutionary bourgeoisie to the revolutionary proletariat.

From: *op. cit.,* 556

4.3.2 **From the** *Communist Manifesto*

The history of all hitherto existing society is the history of class struggles.

Free man and slave, patrician and plebeian, lord and serf, guild master and journeyman, in a word, oppressor and oppressed, stood in constant opposition to one another, carried on an uninterrupted, now hidden, now open fight, a fight that each time ended either in a revolutionary reconstitution of society at large or in the common ruin of the contending classes. . . .

The modern bourgeois society that has sprouted from the ruins of feudal society has not done away with class antagonisms. It has but established new classes, new conditions of oppression, new forms of struggle in place of the old ones.

Our epoch, the epoch of the bourgeoisie, possesses, however, this distinctive feature: it has simplified the class antagonisms. Society as a whole is more and more splitting up into two great hostile camps, into two great classes directly facing each other: bourgeoisie and proletariat. . . .

Hitherto every form of society has been based, as we have already seen, on the antagonism of oppressing and oppressed classes. But in order to oppress a class certain conditions must be assured to it under which it can, at least, continue its slavish existence. The serf, in the period of serfdom, raised himself to membership in the commune, just as the petty bourgeois, under the yoke of feudal absolutism, managed to develop into a bourgeois. The modern labourer, on the contrary, instead of rising with the progress of industry, sinks deeper and deeper below the conditions of existence of his own class. He becomes a pauper, and pauperism develops more rapidly than population and wealth. And here it becomes evident that the bourgeoisie is unfit any longer to be the ruling class in society, and to impose its conditions of existence upon society as an overriding law. It is unfit to rule because it is incompetent to assure an existence to its slave within his slavery, because it cannot help letting him sink into such a state that it has to feed him instead of being fed by him. Society can no longer live under this bourgeoisie: in other words, its existence is no longer compatible with society.

From: *The Communist Manifesto* by Karl Marx and Friedrich Engels. Reprinted in Irving Howe, ed., *Essential Works of Socialism,* New York: Holt, Rinehart and Winston, 1970, pp. 30 ff

Fill in the following flow chart using the information given in 4.3

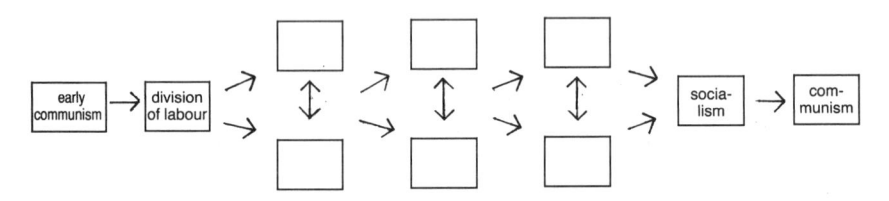

early communism → division of labour → ⤢⤡ ↕ ⤢⤡ ↕ ⤢⤡ ↕ ⤢⤡ → socialism → communism

This flow chart is a response to the teachings of Historic Materialism (Histomat). Put it into words. Can you comment on it?

4.4 Darwinism

Darwin realized that it would be useless, in the state of opinion of his day, to try to convince anybody of the truth of evolution unless he could also explain how it was brought about. In searching for this cause he knew that the key to man's success in producing change in cultivated plants and domestic animals was careful selection of parents from which to breed the desired qualities, and he felt sure that selection must somehow also be operative in nature's creation of species. He knew that all individuals in a species were not identical but showed variation, and he realized that some individuals, well adapted to the places they occupied in the economy of nature (in the mid-20th century called ecological niches), would flourish, while others, less adapted, would perish. This was the principle of natural selection that he had grasped as early as 1837, but he still required to know how nature enforced it. On Sept. 28, 1838, he read Malthus' *Essay on the Principle of Population* in which the author tried to show that, as the rate of increase of human population was in a geometrical ratio, while that of increase in human food supply was only in arithmetical ratio, the result must be misery and death for the poor, unless population growth was checked. Malthus' argument was unsound because it has never been determined to what extent human food supply could be artificially increased if it were given sufficient priority and finance. But Darwin saw at once that this fallacious argument could be applied correctly to plants and animals, which are unable to increase their food supply artificially. He saw, too, that in these organisms mortality must be very high, thereby automatically enforcing the mechanism of selection of parents of successive generations. The note in telegraphic style which Darwin entered that day in his "Notebook on Transmutation of Species" is worth quoting:

On an average every species must have same number killed year with year by hawks, by cold, & c. – even one species of hawk decreasing in number must affect instantaneously all the rest. The final cause of all this wedging must be to sort out proper structure. . . . One may say there is a force like a hundred thousand wedges trying to force every kind of adapted structure into the gaps in the oeconomy of nature, or rather forming gaps by thrusting out weaker ones.

In these words Darwin showed that he had solved the problem of the origin and improvement of adaptation as a result of selection pressure, and that modification during descent (*i. e.*, evolution) does not take place in a vacuum but is strongly related to the ecological niches occupied by the species. Darwin is therefore included among the founding fathers of the science of ecology.

From: *op. cit.*, 493, (cf. 4.2)

4.5 Capitalism

Capitalism, economic system, dominant in the Western world since the breakup of feudalism, in which the means of production are privately owned and production is guided and income distributed through the operation of markets. Although the continuous development of capitalism as a system dates only from the 16th century, antecedents of capitalist institutions existed in the ancient world, and flourishing pockets of capitalism were present during the later Middle Ages.

The development of capitalism was spearheaded by the growth of the English cloth industry during the 16th, 17th, and 18th centuries. The feature of this development that distinguished capitalism from previous systems was the use of the excess of production over consumption to enlarge productive capacity rather than to invest in economically unproductive enterprises, such as pyramids and cathedrals. This characteristic was encouraged by several historical events.

In the ethic encouraged by the Protestant Reformation of the 16th century, traditional disdain for acquisitive effort was diminished, while hard work and frugality were given a stronger religious sanction. Economic inequality was justified on the grounds that the wealthy were also the virtuous.

Another contributing factor was the increase in Europe's supply of precious metals and the resulting inflation in prices. Wages did not rise as fast as prices in this period, and the main beneficiaries of the inflation were the capitalists. The early capitalists (1500–1750) also enjoyed the benefits of the rise of strong national states during the mercantilist era. The policies of national power followed by these states succeeded in providing the basic social conditions, such as uniform monetary systems and legal codes, necessary for economic development and eventually made possible the shift from public to private initiative.

Beginning in the 18th century in England, the focus of capitalist development shifted from commerce to industry. The steady capital accumulation of the preceding centuries was invested in the practical application of technical knowledge during the Industrial Revolution. The ideology of classical capitalism was expressed in Adam Smith's *Inquiry into the Nature and Causes of the Wealth of Nations* (1776), which recommended leaving economic decisions to the free play of self-regulating market forces. After the French Revolution and the Napoleonic Wars had swept the remnants of feudalism into oblivion, Smith's policies were increasingly put into practice. The policies of 19th-century political liberalism included free trade, sound money (the gold standard), balanced budgets, and minimum levels of poor relief.

From: *op. cit.,* Micropaedia, Vol. II, 535–536

5. Tell a Good Joke

Frage an Radio Eriwan:
  Wie werden wir unter dem vollendeten Kommunismus leben?
Radio Eriwan antwortet:
  Brot, Fleisch und Textilien werden ganz billig sein. Mit einem Wort, es werden Zustände herrschen wie unter dem Zaren.

Frage an Radio Eriwan:
  Wäre es nicht am einfachsten, wenn man alle Gegner unseres Arbeiter- und Bauernstaates ins Gefängnis stecken würde?
Radio Eriwan antwortet:
  Im Prinzip ja. Aber wer soll dann die Arbeit auf den Feldern und in den Fabriken verrichten?

Frage an Radio Eriwan:
  Was ist Kapitalismus?
Radio Eriwan antwortet:
  Die Ausbeutung des Menschen durch den Menschen.
Zusatzfrage:
  Was ist Kommunismus?
Radio Eriwan antwortet:
  Das Gegenteil.

Frage an Radio Eriwan:
  Woran zeigt sich, daß der Kommunismus dem Kapitalismus überlegen ist?
Radio Eriwan antwortet:
  Würde es beim Kapitalismus so drunter und drüber gehen, wäre er schon längst daran zugrunde gegangen, aber dem Kommunsimus scheint es nicht zu schaden.

Ein Kapitalist, ein Sozialist und ein Kommunist verabreden sich. Kapitalist und Kommunist sind pünktlich, nur der Sozialist verspätet sich um eine Stunde. Atemlos entschuldigt er sich: "Ich mußte noch soeben beim Fleischer nach einem Schnitzel in der Schlange anstehen."

Fragt der Kapitalist: "Was ist denn das, eine Schlange?"
Fragt der Kommunist: "Was ist denn das, ein *Schnitzel?*"

1. Tell these jokes in English!
2. Explain them!
3. Why are there so many more political jokes from totalitarian states than from the Western liberal democracies?

7 THE MARKS SAVING MARX

Introducing the Topic

A)
Indira Gandhi arrived in Moscow on official business and was making a tour of the Soviet capital. She saw a queue and walked up to it.
'What are you queuing for?' she asked.
'They're giving out sugar,' replied the citizens.
'Well, well!' Gandhi is surprised. 'Here they give out sugar whereas at home we usually sell it.'
She walked further. There was another queue.
'What's going on here?' she asked.
'They're throwing out shoes!'
Indira looked at the shoes, twirled a pair in her hands: 'No wonder', she said. 'In India we throw out shoes like this too.'

B)
There were two brothers, an American and a Russian.
The American was jobless and hungry. But he had an idea: he went to the gates of the White House, sat on the ground outside and began eating hay. Carter saw him there and asked: 'What are you eating hay for?'
'Because I'm hungry and I haven't a job.'
Carter was outraged and ordered that he be fed and given some money.
'What else would you like?'
'A ticket to Russia to visit my brother.'
Carter made the arrangements and the American flew to Russia where he found that his brother was starving too. The American burst out laughing and said: 'Brother, I can give you a good piece of advice. Go to the Kremlin sit on the ground by the gates and eat hay. Out will come Brezhnev who will be angry to see you in such a state and give you everything you need.'
And that's what the Russian brother did. He sat down by the Kremlin gates and began eating hay. Out came Brezhnev and saw him there.
'What are you eating hay for?' he asked.
'Because I'm hungry and I haven't any money.'
'You're a fool!' says Brezhnev. 'It's summer now, you should be eating grass and leaving the hay for winter.'

C)
An Englishman, a Frenchman and an American were arguing about the nationality of Adam and Eve.

'They must have been English,' declares the Englishman. 'Only a gentleman would share his last apple with a woman.'

'They were undoubtedly French,' says the Frenchman. 'Who else could seduce a woman so easily?'

'I think they were Russian,' says the American. 'After all, who else could walk around stark naked, feed on one apple between the two of them and think they were in paradise?'

From: *Russia Dies Laughing,* ed. by Z. Dolgolopolova, André Deutsch, London 1982

1. Read the jokes in silence; then tell them to your classmates.
2. What do the jokes deal with? Explain!
3. Which joke do you consider the best, and why?
4. Do you know any other political jokes? If so, try and tell one in English.
5. The jokes above apply a variety of rhetorical figures. For instance, there are sarcasm, pun, exaggeration, and contrast. Find one example of each.
6. The following joke is left without the so-called punch line (= G. Pointe). Try to make up as many funny ones as you can.

Roosevelt, Churchill and Stalin went to inspect a collective farm. They had to cross over a bridge. But there was a cow standing on it.

Churchill got out of the car and advanced on the cow, intending to drive it away.

'Moo-o-oo . . .' went the cow and lowered her horns at Churchill. Churchill backed off.

Up came Roosevelt.

'Moo-o-oo . . .' went the cow and lowered her horns at him too. Roosevelt backed off.

Up came Stalin and whispered something to the cow. The cow raised its tail in fright and took off.

'What did you say to her, Joseph?' asked Churchill and Roosevelt . . .

7. Now let's do it the other way round. These are the middle part and the punch line of a joke. Try and recreate the missing introduction.

. . . 'I'll transfer my fortune to the USSR on condition that for one day all the shops in Leningrad will give everything away free.'

The authorities thought about this, and since the inheritance was vast, they decided to agree.

The next day all the shops in Leningrad gave their goods away free. There was pandemonium – people climbing over one another, children crushed. The hospitals and soon the morgues too were filled to overflowing . . .

'See what you've done,' the authorities say to the man. 'What on earth did you want this to happen for?'

'I'm an old man,' replies the Leningrader, 'and before I die I badly wanted to see what Communism would be like.'

From: *Op. cit.,* pp. 48/49 + p. 22
Vocabulary: inheritance: Erbschaft – – pandemonium: Höllenspektakel, Tumult, Chaos – – morgue: Leichenschauhaus

Note on the Text

The following article taken from *The Times,* October 17, 1984 deals with the daily problems that the consumers in Communist countries have to grapple with.

Imagine the sense of wonder, the frustration of a tramp who, having spent his night wrapped up in newspapers in a Knightsbridge doorway, enters Harrods for a clandestine wash and brush-up.

Everything around him glitters or shimmers or smells of wealth. The salmon from
5 Scotland, the cheeses, the sweetmeats are tangible, real, available but, for him, as elusive as quicksilver.

Most East Europeans – not just tramps, but workers, academics, housewives, craftsmen – are condemned to similar lives. They commute between two parallel worlds, a world of scarcity, measured by the length of its queues and the breadth
10 of its empty shelves, and a world of unlimited possibilities.

In a country where it is technically impossible to buy a pair of shoes for a schoolchild, it is possible in practice not only to buy those simple shoes but also a silk shirt tailored by Pierre Cardin.

The dollar and the Deutschmark, even sterling, are at the heart of this conundrum.
15 The flow of these currencies through the veins and arteries of East European economies has, in the short term at least, kept the consumer calm.

The grey, brown and black markets – the interweave of legal, semi-legal and outright criminal activities – have actually acted as a stabilizing element in Eastern Europe, defusing the tensions that build up at a time of chronic shortage.
20 But the huge, daily corruption that is eating into these socialist states, the creation of a gulf between those who have ready access to dollars and those who do not, all of this spells trouble for the long-term stability of the bloc.

Appetite for hard currency led them to set up networks of shops where only western cash is accepted. In Poland these are known as Pewex, in Czechoslovakia as
25 Tuwex, in Bulgaria as Korekom, in East Germany as Intershop.

Consider the contrast. Depending on season and the temperament of the plan, it is difficult or impossible to buy the following goods in Polish shops for Polish currency: flour, butter, rice, most cereals, most kinds of meat, washing powder, hair shampoo, children's shoes, light bulbs, lavatory paper, coffee, sugar, oranges,
30 bananas, school exercise books, chocolates, dictionaries, car batteries.

The list could cover a complete page of *The Times.* Now pass the shops by and enter a Pewex. Gaudy signs advertise chocolate bars that "help you work, rest and play", cartons of Marlboro and Kent cigarettes are piled up shoulder-high, the shelves are cluttered with tins of ham, jars of chocolate spread and the amber parades of whisky bottles.

Outside children push their noses against the smoked glass looking into the wonderland.

In the Eastern bloc it is illegal to sell or buy western currency but it is not illegal to possess it or spend it in the state-controlled stores, these staging posts of western consumerism.

Nobody in the shops asks where the money has come from. Theoretically it could have been sent through the post by a benevolent relative, or it could have been earned in legitimate work abroad. But most of the cash comes from the black market which flourishes and expands in a way that the official economies of Comecon have failed to do.

According to semi-official estimates between 50 and 70 per cent of expenditure in Poland is channelled into the second, black, economy. It is a market that thrives on the demand for the dollar, the constant shortages in the official shops, the poor quality of domestic products and official prices that are kept artificially low.

But the problem is that while these shops were set up to absorb some of the western currency that was already circulating and make some profit for the state (most hard currency stores make about $200m a year for their governments), the effect has been to make the dollar and the Deutschmark a central part of everyday survival. A plumber in East Germany will come to your assistance for 10 West German marks but not for double that amount in East German currency.

In Poland a dollar bribe to a car mechanic not only ensures speedier repair work – it also reduces the likelihood that he will swap your perfectly functioning car battery with a defective one.

In Romania, a carton of Kent cigarettes, the safer form of currency, will guarantee the same.

But the social divisions that are opening up as a result of this parallel existence are slowly being recognized.

A Czech commentator said on Bratislava Radio: "It is not easy to fight bribery because it often helps us to achieve something we want very much, and even the most principled of us will bend our principles."

"Usually two are involved, he who bribes and he who is bribed. But who will bribe a miner? A steel foundryman? A woman working in a textile mill? A milkmaid or other honest working people?"

Who indeed? It was inevitable that the Solidarity revolution was sparked off by Gdansk shipyard workers. Nobody bribes such workers, though they may have put in long years of apprenticeship. Nor do they have access to hard currency except by finding an illegal dealer and cashing in a substantial slice of their wage packet. They are urged to work harder but the incentive to do so is a small increase in their zloty wage that can buy next to nothing in the official shops.

"The problem", a Hungarian sociologist comments, "is that black markets have become a substitute for reform. The idea of reform in most East European countries is to introduce more market mechanisms into everyday life."

"But too many entrenched interests are challenged by such far-reaching changes. There are too many bureaucrats with desks to lose. The result is that the underground markets – the grey, the brown and the black – take over the market mechanism, try to match supply with demand by dealing in dollar denominations or large, 'realistic', quantities of local currency."

Hungary which has managed to push its economic reforms the furthest, the key symptoms being relatively full shops but high prices, is also the least troubled by a dollar black market.

The usual chain of bribes can be found when, for example, an individual tries to build a house, but western currency does not play a central role.

Grey markets usually offer legally acquired goods or services in an illegal way. At its most harmless, the grey market is best observed in the early evening when old ladies appear in the streets of Warsaw, Cracow, East Berlin and Prague to sell flowers to those who are invited to dinner.

The flowers are being sold after official closing hours by people who do not have official trading licences at uncontrolled prices, but the practice is tolerated by police in all these countries.

Usually, grey markets involve the sale of services. A gynaecologist working in a state-run hospital who offers to carry out an abortion after hours is a common example in every Eastern bloc country.

Abortion is legal throughout Eastern Europe but it is often a faceless, harsh process. Rarely is an anaesthetic offered and the patient is frequently expected to take the bus home straight afterwards.

A state doctor with a private practice on the side can offer more personal treatment – for a hefty fee in local or hard currency.

The colours grow darker as the scope for corruption increases. The brown market includes sales clerks who hide a new intake of linen or meat or books when it arrives and then telephone regular clients, in return for a bribe.

The Berlin-Warsaw express is a brown market on wheels. Poles who work in East Germany come back to the motherland at the weekends with suitcases full not of dirty washing but of chocolate or coffee for resale to dealers.

As soon as the train crosses the East German-Polish border dealers put their heads into compartments in mute inquiry. By the time the first Polish stop has been reached, the exchange has been carried out, usually in the lavatory – two months' salary for a caseload of chocolate which will end up at five times the price in private Polish shops.

This is a brown market because the chocolate has been legally acquired and
because the illegality of a bag full of sweets is difficult to prove.
The full-blown black market includes those who deal with stolen goods, the wholesale profiteers who buy goods diverted from official shops, the bigtime smugglers, the currency speculators, the prostitutes and the underground entrepreneurs.
Most professional black marketeers live in their own special milieux – in Warsaw it is the Praga district – and haunt specific cafés. They have an independent information exchange and know which policemen are bent or bendable.
In East Berlin the marketeers have contacts with third world diplomats who can travel without impediment through the wall into West Berlin and return stocked to the gunwales with scarce merchandise.
In Bulgaria two or three big gangs have sewn up the seaside resorts and both Burgas and Varna are key black market centres.
Not just Solidarity but also hardline Marxists sense that there is something gravely wrong with a socialist state that not only allows but also contributes to the prosperity of these dealers.
But they make the error of pursuing private businessmen, many of whom operate well within the law, on the assumption that private enterprise equals corruption. Slowly, the workers of Eastern Europe are beginning to see behind this posturing: the real problem lies in governments that lack the courage to change the system in a way that satisfies the basic needs of the population.
Black marketeers are despised in Eastern Europe but they exist because they are needed. Sooner rather than later, the frustrated consumers of Comecon are going to demand that communist authorities introduce genuine market mechanisms and disenfranchise the shady criminal entrepreneurs. (~ 1640 ws)

Annotations

(The words marked * should be memorized.)

Knightsbridge area in London where Harrods is situated – – **doorway** Torweg, Zugang – – **Harrods** famous and expensive department store in London – – **clandestine** secret – – **brush-up** das Sich-Frisch-Machen – – **salmon** ['sæmən] Lachs – – **elusive** tending to escape – – ***to commute** travel back and forth – – ***shelf** (shelves) Regal – – **conundrum** puzzling question, esp. one asked for fun; riddle – – ***currency** here: money that is actually in use in a country – – **interweave** here: things woven together (one with another) – – **outright** rundweg, völlig, unverblümt – – **to defuse** here: remove cause of tension from a crisis; entschärfen – – ***gulf** abyss; division – – ***access** Zugang – – **to spell** here: have as a consequence – – **gaudy** too bright and showy; gay or bright in a tasteless way – – **cluttered** crowded in a disorderly way; vollgestopft mit – – **jar** round container, with a wide mouth, with or without handle(s), of glass, stone or earthenware – – **amber** here: of yellowish-brown colour – – **staging post** here: Anlaufstelle; Zwischenstation – – **Comecon** economic association of East-bloc countries – – **expenditure**

money spent – – **to thrive (on)** prosper – – ***shortage** scarcity – – **plumber** workman who fits and repairs pipes; Installateur – – ***bribe** s. th. given, offered or promised to s. b. in order to influence or persuade him (often to do wrong) in favour of the giver; Bestechungsgeschenk, -geld; Bestechung – – **speedy** fast – – **to swap** exchange – – ***bribery** Bestechung – – **to bend** (bent, bent) *here:* relax s. th. – – **foundryman** man who works at a place where metal or glass is melted and moulded; Gießer, Schmelzer – – **to spark off** *here:* trigger, cause – – **Solidarity** social and political movement in Poland of the early 1980's which fought the official trade union controlled by the Communist regime and established itself as independent trade union. Soon after its foundation (in 1980) it had more than ten million members. Its leader Lech Wałęsa received the Nobel prize for peace in 1982. When the movement threatened to become a danger for the political system, the Communist Government – under pressure from the Soviet Union – banned the union. Thousands of *Solidarity* members were interned. Many leaders went underground. In 1982, Lech Wałęsa was released but completely stripped of influence. Since then *Solidarity* has lost almost all of its previous power. – **Gdansk** Danzig – – **apprenticeship** time spent being the learner of a trade – – **to cash in** *here:* convert, exchange – **slice** *here:* part – – **incentive** encouragement; Anreiz – – **entrenched** established firmly – – **to challenge** invite s. b. to have a fight; herausfordern – – **to match** *here:* bring in balance – – **denomination** *here:* unit (in weight, money, etc.) – – **hefty** (coll.) big – – **fee** charge or payment for professional advice or services, e. g. private teachers, doctors, etc. – – **scope** opportunity – – **intake** Aufnahme, Eingang – – **mute** silent – – **inquiry** asking – – **to carry out** effect – – **lavatory** Waschraum – – **case** *here:* box – – **wholesale** Großhandel – – **to divert** [daɪˈvɜt] turn in another direction – – **entrepreneur** [ŏtrəprəˈnɜr] person who organizes and manages a commercial undertaking – – **marketeer** seller in a market; market dealer – – **to haunt** visit habitually or repeatedly – – **bendable** can be bribed – – **impediment** s. th. that hinders – – **stocked to the gunwales** bis oben hin beladen – – **merchandise** goods bought and sold; trade goods – – **to sew up** [sou] (coll.) *here:* secure or assure exclusive control; monopolize – – **resort** *here:* Erholungsort – – **to sense** become aware – – **posturing** (das Machen von) Verrenkungen – – **to despise** feel contempt for; verachten – – **genuine** real, true – – **to disenfranchise** deprive of privileges, rights, etc. – – **shady** (coll.) of doubtful honesty; fragwürdig, zweifelhaft, schmutzig

WORKSHEET

1. **Language**
1.1.1 Our text contains two interesting nouns whose suffix is *-eer*. Find them and explain their meaning. Guess the meaning of the suffix.
1.1.2 Two other suffixes have the same meaning: *-ian; -ist*. Check your dictionary to find out whether the following nouns can be combined with any of the three suffixes to result in a meaningful noun. Do the suffixes give the *derivatives* the above-mentioned meaning? Explain the meaning of the derivatives.
bank; bracket; economy; engine; flora; freight; light; lock; magic; model; motor; mountain; musket; nature; novel; piano; practice; racket; reform; rocket; statistic; talent; theology; theory; therapy; type.

Now that you have done this task choose *eight* of the *derivatives* and use them in sentences you yourself make up.

1.2 Insert the following words into the sentences below (each word is to be used once.):

amount, business, cash, cost, customer, dealer, demand, department, loss, offer, payment, purchase, sales, shortage, supplier.

a) I was born on October 15, 1924. By this time, my father had opened a hot-dog restaurant called the Orpheum Wiener House. It was the perfect _____ for somebody without much cash. All one really needed to get started was a grill, a bun warmer (bun = roll), and a few stools.

b) At Ford I used to watch with some envy as the car _____ (Pl.) made the really big bucks.

c) When I worked at Ford, I barely knew that Chrysler existed. We never thought much about Chrysler. Their products didn't even show up on the monthly _____ sheets that measured how well our cars were doing against the competition.

d) A couple of months after I arrived at Chrysler, something hit me like a ton of bricks. We were running out of _____ .

e) Another point troubling me about our sales figures was that Chrysler had long been known as an older guy's car. When I came aboard, the median age for Dodge and Plymouth buyers was higher than that of Buick, Oldsmobile, Pontiac, or even Mercury _____ (Pl).

f) I also learned that Chrysler had been running the world's largest leasing company. Instead of selling cars to Hertz and Avis, we had been leasing them. And every six months we were buying them back. Our dealers didn't want these cars, so we had to dump them at auctions. The first year I was at Chrysler, I wrote off $88 million in used-car _____ (Pl.).

g) The rental companies drive a hard bargain, but especially for Chrysler it's essential to be represented in their fleets. We get a tremendous _____ of mail from the rental customers saying: "Why don't you promote this car? Where has it been hiding? I rented a Reliant to drive from Seattle to San Francisco and I was amazed."

h) Another disaster area I uncovered was Chrysler's handling of warranty (= guarantee) _____ (Pl.) which were running as high as $350 million a year.

i) We were flooded with letters from unhappy customers who had visited Chrysler showrooms and complained about the bad treatment they had received from the salesmen. So I sent Gar Laux to hold seminars with the dealers and reminded them of a few fundamentals: when a guy comes through your door, love him. Talk to him. Give him the information he needs to make a $10,000 _____ .

j) To give us a hand on quality I brought Hans Matthias out of retirement and made him an _____ to be our quality consultant.

k) All of us who had worked at Ford were used to a highly systematic way of working. At Chrysler I found almost no systems in place in the purchasing _____ , which even by the lax standards of Chrysler was known for its inefficiency.

l) To make matters worse, the company had failed to treat its _____ (Pl.) well, and over the years they had reciprocated (= sich revanchieren) in kind. As a result, we couldn't always depend on a steady flow of parts.

m) _____ for small cars was low in 1978. Datsun was offering rebates; Toyota and Honda weren't selling anything. Until the Shah was overthrown in 1979, there were long waiting lists of customers who wanted big cars with big V-8s – in fact, there weren't enough gas-guzzlers to go around.

n) One of the public's favorite criticisms of the auto industry is that we should have anticipated the post-Iran oil _____ . But if our own government had no idea about what was going on over there, how should I have known?

o) Some time later, I concluded that we had no choice but to sell our tank operation to General Dynamics for $348 million. That was a very tough decision but we needed the cash as a buffer to get the suppliers to give us an extension on our _____ (Pl.) to them.

1.3 Do you remember that we practiced the use of the prepositions "on", "at", and "in" on page 31? Here are another three which may create difficulties for foreign learners of English.

Insert "of", "for", "from" into the following sentences:

a) They must be arrested _____ stealing.
b) He had died _____ apoplexy. (= Schlaganfall)
c) He separated himself _____ his friends.
d) Our society strives _____ self-preservation.
e) The effort was doomed _____ the start.
f) She made a will, when she came _____ age.
g) He is sacrificing himself _____ me.
h) He longed _____ freedom.
i) It was a step _____ which she shrank.
j) They took leave _____ him.
k) He would be rid _____ her forever.
l) The burden of responsibility was taken _____ him.
m) There was no way _____ moving her.
n) Schools are made _____ the average child.
o) Her eyes were heavy _____ want of sleep.

2. **Content and Comment**
Answer the following questions.
2.1 How does the author introduce the text, and why?
2.2 What's the situation of the majority of the East European consumers?
2.3 Why is a minority of citizens in a better position?
2.4 How come that Communist governments established the special shops?
2.5 The text says that there are three extra markets existing alongside the official one. What are they? Give examples how they work.
2.6 Why is the social and political effect on Communist regimes of such a situation an ambiguous one?
2.7 What are, in your view, the reasons for the shortages in food and other goods, in East European countries?

3. **Further Studies**
3.1 Imagine you are an American citizen who has just returned to New York from a six-month-stay in Moscow. You write a letter to the editors of the *New York Times* in which you air your disappointment about the scarcity and bad quality of the food and of other commodities of daily life in the Soviet Union. Write, as well, about the waste of time involved in shopping, and about the existence of the black market flourishing in certain quarters of the city.
3.2 As you well know, a lot of espionage goes on between East and West. Of course, spies – if they need to pass on information to their colleagues – have a variety of ways of doing so. One such way is sending encoded messages. Secret codes used by spies are usually easy to solve. This is because the spy needs to be able to write messages quickly and without special training or sophisticated equipment. The *letter* below contains a secret message that has been encoded using one of the simplest techniques available to the cipher maker. Your task is a) to find the secret message contained in the letter below and b) to write a letter of your own (in *English!*) which also has an encoded message. Your classmates will have to decipher it. (Imagine you belong to an international gang of black marketeers in East Europe. You want to inform a "colleague" about a "delivery" of 500 electronic calculators from the West. You have to let him know the price [in dollars or deutschmarks, of course], the time and place of the transfer, etc.)

> Dear John:
>
> If you are interested I'll meet with Mr. Smith and you at the next club meeting at the same time as before. Our place and bridge partners are fixed this time on the agenda. Also on Tuesday, I plan to see the city as I now have the time to travel. The information that you sent me concerning the American Ballet troop ("movements very stiff") was correct. That will be my last ballet. It used to be vital for me to see the theater or go to our club, but they are not in my future plans.
>
> – Bill

From: *Discover,* February 1986

8 WHO PROTECTS THE CONSUMER?

Note on the Text

In Topic 7 we have learnt about the economic problems which consumers in Communist countries have to grapple with. What about consumers in the capitalist West? Do they have problems as well? What are they and what can be done to overcome them?
The following excerpt, which is adapted from Milton D. Friedman's book *Free To Choose* (see also *Topic* 5, p. 67), deals with these questions from a typically neo-liberal point of view.

"It is not from the benevolence of the butcher, the brewer, or the baker, that we expect our dinner, but from their regard to their own interest. We address ourselves, not to their humanity but to their self-love, and never talk to them of our own necessities but of their advantages. Nobody but a beggar chooses to depend chiefly upon the benevolence of his fellow citizens."
– Adam Smith, *The Wealth of Nations,* vol. I, p. 16

We cannot indeed depend on benevolence for our dinner – but can we depend wholly on Adam Smith's invisible hand? A long line of economists, philosophers, reformers, and social critics have said no. Self-love will lead sellers to deceive their customers. They will take advantage of their customers' innocence and ignorance
5 to overcharge them and pass off on them shoddy products. They will cajole customers to buy goods they do not want. In addition, the critics have pointed out,

if you leave it to the market, the outcome may affect people other than those directly involved. It may affect the air we breathe, the water we drink, the safety of the foods we eat. The market must, it is said, be supplemented by other arrangements in order to protect the consumer from himself and from avaricious sellers, and to protect all of us from the spillover neighborhood effects of market transactions.

These criticisms of the invisible hand are valid. The question, however, is whether the arrangements that have been recommended or adopted to meet them, to supplement the market, are well devised for that purpose, or whether, as so often happens, the cure may not be worse than the disease.

All of the movements in the past two decades – the consumer movement, the ecology movement, the back-to-the-land movement, the hippie movement, the organic-food movement, the protect-the-wilderness movement, the zero-population-growth movement, the "small is beautiful" movement, the antinuclear movement – have had one thing in common. All have been antigrowth. They have been opposed to new developments, to industrial innovation, to the increased use of natural resources. Agencies established in response to these movements have imposed heavy costs on industry after industry to meet increasingly detailed and extensive government requirements. They have prevented some products from being produced or sold; they have required capital to be invested for nonproductive purposes in ways specified by government bureaucrats.

The results have been far-reaching and threaten to be even more so. Ask yourself what products are currently least satisfactory and have shown the least improvement over time. Postal service, elementary and secondary schooling, railroad passenger transport would surely be high on the list. Ask yourself which products are most satisfactory and have improved the most. Household appliances, television and radio sets, hi-fi equipment, computers, and, we would add, supermarkets and shopping centers would surely come high on that list.

The shoddy products are all produced by government or government-regulated industries. The outstanding products are all produced by private enterprise with little or no government involvement. Yet the public – or a large part of it – has been persuaded that private enterprises produce shoddy products, that we need ever vigilant government employees to keep business from foisting off unsafe, meretricious products at outrageous prices on ignorant, unsuspecting, vulnerable customers. That public relations campaign has succeeded so well that we are in the process of turning over to the kind of people who bring us our postal service the far more critical task of producing and distributing energy.

Ralph Nader's attack on the Corvair, the most dramatic single episode in the campaign to discredit the products of private industry, exemplifies not only the effectiveness of that campaign but also how misleading it has been. Some ten years after Nader castigated the Corvair as unsafe at any speed, one of the agencies that was set up in response to the subsequent public outcry finally got around to testing the Corvair that started the whole thing. They spent a year and a half comparing the performance of the Corvair with the performance of other comparable vehicles, and they concluded, "The 1960–63 Corvair compared favorably with the other contemporary vehicles used in the tests." Nowadays Corvair fan clubs exist throughout the country. Corvairs have become collectors' items. But to most people, even the well informed, the Corvair is still "unsafe at any speed".

Food and Drug Administration

The Food and Drug Act of 1906 arose from concern about the cleanliness of food. It was the era of the muckraker, of investigative journalism. *Upton Sinclair* had been sent by a socialist newspaper to Chicago to investigate conditions in the stockyards. The result was his famous novel, *The Jungle,* which he wrote to create sympathy for the workers, but which did far more to arouse indignation at the unsanitary conditions under which meat was processed. As Sinclair said at the time, "I aimed at the public's heart and by accident hit it in the stomach."

The 1906 act was largely limited to the inspection of foods and the labeling of patent medicines, though, more by accident than design, it also subjected prescription drugs to control, a power which was not used until much later. The regulatory authority, from which the present Food and Drug Administration developed, was placed in the Department of Agriculture. Until the past fifteen years or so, neither the initial agency nor the FDA had much effect on the drug industry.

The 1962 amendments coincided with the series of events that produced an explosion in government intervention and a change in its direction: the thalidomide tragedy, Rachel Carson's *Silent Spring,* which launched the environmental movement, and the controversy about Ralph Nader's *Unsafe at Any Speed.* The FDA participated in the changed role of government and became far more activist than it had ever been before. The banning of cyclamates and the threat to ban saccharin have received most public attention, but they are by no means the most important actions of the FDA.

No one can disagree with the objectives of the legislation that culminated in the 1962 amendments. Of course it is desirable that the public be protected from unsafe and useless drugs. However, it is also desirable that new drug development should be stimulated, and that new drugs should be made available to those who can benefit from them as soon as possible. As is so often the case, one good objective conflicts with other good objectives. Safety and caution in one direction can mean death in another.

The effect of increased government control on the rate of innovation of new drugs is dramatic: the number of "new chemical entities" introduced each year has fallen by more than 50 percent since 1962. Equally important, it now takes much longer for a new drug to be approved and, partly as a result, the cost of developing a new drug has been multiplied manyfold. According to one estimate for the 1950s and early 1960s, it then cost about half a million dollars and took about twenty-five months to develop a new drug and bring it to market. Allowing for inflation since then would raise the cost to a little over $1 million. By 1978, "it [was] costing $54 million and about eight years of effort to bring a drug to market" – a hundredfold increase in cost and quadrupling of time, compared with a doubling of prices in general. As a result, drug companies can no longer afford to develop new drugs in the United States for patients with rare diseases. Increasingly, they must rely on drugs with high volume sales. The United States, long a leader in the development of new drugs, is rapidly taking a back seat. And we cannot even benefit fully from developments abroad because the FDA typically does not accept evidence from abroad as proof of effectiveness. The ultimate outcome may well be the same as in passenger rail traffic, the nationalization of the development of new drugs.

Granted all this, may these costs not be justified by the advantage of keeping dangerous drugs off the market, of preventing a series of thalidomide disasters? The most careful empirical study of this question that has been made, by Sam Peltzman, concludes that the evidence is unambiguous: that the harm done has greatly outweighed the good. He explains his conclusion partly by noting that "the penalties imposed by the marketplace on sellers of ineffective drugs before 1962 seems to have been sufficient to have left little room for improvement by a regulatory agency." After all, the manufacturers of thalidomide ended up paying many tens of millions of dollars in damages – surely a strong incentive to avoid any similar episodes. Of course, mistakes will still happen – the thalidomide tragedy was one – but so will they under government regulation . . .

The really great danger to the consumer is *monopoly* – whether private or governmental. The most effective way to counter it is not through a bigger antitrust division at the Department of Justice or a larger budget for the Federal Trade Commission or the FDA, but through removing existing barriers to international trade. That would permit competition from all over the world to be even more effective than it is now in undermining monopoly at home. Alternative sources of supply protect the consumer far more effectively than all the Ralph Naders of the world.

Annotations
(The words marked * should be memorized.)

benevolence wish to do good; activity in doing good – – **Adam Smith** see Introduction to Topic 5, p. 56 – – **invisible hand** see Topic 5, text B, p. 64 – – ***to deceive** cause s. b. to believe s. th. that is false; play a trick on; mislead (on purpose) – – ***customer** person who buys things – – **innocence** *here:* naiveté [naiˈiːvtei] – – ***to overcharge** demand a price that is too high – – **shoddy** of poor quality – – **to cajole** [kəˈdʒəoul] use flattery or deceit to persuade s. b. to do s. th./ into doin s. th.; beschwatzen, verführen, herumkriegen – – ***outcome** result, end – – ***to affect** have an influence on – – ***to supplement** make an addition or additions to – – **avaricious** [ævə'rıʃəs] greedy – – **spillover** *here:* extra – – *****valid** wellbased; sound – – **to meet** *here:* satisfy; answer in a satisfactory way; nachkommen, entsprechen – – **to devise** think out; plan – – *****purpose** aim, end – – *****increased** made or become greater – – **agency** *here:* governmental office, administrative unit through which power is exerted; Amt, Behörde – – **in response to** in answer to – – **requirement** *here:* order, demand; Auflage – – *****appliance** instrument or apparatus – **vigilant** watchful – – **to foist** (s. th. off on s. b.) trick s. b. into accepting s. th. useless; andrehen – – **meretricious** superficially attractive – – **unsuspecting** ahnungslos – – **vulnerable** ['vʌlnərəbl] not protected against attack – – **public relations campaign** *here:* Kampagne zur Pflege und Verbesserung der Beziehungen zwischen Regierung und Öffentlichkeit – – **Ralph Nader** (1935–) prominent fighter for consumer protection whose protests against shoddy industrial products, environmental pollution, etc. triggered off dozens of environmental and consumer protection laws in the past two decades, such as legislation on car safety, clean water, and freedom of information. In the 1960's he became something of a folk hero of the protest generation. "... His book *Unsafe at Any Speed* was a devastating indictment (= vernichtende Anklage) of the American car industry and its attempts to cover up (= vertuschen) safety defects ... It led to a showdown with General Motors, to Senate hearings, to the eventual scrapping (= Abschaffung) of the Corvair and to federal traffic safety legislation. The car industry fought tooth and nail (= sich mit Händen und Füßen wehren) against federal safety standards ... But the resulting law has sparked off the recall of more than 100 million defective vehicles since 1966, and Nader claims that over 150,000 lives have been saved ..." (adapted from *The Times*, April 1986) – – **to castigate** punish severely with blows or by criticizing – – **performance** *here:* quality of functioning; Leistung – – **muckraker** person who is always looking for scandal, corruption, etc. – – **investigative** examining in detail; nachforschend, Untersuchung ... – – **Upton Sinclair** (b. Sept. 20, 1878, Baltimore, Md.–d. Nov. 25, 1968, Bound Brook, N. J.), novelist and polemicist for Socialism and other causes; his *Jungle* is a landmark among naturalistic, proletarian novels. Producing some 80 books in his lifetime, he made largely his own the documentary novel, that blended journalist fact with fiction. Most of his books did not survive the topical concerns that occasioned them, but they were widely translated and continued to be read in other countries. He was highly popular in Russia both before and immediately after the Revolution of 1917, although Lenin criticized him as an emotional rather than an intellectual Socialist. Later his active opposition to the Communist regime caused a decline in his reputation there, but it was revived temporarily in the late 1930s and 1940s when his anti-Fascist writing was welcomed. Some other novels: *Oil* (1927), *Boston* (1928); *The Flivver King* (1937); *World's End* (1940) – – **stockyard** Viehhof – – **to arouse** *here:* stir up (from inactivity); awaken – – **labeling** description on labels – – **patent medicine** medicine made by one firm or person only; durch Warenzeichen geschütztes, nicht rezeptpflichtiges Präparat – – **by design** *here:* on purpose – – **to subject to control** bring under control – – **though** *here:* however – – **thalidomide tragedy** Kontergantragödie. The babies of mothers who had taken this medicine (a sedative) were born with defective limbs; frequently one hand or arm was missing or crippled – – **Rachel Carson** (1907–64) In her book *Silent Spring* (1962) the author warned that "... the indiscriminate use of pesticides (= insect killers such as DDT, etc.) was poisoning the natural world. The environment would eventually become so damaged that the song of birds in springtime would be silenced forever. She also warned of the serious risks of cancer and other threats to human health from the contamination of underground water.

Silent Spring became one of the most influential books of this century. One of the consequences of the book was the banning of DDT, which had been responsible for the death of many birds and other wildlife. Another important consequence was the establishment of the *EPA* (= Environmental Protection Agency) in the USA..." (adapted from *World & Press,* July 1986). Today there is still too much use of pesticides, but there is a hope that genetic engineering will make it possible to diminish the number of insects dangerous to crops without polluting the environment – – **to quadruple** [ˈkwɔdrupl] multiply by 4 – – **evidence** anything that gives reason for believing s. th., that makes clear or proves s. th.; Beweismittel, Beweismaterial – – **proof** Nachweis – – **unambiguous** eindeutig – – **penalty** punishment – – **incentive** motivation

"Marvellous dinner, darling – you must let me have the formula."

"... and you're positive it contains only natural monosodium glutamate?"

Source: *Punch,* Febr. 1, 1978

Assignments

1. Explain the following words and expressions, or supply synonyms: to depend on (l. 1); to take advantage of (l. 4); antigrowth (l. 20); currently (l. 28); outstanding (l. 35); private enterprise (l. 35); employee (l. 38); natural resources (l. 22); high volume sales (l. 96); sufficient (l. 106)
2. Give the opposite: benevolence (l. 1); consumer (l. 10); to recommend (l. 13); satisfactory (l. 28); to succeed (l. 40); employee (l. 38); shoddy (l. 37); improvement (l. 106); by accident (l. 61); inflation (l. 89); to raise (l. 90); increase (l. 92)
3. Let's do another wordgame. This time you have to find a word which forms a "bridge" between two other words. The word in question must operate both as the final part of the word on the left, and as the first part of the word on the right. If your solution is correct, the initial letters of the words in question will result in two new words which signify legal tender (= gesetzliches Zahlungsmittel) and a currency.

Example	master		writer
Solution	master	copy	writer
	1. black		place
	2. olive		field
	3. tennis		work
	4. money		rate
	5. stock		stick
	6. front		way
	7. telephone		form
	8. bank		word
	9. passenger		price
	10. fire		clock
	11. conference		mate

Explanations of the words in question:
1. a place where buyers and sellers come together to trade in goods
2. liquid which does not mix with water, obtained from animals, plants, or found in rock underground
3. open-work material of knotted string, wire, etc.
4. act of swopping
5. (usu. unroofed) enclosed or partly enclosed space near or round a building or group of buildings
6. that which closes the entrance to a building, room, cupboard, safe, etc.
7. command; direction
8. sum of money lent

9. number of names (of persons, items, things, etc.) written or printed
10. (sound or signal giving a) warning of danger; apparatus used to give such a warning
11. part of a house

4. Sum up the main points of the text's content.
5. Comment on Friedman's chief arguments. Do you think the examples accompanying his argument hold water?
6. Do you think the Austrian and Italian wine scandals of 1985/1986 argue for or against Friedman's thinking? Consider the reasons for and the reactions to these scandals. (If you don't remember the facts, read the following texts!)

AUSTRIA
Bitter Taste
Scandal in the wine industry

In the past, unscrupulous winemakers have added all sorts of ingredients to their products or have put expensive labels on bottles of *vin ordinaire* in an attempt to increase their profits. Now some Austrian vintners have found a highly unorthodox and potentially lethal way to turn their cheaper drink into the expensive stuff. Last
5 week the Austrian government announced it had impounded (= beschlagnahmt) more than 1 million gal. of Austrian wine that was adulterated (= made impure) with diethylene glycol, a chemical found in aircraft antifreeze, which can be fatal if swallowed. Panic among wine drinkers in Europe and the U.S. soon turned to indignation when it was revealed that the Austrian government had known about
10 the doctored wine for months.
Some of the contaminated wine came from the eastern province of Lower Austria, but most came from the neighboring province of Burgenland. Indeed many of the labels were marked RUST, the name of the village where much of the wine allegedly originated. Last week eight wine dealers and two chemists were arrested for their
15 part in the scandal. Among them: Johann Sautner, Josef Tschida and Georg Steiner, all from Burgenland, and Richard Grill, from the province of Lower Austria. The scheme first came to light after Austrian health authorities, apparently acting on anonymous tips, began testing wine for the dangerous chemical. By April they were sure enough of their results to reveal them publicly. Bu the scandal did not
20 become widely known until early July, when the West German government announced that 78,000 gal. of Austrian wine that had been imported into West Germany contained the chemical. Austrian officials promptly replied that the Vienna government had warned Bonn about the poisoned wine as early as April 25. West German officials acknowledged that they had received the information but
25 countered that the Austrians had not gone through the proper channels and thus had failed to sound a sufficiently urgent alarm.
The Bonn government has released a blacklist of 350 Austrian wines that are said to contain diethylene glycol. Bottles of wine with the toxic labels have been found in Poland, Greece, France, Japan and the U.S. als well as West Germany. The U.S.
30 Bureau of Alcohol, Tobacco and Firearms has forbidden shipments of any Austrian wine to U.S. retailers (= Einzelhändler) until the alcohol is tested by an approved U.S. laboratory.

In the meantime, overall sales of Austrian wine have dropped significantly. In West Germany alone which is Austria's biggest export market, losses to Austrian winemakers have been estimated at $5 million.

At this time no deaths have been linked to the contaminated vintages (= grape harvesting) according to West German health authorities, though a 1-to-2-oz. dose of diethylene glycol can be fatal.

Austrian officials are hoping that a tough new wine-control law will restore Austria's reputation in international markets. Yet observers in the wine business believe that the scandal may have done irreparable damage to the Austrian wine industry. Said one U.S. wine dealer: "It's sabotaged the wine industry for Austria. It's almost treason."

TIME, AUGUST 5, 1985

ITALY
The Most Dangerous Vintage
A deadly mixture and a wine industry in turmoil

Throughout West Germany, many supermarkets returned the wine to suppliers, and customs officers effectively barred all shipments until samples (= Proben) could be tested. Some states, including North Rhine-Westphalia, Bavaria and Lower Saxony, seized the wine from grocers' shelves. In France, officials confiscated 4.4 million gal. and said they would destroy an additional 1.3 million. Other countries took similar steps: in Switzerland, health officers impounded 2 million gal., while officials in Belgium, Denmark and Britain urged consumers to "play safe" by not buying the wine. Across Western Europe last week the word was out: drinking Italian wine can be dangerous, even deadly.

Since mid-March at least 21 Italians have died and more than 90 have been hospitalized after consuming poisoned wine. The suspect labels (= Marken) are largely inexpensive, supermarket-grade products. They were apparently fortified with methanol, or wood alcohol, a highly toxic substance used in paint solvent (= Lösungsmittel) and antifreeze. The winemakers, some of whom have been arrested, added the methanol to boost the alcohol content of their products – and thus their profits. Said *L'Osservatore Romano:* "A man's life is worth less than the price of a bottle of wine."

The first deaths last month were caused by tainted red Odore Barbera from the northern Piedmonte district. Since then Italian authorities have drawn up a list of suspect wines from various bottlers, including whites from Veneto, some Chiantis, even such well-known types as Soaves and Lambruscos, Thousands of bottles have been taken from stores, warehouses and wineries and analyzed for impurities. Of those tested so far, 2% carried dangerous levels of methanol. Last week one sample was found to contain 28% methanol, nearly 100 times the legal limit of 3% – and a dose large enough to cause the death of a person drinking just two glasses. The effect on wine drinkers has been profound. The Vatican felt compelled to reassure Roman Catholics that sacramental wine used for Communion was not contaminated. Convicts in Milan's San Vittore prison gave up wine in favor of beer, and wine sold at the bars in Rome's Parliament building was tested. In an effort to restore faith in their product, some producers last weekend opened stands for public wine tasting in the main squares of Turin, Milan, Rome and Florence.

More is at stake for Italy than changed drinking habits and shattered pride. The country is the world's largest producer of wine (1.8 billion gal. in 1985, vs. France's 1.7 billion, Spain's 924 million and the U.S.'s estimated 500 million). Officials are worried that the disaster could cripple an industry that generated about $950 million in export earnings last year. There is reason for concern: in 1985 Austria's wine-export business came close to collapse after 1 million gal. of white were found to have been diluted with an antifreeze additive. "This is an emergency," said Giuseppe Battistuzzi, the director of Federcantine, one of Italy's largest wine cooperatives. "We must work to repair our image abroad."

Italian wines, especially those shipped in bulk (= large amounts), are traditionally sold by alcohol content: the higher the proof per gallon, the higher the value. The Italian government forbids any additives for blending other than wines. Nonetheless, some producers and bottlers regularly add ethanol, or common alcohol. In 1984 the Italian government dropped its tax on methanol, making it cheaper than ethanol.

Late last year a group of about ten people in the northern region of Piedmonte began selling methanol to wine producers, who mixed the deadly alcohol with their wines and sold the blend at what seemed like bargain prices. The number of suspect firms now stands at 65, according to the police. Most of the gang members have been arrested, and two men, believed to be largely responsible for the tragedy, have been accused of purchasing more than 262 tons of methanol through a fictitious company and selling it to wine producers. The two face multiple charges, including manslaughter.

"The heart of the poisonous adulteration has been identified, isolated and crushed", declared Prime Minister Bettino Craxi last week after the latest arrests were announced. His statement may be premature. Despite a move earlier this month to pass legislation that would permit the government to close down firms convicted of adulterating wine, the incentive for illegal blending remains high. There is, for example, some concern regarding Sicilian production, which was reported to be 20% greater last year than the previous year, even though the grape harvest fell by 20%. Despite the scare, some Italians are refusing to give up their daily glass of wine. People are still ordering wine in restaurants, says Luigi Sestini, who heads the Italian Hotel and Restaurant Sommeliers Association, but "they only drink half, as if to reduce the danger". The most cautious of all, he says, call over the manager, ask what he drinks, then order it for themselves.

From: *TIME,* APRIL 21, 1986

The "Innocent" Consumer

Source: *World and Press,* 1 July, 1986.

9 THE ROOM

Note on the Text

This short story is intended for your reading pleasure. It has been left without annotations to make you use your dictionary if necessary. Unfortunately, no information was available on the author, Ray Russel.

The story has been taken from: I. Asimov, ed., *100 Great Science Fiction Short Stories,* Avon Books, New York 1980, p. 195 ff.

Crane awoke with the Tingle Tooth-foam song racing through his head. Tingle, he realized, must have bought last night's Sleepcoo time. He frowned at the Sleepcoo speaker in the wall next to his pillow. Then he stared at the ceiling: it was still blank. Must be pretty early, he told himself. As the Coffizz slogan slowly faded in on the
5 ceiling, be averted his eyes and got out of bed. He avoided looking at the printed messages on the sheets, the pillowcases, the blankets, his robe, and the innersoles of his slippers. As his feet touched the floor, the TV set went on. It would go off, automatically, at ten P. M. Crane was perfectly free to switch channels, but he saw no point in that.

105

10 In the bathroom, he turned on the light and the TV's audio was immediately piped in to him. He switched the light off and performed his first morning ritual in the dark. But he needed light in order to shave, and as he turned it on again, the audio resumed. As he shaved, the mirror flickered instantaneously once every three seconds.

15 It was not enough to distrub his shaving, but Crane found himself suddenly thinking of the rich warm goodness of the Coffizz competitor, Teatang. A few moments later, he was reading the ads for Now, the gentle instant laxative, and Stop, the bourbon-flavored paregoric, which were printed on alternating sheets of the bathroom tissue.

20 As he was dressing, the phone rang. He let it ring. He knew what he would hear if he picked it up: "Good morning! Have you had your Krakkeroonies yet? Packed with protein and –" Or, maybe, "Why wait for the draft? Enlist now in the service of your choice and cash in on the following enlistee benefits –" Or: "Feeling under the weather? Coronary disease kills four out of five! The early symptoms are –"

25 On the other hand, it *could* be an important personal call. He picked up the phone and said hello. "Hello yourself," answered a husky, insinuating feminine voice. "Bob?"

"Yes."

"Bob Crane?"

30 "Yes, who's this?"

"My name's Judy. I know you, but you don't know me. Have you felt logy lately, out of sorts –" He put down the phone. That settled it. He pulled a crumpled slip of paper from his desk drawer. There was an address on it. Hitherto, he had been hesitant about following up this lead. But this morning he felt decisive. He left his

35 apartment and hailed a cab.

The back of the cab's front seat immediately went on and he found himself watching the Juice-O-Vescent Breakfast Hour. He opened a newspaper the last passenger had left bebind. His eyes managed to slide over the four-color Glitterink ads with their oblique homosexual, sadistic, masochistic, incestuous and autoerotic

40 symbols, and he tried to concentrate on a new story about the initiating of another government housing program, but his attempts to ignore the Breeze Deodorant ads printed yellow-on-white between the lines were fruitless. The cab reached its destination. Crane paid the driver with a bill bearing a picture of Abraham Lincoln on one side and a picture of a naked woman bathing with Smoothie Soap on the

45 other. He entered a rather run-down frame building, found the correct door, and pressed the doorbell. He could hear, inside the flat, the sound of an old-fashioned buzzer, not a chime playing the EetMeet or Jetfly or Krispy Kola jingles. Hope filled him.

A slattern answered the door, regarded him suspiciously and asked, "Yeah?"

50 "I – uh – Mrs. Ferman? I got your name from a friend, Bill Seavers? I understand you –" his voice dropped low, "– rent rooms."
"Get outta here; you wanna get me in trouble? I'm a private citizen, a respectable –"
"I'll, I'll *play*. I have a good job. I –"
55 "How much?"
"Two hundred? That's twice what I'm paying at the housing projcet."
"Come on in." Inside, the woman locked, bolted and chained the door. "One room," she said. "Toilet and shower down the hall, you share it with two others. Get rid of your own garbage. Provide your own heat in the winter. You want hot water, it's
60 fifty extra. No cooking in the rooms. No guests. Three months' rent in advance, cash."
"I'll take it," Crane said quickly; then added, "I can turn off the TV?"
"There ain't no TV. No phone either."
"No all-night Sleepcoo next to the bed? No sublims in the mirrors? No Projecto in
65 the ceiling or walls?"
"None of that stuff."
Crane smiled. He counted out the rent into her dirty hand. "When can I move in?"
She shrugged. "Any time. Here's the key. Fourth floor, front. There ain't no elevator."
70 Crane left, still smiling, the key clutched in his hand.
Mrs. Ferman picked up the phone and dialed a number. "Hello?" she said. "Ferman reporting. We have a new one, male, about thrity."
"Fine, thank you," answered a voice. "Begin treatment at once, Dr. Ferman."

(~ 820 words)

Assignments

1. In what sense is this story a satire? and what does it satirize?
2. What does the surprise end of the story consist in?
3. The plot surely constitutes a cliché. What cliché?
4. List the exaggerated ads mentioned in the text.
5. Set the following bloopers (American slang for 'mistaken') right!

Business Bloopers

Business meetings are diamond mines for these bloopers, says John Ehrman, a San Jose, Calif., computer professional. Ehrman has been scribbling down misstatements for ten years. With the help of some friends, he has collected a list of more than 1600 from meetings, speeches and memos of San Jose companies and professional associations. Here are a few:

1. Things were all up in a heaval.
2. She had a missed conception.
3. That's just putting the gravy on the cake.
4. To be a leader, you have to develop a spear de corps.
5. I'm having a hard time getting my handles around that one.
6. If we keep going on this way, somebody is going to be left standing at the church with his pants down.
7. That's the whole kettle of fish in a nutshell.
8. I wish someone would make a decision; I'm tired of hanging in libido.
9. It's as easy as falling off a piece of cake.
10. There were tears strolling down their faces.
11. He likes sitting there in his big executive snivel chair.
12. Here's the crutch of the matter.
13. Don't put your umbrella and goulashes away yet.
14. We didn't sleep very well last night; it was one of those castrated beds, and it kept rolling around.
15. Would you like a craft of house wine?
16. I can't hear what you're saying because of the noise of the celery I'm chewing in my ears.
17. That needs some thinking about; let me go away and regurgitate for a couple of hours.

And finally, one item captures many people's sentiments about most business meetings: I'm not sure we really need to understand what we're talking about.

(from: Reader's Digest, US ed., 8/84)

6. Discuss:
Ads make us buy things we don't need with money we haven't got to impress or catch up with neighbours we don't like.

7. Translate the following expressions and use them to create sentences or minisituations
   1. to eat one's hat
   2. like a dying duck in the thunderstorm
   3. to go like clockwork
   4. let's play it safe
   5. his fingers are all thumbs
   6. a storm in a tea cup
   7. he's cracking up
   8. to make both ends meet
   9. to kiss the dust
   10. to make a mountain out of a molehill
   11. to have a finger in the pie

12 to turn a blind eye on s. th.
13 to mince matters
14 to get on the gravy train
15 to lead s. o. up the garden path
16 to call a spade a spade
17 to hit the roof
18 to have a bone to pick with s. o.
19 hit or miss
20 to go the whole hog.

10 HOW TO PERSUADE THE CONSUMER

Introducing the Topic

In text 9, *The Room,* we were confronted with a future world where the citizen is, as it were, controlled by a constant flow of advertising; where every minute of his life is exposed to the "terror" of persuasive appeals in newspapers, on radio, television, and even on the telephone and in taxis; where citizens who want to escape this "consumer's terror" are subdued to psychotherapeutic treatment. Of course, this nightmare is an extrapolation of certain phenomena in the advertising business of today's capitalist society. Like Crane in *The Room* we are frequently exposed to advertising without having a chance of escape. A striking example are British and American TV commercials, which are inserted in the middle of programmes (see the cartoon below). Other examples of advertising which is difficult to ignore are billboards, neon-lights, and advertisements in magazines.

"Why can't they save all the commercials to the end, and then we could be honor-bound to look at them?"

Source: *The New Yorker 1925–1975,* The Viking Press, New York 1975

"... and then again, madam, if you prefer adventurous cooking with that element of uncertainty, this new instant Yorkshire pudding mix has a built-in 0.998 per cent failure-to-rise probability-factor."

Source: *Punch,* Febr. 1, 1978

Another negative aspect of advertising is that it often persuades people to buy things they don't actually need and/or cannot afford.

However, it would be naive to believe that a competitive, free-market system could do without advertising, or to demand its elimination because of its negative aspects. Without doubt, advertising also has its positive sides: it informs the consumer about the existence of certain products and services; it can be used for good causes, such as collecting money for hungry people in underdeveloped countries (cf. *MW2,* p. 64); last but not least, it contributes to keeping the economy running, provides jobs, and helps increase living standards.

Moreover, the influence of ads is sometimes overrated. People are also influenced in their decision-making by personal likes or dislikes, prejudices ("French cars are sloppily built"), the views of friends, of family members, public opinion, etc.

Nevertheless, clever copy-writers are definitely able to arouse desires in most of us, even though we may not be aware of this effect. In particular, they will do so through their appeal or reference to the consumer's sensations, instincts, sexual appetite, ambitions, etc. These appeals or references are both verbal and visual, i. e. they are produced by the ad's lay-out and language. The trend in advertising language is towards "catchiness" and ambiguity in the words. The main idea is that the names of products and producers are "bound" into slogans which stick in the consumer's memory, such as "Players please". (Note the double meaning of "please".) Other rhetorical tricks, of course, are also used, such as repetitions, suggestive questions, alliteration, the so-called "you"-angle, exaggerations, etc. All of these tricks serve the single purpose of persuading the consumer to buy product X, Y, or Z.

Let's now have a look at some examples of magazine ads and find out how they work on the reader, and what psychological tricks they use.

A)

"Reaganomics is like sex. Everyone thinks there is more of it than there really is, and that someone is getting most of it."

Georgetown University's Paul Craig Roberts equated Reaganomics with sex as Senator Russell Long (D. Louisiana) led the list of two score speakers discussing... **The Economy. Government Regulation. Productivity. Finance. The how-to's of corporate communications programs that really work. And much more.**

Ideas crackled through FORTUNE's 1982 Corporate Communications Seminar.

The richness of these valuable insights is now gathered in the eleventh edition of Crosscurrents in Corporate Communications—FORTUNE's 100+ page special seminar report.

For your copy fill in the coupon below and mail it with your check for U.S. $15.

Quantity discounts: 10-24 copies @ U.S. $13 each
                         25 or more copies @ U.S. $11 each

Special offer: Crosscurrents No. 10 is available @ U.S. $10 with your eleventh-edition order (U.S. $14 if purchased separately).

FORTUNE
Rockefeller Center, New York, N.Y. 10020

Please send me _____ copies of Crosscurrents in Corporate Communications No. 11.
My check for $_____ is enclosed.

| NAME |
| COMPANY |
| ADDRESS |
| CITY   STATE   ZIP   T1 |

Source: *Time,* Febr. 28, 1983.

B)

CAN YOU SEE TOSHIBA IN THIS PICTURE?

We're there. In their smiles. We helped make those smiles. By making their lives a little nicer.

We did it through electronics.

Electronics is a field you touch wherever you turn these days.

And in the years to come, you're going to touch it more.

And much of what you touch is going to be Toshiba. Because Toshiba is one of the biggest electronics makers in the world.

We make everything from semiconductors to computers to color TVs to medical equipment to satellite communications systems.

And everything we make, makes life a little nicer. That's what electronics are all about. That's what we're about. We're Toshiba. We're making electronics come to life.

In Touch with Tomorrow
TOSHIBA

Source: *Business Week,* July 22, 1985

C)

ONE NAME STANDS TALL
IN SAUDI BUSINESS TRADITION

In the early 1950's The National Commercial Bank stood alone as the only Saudi bank in the Kingdom. Today, we still stand tall—as the largest commercial bank in the Middle East and the #1 bank in Saudi Arabia. Our spectacular growth is guided and nurtured by a progressive outlook and a clear vision of the future. This dynamism is reflected even in the design of our general management building in Jeddah.

Just as importantly, however, The National Commercial Bank is built on a firm foundation. Solid as rock. Our current assets amount to over $25 billion* with thousands of depositors and $12 billion in deposits. We network the Kingdom with over 160 branches, more than any other bank in Saudi Arabia, and span the globe to serve your every banking need with offices and branches in Frankfurt, London, Singapore, Seoul, New York, Beirut and Bahrain. This is the kind of foundation you need when doing business in Saudi Arabia and the Middle East.

So when you are looking for a bank in the Middle East, remember who was first in the Kingdom and is still #1 today, particularly in service and stability. NCB: Modern banking with a tradition of trust; make it *your* tradition.

For more information on The National Commercial Bank, please contact any of our offices listed below.

*Includes Contra Accounts.

THE NATIONAL COMMERCIAL BANK
MODERN BANKING WITH A TRADITION OF TRUST.

JEDDAH	LONDON	FRANKFURT	NEW YORK	BEIRUT	MANAMA	SINGAPORE	SEOUL
Tel: 644-6644	Tel: 638-4477	Tel: 250-181	Tel: 916-9000	Tel: 809-354	Tel: 231-182	Tel: 223-6243	Tel: 764-0018
Tlx: 405571 NCB H	Tlx: 8952594 NCB LON	Tlx: 416507 NCB FD	Tlx: 420037 NCB UW	Tlx: 20642 SAUDI B	Tlx: 9298 NCB GN BN	Tlx: RS 2719 NCB SIN	Tlx: K 25148 NCB SEL

Source: *Business Week,* July 22, 1985

D)

Plants have fed the world and cured its ills since life began.
Now we're destroying their principal habitat at the rate of 50 acres every minute.

We live on this planet by courtesy of the earth's green cover. Plants protect fragile soils from erosion, regulate the atmosphere, maintain water supplies for agriculture and prevent formation of deserts. Without plants man could not survive.

Yet, knowing this, we are destroying our own life-support system at such an alarming rate that it has already become a crisis – a crisis for ourselves and an even bigger one for our children.

The figures alone should tell the story – we destroy a tropical rain forest three times the size of Switzerland every year; within 25 years only fragments of the vast Malaysian and Indonesian forests will remain.

Photo: Courtesy of Richard Evans Schultes

<u>Dr. Richard Evans Schultes</u>, *director of the Botanical Museum at Harvard University, has spent 13 years in the Amazon jungle collecting the 'magic' plants of myth and legend and making them available to Western medicine and science. "The drugs of the future," he says, grow in the primeval jungle."*

What we are destroying
Much of the food, medicines and materials we use every day of our lives is derived from the wild species which grow in the tropics. Yet only a tiny fraction of the world's flowering plants have been studied for possible use. Horrifyingly, some 25,000 of all flowering species are on the verge of extinction.

Once the plants go, they are gone forever. Once the forests go only wastelands remain.

Photo: Mark. J. Plotkin

<u>Catharanthus roseus</u>. *Many of the world's children who have suffered from leukaemia are now alive due to the properties discovered in the rosy periwinkle, which originated in Madagascar where 90% of the forests are already destroyed.*

Who is the villain?
There is no villain – except ignorance and short-sightedness. The desperately poor people who live in the forests have to clear areas for crops and fuel, but they are doing this in such a way that they are destroying their very livelihood.

Add to this the way in which the heart is being ripped out of the forests to meet the demand for tropical timbers and we have a recipe for disaster.

Photo: WWF/H. Jungius

<u>Disease-resistant potatoes</u>, *obtained by cross-breeding wild potatoes from the Andes with domestic varieties, ensure that Ireland will never again experience the blight disease which wiped out its entire crop, leaving a million people to die of starvation.*

What can be done about it?
The problem seems so vast that there is a tendency to shrug and say "What can I do?" But there is an answer. There is something that each and every one of us can do.

The WWF Plant Conservation Programme
The World Conservation Strategy, published in 1980, is a programme for conserving the world's natural resources whilst managing them for human needs. A practical, international plant conservation programme has been prepared based on WCS principles and is now well under way all around the world.

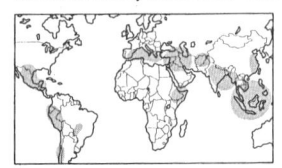

The Vavilov Centres. Named after the Russian scientist who identified them. These are the regions in which our major crop plants were first domesticated. Many of these regions contain wild or semi-domesticated relatives of commercial species which can be cross-bred with crop plants to increase yield and resistance to pests and diseases.

You can become part of it
The WWF Plant Conservation Programme is a plan for survival which you can help make a reality. Join the World Wildlife Fund now. We need your voice and your financial support.

Get in touch with your local WWF office for membership details, or send your contribution direct to the World Wildlife Fund at: WWF International, Membership Secretary, World Conservation Centre, 1196 Gland, Switzerland.

Save the plants that save us.
WWF FOR WORLD CONSERVATION

Source: *South*, December 1985

E)

A report to the American people on the progress of the Statue of Liberty– Ellis Island restoration.

As the scaffolding around the Statue comes down, it's going up just a half a mile away on Ellis Island. Here the work is just beginning for the second half of this great project that began nearly three years ago.

We can be proud of what we have accomplished. The Torch of Liberty has been completely rebuilt by French and American workers starting from scratch. It's an exact duplicate of the torch that was installed in 1886.

A monumental achievement

In addition, we've strengthened every part of the Statue. We've removed the rust, replaced 1,800 corroded iron armatures with stainless steel, and repaired or replaced the rivets that bind the skin to the framework.

A new spiral stairway leads up to the crown, as well as a new emergency elevator. And you'll be able to visit an expanded American Museum of Immigration where the name of every contributor is listed in a permanent registry.

July 4, 1986, the day of the Centennial Celebration, will climax a monumental achievement of volunteerism at work. The restoration of the Statue is on time. And paid for. And so is the upcoming celebration. The Lady will be ready for the great unveiling. And with your continued support we will be able to turn our full efforts to finishing the job on Ellis Island.

The Statue of Liberty was the symbol of freedom. But Ellis Island was the reality.

Although the years have been hard on the Lady with the Torch, they've been much harder on Ellis Island. The Great Hall, where almost half of all Americans can trace their ancestry is in ruins. It's here in the Great Hall the restoration work is beginning.

A staircase, similar to the one the immigrants climbed, will be built and the Great Hall, where formal medical and legal inspections were held, will be restored.

On the second and third floors, a library and museum will contain memorabilia the immigrants brought from their homeland. An oral history room will permit visitors to hear their actual voices as they relate their experiences.

And we'll provide facilities enabling the aged and handicapped to visit throughout the building.

**Liberty will be reborn.
Ellis Island will be restored.**

The progress of the restoration is an affirmation of the American people's belief that these symbols stand for America's future, not just its past. It's a tribute to the generosity of everyone from school children to giant corporations who reached into their pockets to get this work off to such a good start.

When the work is done, Ellis Island will be a living monument to the courage of our forefathers who came here and helped build a country. It must not die.

That's why I'm asking you to join me in this great campaign. We need your support and your contributions to continue. Together we will Keep the Dream Alive."

Lee A. Iacocca

Lee A. Iacocca, Chairman
Statue of Liberty–Ellis Island Foundation, Inc.
Send your tax-deductible contribution to: The Statue of Liberty–Ellis Island Foundation, Inc., P.O. Box 1986, New York, N.Y. 10018.

Source: *Discover*, July 1986

Annotations
(The words marked* should be memorized.)

Advertisement A) **Reaganomics** portmanteau word or blend of Reagan and economics: the term for the conservative economic policy practiced by the Reagan administration between 1980 and 1987 (see also p. 117) – – ***to equate** (with) gleichsetzen (mit) – – **two score** 40 – – **how-to's** (US) how-to-do-it – – **to crackle** prasseln – – ***insight** Erkenntnis, Einsicht – – ***to gather** sammeln – – **crosscurrents** conflicting trends; gegensätzliche Strömungen, Streitfragen – – **corporate communications** betrieblicher Informationsaustausch – – ***quantity discount** Mengenrabatt – – ***zip** Postleitzahl
B) **semiconductor** Halbleiter
C) **commercial bank** Handelsbank – – **to nurture** nähren; *hier:* erzeugen – – **outlook** Aussichten; *hier:* Planung – – **foundation** *hier:* Grund, Fundament – – **current assets** kurzfristiges Umlaufvermögen – – **contra-account** Wertberichtigungskonto – – ***depositor** Einleger, Kontoinhaber – – **to network** ... **with** ... **branches** Zweigstellen haben – – **to span the globe** weltweit tätig sein – – **banking need** Bedarf an Dienstleistungen der Banken – – **NCB** National Commercial Bank
D) **principal habitat** Hauptlebensraum – – **acre** Morgen; ungefähr 4050 qm – – **by courtesy** mit freundlicher Erlaubnis; *hier:* dank – – ***fragile** brüchig, leicht zerstörbar – – ***soil** Boden, Ackerland – – ***to maintain** erhalten – – **water supply** Wasserzufuhr – – **life-support system** Lebenserhaltungssystem – – **fragment** Bruchstück – – **primeval** Ur... – – ***to derive (from)** abstammen (von) – – **species** ['spi:ʃiz] Art, Arten – – **fraction** Bruchteil – – **on the verge** am Rande – – **wastelands** Ödland – – **periwinkle** (bot.) Immergrün – – **villain** der Böse, Schurke – – **livelihood** *hier:* Existenz – – **heart** Kernholz – – **timber** Nutzholz – – **recipe** ['resəpi] Rezept – – **disease resistant** widerstandsfähig gegen Krankheiten – – **crossbreeding** Kreuzung – – **variety** *hier:* Spielart, Variante – – **blight disease** (bot.) Trockenfäule – – ***to shrug** mit den Schultern zucken – – **whilst** während; unterdessen – – **crop plant** Nutzpflanze – – **pest** Schädling – – ***yield** Ertrag
E) **scaffolding** Baugerüst – – **torch** Fackel – – **to start from scratch** ganz von vorn anfangen – – **armatures** Bewehrung – – **stainless steel** rostfreier Stahl – – **rivet** Niete – – **framework** *hier:* Stahlrahmen – – **emergency elevator** Notfahrstuhl – – ***registry** Verzeichnis – – **to climax** den Höhepunkt bilden für; den Höhepunkt finden in – – **volunteerism** Freiwilligkeitsprinzip; freiwilliges Engagement – – **unveiling** Enthüllung – – ***ancestry** Abstammung; Vorfahren – – ***floor** Stockwerk – – **memorabilia** Erinnerungsstück – – ***actual** wirklich – – **handicapped** Behinderte – – **affirmation** Bestätigung – – ***chairman** Vorsitzender – – **tax-deductible** steuerabzugsfähig – – ***contribution** Spende – – **foundation** *hier:* Stiftung

Assignments

1. Use your English-English dictionary to look up the annotations marked*, then write in your index cards their English explanations or synonyms.
2. What do the ads A–E want to sell?
3. Sum up the contents of the ads.
4. What groups of addressees have the copy-writers in mind?

5. Into what parts can the ads be broken down?
6. The line of persuasion any copywriter should follow is expressed in the formula of "AIDA" (= creation of ATTENTION; INTEREST; DESIRE; ACTION). Would you say that our ads achieve these responses? If so, how? (Choose one or two ads to verify your answer.)
7. Analyse the language of one or two ads. Which psychological tricks are used? Which words and sentence fragments are most important? What about the sentence structure? Is it simple, complex, compound? What are the reasons for the sentence structure used?
8. Which ads appeal more to our feelings and instincts, and which appeal mainly to our minds? Why is that so?
9. Sum up the results of your analysis of the ads in a list. Divide the list into
   a) types of the ads
   b) parts of the ads
   c) purposes of the parts
   d) techniques (lay-out, style) for achieving these purposes
10. Explain which ad – in your opinion – is most impressive and persuasive.
11. Make up the headline, caption, and main text of an ad for a car. Compare it with your classmates'.

11 ACTION NOW

Introduction

The victory of the Republican Ronald Reagan over the Democratic President Jimmy Carter in 1980 marked a political turning-point from an increasingly welfare state-oriented policy, which was more and more felt to be a heavy burden for the American tax payer, to a policy which put into focus private initiative, individual responsibility, and a reduction of "interventionist government". President Reagan's message to the American people was: "Let's cut back on Big Government, on Government spending and Government intervention in people's lives and America will overcome the economic problems of the second half of the 1970's and find a way back to the prosperity of the 1960's."

Almost 50 years earlier (in 1932) it was Franklin D. Roosevelt, the democratic challenger of the incumbent President Herbert Hoover, who – using arguments diametrically contrary to those of Ronald Reagan fifty years later – – swept the Republican President out of the White House by a landslide of 472 electoral votes to 59. To master the economic crisis of the early 1930's Roosevelt (1882–1945) promised his voters to put an end to ". . . nineteenth century expansive, laissez-faire individualism" and to establish a Government that ". . . must play a major role in the soberer, less dramatic business of . . . seeking to re-establish foreign markets for our surplus production, adjusting production to consumption, of distributing wealth and products more equitably, of adapting existing economic organizations to the service of the people." ("The Roosevelt Revolution", in R. D. Heffner, *A Documentary History of the United States,* New American Library, p. 269.)

Roosevelt assumed leadership during one of the greatest economic and social crises in modern history – a crisis that seemed to mark the total breakdown of the Capitalist system (with an unemployment rate of 25% = 12 million jobless in the USA in 1932). His response to that emergency was the introduction of the *New Deal,* i. e. of a limited welfare state coupled with an unprecedented measure of Government competence – – a genuine political and social revolution in the America of "Rugged Individualism" (Herbert Hoover in his *Inauguration Speech,* 1928). In the first 100 days of his Government, Roosevelt pushed through Congress no less than 15 major legislative innovations. He inaugurated a programme of old-age insurance, unemployment insurance, and financial assistance for dependent children, the crippled, and the blind. To avert the total collapse of an already badly shaken banking system Roosevelt proclaimed a national "bank holiday", closing the banks until steps might be taken to protect the savings of vast numbers of small depositors. To help impoverished farmers the *Agricultural Adjustment Administration* (AAA) was created, which brought about an enormously expanded national farm income through a programme of crop curtailment and government-supported price levels (Heffner, *op. cit.,* p. 271). The *National Recovery Administration* (NRA) attempted to increase the living standards of the urban industrial worker. Workers were encouraged to enter and form trade unions.

President Roosevelt was one to the most forceful speakers of the time. His "fireside chats" were the first radio broadcasts ever made by a President directly to the people. His *First Inauguration Speech* of 1933 (he was elected President four times and was in office from 1933–1945), in which he outlines his political credo, has always ranked among the greatest political speeches delivered in 20th century America. We present the complete text as it is published in *The World's Great Speeches,* edited by L. Copeland and L. W. Lamm, Dover Publications Inc., New York 1973.

PRESIDENT HOOVER, Mr. Chief Justice, my friends:
This is a day of national consecration, and I am certain that my fellow-Americans expect that on my induction into the Presidency I will address them with a candor and a decision which the present situation of our nation impels.

5 This is preeminently the time to speak the truth, the whole truth, frankly and boldly. Nor need we shrink from honestly facing conditions in our country today. This great nation will endure as it has endured, will revive and will prosper.

So first of all let me assert my firm belief that the only thing we have to fear is fear itself – nameless, unreasoning, unjustified terror which paralyzes needed efforts
10 to convert retreat into advance.

In every dark hour of our national life a leadership of frankness and vigor has met with that understanding and support of the people themselves which is essential to victory. I am convinced that you will again give that support to leadership in these critical days.

15 In such a spirit on my part and on yours we face our common difficulties. They concern, thank God, only material things. Values have shrunken to fantastic levels; taxes have risen; our ability to pay has fallen; government of all kinds is faced by serious curtailment of income; the means of exchange are frozen in the currents of trade; the withered leaves of industrial enterprise lie on every side; farmers find
20 no markets for their produce; the savings of many years in thousands of families are gone.

More important, a host of unemployed citizens face the grim problem of existence, and an equally great number toil with little return. Only a foolish optimist can deny the dark realities of the moment.

25 Yet our distress comes from no failure of substance. We are stricken by no plague of locusts. Compared with the perils which our forefathers conquered because they believed and were not afraid, we have still much to be thankful for. Nature still offers her bounty and human efforts have multiplied it. Plenty is at our doorstep, but a generous use of it languishes in the very sight of the supply.

30 Primarily, this is because the rulers of the exchange of mankind's goods have failed through their own stubbornness and their own incompetence, have admitted their failure and abdicated. Practices of the unscrupulous money changers stand indicted in the court of public opinion, rejected by the hearts and minds of men.

True, they have tried, but their efforts have been cast in the pattern of an outworn
35 tradition. Faced by failure of credit, they have proposed only the lending of more money.

Stripped of the lure of profit by which to induce our people to follow their false leadership, they have resorted to exhortations, pleading tearfully for restored confidence. They know only the rules of a generation of self-seekers.

40 They have no vision, and when there is no vision the people perish.

The money changers have fled from their high seats in the temple of our civilization. We may now restore that temple to the ancient truths.

The measure of the restoration lies in the extent to which we apply social values more noble than mere monetary profit.

45 Happiness lies not in the mere possession of money; it lies in the joy of achievement, in the thrill of creative effort.

The joy and moral stimulation of work no longer must be forgotten in the mad chase of evanescent profits. These dark days will be worth all they cost us if they teach us that our true destiny is not to be ministered unto but to minister to ourselves and
50 to our fellow-men.

Recognition of the falsity of material wealth as the standard of success goes hand in hand with the abandonment of the false belief that public office and high political position are to be valued only by the standards of pride of place and personal profit; and there must be an end to a conduct in banking and in business which too often
55 has given to a sacred trust the likeness of callous and selfish wrongdoing.

Small wonder that confidence languishes, for it thrives only on honesty, on honor, on the sacredness of obligations, on faithful protection, on unselfish performance. Without them it cannot live.

Restoration calls, however, not for changes in ethics alone. This nation asks for action, and action now.

Our greatest primary task is to put people to work. This is no unsolvable problem if we face it wisely and courageously.

It can be accomplished in part by direct recruiting by the government itself, treating the task as we would treat the emergency of a war, but at the same time, through this employment, accomplishing greatly needed projects to stimulate and reorganize the use of our natural resources.

Hand in hand with this, we must frankly recognize the overbalance of population in our industrial centres and, by engaging on a national scale in a redistribution, endeavor to provide a better use of the land for those best fitted for the land.

The task can be helped by definite efforts to raise the values of agricultural products and with this the power to purchase the output of our cities.

It can be helped by preventing realistically the tragedy of the growing loss, through foreclosure, of our small homes and our farms.

It can be helped by insistence that the Federal, State and local governments act forthwith on the demand that their cost be drastically reduced.

It can be helped by the unifying of relief activities which today are often scattered, uneconomical and unequal. It can be helped by national planning for and supervision of all forms of transportation and of communications and other utilities which have a definitely public character.

There are many ways in which it can be helped, but it can never be helped merely by talking about it. We must act, and act quickly.

Finally, in our progress toward a resumption of work we require two safeguards against a return of the evils of the old order; there must be a strict supervision of all banking and credits and investments; there must be an end to speculation with other people's money, and there must be provision for an adequate but sound currency.

These are the lines of attack. I shall presently urge upon a new Congress in special session detailed measures for their fulfillment, and I shall seek the immediate assistance of the several States.

Through this program of action we address ourselves to putting our own national house in order and making income balance outgo.

Our international trade relations, though vastly important, are, in point of time and necessity, secondary to the establishment of a sound national economy.

I favor as a practical policy the putting of first things first. I shall spare no effort to restore world trade by international economic readjustment, but the emergency at home cannot wait on that accomplishment.

The basic thought that guides these specific means of national recovery is not narrowly nationalistic.

It is the insistence, as a first consideration, upon the interdependence of the various elements in and parts of the United States – a recognition of the old and permanently important manifestation of the American spirit of the pioneer.

It is the way to recovery. It is the immediate way. It is the strongest assurance that the recovery will endure.

In the field of world policy I would dedicate this nation to the policy of the good neighbor – the neighbor who resolutely respects himself and, because he does so, respects the rights of others – the neighbor who respects his obligations and respects the sanctity of his agreements in and with a world of neighbors.

If I read the temper of our people correctly, we now realize, as we have never realized before, our interdependence on each other; that we cannot merely take, but we must give as well; that if we are to go forward we must move as a trained and loyal army willing to sacrifice for the good of a common discipline, because, without such discipline, no progress is made, no leadership becomes effective.

We are, I know, ready and willing to submit our lives and property to such discipline because it makes possible a leadership which aims at a larger good.

This I propose to offer, pledging that the larger purposes will bind upon us all as a sacred obligation with a unity of duty hitherto evoked only in time of armed strife.

With this pledge taken, I assume unhesitatingly the leadership of this great army of our people, dedicated to a disciplined attack upon our common problems.

Action in this image and to this end is feasible under the form of government which we have inherited from our ancestors.

Our Constitution is so simple and practical that it is possible always to meet extraordinary needs by changes in emphasis and arrangement without loss of essential form.

That is why our constitutional system has proved itself the most superbly enduring political mechanism the modern world has produced. It has met every stress of vast expansion of territory, of foreign wars, of bitter internal strife, of world relations.

It is to be hoped that the normal balance of executive and legislative authority may be wholly adequate to meet the unprecedented task before us. But it may be that an unprecedented demand and need for undelayed action may call for temporary departure from that normal balance of public procedure.

I am prepared under my constitutional duty to recommend the measures that a stricken nation in the midst of a stricken world may require.

These measures, or such other measures as the Congress may build out of its experience and wisdom, I shall seek, within my constitutional authority, to bring to speedy adoption.

But in the event that the Congress shall fail to take one of these two courses, and in the event that the national emergency is still critical, I shall not evade the clear course of duty that will then confront me.

I shall ask the Congress for the one remaining instrument to meet the crisis – broad

140 executive power to wage a war against the emergency as great as the power that would be given to me if we were in fact invaded by a foreign foe.
For the trust reposed in me I will return the courage and the devotion that befit the time. I can do no less.
We face the arduous days that lie before us in the warm courage of national unity;
145 with the clear consciousness of seeking old and precious moral values; with the clean satisfaction that comes from the stern performance of duty by old and young alike.
We aim at the assurance of a rounded and permanent national life.
We do not distrust the future of essential democracy. The people of the United States
150 have not failed. In their need they have registered a mandate that they want direct, vigorous action.
They have asked for discipline and direction under leadership. They have made me the present instrument of their wishes. In the spirit of the gift I take it.
In this dedication of a nation we humbly ask the blessing of God. May He protect
155 each and every one of us! May He guide me in the days to come!   (~ 1815 ws)

Annotation
(The words marked * should be memorized.)

Chief Justice head of the Supreme Court – – **consecration** dedication; Hingabe – – **induction** the act of installing with ceremony in position or office – – **cando(u)r** sincerity – – **to impel** to force (forward) – – **preeminently** above all – – **to shrink** (shrank, shrunk) **[from]** keep o. s. away from – – **to endure** last – – **to assert** declare – – **unreasoning** not guided by reason; unvernünftig – – **to paralyze** lähmen – – **values** *here:* what things are worth – – **shrunken** diminished – – **curtailment** reduction – – **currents of trade** Handelsströme – – **means of exchange** Tauschmittel, Waren – – **to wither** become dry – – **on every side** everywhere – – **host** great number – – **return** gain, profit – – **distress** (cause of) great sorrow – – **stricken** affected – – **locust** Heuschrecke – – **peril** danger – – **bounty** generosity; Freigebigkeit – – **to languish** be or become lacking in energy; lose health and strength; verkümmern, dahinsiechen – – **stubbornness** Sturheit – – **unscrupulous** not guided by conscience – – **money changer** *here:* banker – – **to indict** [in'dait] accuse – – **pattern** *here:* form, structure – – **lure** attraction s. th. has – – **to resort (to)** Zuflucht nehmen (zu) – – **exhortation** Ermahnung – – **selfseeker** selfish person – – **to perish** be destroyed, come to an end – – **evanescent** [ivə'nesnt] quickly fading – – **to minister** (to) give help or service – – **abandonment** the act of giving up – – **place** *here:* position or station (in society, etc.) – – **conduct** behaviour; Verhalten – – **likeness** *here:* external appearance; Gestalt – – **callous** insensible – – **to thrive** (throve, thriven) prosper – – **emergency** unforseen and sudden danger – – **to endeavo(u)r** try hard – – **output** (quantity of) goods produced – – **values** *here:* prices – – **foreclosure** Verfallserklärung einer Hypothek bei Nichteinhaltung der Zahlungsverpflichtung – – **forthwith** at once – – **supervision** control – – **resumption** the act of taking up again – – **safeguard** undertaking that tends to prevent harm; Sicherheitsvorrichtung – – **provision** *here:* preparation – – **speculation** the act of investing money in a business deal, in the hope of making a big profit – – **obligation** Verpflichtung – – **sanctity** holiness – – **to pledge** promise seriously – – **to evoke** call up – – **feasible** machbar – – **ancestor** forefather – – **undelayed** immediate – – **adoption** acceptance – – **foe** enemy – – **to befit** be right and suitable for – – **arduous** using up much energy – – **stern** severe, strict – – **assurance** *here:* Sicherstellung – – **rounded** voll, abgerundet – – **to register a mandate** einen (politischen) Auftrag erteilen

WORKSHEET

1. **Language**
1.1 Explain or paraphrase the following expressions, as they are used within their context:
to convert retreat into advance (l. 10); the withered leaves of industrial enterprise (l. 19); rulers of the exchange of mankind's goods (l. 30); stripped of the lure of profit (l. 37); restored confidence (l. 38); relief activities (l. 76); making income balance outgo (l. 91); spirit of the pioneer (l. 101)
1.2.1 In the course of his speech Roosevelt makes use of a couple of so-called "notional phrases", such as "I am certain" in line 1, which underlines his *conviction* that his policy is able to grapple with the crisis. Do you know any other such phrases expressing conviction or certainty?
1.2.2 Find the other notional phrases expressing certainty used in the text.
1.2.3 What does the speaker demonstrate by employing phrases like "I am prepared . . ." (l. 131); "I shall spare no effort . . ." (l. 94)?
Do you know any other notional phrases of that type?
1.2.4 Decide what type the following notional phrases are: I don't care; never mind; I don't mind; that's great; you'd rather; be careful; I fear that . . .; we're going to; that doesn't interest me; I trust that . . .; I don't agree; I don't know for sure; that's fantastic; what a shame; you wouldn't believe it; I'm sorry; I definitely disagree; that's bad news; thanks a lot; don't worry

Agreement	Disagreement	Annoyance
Advice	Apology	Certainty/Conviction
Determination	Disappointment	Doubt/Uncertainty
Fear/Worry	Gratitude	Indifference
Intention	Pleasure	Reassurance
Sympathy	Surprise	Warning

1.2.5 Insert the appropriate notional phrase:
a) "Oh God, tomorrow we'll have to take our final exam."
"Oh, _____, you'll manage an A."
b) "He's just passed his exams." "Oh, _____."
c) "I'll tell you something that I hate to say, but in school they think you're a failure."

"Well, _____ what they think."
d) "The cellar is full of boys. They don't know what to do with themselves."
"Ah, they can wait."
"_____ go down and tell them what to do. Otherwise they might cause trouble."
e) "I'll try to get a rise in salary." "I'_____ you will."
f) "He will get married next week." "Oh, _____."
g) "_____ on the underground."
h) "Hello, Pete, come in." "I'd like to have a little talk with you, Bob."
"_____ to keep you waiting. I'll be with you in a minute."
i) "I think that a tape recorder is a useful machine."
"I _____. I could use it at school as well."
j) "Do you think Schmeling will knock him out?" "Well, _____ that."

1.3 Roosevelt is a good orator who employs quite a number of stylistic devices. Decide which of the following are used in his speech:

parallelism	metaphor	understatement
repetition	alliteration	overstatement
pun	symbol	simile (comparison)
personification	accumulation	irony
allusion	climax	sarcasm

1.4 Now that you have worked so hard, do this for relaxation:

JUMBLE THAT SCRAMBLED WORD GAME
by Henri Arnold and Bob Lee

Unscramble these four Jumbles, one letter to each square, to form four ordinary words.

JYTET

SONEO

KRUTEY

TORREC

WHAT HE GOT WHEN HE BOUGHT THAT STOCK.

Now arrange the circled letters to form the surprise answer, as suggested by the above cartoon.

Print answer here:

Source: *The International Herald Tribune,* Nov. 6, 1985

2. **Text Analysis**
2.1 Roosevelt's speech falls into 6 parts. Identify them. Give each of them a fitting headline.
2.2 Sum up Roosevelt's depiction of the economic and social situation of the early 1930's. Try to use your own words.
2.3 What are the causes of the crisis, according to the speaker?
2.4 What is his economic recipe for overcoming the problems?
2.5 What are the political prerequisites to cope with the crisis successfully?
2.6 What does Roosevelt appeal to and why does he do so?
2.7 How would you describe the tone of the speech? Explain your view.
2.8 What do you think was the reaction of the majority of his listeners? (His speech was broadcast on national radio.) Justify your view.

The Depression suddenly brought millions of Americans face to face with stark ruin. From left, apples sold by jobless on Washington street corners; unemployed Detroit worker pleaded for help; breadlines stretched for blocks in New York City; farm mother lacked food for her children

Source: *Time,* Febr. 1, 1982

3. **Discussion and Comment**
3.1 Roosevelt, determined to fight the crisis by creating a limited welfare state and by starting public projects ranging from road repairing, raking leaves or building public toilets to creating dams, power plants, airports, port facilities, sewage systems, schools, etc. Do you think such a policy can overcome unemployment?
3.2 Ronald Reagan's answer to the slump in the late 1970's and the early 1980's was a curtailment of subsidies and welfare expenditure, a reduction in taxes, and the removal of excessive Government regulation of industry. Between 1979 and 1986 the inflation rate dropped from about 11.5% to 3.8% and unemployment fell from 9.5% to 6.8%. Can you explain why the effect of the measures taken was so obviously positive for the country's economy?
Or do you think there were other or additional reasons for the fall in unemployment and inflation?
3.3 In the Federal Republic of Germany inflation decreased from about 5.5% in 1981 to 0.0% in 1986. On the other hand, unemployment stagnated or barely fell. What, in your opinion, were the reasons for the different developments of inflation and unemployment in that period?

4. **Further Studies**

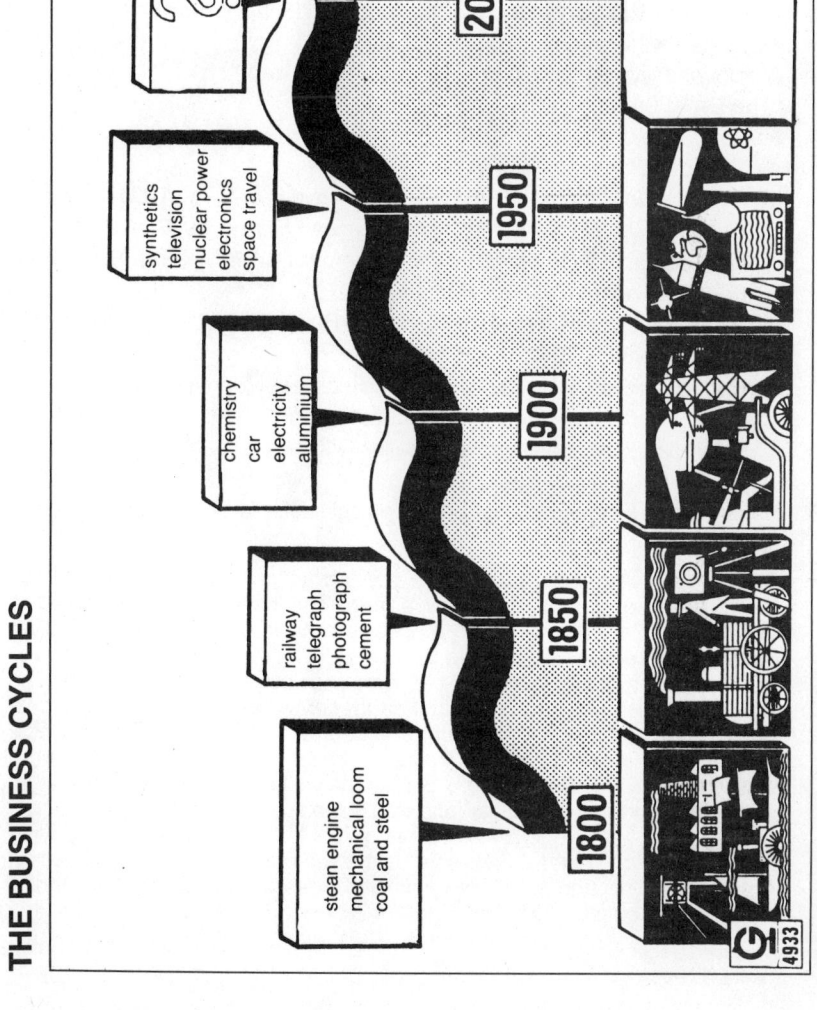

THE BUSINESS CYCLES

1800	1850	1900	1950	2000	

- steam engine, mechanical loom, coal and steel
- railway, telegraph, photograph, cement
- chemistry, car, electricity, aluminium
- synthetics, television, nuclear power, electronics, space travel

Source: *Mannheimer Morgen*, 1984

4.1 So far you have learnt that business in Capitalist countries is subject to ups and downs, to booms and slumps. As early as the 1920's, an interesting theory about the reasons for these oscillations had been developed by the Russian economist Kontratieff, who claimed that – since the onset of industrialization – the course of the world economy had followed a pattern of long waves. Worldwide crises in the years 1825, 1873, 1929, (and we may add the year 1973!) had marked the turning points. The chart above attempts to make Kontratieff's theory clear.

Assignment: Explain his theory. Make suggestions as to which innovations might determine the future course of our economy.

4.2 A student delivers a speech (only notes are allowed!) on
"The Great Depression and the New Deal."
For reference use:
a) The *Encyclopaedia Britannica*
b) Richard D. Heffner, "The Roosevelt Revolution", in *A Documentary History of the United States,* New American Library, 1976, p. 268 ff.
c) M. Friedman & R. Friedman, "The Anatomy of Crisis", in *Free To Choose,* Penguin Books, 1980, p. 95 ff.
d) "Roosevelt's Legacy – – The New Deal Reconsidered", *Time Magazine,* Febr. 1, 1982.
e) Robert Lekachman, *Capitalism for Beginners,* Pantheon Books, New York, 1980 (in particular the chapter on "1929: The Collapse of Capitalism?" and the chapters dealing with the theory of John M. Keynes, pp. 84–97.)

4.3 Having worked through all this philosophical stuff, you are probably dying for some relaxation. Why not try this?

Sometime during the last century two towns on opposite sides of the Canadian-American border began a feud. The American town decided to devalue the Canadian dollar to 90 cents. In retaliation the Canadian town devalued the American dollar to 90 cents. A Canadian ne'er-do-well woke the following morning with only one American dollar left from the previous night's debauchery. Knowing that it had recently been devalued in his own town, he walked across the border and bought a 10-cent drink from a local bar. He was surprised to get a Canadian dollar in change, which of course was worth only 90 cents in the U.S. He then walked back to his own village, bought a second 10-cent drink, and was given an American dollar in change. By repeating this sequence of events he continued back and forth buying drinks all day and night. Just before he passed out he noticed he still had an American dollar, and wondered who had been buying his drinks. Who, if anyone, was buying the drinks?

From: *Discover,* December 1985.

12 THE DISPOSSESSED

Note on the Text

Ursula K. LeGuin was born in Berkeley in 1929. She was brought up in academic surroundings and started reading sf early. She studied romance languages and literature and holds two university degrees. In the 1950s she started writing mainstream novels. Her sf career began in 1966.
The Dispossessed – An Ambiguous Utopia is without doubt her greatest achievement. It constitutes a highly important study of politics and sociology in sf. In a parallel structure it contrasts the utopian world of the planet Anarres with the "normal" (dystopian?) world of the planet Urras, both in the same solar system, far away from the nearly-forgotten earth. The hero of the novel, the famous scientist Shevok form Anarres, tries to reconcile differences between the two cultures and break down walls (a recurrent theme and image in the book) by flying to Urras as an ambassador. Our excerpt shows him in a discussion with his hosts on Urras.

Our extract has been taken from U. K. LeGuin; *The Dispossessed,* Avon Books, New York, 1975, p. 120 ff.

"We know that nominally there's no government on Anarres. However, obviously there's administration. And we gather that the group that sent you, your Syndicate, is a kind of faction; perhaps a revolutionary faction."
"Everybody on Anarres is a revolutionary, Oiie. . . . The network of administration
5 and management is called PDC, Production and Distribution Coordination. They are a coordinating system for all syndicates, federatives, and individuals who do productive work. They do not govern persons; they administer production. They have no authority either to support me or to prevent me. They can only tell us the public opinion of us – where we stand in the social conscience."
10 "But what," Oiie said abruptly, as if the question, long kept back, burst from him under pressure, "what keeps people in order? Why don't they rob and murder each other?"
"Nobody owns anything to rob. If you want things you take them from the depository. As for violence, well, I don't know, Oiie; would you murder me, ordinarily? And if
15 you felt like it, would a law against it stop you? Coercion is the least efficient means of obtaining order."
"All right, but how do you get people to do the dirty work?"
"What dirty work?" asked Oiie's wife, not following.
"Garbage collecting, grave digging," Oiie said; Shevek added, "Mercury mining,"
20 and nearly said, "Shit processing," but recollected the Ioti taboo on scatological words. He had reflected, quite early in his stay on Urras, that the Urrasti lived among mountains of excrement, but never mentioned shit.

"Well, we all do them. But nobody has to do them for very long, unless he likes the work. One day in each decade the community management committee or the block committee or whoever needs you can ask you to join in such work; they make rotating lists. Then the disagreeable work postings, or dangerous ones like the mercury mines and mills, normally they're for one half year only."

"But then the whole personnel must consist of people just learning the job."

"Yes. It's not efficient, but what else is to be done? You can't tell a man to work on a job that will cripple him or kill him in a few years. Why should he do that?"

"He can refuse the order?"

"It's not an order, Oiie. He goes to Divlab – the Division of Labor office – and says, I want to do such and such, what have you got? And they tell him where there are jobs."

"But then why do people do the dirty work at all? Why do they even accept the one-day-in-ten jobs?"

"Because they are done together . . . And other reasons. You know, life on Anarres isn't rich, as it is here. In the little communities there isn't very much entertainment, and there is a lot of work to be done. So, if you work at a mechanical loom mostly, every tenthday it's pleasant to go outside and lay a pipe or plow a field, with a different group of people. . . . And then there is challenge. Here you think that the incentive to work is finances, need for money or desire for profit, but where there's no money the real motives are clearer, maybe. People like to do things. They like to do them well. People take the dangerous, hard jobs because they take pride in doing them, they can – egoize, we call it – show off? – to the weaker ones. Hey, look, little boys, see how strong I am! You know? A person likes to do what he is good at doing. . . . But really, it is the question of ends and means. After all, work is done for the work's sake. It is the lasting pleasure of life. The private conscience knows that. And also the social conscience, the opinion of one's neighbors. There ist no other reward, on Anarres, no other law. One's own pleasure, and the respect of one's fellows. That is all. When that is so, then you see the opinion of the neighbors becomes a very mighty force."

"No one ever defies it?"

"Perhaps not often enough," Shevek said.

"Does everybody work so hard, then?" Oiie's wife asked. "What happens to a man who just won't cooperate?"

"Well, he moves on. The others get tired of him, you know. They make fun of him, or they get rough with him, beat him up; in a small community they might agree to take his name off the meals listing, so he has to cook and eat all by himself; that is humiliating. So he moves on, and stays in another place for a while" . . .

"The same old hypocrisy. Life is a fight, and the strongest wins. All civilization does is hide the blood and cover up the hate with pretty words!"

"Your civilization, perhaps. Ours hides nothing. It is all plain. Queen Teaea wears

her own skin, there. We follow one law, only one, the law of human evolution."
65 "The law of evolution is that the strongest survives!"
"Yes, and the strongest, in the existence of any social species, are those who are most social. In human terms, most ethical. You see, we have neither prey nor enemy, on Anarres.– We have only one another. There is no strength to be gained from hurting one another. Only weakness."
70 "I don't care about hurting and not hurting. I don't care about other people, and nobody else does, either. They pretend to. I don't want to pretend. I want to be free!"
"But Vea," he began with tenderness, for the plea for freedom moved him very much, but the doorbell rang. Vea stood up, smoothed her skirt, and advanced smiling to welcome her guests . . .
75 "It is our suffering that brings us together. It is not love. Love does not obey the mind, and turns to hate when forced. The bond that binds us is beyond choice. We are brothers. We are brothers in what we share. In pain, which each of us must suffer alone, in hunger, in poverty, in hope, we know our brotherhood. We know it, because we have had to learn it. We know that there is no help for us but from one another,
80 that no hand will save us if we do not reach out our hand. And the hand that you reach out is empty, as mine is. You have nothing. You possess nothing. You own nothing. You are free. All you have is what you are, and what you give.

"I am here because you see in me the promise, the promise that we made two hundred years ago in this city – the promise kept. We have kept it, on Anarres. We
85 have nothing but our freedom. We have nothing to give you but your own freedom. We have no law but the single principle of mutual aid between individuals. We have not government but the single principle of free association. We have no states, no nations, no presidents, no premiers, no chiefs, no generals, no bosses, no bankers, no landlords, no wages, no charity, no police, no soldiers, no wars. Nor do we have
90 much else. We are sharers, not owners. We are not prosperous. None of us is rich. None of us is powerful. If it is Anarres you want, if it is the future you seek, then I tell you that you must come to it with empty hands. You must come to it alone, and naked, as the child comes into the world, into his future, without any past, without any property, wholly dependent on other people for his life. You cannot take what
95 you have not given and you must give yourself. You cannot buy the Revolution. You cannot make the Revolution. You can only be the Revolution. It is in your spirit, or it is nowhere." (~ 1300 words)

Sayings and proverbs that illustrate the ideology of the Anarres way of life:
"Having's wrong, sharing's right."
"Speech is sharing"
"Excess is excrement"
"To be whole is to be part – true voyage is return"
"To make a thief, make an owner; to create crime, create laws"

Annotations

1 **syndicate** business association, combination of commercial firms – – 2 **faction** group of persons within a party (esp. political) – – 3 **depository** storehouse – – 4 **coercion** [kəu'ə:ʃn] force – – 5 **to recollect** to remember – – 6 **scatological** scatology: preoccupation with excrement – – 7 **loom** machine for weaving cloth – – 8 **incentive** that which incites, rouses or encourages a person – – 9 **to defy** resist openly, refuse to obey or show respect – – 10 **to humiliate** cause to feel ashamed, put to shame, lower the dignity or self-respect – – 11 **hypocrisy** falsely making oneself appear to be virtuous or good

WORKSHEET

1. Language

1.1 Let's have a look at English *proverbs!* Find the matching pairs and give their German counterparts:

Brevity	is worth two pressed men
Don't count your chickens	when he tells the truth
A liar is not believed	who laughs last
Once bitten	to kill a butterfly
One volunteer	is the thief of time
Take not a musket	that lays the golden egg
Procrastination	is the soul of wit
He laughs best	is not gold
Kill not the goose	before they are hatched
Might	twice shy
All that glitters	flock together
Birds of a feather	is right.

Find apt situations for these proverbs!

1.2 Find the hidden proverb! Find it by listing the **7**th letter of the **1**st word of the annotations, the **2**nd letter of the **2**nd word, the 1st letter of the 3rd word etc.!
1,7 b2,2/3,1 w4,2/11,6/k/10,3/6,3/8,2 10,7/5,5/w/6,11/11,2/1,1 b/7,1/6,12/7, 4/9,2/3,5 10,1/2,5/6,1 8,6/5,4/3,4/5,6/11,8. (The given letters are needed for the solution!)

1.3 Error recognition
The following 10 sentences contain 16 errors. Find them! The sentences have been taken from a "Klassenarbeit" of a "9. Klasse".
The story to be retold was about a young man called Adrian who is travelling home in the buffet car of a train. He meets a young woman who wants to spend her holidays in the town where Adrian lives but has no hotel room yet. As Adrian likes the woman, he invites her to stay in his mother's house which has plenty of room. The young woman accepts, but then her husband shows up, and then their three children with a lot of pets. So much for the story. The students were

to retell the story and, and if they wanted to they could finish it according to their own taste and liking.
1. Drinking his tea, a pretty joung women was coming in.
2. She had to come immediately with two siutcases to the station.
3. His mother didn't want that they came.
4. One day A. F. travelled from London to Devon with the train when the following story happened to him.
5. She came to the table were A. sat.
6. When he saw the other man coming to their table it was clearly for A. that it was her man.
7. He called his mother that a big family will come.
8. He suggested the girl living there.
9. She told her husband that A. gave them a spare room.
10. His mother explained him that she has no room.

1.4 Have a laugh!
Did you know that speaking a language correctly was so important?
A German in an English restaurant:
"Waiter, when do I become a beefsteak?" – "I hope never, sir!"
"Waiter, I want to become a beefsteak, please!" – "I'm afraid you don't taste that good, sir!"
... and the other way around:
Ein Engländer ist zu Besuch bei einem Freund in Deutschland. Er bessert sein Deutsch auf und lernt u. a., daß "Schwein haben" ein anderer Ausdruck für "Glück haben" ist. Während seines Besuches feiert die Tochter seines Freundes Geburtstag mit einem großen Fest, auf dem auch getanzt wird. Im Verlauf des Abends fragt sein Freund ihn, ob er schon mit seiner Tochter getanzt habe. Darauf antwortet der Engländer: "Das Schwein habe ich noch nicht gehabt!"

2. Text Analysis
2.1 Enlarge on and interpret the sayings and proverbs of Anarres!
2.2 What, obviously, holds Anarres' society together?
2.3 Make a list of the differences between Anarres and Urras!
2.4 Give an interpretation of the expression "mountains of excrement"! What do you think it means?
2.5 What meaning does the term "efficiency" have on Anarres? (l. 29 + 66)

3. Discussion and Comment
3.1 Discuss: "Coercion is the least efficient means of obtaining order" and "If you want things you just take them from the depository" (l. 13 + 15).
3.2 On Anarres, dirty work is done because people do it together. Does that sound convincing?

3.3 Compare "Utopia" and "The Dispossessed": find differences and similarities!
3.4 Read the whole novel, and then retell the story to your fellow students.
3.5 If you were to be banished but could choose between Utopia and Anarres, where would you go?

13 DISMISSAL OF A SALESMAN

Introduction

In *Modern World,* Volume 1, you were acquainted with a few forms of *short narrative prose* like the joke (see p. 90 ff.), the prose satire (p. 88), and the short story (pp. 13–14). Dealing with them, you learnt some features typical of their themes, structure, and language.
Topic 15 in *MW 2* made you familiar with another literary genre: *poetry,* and its main characteristics, such as subjective feeling, poetic imagination, rhyme, meter, rhythm, imagery, etc.
Today we want to have a closer look at a third genre, the *drama.* Like the novel, novella, short story, etc. the *classical drama* (1) *tells* a story, but unlike them (2) tells its story in *action,* and (3) tells it through *actors* who impersonate the characters of the story. The story or *plot* (see *MW 1*, p. 18, and below) is presented in the form of *monologue* and *dialogue,* thus informing the onlooker about the problems of the characters and the conflicts between them, i. e. between the *protagonist* (= the hero), who pursues certain aims, interests, or ideas, and the other persons who have different objectives or concepts which clash with those of the protagonist. If these conflicts end with the protagonist's defeat we speak of a *tragedy* or *serious* drama, whereas the *comedy* solves its problems and presents the audience with the so-called *happy ending.*
According to Aristotle[1] a *good* tragedy arouses feelings of *pity* and *fear* in the onlookers, because the tragic incidents of the plot (if they are sufficiently likely!) cause the spectator to identify with the hero and his fate.
Classical dramas, as well as *Shakespearean* plays, are divided into five acts, which, in turn, are split into scenes. The plot of the play also falls into five chief parts, which, however, are not necessarily identical with the five acts:
1) the *introduction* or *exposition* creates the tone, gives the setting, introduces some of the characters, and supplies other facts necessary to the understanding of the play, such as events in the story supposed to have taken place before the action included in the play (since a play is likely to plunge *in medias res*). Possible conflicts are also suggested.
2) the *rising action* or *complication* is set in motion by contrasting interests of the hero and his adversaries (= antagonists); by the greed for power and/or other flaws of the characters (in tragedy); or by a chain of misunderstandings (in comedy). It continues through successive stages of *conflict* up to
3) the *climax,* which is either the culmination of the struggle for power (tragedy) or of the misunderstandings (comedy). The climax produces in the onlooker his greatest emotional response, and is either accompanied or is closely followed by the *crisis* or *turning point* of the plot; this presents an action by the protagonist which

---
[1] *Poetics*

turns out to be irreparable (tragedy) or gives the course of events an unexpected turn (in comedy), thus foreshadowing the tragic or happy ending.

4) The crisis sets in movement the *falling action* which either stresses the activities of the forces opposing the hero, and must logically lead to the *catastrophe* (tragedy); or strengthens the superiority of the positive forces (for instance of the loving couple and their supporters), and must logically lead to the happy ending (comedy). The falling action is sometimes marked by an event which delays the solution and *seems* to offer a way of escape for the hero (tragedy), or to suggest a disastrous course for the positive forces (comedy). This event is called the *moment of final suspense* (G. retardierendes Moment) and helps maintain the audience's interest.

5) the *catastrophe,* or the *happy ending,* represents the solution of the story, the first marking the tragic failure, usually the death of the hero, the latter the victory of the positive over the negative forces, which in many cases means the union of the lovers.

The **modern** serious drama of the late 19th and the 20th centuries has brought about a substantial change in dramatic structure and the aims of the play. At first the five-act structure gave way to the three-act structure. Then the acts disappeared altogether, the drama being divided into single scenes. This change of structure was due to the shift from the classical tragedy, which aimed at arousing in the audience the emotions of fear and pity, to the modern drama with its emphasis on the spectator's *critical reflection.* The modern drama no longer aims to show the onlooker that the evil emotions of the hero are destructive and should therefore be avoided. It tends to teach the spectator a lesson in politics and the psychology of the masses, or to demonstrate the absurdity of modern life, rather than to show the fate of the individual and to teach worldly wisdom and general truths. Identification with the hero is to be avoided since it doesn't allow objective consideration and critical reflection on the protagonist's actions and character, and on the political and social problems dealt with. In the so-called *epic theatre* of Brecht and his successors this is sometimes achieved by the interruption of the course of events (the actors, e. g., stop enacting their roles, approach the spectators, and simply comment on the events of the play) or more frequently by the use of songs and placards, which explain events or foretell events to come. The result is the destruction of illusion and, in many cases, of tension.

So-called *documentary theatre* even tries to sell its message by means of news reels, radio broadcasts, TV spots, etc., which are inserted into the play.

Of course, there have developed a lot of mixed forms, some relatively close to the traditional drama, others very experimental and making use of many of the theatrical devices of the type mentioned above. But however radical the changes have been, most of them have contributed to keeping the genre interesting and flourishing.

One of the more daring dramas, which had great influence on the theatre of its time, is Arthur Miller's *Death of a Salesman.* Combining Henry Ibsen's scrutinizing character analysis and Clifford Odet's realism and social criticism with elements of Brecht's epic drama, it can serve as a model of the modern American play.

Arthur Miller (1915–) began writing plays as an undergraduate student at the University of Michigan in 1936, but he traces his development as a playwright back to the year 1929. Then a boy of fourteen, Miller was deeply impressed by the great economic depression, which ruined his father's business. Little wonder that the majority of his plays deal with the economic, social, and psychic problems of the "little man" and his false dreams of material success idolized in a Capitalist society. Miller's first successful play was *All My Sons* (1947) which – like *Death of a*

Salesman (1949) – is a family play centering on a father-son conflict. Both dramas – *AMS* and *DOS* – earned A. Miller the Pulitzer prize for the best American play of the year. Other important plays followed, such as *The Crucible* (1953) and *A View from the Bridge* (1955), which again won the Pulitzer prize. In 1961, he wrote the scenario for the film *The Misfits* starring Marylin Monroe, his second wife. But without any doubt *DOS* is his most fascinating play as regards form, and (next to *The Crucible*) his most ambitious in content.

Willy Loman is the play's protagonist. Though he used to be quite a good salesman, he has never made much money. Now – at the age of 63 – he is no longer able to fulfill the requirements of modern salesmanship. The course of his life, in particular his failure to make money, shows Loman to be a typical representative of the decent man-in-the-street who falls victim to the dream of (material) success and consequent happiness. The ironic twist of the play is that Loman comes to realize the falsity of his dream, but nevertheless stubbornly clings to it.

The following extract, taken from Act Two of the play, shows Loman seeing his boss Howard Wagner. He wants Howard to employ him in the office from now on, instead of sending him out on the road, which increasingly exhausts him.

The other persons: *Linda* = Willy's wife; *Ben* = Willy's brother; *Biff* and *Happy* = Willy's and Linda's sons

[*In the middle of her speech,* HOWARD WAGNER, *thirty-six, wheels on a small typewriter table on which is a wire-recording machine and proceeds to plug it in. This is on the left forestage. Light slowly fades on* LINDA *as it rises on HOWARD. HOWARD is intent on threading the machine and only glances over his shoulder*
5 *as* WILLY *appears.*]
WILLY: Pst! Pst!
HOWARD: Hello, Willy, come in.
WILLY: Like to have a little talk with you, Howard.
HOWARD: Sorry to keep you waiting. I'll be with you in a minute.
10 WILLY: What's that, Howard?
HOWARD: Didn't you ever see one of these? Wire recorder.
WILLY: Oh. Can we talk a minute?
HOWARD: Records things. Just got delivery yesterday. Been driving me crazy, the most terrific machine I ever saw in my life. I was up all night with it.
15 WILLY: What do you do with it?
HOWARD: I bought it for dictation, but you can do anything with it. Listen to this. I had it home last night. Listen to what I picked up. The first one is my daughter. Get this. [*He flicks the switch and 'Roll out the Barrel' is heard being whistled.*] Listen to that kid whistle.
20 WILLY: That is lifelike, isn't it?
HOWARD: Seven years old. Get that tone.
[*The whistling breaks off, and the voice of* HOWARD's *daughter is heard.*]
HIS DAUGHTER: 'Now you, Daddy.'
HOWARD: She's crazy for me! [*Again the same song is whistled.*]
25 That's me! Ha! [*He winks.*]

WILLY: You're, very good!
[*The whistling breaks off again. The machine runs silent for a moment.*]
HOWARD: Sh! Get this now, this is my son.
HIS SON: 'The capital of Alabama is Montgomery; the capital of Arizona is Phoenix;
30 the capital of Arkansas is Little Rock, the capital of California is Sacramento . . .'
[*and on, and on.*]
HOWARD [*holding up five fingers*]: Five years old, Willy!
WILLY: He'll make an announcer some day!
HIS SON [*continuing*]: 'The capital . . .'
35 HOWARD: Get that – alphabetical order! [*The machine breaks off suddenly.*] Wait a minute. The maid kicked the plug out.
WILLY: It certainly is a –
HOWARD: Sh, for God's sake!
HIS SON: 'It's nine o'clock, Bulova watch time. So I have to go to sleep.'
40 WILLY: That really is –
HOWARD: Wait a minute! The next is my wife.
[*They wait.*]
HOWARD'S VOICE: 'Go on, say something.' [*Pause.*] 'Well, you gonna talk?'
HIS WIFE: 'I can't think of anything.'
45 HOWARD'S VOICE: 'Well, talk – it's turning.'
HIS WIFE [*shyly, beaten*]: 'Hello.' [*Silence.*] 'Oh, Howard, I can't talk into this . . .'
HOWARD: [*snapping the machine off*]: That was my wife.
WILLY: That is a wonderful machine. Can we–
HOWARD: I tell you Willy, I'm gonna take my camera, and my bandsaw, and all
50 my hobbies, and out they go. This is the most fascinating relaxation I ever found.
WILLY: I think I'll get one myself.
HOWARD: Sure, they're only a hundred a half. You can't do without it. Supposing you wanna hear Jack Benny, see? But you can't be at home at that hour. So you tell the maid to turn the radio on when Jack Benny comes on, and this automatically
55 goes on with the radio . . .
WILLY: And when you come home you . . .
HOWARD: You can come home twelve o'clock, one o'clock, any time you like, and you get yourself a Coke and sit yourself down, throw the switch, and there's Jack Benny's programme in the middle of the night!
60 WILLY: I'm definitely going to get one. Because lots of time I'm on the road, and I think to myself, what I must be missing on the radio!
HOWARD: Don't you have a radio in the car?
WILLY: Well, yeah, but who ever thinks of turning it on?
HOWARD: Say, aren't you supposed to be in Boston?
65 WILLY: That's what I want to talk to you about, Howard. You got a minute? [*He draws a chair in from the wing.*]
HOWARD: What happened? What're you doing here?

WILLY: Well . . .

HOWARD: You didn't crack up again, did you?

WILLY: Oh, no. No . . .

HOWARD: Geez, you had me worried there for a minute. What's the trouble?

WILLY: Well, tell you the truth, Howard. I've come to the decision that I'd rather not travel any more.

HOWARD: Not travel! Well, what'll you do?

WILLY: Remember, Christmas-time, when you had the party here? You said you'd try to think of some spot for me here in town.

HOWARD: With us?

WILLY: Well, sure.

HOWARD: Oh, yeah, yeah, I remember. Well, I couldn't think of anything for you, Willy.

WILLY: I tell ya, Howard. The kids are all grown up, y'know. I don't need much any more. If I could take home – well, sixty-five dollars a week, I could swing it.

HOWARD: Yeah, but Willy, see I –

WILLY: I tell ya why, Howard, Speaking frankly and between the two of us, y'know – I'm just a little tired.

HOWARD: Oh, I could understand that, Willy. But you're a road man, Willy, and we do a road business. We've only got a halfdozen salesmen on the floor here.

WILLY: God knows, Howard, I never asked a favor of any man. But I was with the firm when your father used to carry you in here in his arms.

HOWARD: I know that, Willy, but –

WILLY: Your father came to me the day you were born and asked me what I thought of the name of Howard, may he rest in peace.

HOWARD: I appreciate that, Willy, but there just is no spot here for you. If I had a spot I'd slam you right in, but I just don't have a single solitary spot.

[*He looks for his lighter,* WILLY *has picked it up and gives it to him. Pause.*]

WILLY [*with increasing anger*]: Howard, all I need to set my table is fifty dollars a week.

HOWARD: But where am I going to put you, kid?

WILLY: Look, it isn't a question of whether I can sell merchandise, is it?

HOWARD: No, but it's business, kid, and everybody's gotta pull his own weight.

WILLY [*desperately*]: Just let me tell you a story, Howard –

HOWARD: 'Cause you gotta admit, business is business.

WILLY [*angrily*]: Business is definitely business, but just listen for a minute. You don't understand this. When I was a boy – eighteen, nineteen – I was already on the road. And there was a question in my mind as to whether selling had a future for me. Because in those days I had a yearning to go to Alaska. See, there were three gold strikes in one month in Alaska, and I felt like going out. Just for the ride, you might say.

HOWARD [*barely interested*]: Don't say.

WILLY: Oh, yeah, my father lived many years in Alaska. He was an adventurous man. We've got quite a little streak of self-reliance in our family. I thought I'd go out with my older brother and try to locate him, and maybe settle in the North with the old man. And I was almost decided to go, when I met a salesman in the Parker House. His name was Dave Singleman. And he was eighty-four years old, and he'd drummed merchandise in thirty-one states. And old Dave, he'd go up to his room, y'understand, put on his green velvet slippers – I'll never forget – and pick up his phone and call the buyers, and without ever leaving his room, at the age of eighty-four, he made his living. And when I saw that, I realized that selling was the greatest career a man could want. 'Cause what could be more satisfying than to be able to go, at the age of eighty-four, into twenty or thirty different cities, and pick up a phone, and be remembered and loved and helped by so many different people? Do you know? when he died – and by the way he died the death of a salesman, in his green velvet slippers in the smoker of the New York, New Haven, and Hartford, going into Boston – when he died, hundreds of salesmen and buyers were at his funeral. Things were sad on a lotta trains for months after that. [*He stands up, HOWARD has not looked at him.*] In those days there was personality in it, Howard. There was respect, and comradeship, and gratitude in it. Today, it's all cut and dried, and there's no chance for bringing friendship to bear – or personality. You see what I mean? They don't know me any more.

HOWARD: [*moving away, toward the right*]: That's just the thing, Willy.

WILLY: If I had forty dollars a week – that's all I'd need. Forty dollars, Howard.

HOWARD: Kid, I can't take blood from a stone, I –

WILLY [*desperation is on him now*]: Howard, the year Al Smith was nominated, your father came to me and –

HOWARD [*starting to go off*]: I've got to see some people, kid.

WILLY [*stopping him*]: I'm talking about your father! There were promises made across this desk! You mustn't tell me you've got people to see – I put thirty-four years into this firm, Howard, and now I can't pay my insurance! You can't eat the orange and throw the peel away – a man is not a piece of fruit! [*After a pause*] Now pay attention. Your father – in 1928 I had a big year. I averaged a hundred and seventy dollars a week in commissions.

HOWARD [*impatiently*]: Now, Willy, you never averaged –

WILLY [*banging his hand on the desk*]: I averaged a hundred and seventy dollars a week in the year of 1928! And your father came to me – or rather, I was in the office here – it was right over this desk – and he put his hand on my shoulder –

HOWARD [*getting up*]: You'll have to excuse me, Willy, I gotta see some people. Pull yourself together. [*Going out*] I'll be back in a little while.

[*On* HOWARD's *exit, the light on his chair grows very bright and strange.*]

WILLY: Pull myself together! What the hell did I say to him? My God, I was yelling at him! How could I! [WILLY *breaks off, staring at the light, which occupies the chair, animating it. He approaches this chair, standing across the desk from it.*] Frank, Frank, don't you remember what you told me that time? How you put your hand on my shoulder, and Frank . . . [*He leans on the desk and as he speaks the dead mans's name he accidentally switches on the recorder, and instantly –*]

155 HOWARD'S SON: '. . . of New York is Albany. The capital of Ohio is Cincinnati, the captial of Rhode Island is . . .' [*The recitation continues.*]
WILLY [*leaping away with fright, shouting*]: Ha! Howard! Howard! Howard!
HOWARD [*rushing in*]: What happened?
WILLY [*pointing at the machine, which continues nasally, childishly, with the capital
160 cities*]: Shut it off! Shut it off!
HOWARD [*pulling the plug out*]: Look, Willy . . .
WILLY [*pressing his hands to his eyes*]: I gotta get myself some coffee. I'll get some coffee . . .
[WILLY *starts to walk out.* HOWARD *stops him.*]
165 HOWARD [*rolling up the cord*]: Willy, look . . .
WILLY: I'll go to Boston.
HOWARD: Willy, you can't go to Boston for us.
WILLY: Why can't I go?
HOWARD: I don't want you to represent us. I've been meaning to tell you for a long
170 time now.
WILLY: Howard, are you firing me?
HOWARD: I think you need a good long rest, Willy.
WILLY: Howard –
HOWARD: And when you feel better, come back, and we'll see if we can work
175 something out.
WILLY: But I gotta earn money. Howard. I'm in no position to –
HOWARD: Where are your sons? Why don't your sons give you a hand?
WILLY: They're working on a very big deal.
HOWARD: This is no time for false pride, Willy. You go to your sons and you tell
180 them that you're tired. You've got two great boys, haven't you?
WILLY: Oh, no question, no question, but in the meantime . . .
HOWARD: Then that's that, heh?
WILLY: All right, I'll go to Boston tomorrow.
HOWARD: No, no.
185 WILLY: I can't throw myself on my sons. I'm not a cripple!
HOWARD: Look, kid, I'm busy this morning.
WILLY [*grasping* HOWARD's *arm*]: Howard, you've got to let me go to Boston!
HOWARD [*hard, keeping himself under control*]: I've got a line of people to see this morning. Sit down, take five minutes, and pull yourself together, and then go home,
190 will ya? I need the office, Willy. [*He starts to go, turns, remembering the recorder, starts to push off the table holding the recorder.*] Oh, yeah. Whenever you can this week, stop by and drop off the samples. You'll feel better, Willy, and

then come back and we'll talk. Pull yourself together, kid, there's people outside. [HOWARD *exits, pushing the table off left.* WILLY *stares into space, exhausted.*
195 Now the music is heard – BEN'S *music – first distantly, then closer, closer. As* WILLY *speaks,* BEN *enters from the right. He carries valise and umbrella.*]
WILLY: Oh, Ben, how did you do it? What is the answer? Did you wind up the Alaska deal already?
BEN: Doesn't take much time if you know what you're doing. Just a short business
200 trip. Boarding ship in an hour. Wanted to say good-bye.
WILLY: Ben, I've got to talk to you.
BEN [*glancing at his watch*]: Haven't the time, William.
WILLY [*crossing the apron to* BEN]: Ben, nothing's working out I don't know what to do.
205 BEN: Now, look here, William. I've bought timberland in Alaska and I need a man to look after things for me.
WILLY: God, timberland! Me and my boys in those grand outdoors!
BEN: You've a new continent at your doorstep, William. Get out of these cities, they're full of talk and time payments and courts of law. Screw on your fists and
210 you can fight for a fortune up there.
WILLY: Yes, yes! Linda, Linda!
[LINDA *enters as of old, with the wash.*]
LINDA: Oh, you're back?
BEN: I haven't much time.
215 WILLY: No, wait! Linda, he's got a proposition for me in Alaska.
LINDA: But you've got – [*To* BEN] He's got a beautiful job here.
WILLY: But in Alaska, kid, I could –
LINDA: You're doing well enough, Willy!
BEN [*to* LINDA]: Enough for what, my dear?
220 LINDA: [*frightened of* BEN *and angry at him*]: Don't say those things to him! Enough to be happy right here, right now. [*To* WILLY, *while* BEN *laughs*] Why must everybody conquer the world? You're well liked, and the boys love you, and someday – [*to* BEN] – why, old man Wagner told him just the other day that if he keeps it up he'll be a member of the firm, didn't he, Willy?
225 WILLY: Sure, sure. I am building something with this firm, Ben, and if a man is building something he must be on the right track, mustn't he?
BEN: What are you building? Lay your hand on it. Where is it?
WILLY [*hesitantly*]: That's true, Linda, there's nothing.
LINDA: Why? [*To* BEN] There's a man eighty-four years old –
230 WILLY: That's right, Ben, that's right. When I look at that man I say, what is there to worry about?
BEN: Bah!
WILLY: It's true, Ben. All he has to do is go into any city, pick up the phone, and he's making his living and you know why?

235 BEN [*picking up his valise*]: I've got to go.
WILLY [*holding* Ben *book*]: Look at this boy!
[BIFF, *in his high-school sweater, enters carrying suitcase.* HAPPY carries BIFF'S *shoulder guards, gold helmet, and football pants.*]
WILLY: Without a penny to his name, three great universities are begging for him,
240 and from there the sky's the limit, because it's not what you do, Ben. It's who you know and the smile on your face! It's contacts, Ben, contacts! The whole wealth of Alaska passes over the lunch table at the Commodore Hotel, and that's the wonder, the wonder of this country, that a man can end with diamonds here on the basis of being liked! [*He turns to* BIFF.] And that's why when you get out on that
245 field today it's important. Because thousands of people will be rooting for you and loving you. [*To* BEN, *who has again begun to leave*] And Ben! when he walks into a business office his name will sound out like a bell and all the doors will open to him! I've seen it, Ben, I've seen it a thousand times! You can't feel it with your hand like timber, but it's there!
250 BEN: Good-bye, William.
WILLY: Ben, am I right? Don't you think I'm right? I value your advice.
BEN: There's a new continent at your doorstop, William. You could walk out rich. Rich! [*He is gone.*]
WILLY: We'll do it here, Ben! You hear me? We're gonna do it here!

Annotations

(The words marked* should be memorized.)

to wheel push or pull a vehicle with wheels – – **wire-recording machine** predecessor of the tape recorder – – ***to proceed** continue – – ***to plug in** connect plug and wall socket – – **to be intent (on)** busily occupied (with) – – **to thread** put the wire (or tape) into place so the machine can work – – **terrific** great – – **to flick** to touch lightly – – **Roll out the Barrel** first line of a popular song – – **kid** (coll.) child – – **to wink** close and open one eye, to signal amusement or to call attention to s. th. – – **Bulova** firm of US watch and clock makers – – **bandsaw** Bandsäge – – **wanna** colloquial for "want to" – – **to crack up** (coll.) break down, collapse – – **to swing it** (coll.) manage, get along – – ***on the floor** *here:* on the wholesale outlet – – **to slam in** (coll.) put in, find a place – – **to set one's table** (coll.) to earn enough to get along – – ***merchandise** trade goods – **to pull one's own weight** (coll.) to take one's fair share of work, duty; sein bestes geben – – **yearning** strong desire – – **streak** element or trace; Spur – – ***to locate** to find – – **to drum** *here:* to sell – – ***velvet** Samt – – **smoker** smoking compartment on a train – – **cut and dried** mere routine work – – **I can't take blood from a stone** *here:* I can't get hold of money which doesn't exist – – ***peel** skin of fruit – – ***commissions** orders – – ***to yell (at)** shout (at) – – ***sample** Muster – – **valise** [vəˈliːze] small leather bag for clothes, etc., during a journey – **to wind up** (coll.) to bring to an end successfully – – **apron** *here:* forestage; vorderer Teil der Bühne – – **timberland** Waldland, das Nutzholz liefert – – ***outdoors** the world away from human habitations; von der Zivilisation unberührte Weiten – – **time payments** sums of money to be paid for goods you already have; instalments – – **to screw on one's fists** to get ready to fight – – **proposition** *here:* offer of a position – – **shoulder guards** pads protecting a player's body in a football game – – *****pants** trousers – – **without a penny to one's name** without having any money at all – – **the sky's the limit** there is no limit to where you can get – – **to root (for)** (US sl.) to support by cheering, applauding.

WORKSHEET

1. **Text Analysis**
   Decide whether the following statements are true or false. Give reasons for your view, and correct the statements which are false.

                                                                             True   False

   a) Willy Loman goes to see his boss Howard Wagner to ask him for a rise in salary.
   b) Willy can't think of more than 2 arguments to convince Howard why he should accept his request.
   c) Howard turns down Willy's request because he doesn't like Willy.
   d) Howard is a typical representative of the American capitalism in the first half of the 20th century.
   e) Willy is dismissed because he offends Howard.
   f) Personality, popularity and contacts (l. 126 ff.) have – according to the text – ever been sufficient to be successful in business life.
   g) When Willy Loman arrives at Howard's office the latter is occupied with dictating letters on a wire-recorder.
   h) The negative emotional response of Howard's wife to the machine (ll. 41–47), the boy's monotonous recitation of American *capitals* (ll. 29–39), and Willy's horror at the boy's recitation (ll. 155–156) after the denial of his request suggest that the machine has a *symbolic* meaning.
   i) Our extract is clearly divided into four parts.
   j) The climax of the excerpt is at line 102, where Howard explains that ". . . business is business."
   k) The last part isn't set in the present, but in the past.
   l) Willy's brother Ben ist the genuine personification of the American success story.
   m) Willy's recollection of the missed opportunity with Ben is triggered off by his tiredness.

                                                                True   False

   n) Such a shift in the chronological sequence is called
      "timing".
   o) This device is a typical feature of classical drama.
   p) Vocabulary, grammar, and sentence structure are
      typical of a formal speech level.

2. **Further Studies**
2.1.1 You have just read this news story in *Stars and Stripes*. (Vocabulary see below.)

Student entrepreneurs

Many college kids take parttime jobs to earn a little pocket money, but some clever Stanford University students are amassing millions while working toward their degrees.
Sometimes operating from their dormitory rooms, the students have found there's big money to be made in the worlds of publishing, electronics, entertainment and engineering.
A few success stories:
— **George Hara** co-founded Gekee Fiber Optics as he studied for his master's degree in electrical engineering. The firm reported $1 million in sales last year and projects $5 million revenue for 1983.
— **John Halamka** used to edit Stanford's humor magazine when he wasn't studying political science and medical microbiology. Now he writes computer programs for 20 clients, including physicist Edward Teller and economists Milton Friedman and Arthur Laffer. He grossed $100,000 last year and, next year, Halamka will be old enough to buy himself a beer.
— **Mike Boone's** computer software firm is appraised at more than $1 million. The 21-year-old operates Boone Corp. from his dorm room.
"All you have to do is look at all the young millionaires driving around Silicon Valley to get inspired," Stanford business school dean Robert Jaedicke said. "I think that's the big reason why we're seeing a renewed interest in entrepreneurship here."
To help businesses grow, the students have organized their own Center For Entrepreneurship.
"Most of us here have been entrepreneurs all our lives," said center co-founder **Connie Carroll,** 27. "We're the ones running lemonade stands when we were little kids."

Stars and Stripes, April 14, 1983

Vocabulary:

*__entrepreneur__ [ōtrəprə'nɜr] person who organizes and manages a commercial undertaking
*__parttime job__ a job for only a part of the working day
*__dormitory room__ sleeping room in college or private highschool
__revenue__ *here:* annual income
__to gross__ [grous]: to make as total amount
__to be appraised at__ said to be worth

144

Silicon Valley place in California where many firms specializing in electronics produce silicon chips for computers

Construct a conversation with an *American friend* of yours about it.
Begin like this:
You: Hey, George, have you already heard of those college whiz kids making millions of bucks every year?
George: Are you kidding? College kids? How are they doing it?
Y.: Just like this. Using their brains. Had the guts to open up their own business in electronics and engineering.
G.: Gee. We should've had the guts to do the same, shouldn't we?
Y.: That's damn right. Look at this guy. Writes goddam computer programs for bastards like old Milton Friedman.
G.: Who's that?
Y.: That's this Prof from Chi who says the Government better kill social welfare and all that . . .

Continue like this for another 5 statements and 5 questions. Use some more American colloquial expressions like: blockhead / airhead (= stupid person); dough (= money); fella (= fellow); to give sb the bang (= to surprise sb completely); gorgeous (= great); gotta (got to); to be hot (= eager); lotta (= lot of); lousy (= poor, bad); a big shot (= of persons: big success); smart (intelligent); sort of (= kind of); stuff (= things, material).

2.1.2 Now you are not talking to your American friend, but to your *teacher* or a *superior*. Begin like this:
You: Hello, Mr. Martin, have you yet heard of those college students who earn millions of dollars every year? (Go ahead)

2.2 Howard's son obviously knows a lot of the US state capitals. What about you? Try to solve the puzzle without an atlas.

5 Letters	7 Letters	8 Letters	10 Letters	11 Letters
Idaho	Georgia	North Dakota	Louisiana	Illinois
Delaware	Maine	Wyoming	Nevada	Florida
Oregon	New Hampshire	South Carolina	West Virginia	
	Mississippi	Ohio	Pennsylvania	**12 Letters**
6 Letters	Michigan	Connecticut	Arkansas	Indiana
New York	Nebraska	Hawaii	Alabama	Oklahoma
Texas	Wisconsin	Virginia	Vermont	Utah
Massachusetts	Washington		Rhode Island	
Colorado	Arizona	**9 Letters**	California	**13 Letters**
Montana	North Caroline	Maryland		Missouri
Alaska	New Mexico	Iowa		
South Dakota	New Jersey	Kentucky		
Minnesota		Tennessee		
Kansas				

145

Capital Punishment

THIS skeleton puzzle features all 50 U.S. state capitals. You must identify them and place them in the grid so they'll all fit reading across from the left or down. Only the states are listed above, but they appear according to the letter-count and alphabetical order of their capitals. For example: Maine's seven-letter capital is Augusta. The four black squares are not used.

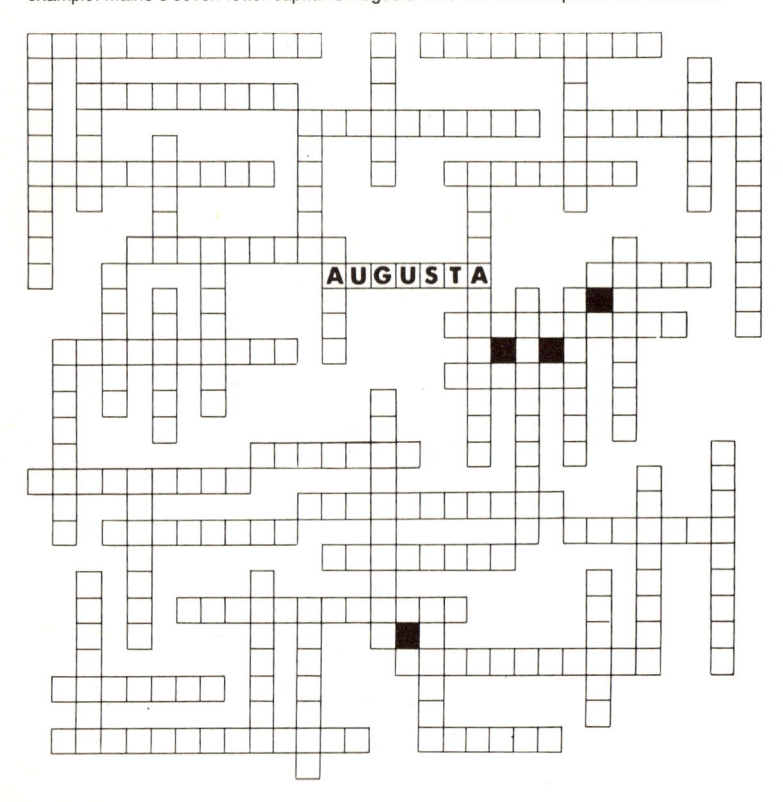

Source: *Soldiers*, April 1983

2.3

1. Explain what the following comic strip has to do with our extract from *DOS*.
2. Change the dialogue between the King and Hagar into a **short** story. Start like this:
   One day Hagar addressed the King . . .
   (Go ahead)

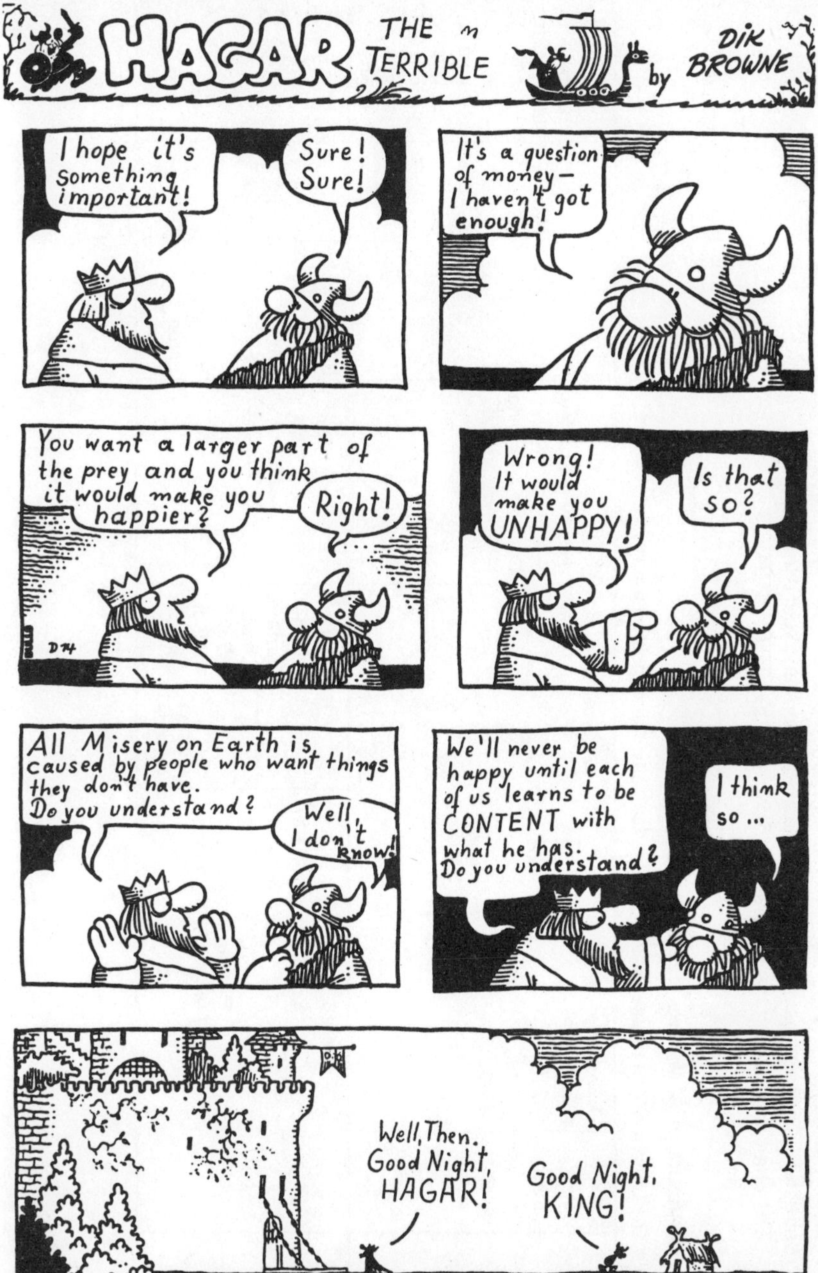
HAGAR THE TERRIBLE by DIK BROWNE
I hope it's something important!
Sure! Sure!
It's a question of money— I haven't got enough!
You want a larger part of the prey and you think it would make you happier?
Right!
Wrong! It would make you UNHAPPY!
Is that so?
All Misery on Earth is caused by people who want things they don't have. Do you understand?
Well, I don't know!
We'll never be happy until each of us learns to be CONTENT with what he has. Do you understand?
I think so ...
Well, Then.. Good Night, HAGAR!
Good Night, KING!

2.4 Read the complete play and tell your classmates about its contents and structure. The chart below will help the class to understand your explanations. The chart is based on the *Diesterweg Schulausgabe*, B. Nr. 4134.

The Structure of A. Miller's Death of a Salesman

Act I: The Loman's little house; late evening after Willy's unexpected return.

	5	11.25		18.5	26.3	27.9	28.16	31.4	32.34		37.3
reality	Willy + Linda "car, business, sons"	Happy + Biff "father, plans"					Happy – Willy Charley – Willy "cards, job, lack of money"	Charley, Willy "playing cards"			Linda + Happy, Biff, Willy "W's attempts at suicide" "plans to sell sporting goods"
dream				Young Happy + Biff + Willy "girls, car" Bernard "education" Linda + Willy "money"	The woman episode	Young Bernard, Linda, Willy "Biff at school"		Ben "their parents"	Ben Willy Charley } "Alaska" "success" "education" "jungle" Bernard Linda		

148

Act II: The Loman's house; Howard's und Charley's offices; at Frank's Chop House; next day from morning to night.

	50	53.16	54.5		60.22	64.25	71.15	79.9	83.7	88.8	89.7		93.9	97.36	99.36 100.1
reality	Linda + Willy "optimism" "dinner" "job in New York"	Linda's phone call with Biff	Willy's "negociations" with Howard" "fired"			Willy in Charley's office Bernard: "Biff's failure" Charley: "job"	Restaurant Stanley, Happy "girls" Biff: "Oliver" Willy: "Howard"	Biff's failure (Oliver)	Happy + Biff "leave with the girls"	Restaurant Willy + Stanley "plan to buy seeds"	Linda's reproaching to Happy + Biff		Biff's argument with Willy	Happy Linda Willy	Biff "No! Pop!"
dream					Ben's offer of Alaska-job Linda's interference Mc Ebbet's Field game			Biff's failure (at school) Boston-Hotel operator's paging		84.9 The Boston-hotel-affair "Biff breaks with Willy"		91.26 Willy Ben suicide "big deal"		Ben Willy	

dream? – reality?
III Requiem: Grave yard; a few days later

100.5
Biff realizes the facts
Happy clings to the dreams + illusions

2.5 Write a research paper and deliver a speech on: (Notes only!) (Social)Darwinism, the Frontier, and the American Dream as Portrayed in Arthur Miller's *Death of a Salesman*.
For reference use:
1) The *Encyclopaedia Britannica*
2) John V. Hagopian / Martin Dolch: *Insight I,* Hirschgraben Verlag, Frankfurt/Main, pp. 174–186.
3) *MW 3,* pp. 160–161.

14 LEE IACOCCA: THE AMERICAN DREAM PERSONIFIED

Introduction

B O O K S

A Dream Talking

Jane McLoughlin

CHAIRMAN LEE IACOCCA

Iacocca, An Autobiography
Lee Iacocca
Sidgwick & Jackson £12,95

"YOU'LL NEVER GET FIRED for losing a billion dollars. You'll get fired one night when he's drunk. He'll call you a wop and you'll get into a fight. Mark my words, it'll be over nothing."

In the end, it was because "Sometimes, you can just not like someone." Which was marginally more reasonable, for the previous president of the corporation was fired because he forgot to knock on the door of the boss's office. Even that seems mild compared with this exchange.

"Fire that man. He's a fag."

"What are you talking about? We have dinner together. He's married with a kid."

"Look at him his pants are too tight." He was fired.

Is this fag-baiting, wop-hating, drunken, irrational brat one of the power brokers of *Dallas* or *Dynasty*? Alas, our TV screens would be more riveting if this was video fodder. It is not: it is real life at Ford. The boss who thought only fags wear tight trousers was Henry Ford the Second, son of the famous pioneer, at least it is Henry II as he appears in the story of Lee Iacocca, a former head man at Ford but known chiefly as The Man Who Saved Chrysler. Lee Iacocca was the son of poor immigrants from Naples who called him Lido in nostalgia for romantic Venice where they had spent their honeymoon. Lee Iacocca was eventually fired from Ford because he threatened to topple the succession of King Henry's son Edsel. He then moved to Chrysler Corporation where he scraped it off the floor and recreated it as a great car maker. According to many he is the greatest corporate chief of all. According to others, to quote a Ford colleague, he was "pretty heartily disliked . . . utterly tactless . . . at least," they said, "Henry would listen . . ." But then, I got that elsewhere, these unkind words about Lee; the kind words about Ford II you will not find in this book.

Lee Iacocca has made such a name for himself saving the near bankrupt Chrysler Corporation that he is right now being talked of as Presidential timber. There are some who would like to see him run for President. For his many fans Iacocca represents a return to the old American dream. And this book is the American Dream talking.

His is a story with all the ingredients of good soap opera. Hard work wins glittering prizes; then a great fall from power, and after that he does it all over again, proving that the underdog (both himself and Chrysler Corporation) can and does win. Revenge is sweet – as when Henry Ford turns tail and flees rather than face him at a glittering social occasion for the world's top car men.

If you tend to write about this book in terms of *Readers' Digest* exclamations, it's inevitable. The story of Lee Iacocca (the name rhymes with Try a Coke-ah) is an extended version of the Most Unforgettable Character I Ever Met. Young Lee actually learned his vocabulary from the "Word Power Game", and he learned the vital skill of communication on a Dale Carnegie Course which may well have been advertised in *Readers' Digest*.

There are bound to be those who will read this book for clues as to how to get ahead. Certainly by trying – Iacocca trained as an engineer, taught himself salesmanship, and then worked his way from trainee to President of Ford.

For every set back there was a salty saying from his immigrant father – "You've got to accept a little suffering in this life. You'll never really know what happiness is unless you have something to compare."

Iacocca's story is a moral tale; it records the pursuit of happiness through virtue. A little decisiveness, a bit of intuition and a pinch of motivation, all stirred with facts and done to a turn to create a corporate team as simple as that.

What's remarkable about him is how simple he is. His emotional reactions are very basic – he hates Henry Ford for hurting his family by hurting him, he loved his wife, he was angry at an investigation set up by Henry Ford to try and pin some moral misdemeanour on him. But he was blameless.

He loves his wife (now sadly, dead) and children; he *is* his work. He puts his conscience in the care of a priest, his family in the care of his wife, his money in the bank, chooses them as vice-presidents and runs them all with passion and dedication as subdivisions of his corporate function.

He is hurt when his friends, after he is fired, disloyal or intimidated, cut him out of their lives. Yet he shows no surprise or guilt at having to fire his own close friend Hal Sperlich because Henry says so, though all seems forgiven and forgotten when Hal and he work together later at Chrysler. Lee Iacocca never had anything to do with the Mafia (which Henry hoped to discover he had through his Watergate-style investigation) but he falls naturally into the role of Godfather, just as Mrs Thatcher as Prime Minister cannot be separated from Mrs Thatcher, shopkeeper.

He's a motivator, he's a do-er, a producer, a man who fights back, and never surrenders. You finish this book as many junior executives in Ford and Chrysler must have left conferences he conducted, feeling better. You believe that you can do it too. But how? The man's some sort of genius, but after 341 pages I don't know why. He still seems just like the guy next door.

From: *Punch Magazine,* March 6, 1985.

1. What does the book review tell us about the nature of the book?
2. Retrace the story line of Iacocca's autobiography as summed up in the review.
3. How does Lee Iacocca portray himself?
4. Iacocca's autobiography was in the American bestseller list for months. Can you suggest why?

At the age of thirty-six I was the general manager of the biggest division in the world's second largest company. At the same time, I was virtually unknown. Half the people at Ford didn't know who I was. The other half couldn't pronounce my name.

When Henry Ford called me over to his office in December of 1960, it was like being summoned to see God. We had shaken hands a few times, but this was the first time we ever had a real conversation. McNamara and Beacham had already told me they had sold Henry on the idea of making me head of the Ford Division, but they asked me to play dumb. They knew that Henry would want to give me the impression it was his idea.

I was thrilled by the promotion, but I could see that it put me in a delicate position. On the one hand, I was suddenly running the company's elite division. Henry Ford had personally entrusted me with the crown jewels. On the other hand, I had bypassed a hundred older and more experienced people on my way up the ladder. Some of them, I knew, were resentful of my quick success. In addition, I still had

15 no real credentials as a product man. At this point in my career there was no car that people could point to and say: "Iacocca did that one."

My years as general manager of the Ford Division were the happiest period of my life. For my colleagues and me, this was fire-in-the-belly time. We were high from smoking our own brand – a combination of hard work and big dreams.

20 In those days, I couldn't wait to get to work in the morning. At night I didn't want to leave. We were continually playing with new ideas and trying out models on the test track. We were young and cocky. We saw ourselves as artists, about to produce the finest masterpieces the world had ever seen.

"Well, let's now diminish the sales and then we'll take his stress symptoms."

Source: *Stern,* 1982.

In 1960, the whole country was optimistic. With Kennedy in the White House, a fresh
25 breeze was blowing across the land. It carried an unspoken message that anything was possible. The striking contrast between the new decade and the 1950s, between John Kennedy and Dwight Eisenhower, could be summed up in a single word – youth.

Any car that would appeal to the young customers had to have three main features:
30 great styling, strong performance, and a low price. Developing a new model with all three would not be easy. But if it could be done, we had a shot at a major success. Once we settled on the styling, we had to make some basic decisions about the

interior. We were eager to provide for those customers who wanted luxury, but we didn't want to cut out the people who were more interested in performance or economy. At the same time, we didn't want to produce a totally stripped car. The Mustang was already being seen as a poor man's Thunderbird; there would be little point in bringing out a poor man's Mustang. We decided that even the economy model had to be comparable to the luxury and performance versions, and so we included such items as bucket seats, vinyl trim, wheel covers, and carpeting as standard features in each car.

Beyond that, we had in mind a kind of do-it-yourself car that would appeal to all segments of the market. If a customer could afford luxury, he could buy extra accessories and more power. If he loved luxury but couldn't afford these extras, he would still be happy because several options he'd normally have to pay for were available here at no extra charge.

On March 9, 1964, the first Mustang rolled off the assembly line. We had arranged to produce a minimum of 8,160 cars before introduction day – April 17 – so that every Ford dealer in the country would have at least one Mustang in his showroom when the car was officially launched.

On April 17, Ford dealerships everywhere were mobbed with customers. In Chicago, one dealer had to lock his showroom doors because the crowd outside was so large. A dealer in Pittsburgh reported that the crush of customers was so thick he couldn't get his Mustang off the wash rack. In Detroit, another dealer said that so many people who had come to see the Mustang had arrived in sports cars that his parking lot looked like a foreign-car rally.

In Garland, Texas, a Ford dealer had fifteen potential customers bidding on a single Mustang in his display window. He sold it to the highest bidder – a man who insisted on spending the night in the car so that nobody else could buy it while his check was clearing. At a dealership in Seattle, the driver of a passing cement truck became so fascinated by the Mustang on display that he lost control of his vehicle and crashed through the showroom window.

The Mustang was destined to be an incredible hit. During the first weekend it was on sale, an unprecedented four million people visited Ford dealerships. The car's public reception was exceeding our wildest hopes.

During *its* first year, the Falcon had sold a record 417,174 cars, and that was the figure I wanted to beat. We had a slogan: "417 by 4/17" – the Mustang's birthday. Late in the evening of April 16, 1965, a young Californian bought a sporty red Mustang convertible. He had just purchased the 418,812th Mustang, and we finished our first year with a new record.

Before the first year was over, there were Mustang clubs – hundreds of them – as well as Mustang sunglasses, key chains, and hats, along with toy Mustangs for kids. I knew we had it made when somebody spotted a sign in a bakery window that read: "Our hotcakes are selling like Mustangs."

I'm generally seen as the father of the Mustang, although, as with any success, there were plenty of people willing to take the credit. A stranger asking around Dearborn for people who were connected with the Edsel would be like old Diogenes with his lantern searching for an honest man. On the other hand, so many people have claimed to be the father of the Mustang that I wouldn't want to be seen in public with the mother!

The success of the Mustang was apparent so quickly that even before its first birthday I was given a major promotion. In January 1965, I became vice-president of the corporate car and truck group. I was now in charge of the planning, production and marketing of all cars and trucks in both the Ford and Lincoln-Mercury Divisions.

My new office was in the Glass House, which is how everybody at Ford referred to World Headquarters. I was finally one of the big boys, part of that select group of officers who ate lunch every day with Henry Ford. Until now, as far as I was concerned, Henry had simply been the top boss. Suddenly I was seeing him almost every day. Not only was I part of the rarefied atmosphere of top management, but I was also the new kid on the block, the young comer who was responsible for the Mustang.

Moreover, I was His Majesty's special protégé. After McNamara left in 1960 to join the Kennedy administration, Henry had more or less adopted me, and he kept a close eye on what I was up to from the start.

As a group vice-president, I had a number of new assignments and responsibilities, especially in the area of advertising and promotion. But my chief mandate, as Henry made clear, was to "rub some of that Mustang ointment onto the Lincoln-Mercury Division."

I decided it was time for us to revive the Mark line with a Mark III, based on our Thunderbird but with enough changes to make it fresh and different. The Mark III had a very long hood, a short rear deck, a powerful V-8 engine, and the same continental spare tire in the back that had been part of the original Marks. It was big, dramatic, and very distinctive.

We brought out the Mark III in April 1968, and in its very first year it outsold the Cadillac Eldorado, which had been our long-range goal. For the next five years we had a field day, in part because the car had been developed on the cheap. We did the whole thing for $30 million, a bargain-basement price, because we were able to use existing parts and designs.

Before the Mark III, the Lincoln-Mercury Division was actually losing money on every luxury car. We were selling only about eighteen thousand Lincolns a year, which wasn't enough to amortize the fixed costs. In our business, these costs are enormous. Whether you produce one car or a million, you've got to have a plant and you have to develop the dies to stamp out the metal. If your volume projections are wrong and you don't hit your objective, you have to pay off these fixed expenses over a smaller number of cars. Simply stated: you lose your shirt.

The old cliché is certainly true: bigger cars do mean bigger profits. We made as much from selling one Mark as we did from ten Falcons. Our profit worked out to an astonishing $2,000 per car. Moreover, the money started coming in so quickly, we could barely keep track of it. In our best year, we made almost $1 billion from the Lincoln Division alone, which is as big a success as I've ever had in my career.

By 1968, I was the odds-on favorite to become the next president of the Ford Motor Company. The Mustang had shown I was someone to watch. The Mark III made it clear I was no flash in the pan. I was forty-four, Henry Ford had taken me under his wing, and my future never looked better. But it took another two years until I did become president.

On December 10, 1970, I finally got what I was waiting for: the presidency of Ford. A few days before he made the announcement, Henry came into my office to tell me what he had in mind. I remember thinking: "This is the greatest Christmas present I've ever had!" We just sat there for a moment or two, he with a cigarette and me with a cigar, and blew smoke at each other.

The moment Henry walked out the door I called my wife. Then called my father in Allentown to tell him the good news. During his long and active life my father had a lot of happy moments, but I'm sure my phone call that day ranks near the top.

I now had so many diverse responsibilities that I had to learn a different style of operating. I didn't like to admit it, but I no longer had the stamina of the Mustang years, when I thought nothing of grabbing a hamburger for dinner and staying at the office until midnight.

The Ford Motor Company had close to half a million employees around the world, and I had to keep in mind that I was only one of them. Sometimes this meant that I wouldn't be able to return a phone call for a couple of weeks. But I decided it was more important to preserve my mental health than to give everybody curb service. Instead of driving home a different car every night to become more familiar with our various products, I now had a driver. I used the commuting time to read and answer my mail. But I continued to follow my old weekly routine. Unless I was out of town, my weekends were devoted to the family. I wouldn't open my briefcase until Sunday night. At that point I would sit in my library at home, do the serious company reading, and plan out the week ahead. By Monday morning I was ready to hit the ground running. I expected no less of the people who worked for me: I've always found that the speed of the boss is the speed of the team.

During my years as president of Ford, I was constantly meeting people who would tell me: "I wouldn't want your job for all the money in the world." I never knew how to respond to that kind of remark. I loved my job, even though many people viewed it as the kind of position that grinds you up and kills you off. But I never saw it that way. To me, it was sheer excitement.

Actually, after reaching the presidency I experienced a certain letdown. I had spent years climbing the mountain. When I finally made it to the top, I started to wonder why I had been in such a hurry to get there. I was only in my mid-forties, and I had no idea what I would do for an encore.

I certainly enjoyed the prestige and the power of my position. But being a public figure was definitely a mixed blessing. This was brought home to me very dramatically one Friday morning as I was riding to work. The radio was on and I was half listening when suddenly the announcer interrupted the regular program with a special bulletin. Apparently a group of the nation's top business leaders, myself included, had been marked for assassination by the Manson "family".

This cheerful news had come from Sandra Good, roommate of "Squeaky" Fromme, the young lady who had been arrested for trying to kill President Ford in Sacramento. If you ever want a quick wakerupper in the morning, all you've got to hear is that you've made somebody's hit list!

But I don't want to complain too much about one of the best jobs in the world. If Henry was king, I was the crown prince. And there was no question that the king liked me. Once he and his wife, Cristina, came to our house for dinner. My parents were there, too, and Henry spent half the night telling them how great I was and that without me there wouldn't be a Ford Motor Company.

Those were the days of wine and roses. All of us who constituted top management in the Glass House lived the good life in the royal court. We were part of something beyond first class – royal class, perhaps, where we had the best of everything. White-coated waiters were on call throughout the day, and we all ate lunch together in the executive dining room.

Now, this was no ordinary cafeteria. It was closer to being one of the country's finest restaurants. Dover sole was flown over from England on a daily basis. We enjoyed the finest fruits, no matter what the season. Fancy chocolates, exotic flowers – you name it, we had it. And everything was served up by those professional waiters in their white coats.

A few of us got into a discussion of how much those lunches really did cost the company. In typical Ford style, we ran a study to determine the real expense of serving lunch in the executive dining room. It came out to $104 dollars a head – and this was twenty years ago!

You could order anything you wanted in that room, from oysters Rockefeller to roast pheasant. But Henry's standard meal was a hamburger. He rarely ate anything else. One day at lunch he turned to me and complained that his personal chef at home, who was earning something like $30,000 or $40,000 a year, couldn't even make a decent hamburger. Furthermore, no restaurant he had ever been to could make a hamburger the way he liked it – the way it was prepared for him in the executive dining room.

I like to cook, so I was fascinated by Henry's complaint. I went into the kitchen to speak to Joe Bernardi, our Swiss-Italian chef. "Joe," I said, "Henry really likes the way you make hamburgers. Could you show me how?"

"Sure," said Joe. "But you have to be a great chef to do it right, so watch me very carefully."

He went over to the fridge, took out an inch-thick New York strip steak, and dropped it into the grinder. Out came the ground meat, which Joe fashioned into a hamburger patty. Then he slapped it onto the grill.
"Any questions?" he asked.
Then he looked at me with a half smile and said: "Amazing what you can cook up when you start with a five-dollar hunk of meat!"

Annotations
The words marked * should be memorized.)

to bail out *here:* free from an unpleasant or difficult situation; come to the help of s. o. (usu. through financial aid) – – **premature** ['prematʃər] US: ['prɪmətʊər] before the right time; too early – – **wop** (sl.) derogatory term for an Italian; from Spanish *guapo* (= dandy) – – **marginal** slight – – **fag** (sl.) *here:* homosexual – – **pants** trousers – – **to bait** *here:* torment s. b. by making cruel or insulting remarks – – **brat** (contemptuous) child – – **to rivet** compel, secure (attention) – – **to topple** overturn; stürzen, kippen – – **to scrape sth. off the floor** remove (mud, etc.) by drawing or pushing s. th. rough along the surface, i. e. to recover sth. from the very bottom – – **as Presidential timber** aus dem Holz, aus dem man Präsidenten schnitzt – – **soap opera** seriel TV or radio drama dealing with domestic problems, etc. in a sentimental or melodramatic way – – **glittering** brilliant – – **to turn tail** turn (to run away) – – **Reader's Digest** monthly magazine publishing a number of texts gathered together from other magazines – – **clue** fact, idea, etc. that suggests a possible answer to a problem – – **setback** Rückschlag – – **virtue** Tugend – – **done to a turn** cooked just right – – **investigation** careful and thorough inquiry – – **misdemeanour** ['mɪsdi'miːnə] offence less serious than a felony; Delikt, (strafbares Vergehen) – – **blameless** free from faults; innocent – – **to intimidate** frighten s. b. – – **to surrender** give up – – **junior executive** untergeordneter (jüngerer) leitender Angestellter
general manager a chief manager who controls the work of a number of other managers – – **virtually** almost entirely – – **to summon** demand the presence of; call or send for – – **to sell s.b. on** (US; coll.) make s. b. believe that s. b/s. th. is good; make s. b. accept s. th. – – **to play dumb** pretend not to know – – **resentful** (of) feeling bitter or angry at – – **credentials** *here:* proofs that a person is entitled to reputation and a powerful position – – **fire-in-the-belly time** a period when one works hard and is fully engaged in one's task – – **to smoke one's own brand** consider one's own ideas and doings to be the best – – **cocky** conceited, arrogant – – **we had a shot (at)** *here:* we had a chance of – – **to cut out** (coll.) ignore – – **item** single article – – **bucket seat** sports car seat (as contrasted with a normal or bench seat) – – **vinyl trim** ['vaɪnɪl] Innenausstattung aus Vinyl – – **wheel cover** hubcap – – **option** choice – – **crush** *here:* crowd; Andrang – – **washrack** *here:* a place having water and drainage facilities for the washing of vehicles – – **on display** being shown, exhibited – – **destined** ['destɪnd] predetermined – – **Falcon/ Thunderbird/Mustang** Ford models built in the 1960's – – **convertible** a car having a top that may be folded back, lowered, or removed; Kabriolett – – **Edsel** (spectacularly unsuccessful) Ford model – – **officer** *here:* executive – – **rarefied** ['reərɪfaɪd] refined – – **on the block** *here:* up for sale – – **to be up to** be busy with – – **ointment** Salbe – – **hood** (US) (Br.: bonnet) Motorhaube – – **rear deck** (US)

the lid of the compartment at the rear of the body of an automobile; the compartment covered by such a deck; Kofferraum, -deckel – – **tire** (Br: tyre) band of rubber on the rim of a wheel – – **spare** in reserve for use when needed – – **goal** object of efforts – – **to have a field day** spend time with great success; sich mit Erfolg betätigen – – **bargain-basement** (coll.) markedly cheap or inexpensive – – **die** metal form; Gußform – – **odds-on** better than even; aussichtsreich – – **flash in the pan** (coll.) something that only lasts for a very short time, e. g. a success or something that has not happened before and is unlikely to happen again; Strohfeuer – – **stamina** vigour, energy enabling a person to work hard for a long time – – **curb service** (US) any special service or favour – – **to commute** to travel regularly by car or train, from home to work and vice versa – – **briefcase** flat leather case, for documents, etc. Aktenkoffer – – **to hit the ground running** to start work at once, energetically – – **letdown** disappointment – – **encore** [ɔŋ'kɔː] repetition (e. g. of a singer) – – **bulletin** ['bulitin] *here:* announcement – – **assassination** act of killing (a usu. prominent person) – – **Manson family** gang of fanatics (mainly girls) with Manson as their leader. The gang killed Sharon Tate (Mrs Polanski), the well-known film producer's wife and female star in Polanski's film *Rosemary's Baby* – – **Dover sole** flat sea-fish with a delicate flavour; Seezunge – – **oyster** Auster – – **roast pheasant** gebratener Fasan – – **strip steak** entstieltes Steak – – **grinder** apparatus for grinding meat; Fleischwolf – – **patty** small flattened cake of minced meat; Frikadelle – – **hunk** thick piece cut off; Brocken

Assignments

1. a) Try and find the English equivalents of the German words given in the wordprobe puzzle below. They may appear horizontally, vertically, diagonally, forward and backward.
   b) Search for a well-known English saying included in the puzzle. It consists of 10 words whose first letters are: T; L; F; M; I; T; R; O; A; E.
   c) Choose 10 words from the puzzle to use in a written text (account, interview, story, etc.)

Wirtschaftlichkeit	Motor	Extra
Modell	Auslage	Händler
Prüfung	Innenausstattung	LKW
Bauform	Rad	Schlüssel
Leistung (2 Wörter)	Teppichauskleidung	für Kofferraum
Teil	Formgebung	Motorhaube
	Reifen	Gestell; *hier:* Boden (einer Waschanlage)

The Automobile Game

	1	2	3	4	5	6	7	8	9	10	11	12	13
1	W	P	E	R	F	O	R	M	A	N	C	E	C
2	T	W	N	N	O	Y	M	O	N	O	C	E	A
3	A	H	T	R	G	E	D	E	R	M	E	P	R
4	R	E	E	T	R	I	M	D	O	O	H	E	P
5	A	E	V	W	S	R	N	E	O	N	D	X	E
6	E	L	O	P	T	T	H	E	T	E	I	T	T
7	R	P	L	D	R	I	P	L	C	Y	G	R	I
8	W	A	L	U	A	R	E	E	A	D	N	A	N
9	Y	D	C	A	C	E	R	D	D	E	I	S	G
10	P	K	E	T	K	S	F	O	R	A	L	L	L
11	A	C	S	T	R	I	O	M	M	L	Y	K	I
12	R	E	X	D	E	S	I	G	N	E	T	E	V
13	T	E	P	O	W	E	R	O	F	R	S	Y	E

2. Sum up what Lee Iacocca tells us about his career in our extract.
3. Iacocca relates some anecdotes underlining the popularity of the *Mustang*. Retell them.
4. Refer to the following definitions of the term "American Dream" and show in what sense Iacocca can be said to be "the American Dream Personified".

– – "The American dream – – a house, a new car, a college education . . ." (*US News & World Report,* August 18, 1986)
– – Recently I have been asking my friends what they thought was meant by "the American Dream". There was little agreement; some spoke of it in the past tense, most in the present; equality was mentioned, success, progress, the frontier, individualism, capitalism, the founding fathers. But on three things they agreed: none claimed to be very sure what it meant, they all touched on freedom of one sort

or another, and they agreed that the Dream was important and affected the way lots of Americans behaved. (George P. Elliott: "Waking from the American Dream", *The Nation,* November 16, 1974.)

– – No, the American dream that has lured tens of millions of all nations to our shores in the past century has not been a dream of merely material plenty, though that has doubtless counted heavily. It has been much more thant that. It has been a dream of being able to grow to fullest development as man and woman, unhampered by the barriers which had slowly been erected in older civilizations, unrepressed by social orders which had developed for the benefit of classes rather than for the simple human being of any and every class. And that dream has been realized more fully in actual life here than anywhere else, though very imperfectly even among ourselves . . .

The point is that if we are to have a rich and full life in which all are to share and play their parts, if the American dream is to be a reality, our communal, spiritual, and intellectual life must be distinctly higher than elsewhere, where classes and groups have their separate interests, habits, markets, arts, and lives . . . The American dream can never be wrought into reality by cheap people or by "keeping up with the Joneses."

(James Truslow Adams: *The Epic of America,* New York Blue Ribbons Books, 1931)

5. To most Americans "the American dream" perhaps means "a house, a new car, a college education". But even the fulfilment of these comparatively modest dreams is getting more and more difficult in the US of today. Refer to the charts below and a) explain why this is so; b) describe the reaction of people to these difficulties.

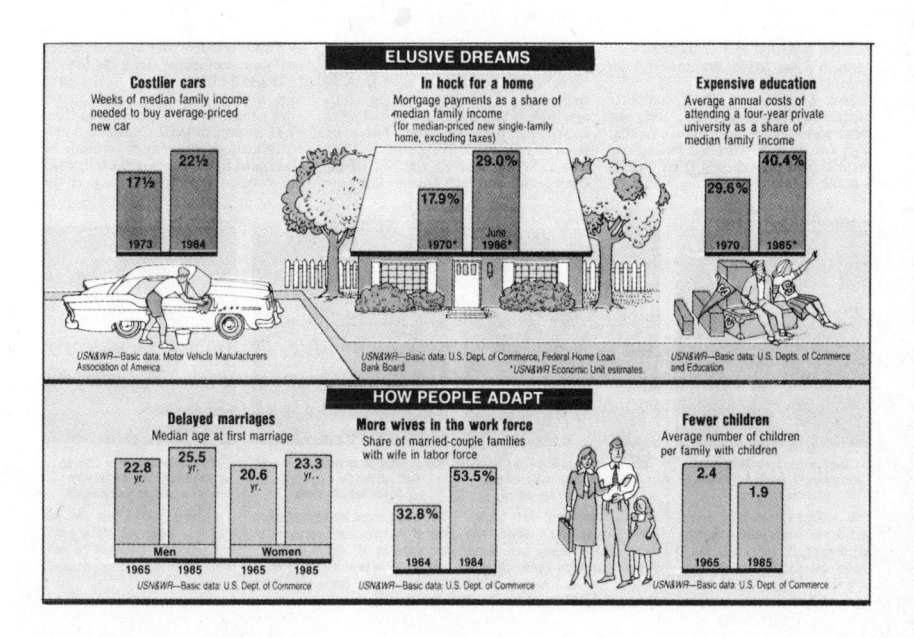

ELUSIVE DREAMS

Costlier cars
Weeks of median family income needed to buy average-priced new car
17½ (1973)   22½ (1984)
USN&WR—Basic data: Motor Vehicle Manufacturers Association of America

In hock for a home
Mortgage payments as a share of median family income (for median-priced new single-family home, excluding taxes)
17.9% (1970*)   29.0% (June 1986*)
*USN&WR—Basic data: U.S. Dept. of Commerce, Federal Home Loan Bank Board   *USN&WR Economic Unit estimates.*

Expensive education
Average annual costs of attending a four-year private university as a share of median family income
29.6% (1970)   40.4% (1985*)
USN&WR—Basic data: U.S. Depts. of Commerce and Education

HOW PEOPLE ADAPT

Delayed marriages
Median age at first marriage
Men: 22.8 yr. (1965), 25.5 yr. (1985)
Women: 20.6 yr. (1965), 23.3 yr. (1985)
USN&WR—Basic data: U.S. Dept. of Commerce

More wives in the work force
Share of married-couple families with wife in labor force
32.8% (1964)   53.5% (1984)
USN&WR—Basic data: U.S. Dept. of Commerce

Fewer children
Average number of children per family with children
2.4 (1965)   1.9 (1985)
USN&WR—Basic data: U.S. Dept. of Commerce

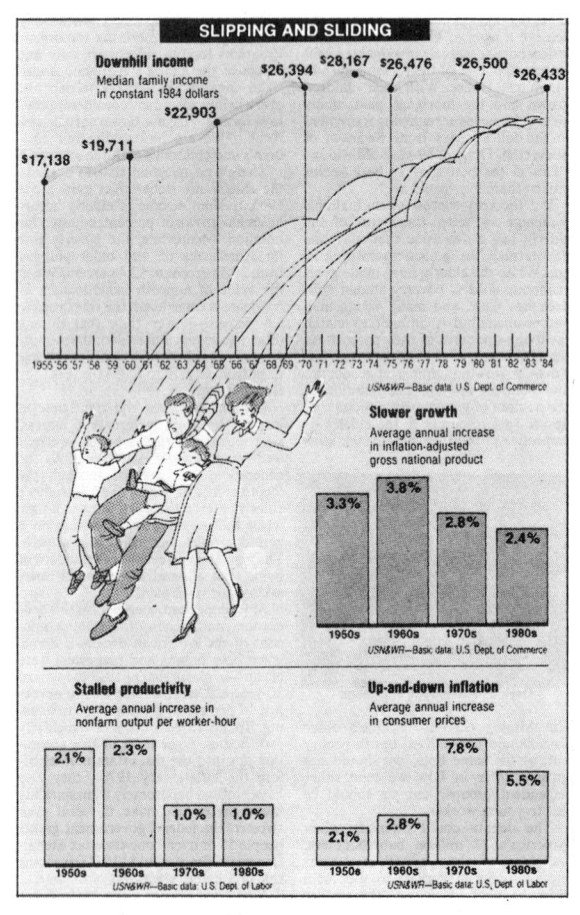

Source: *U.S. NEWS & WORLD REPORT,* Aug. 18, 1986

6. Do you think the same dreams can be put into reality more easily in Germany?
7. Read the book *Lee Iacocca, an Autobiography,* Bantam Books, New York, 1984, and make an outline of Lee Iacocca's life. Then use the latter as the basis for a speech delivered to the class.
8. Make another speech on "Immigration to the USA since 1776". For reference use
    a) *The Encyclopaedia Britannica*
    b) *Time Magazine,* July 8, 1985
    c) *World and Press,* August 1986, 2nd edition
    d) Other sources you provide yourself

9. *Interpreting cartoons*

Have a look at the cartoons below and that on page 153 and work out their meaning. The following questions may help you:
a) What experiment are the rats making with the manager?
b) Could you explain why it is rats, not pigs or other animals that are performing the experiment?
c) What is the result of the experiment likely to be, and why?
d) What topic does the cartoon showing the crying woman salesmanager deal with?
e) Do you think the cartoonist is making fun of the woman?
f) What is your opinion: can women be as successful in business as men?
g) Why are there so few female managers? Do you know of any? Tell your classmates how she got ahead in business.
h) The last cartoon shows a meeting of shareholders (US stockholders). Do you know what is done at such a meeting?
i) Why does the man talking hate this part of capitalism?
j) Which part of capitalism does he probably like?

"This is not the typing-pool, Miss Watson. You're a man now and men don't cry."

Source: *PUNCH,* March 6, 1985

"This is the part of capitalism I hate."

Source: *The New Yorker 1925–1975,* The Viking Press, New York 1975

10. *Taking minutes*

Imagine you are Lee Iacocca's secretary. There is a meeting of the board of directors at Ford's headquarters in Detroit. Your job is to take the minutes, i. e. to write a report on the meeting which sums up the proceedings. The report you hand in to your boss one day later might read as follows:

MINUTES OF THE MEETING OF THE BOARD OF DIRECTORS OF THE FORD MOTOR COMPANY
A special meeting of the Board of Directors of the Ford Motor Company was held on Wednesday, April 16, 19–, at the offices of the Company at 15 Broad Street, Detroit, Michigan, at 11:30 a. m. Mr. Lee Iacocca, president of the Company, presided. All the directors were present.
The minutes of the last meeting were read by the secretary and were approved.
Mr. Iacocca read the annual report of the company to be presented to the stockholders in June. After discussion Mr. Howard Henderson moved (= stellte den Antrag) to include a section entitled "The Ford Motor Company Greets the

Next Ten Years." The motion was seconded (= unterstützt) by Mr. Miles Lathrop and carried (= angenommen).

Mr. Lathrop presented a resolution to increase the minimum pension payable under the Ford Motor Company's Benefit Plan (= Betriebsrente) from three hundred-fifty dollars to four-hundred dollars a month.

Mr. T. R. Bernard moved to submit copies of the resolution to all stockholders for a vote at the annual meeting of stockholders. The motion was carried.

Upon motion regularly made and seconded it was voted to adjourn (= vertagen) the meeting at 2:30 p. m.

Mr. Iacocca announced that the next regular meeting would be held immediately after the meeting of the Executive Committee on Wednesday, May 14, at the Company offices.

Jane Johnson
Secretary

Note: The best preparation for taking minutes is getting as much information as possible ahead of time. Don't expect the chairman to repeat just for you. To help yourself and the chairman, secure in advance, when possible, a list of persons to be present, copies of resolutions to be presented, and reports, particularly financial, to be read at the meeting.

Adapted from: Tressler-Lipman, *Business English in Action,* Heath and Company, Boston 1949, p. 348

Assignment

1. Read the above minutes once again carefully, and make a list of what the secretary has included in them.
2. Write the minutes of this English lesson. Then compare the reports and select the better minutes.
3. Study text 19 *The Space Merchants* in *Modern World,* Volume 1, p. 116 ff. Imagine you have participated in the business meeting as Mr Fowler's secretary. Your task is to take the minutes.

11. *Just For Fun*

a) The sayings of chairman Lee

"Five years ago, we couldn't get any credit at the corner deli for the ol' pastrami sandwich." (On recent quick sale of a Chrysler bond issue.)

"Let me say to our Japanese friends . . . put up your feet and relax. Take a week off. And if you're in the car business, hell, take the whole month off."

"I've got to stop getting fired like this. People are going to start thinking I'm a drifter." (On being dismissed from a commission restoring Ellis Island.)

"We've already made a lot of money from our country's cheap-gas policy, and I'm happy to announce we're going to make a helluva lot more. It's a dumb policy, and I've told them that in Washington until I'm blue in the face, so at least I can go to the bank with a clear conscience."

"I would tell everybody what to do, and she would tell them how." (About TV sex expert Ruth Westheimer as a running mate for President.)

"I'm not president of anything. Everybody keeps trying to run me. And I wish you'd all stop it, because you're making my campaign staff nervous as hell."

Source: U.S. NEWS & WORLD REPORT, July 14, 1986

b) Do "That Scrambled Word Game"

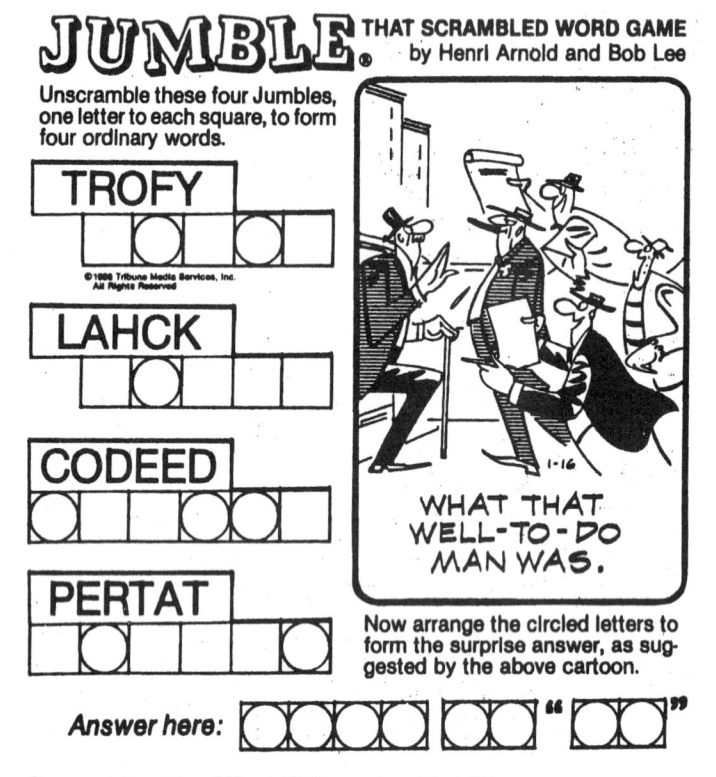

JUMBLE — THAT SCRAMBLED WORD GAME
by Henri Arnold and Bob Lee

Unscramble these four Jumbles, one letter to each square, to form four ordinary words.

- TROFY
- LAHCK
- CODEED
- PERTAT

WHAT THAT WELL-TO-DO MAN WAS.

Now arrange the circled letters to form the surprise answer, as suggested by the above cartoon.

Answer here: ⚪⚪⚪⚪⚪ ⚪⚪ " ⚪⚪ "

Source: *International Herald Tribune*, Jan. 16, 1986

15 NO MATTER HOW GREAT THE RISK

Note on the Text

The following text on Lloyd's of London is taken from *Spotlight,* an English magazine written by Germans for German learners of English. The text is left without a detailed worksheet because it is to be used for practice in listening comprehension and pronunciation. Before you get started with the assignments have a look at the vocabulary on page 169 f.

Assignments

1. Three students who are good at English pronunciation read out the text below. The class doesn't look at the text. The reading of the three students is recorded on cassette or tape.
2. Listen to the cassette/tape. Take notes. Then write down questions about the contents of the text. (At least 8!)
3. Now ask each other those questions. Questions and answers are recorded.
4. Listen to the reading a third time. Then decide whether the questions and answers recorded show that the content of the text has been understood.
5. Write a summary of the contents which doesn't exceed 300 words.
6. Listen to the cassette/tape one last time. Try to find mistakes in pronunciation and correct them. Decide which student in your opinion has the best pronunciation. Justify your view.
7. Now read the text in silence.
8. Between 4 and 6 students read the text aloud. The others note their mistakes and correct them.

Insure yourself, next time in London, against missing out on one of the most unlikely tourist attractions ever: Lloyd's of London. Lloyd's, having finished their new glass-and-stainless steel building in May, are now welcoming tourists to the modernized, spectacular headquarters. All they have to do is pay a call on the
5 visitors' gallery and enjoy the second-best show in London. In fact, during the rest of 1986, visitors will have plenty of company, for more than 250,000 tourists are expected to look in on the sleek, bee-hive building that stands out on the London skyline.
    Yes, it's true: this is the very same Lloyd's of London that will insure anything or
10 anybody, as was done when Elizabeth Taylor insured her eyes for a cool million dollars for two hours; when the Vatican got coverage on Pope Paul VI for $6 million during his visit to India; when the producers of a movie, *Jonathan Livingston Seagull,* took out insurance on the film's star (a bird): when dancer Rudolf Nureyev got a policy on his legs, as did Marlene Dietrich and Betty Grable.
15 Pop groups and rock bands regularly insure their instruments against damage on tour, and Lloyd's say they're surprisingly good risks – these days The Rolling

Stones, Culture Club and Fleetwood Mac (all regular clients) take enormous care of their equipment. Other supermen who've insured their assets with Lloyd's include dancer Gene Kelly, the late Richard Burton and Superman himself, Christopher
20 Reeve.
Most of the action at Lloyd's takes place in what is known as "The Room", which is the nickname for the hectic, underwriting salon. During the tour, from behind a glass enclosure up above, visitors can view this truly incredible stage. Stretching 340 feet in length and 120 feet in width, the gigantic chamber is said to be the largest
25 single room in Europe, where more than 26,000 insurance brokers and underwriters are busy insuring someone against anything.
The friendly guide makes clear that Lloyd's is not an insurance company in the usual sense but a communal market of underwriters. "Individually," he explains, "the people in 'The Room' are private insurance people, but collectively, they are Lloyd's
30 of London, ready to earn small fortunes or take a financial bath." Nearly every year Lloyd's underwrite insurance that produces premiums well in excess of $2 billion. Lloyd's risk insurance covers everything from A to Z. Although most transactions involve companies, especially shipping firms, most unusual policies you hear about come from individuals: Lloyd's even insure anyone against having twins, triplets
35 or quadruplets. Still another common policy is written for those determined persons who want an indemnity against bad weather during their vacations.
"Let the customer be willing to pay the price," adds the guide, "and a Lloyd's underwriter will take you on, no matter how great the risk or silly the conditions. If the risk is really a big one, then several underwriters form a syndicate, each to take
40 on a percentage, and go in on the policy together to share the possible burden of a large payoff."

In Lloyd's new building, despite its modern architecture, the organization will continue to pay homage to its historical past that now goes back nearly 300 years. The famous Lutine Bell, which has tolled good and bad maritime news for almost two centuries, will again be in the underwriting room. When the news is good, the bell rings twice, but when it is bad, the bell rings once. That's when everybody stops what he's doing: was it a bombing of an installation, or the breakup of an oil tanker, was it a collision at sea, did a ship sink?

All of Lloyd's exhibits in the old building, the ones that show how the unique business enterprise works, will be kept intact in the new headquarters, together with a shop where books and leaflets about Lloyd's will be available, including Lloyd's own daily newspaper, which was first established in 1734 and which is sent to over a hundred countries each day (the Kremlin has its own subscription for 50 copies).

With newly installed film equipment, the old library with its works of art will be used as a lecture room. Not to be overlooked is the showcase with Admiral Nelson's famous expense account. He wrote the first part of it with his right hand, and after losing the hand in a battle, he finished the report left-handed.

One of the new attractions will be Edward Lloyd's original coffeehouse, which was the birthplace of the present-day Lloyd's of London and which has been re-constructed with a coffeeshop frontage from the past. When Edward Lloyd opened up his coffeehouse down by the docks in 1688, it soon became a meeting place for ship owners, merchants and seamen. Because Lloyd's Coffeehouse was jammed with persons who often needed marine insurance, brokers were soon attracted to the place where they knew they could find underwriters.

Lloyd himself used to pick up a lot of shipping gossip and news, and he was quick to hand on this information to his customers, often with a printed sheet, to help his business along. When he died in 1713, Edward Lloyd's place was *the* place in London for maritime insurance, and though the man himself never sold any insurance, the insurance underwriters who congregated there as a kind of market place simply called themselves "Lloyd's of London".

Except for 1985 when a group of Lloyd's syndicates faced accumulated losses that exceeded a massive $ 163 million, and then for three years when some mega-disasters struck simultaneously, Lloyd's consistently show an annual profit. So it's not hard to understand why they don't mind insuring a dancer's legs – even if it means going out on a limb . . .   (~ 975 ws)

From: *Spotlight 8,* 1986

Vocabulary

accumulated loss Bilanzverlust – – **beehive** Bienenkorb, -haus – – **breakup** Auseinanderbrechen, Untergang – – **to congregate** sich versammeln – – **coverage** ['kʌverɪdʒ] Versicherungsschutz – – **to exceed** [ik'siːd] übersteigen – – **expense account** – Spesenabrechnung – – **gossip** – Klatsch – – **homage, to pay**

homage to s.th. einer Sache huldigen, Anerkennung zollen – – **indemnity** Versicherung – – **insurance broker** Versicherungsmakler – – **to insure** versichern, sich versichern lassen – – **to jam** verstopfen – – **Kremlin** Kreml (in Moskau) – – **lecture room** Vortragssaal – – **limb, to go out on a limb** sich in eine gefährliche Lage bringen, ein Risiko eingehen – – **to look in on** (als Besucher) vorbeikommen, vorbeischauen – – **marine insurance** See(transport)versicherung – – **mega** groß, Million – – **to overlook** übersehen – – **payoff** Auszahlung – – **premium** Prämie – – **quadruplets** Vierlinge – – **risk insurance** Risikoversicherung – – **shipping firm** Reederei – – **showcase** Schaukasten, Vitrine – – **sleek** elegant, schick – – **stainless steel** rostfreier Stahl – – **to take on** annehmen, aufnehmen – – **to take out insurance on s.th.** etwas versichern lassen – – **to toll** (durch Glockenläuten) verkünden – – **triplets** Drillinge – – **underwriting salon** Saal, in dem die Versicherungsgeschäfte abgewickelt werden

16 UTOPIA

Note on the Text

Sir Thomas More (1478–1535), English writer, lawyer, diplomat and politician, was a humanist and friend of Erasmus.
In 1504 he entered Parliament and occupied several posts under King Henry VIII. In 1521 he was knighted.
As he refused to acknowledge the Act of Supremacy he was indicted for high treason, found guilty, imprisoned in the Tower of London and beheaded in 1535. In 1935 he was canonized.
As an envoy to Flanders he wrote his principal literary work, *Utopia,* which was published in 1516 in Latin. Its first English translation came out in 1551. Its form was probably inspired by the narrative of the voyages of Vespucci, which was printed in 1507.
"Utopia" is an ambiguous term and a pun on the Greek words "eutopia" (well-place, better place) and "outopia" (no place, nowhere).
More's speculative political essay tells about a voyage to an imaginary island with an idealist and ideal state (community, government). It is the first modern depiction of an ideal state (after Plato' *Politeia*) and set the model and example for many "utopias" to follow.

The island contains fifty-four city-states, all spacious and magnificent, identical in language, traditions, customs, and laws. They are similar also in layout and everywhere, as far as the nature of the ground permits, similar even in appearance. None of them is separated by less than twenty-four miles from the nearest, but none
5   is so isolated that a person cannot go from it to another in a day's journey on foot. From each city three old and experienced citizens meet to discuss the affairs of common interest to the island once a year at Amaurotum, for this city, being in the very center of the country, is situated most conveniently for the representatives of all sections. It is considered the chief as well as the capital city.
10 The lands are so well assigned to the cities that each has at least twelve miles of country on every side, and on some sides even much more, to wit, the side on which

the cities are farther apart. No city has any desire to extend its territory, for they consider themselves the tenants rather than the masters of what they hold.

Everywhere in the rural districts they have, at suitable distances from one another, farmhouses well equipped with agricultural implements. They are inhabited by citizens who come in succession to live there. No rural household numbers less than forty men and women, besides two serfs attached to the soil. Over them are set a master and a mistress, serious in mind and ripe in years. Over every group of thirty households rules a phylarch.

Twenty from each household return every year to the city, namely, those having completed two years in the country. As substitutes in their place, the same number are sent from the city. They are to be trained by those who have been there a year and who therefore are more expert in farming; they themselves will teach others in the following years. There is thus no danger of anything going wrong with the annual food supply through want of skill, as might happen if all at one time were newcomers and novices at farming. Though this system of changing farmers in the rule, to prevent any individual's being forced against his will to continue too long in a life of rather hard work, yet many men who take a natural pleasure in agricultural pursuits obtain leave to stay several years.

Every city is divided into four equal districts. In the middle of each quarter is a market of all kinds of commodities. To designated market buildings the products of each family are conveyed. Each kind of goods is arranged separately in storehouses. From the latter any head of a household seeks what he and his require and, without money or any kind of compensation, carries off what he seeks. Why should anything be refused? First, there is a plentiful supply of all things and, secondly, there is no underlying fear that anyone will demand more than he needs. Why should there be any suspicion that someone may demand an excessive amount when he is certain of never being in want? No doubt about it, avarice and greed are aroused in every kind of living creature by the fear of want, but only in man are they motivated by pride alone – pride which counts it a personal glory to excel others by superfluous display of possessions. The latter vice can have no place at all in the Utopian scheme of things.

To continue, each street has spacious halls, located at equal distance from one another, each being known by a special name of its own. In these halls live the syphogrants. To each hall are assigned thirty families, fifteen on either side, to take their meals in common. The managers of each hall meet at a fixed time in the market and get food according to the number of persons in their individual charge.

To these halls, at the hours fixed for dinner and supper, the entire syphograncy assembles, summoned by the blast of a brazen trumpet, excepting persons who are taking their meals either in the hospitals or at home. No one is forbidden, after the halls have been served, to fetch food from the market to his home: they realize that no one would do it without good reason. For, though nobody is forbidden to

Woodcut map of Utopia from the March 1518 edition

Source: see text

dine at home, yet no one does it willingly since the practice is considered not decent and since it is foolish to take the trouble of preparing an inferior dinner when an excellent and sumptuous one is ready at hand in the hall nearby.

Meanwhile, gold and silver, of which money is made, are so treated by them that no one values them more highly than their true nature deserves. Who does not see that they are far inferior to iron in usefulness since without iron mortals cannot live any more than without fire and water? To gold and silver, however, nature has given no use that we cannot dispense with, if the folly of men had not made them valuable because they are rare. On the other hand, like a most kind and indulgent mother, she has exposed to view all that is best, like air and water and earth itself, but has removed as far as possible from us all vain and unprofitable things.

If in Utopia these metals were kept locked up in a tower, it might be suspected that the governor and the senate – for such is the foolish imagination of the common folk – were deceiving the people by the scheme and they themselves were deriving some benefit therefrom. Moreover, if they made them into drinking vessels and other such skillful handiwork, then if occasion arose for them all to be melted down again and applied to the pay of soldiers, they realize that people would be unwilling to be deprived of what they had once begun to treasure.

To avoid these dangers, they have devised a means which, as it is consonant with the rest of their institutions, so it is extremely unlike our own – seeing that we value gold so much and are so careful in safeguarding it – and therefore incredible expect to those who have experience of it. While they eat and drink from earthenware and glassware of fine workmanship but of little value, from gold and silver they make chamber pots and all the humblest vessels for use everywhere, not only in the common halls but in private homes also. Moreover, they employ the same metals to make the chains and solid fetters which they put on their slaves. Finally, as for those who bear the stigma of disgrace on account of some crime, they have gold ornaments hanging from their ears, gold rings encircling their fingers, gold chains thrown around their necks, and, as a last touch, a gold crown binding their temples. Thus by every means in their power they make gold and silver a mark of ill fame. In this way, too, it happens that, while all other nations bear the loss of these metals with as great grief as if they were losing their very vitals, if circumstances in Utopia ever required the removal of all gold and silver, no one would feel that he were losing as much as a penny. (~ 1270 words)

From: E. Surtz, ed., *Utopia*, New Haven and London 1964, Yale University Press, p. 61 ff

Annotations

The following annotations, for a change, give you the German translations of unkown vocabulary. Thus, they also want to make it easier for you to learn the words and not just understand them.

spacious geräumig –– **Amaurotum** "Nebelstadt" –– **to assign** zuweisen, zuteilen – – **to wit** (arch.) nämlich, das heißt – – **tenant** Mieter, Pächter – – **implement** Gerät, Werkzeug – – **serf** Leibeigener – – **phylarch** Head of the Tribe – – **novice** Novize, Neuling, Anfänger – – **commodity** Ware, Erzeugnis (bes. landwirtschaftlich) – – **to designate** kennzeichnen, benennen, bestimmen – – **to convey** befördern – – **avarice** Habgier, Habsucht – – **greed** Gier, Habgier – – **to arouse** wecken, erregen – – **vice** Laster – – **syphogrant** Beamter, Funktionär (weiser/dummer alter Mann) – – **to summon** (herbei-)rufen – – **brazen** blechern, Messing- – – **sumptuous** verschwenderisch – – **mortal** Sterblicher – – **to dispense (with)** verzichten auf – – **folly** Verrücktheit, Torheit – – **indulgent** nachgiebig, -sichtig – – **to deceive** täuschen, betrügen – – **scheme** Plan, Komplott, Intrige – – **to derive s.th.** from s.th. her-, ableiten, (Nutzen usw.) ziehen aus – – **vessel** Gefäß – – **handiwork** Gegenstand – – **to treasure** (hoch-)schätzen – – **to deprive s.b. of s.th.** jdm etwas entziehen – – **to devise** sich ausdenken – – **to be consonant with** (arch.) übereinstimmen mit – – **to safeguard** schützen – – **chamber pot** Nachttopf – – **humble** bescheiden, demütig, einfach – – **fetter** Fessel – – **stigma** Brandmal, Stigma – – **disgrace** Schande, Ungnade – – **temple** Schläfe – – **vitals** lebenswichtige Organe.

Language

Error recognition

The following sentences have all been taken from the text. In each of them one word has been exchanged for another. Find out the original word by comparing the sentences with the text. The first letters of the original words will give you the name of a famous novel by H. G. Wells.
1. They have farmhouses well equipped with industrial implements.
2. In the middle of each quarter is a church.
3. Beside them are set a master and a mistress, serious in mind and ripe in years.
4. The practice (of dining at home) is considered not moral.
5. Pride counts it a personal glory to be equal with others in superfluous display of possessions.
6. Everywhere in the city's districts they have farmhouses.
7. Everybody is forbidden to dine at home.
8. Who does not see that they (gold and silver) are far inferior to iron in value?
9. No city has any desire to extend its territory for they consider themselves to be the masters of what they hold.
10. Men who take a natural pleasure in agricultural pursuits are not refused to stay several years.
11. Only in man are they (avarice and greed) motivated by envy alone.
12. The country contains fifty-four city-states.
13. Utopia is considered the chief as well as the capital city.

Text Analysis

Find out as many details as you can about Utopia's geography (see also picture on p. 172), cities, families, agriculture, business and industry, politics, "Menschenbild" (image of man)!

Discussion and Comment

1. The findings of your text analysis should lead to an understanding of the basic difference between "Utopia" and our kind of society. Can you say what it is?
2. Would you like to live in "Utopia"? Why? Why not?
3. In what sense is the following statement correct? "Mit der Utopie Mores beginnt der moderne Sozialismus." (Karl Kautsky, 1854–1938, German socialist, co-author together with E. Bernstein of the so-called 'Erfurter Programm' of the German SPD from 1891). (see also p. 79 ff.)
4. Have you got any critical questions or remarks concerning "Utopia"?
5. Compare *Utopia* and *The Dispossessed!*
6. Comment on the following text!

   "More's planned state was a danger to world-peace – it resembled strangely the Germany of Hitler. It was an organized community wherein everyone had his place; where there was no unemployment; where the rough work was done by alien laborers or by the forced toil of persons who did not conform to the standards set by the state; where all citizens were trained to arms yet where few citizens lost their lives in wars which were conducted by 'secret weapons', propaganda, and 'fifth column', where aggression was justified whenever *Lebensraum* was needed on the ground that an intelligent people could use land better than their uninstructed neighbours."

   From: J. D. Mackie, *The Oxford History of England, The Earlier Tudors 1485–1558,* Oxford 1952

7. How would you account for the slavery in "Utopia"?
8. Why do men dream utopian dreams?
9. Work on this text!

   The utopian vision is possible because utopian thinkers hold to a number of implicit presuppositions about the human condition. It is obvious that some assumptions rule out *a priori* any hope of utopia. If one believes in the simplest theory of the 'law of the jungle' and assumes man is for ever a ravening beast, concerned only with his own brute survival, there is no hope of utopia. Some types of Christian theology – those that picture us as irrational and sinful beings who can be 'saved' but not basically changed this side of the grave – also preclude utopia. The utopian dreamer must have grounds of hope, hope for the here and now. If he takes too dour a view of man's nature, the dream cannot exist.

   It is fairly easy to deduce the principal articles of faith entertained by the utopian. One simply reads between the lines. Most utopian schemes assume the truth of the following statements, or at least most of them . . .
   What are the principal articles?

   (Ch. Walsh, *From Utopia to Nightmare,* Harper & Row, New York 1962, p. 70)

17 THE UNDERDEVELOPMENT OF U.S. AGRICULTURE

Introducing the Topic

HILLS, Iowa (NYT) – When the radio news flashed across the snow-covered prairies Monday during the noon meal, it carried a bulletin that John Hughes, the president of Hills Bank and Trust Co. had been shot and killed.

One farmer just outside this town of 550 residents turned to his wife and said, "I
5 wonder if it was Dale Burr." It was.

Burr, a 63-year-old farmer whose financial troubles were about to claim his land, his machinery, his stored grains and his beloved quarter horses, went on a killing rampage Monday, shooting three people to death before committing suicide on a lonely road near his rural home.

10 It was but the latest in a series of violent outbursts across the nation's heartland. In 1983, James Jenkins, a Minnesota farmer, and his son Steve, who had lost their land, cattle and credit rating, lured Rudolph H. Blythe Jr., the local bank president, and his loan officer to the abandoned farm and killed them both. The elder Jenkins then shot himself.

15 Last year, an armed Nebraska farmer, Arthur Kirk, was shot and killed after holding police at bay for several hours.

In the last three years, thousands of farmers, dozens of banks and hundreds of rural businesses have failed. And, according to mental health counselors and rural advocates, numerous other potentially violent incidents are defused regularly by
20 families, friends and mediators.

Deadly chain of events

Monday's events began when Burr, described as an outdoors workaholic, shot his wife of 40 years, Emily, apparently as she sought to stop him from leaving the house with his 12-gauge shotgun.

25 Burr left a note at home and drove into town. At 11:22 a.m., he walked in the back door of the shiny, modern bank on Main Street, where his checking account was overdrawn. He pulled the long, pump action gun from inside his overalls and fired one blast at Hughes head as the 46-year-old bank president looked up from his office chair. Hughes died immediately.

30 Burr pointed his gun at two other bank officers, Dale Kretschmar and Roger Reilly, who froze. The farmer did not fire.

Burr then drove east a few miles, and a farmer saw him fire once into the air. At 11:35, Burr entered into the farmyard of Richard Goody, with whom he had had a minor land dispute several years ago. Goody had just been spreading manure on
35 his fields for next year's crop.

As the 36-year-old man greeted his visitor near some hog-feeding pens, Burr shot him twice. He also fired at Goody's fleeing wife and 6-year-old son. He missed.

Ten minutes later, when David Henderson, a sheriff's deputy, pulled Burr onto the shoulder of a gravel road near his home, a muffled blast from within the pickup truck
40 signaled the farmer's suicide.

"It's another tragedy," said Peter Zevenbergen, who runs local mental health programs. "It was bound to happen somewhere. And it'll happen again, too."

"For many of these people," said Dan Levitas of Prairie Fire, a Des Moines group active in rural counseling and legal aid, "the hammer is coming down. They're shell-

45 shocked. Many keep it all inside. But now it's breaking out. I'm afraid this violence is the beginning of what is to come."
When such incidents erupt, along with a growing number of less publicized rural suicides, Levitas and others say they can almost predict from experience the characteristics: a farmer of any age above 35, a strong family man, devout
50 churchgoer, well-liked by friends but quiet.
Typically, they say, the man is the son and grandson of farmers on the same land, his family has a reputation for hard work, and he is not thought to be in financial trouble until after the incident.
Typically, too, the wife has confided the mounting financial and emotional pressures
55 to close friends or family, who profess shock and offer support. Then, shortly before the incident, the husband seems relieved about something.
Such was the case of Burr, the hardworking son of Vernon Burr, a farmer and bank director. The 6-foot-2 farmer was willing to chat, friends recalled, but only for a moment because he always seemed on the way to somewhere. The Burrs were
60 members of Our Redeemer Lutheran Church in Iowa City, eight miles north of this town in eastern Iowa. Their main social activity was a card club.
Burr farmed about 600 acres with his son John, 39. Courthouse records show that while few knew that Burr was in financial trouble, he had debts of some $800,000, many of them due last Friday.

65 **Dispute over $39,000 check**
Close family friends said the immediate financial pressure involved a $39,000 check for corn that Burr had deposited with the government. Because the corn was mortgaged to the Hills Bank, the check should have been made payable to the bank, too. It wasn't. Burr deposited the check in the Hills Bank to pay off fertilizer and
70 herbicide bills. The bank found out and sought the money immediately.
"Hughes has been leaning on some folks harder than he has to," said one bank customer who asked not to be identified. "You get so you don't know where to turn, and the banks push harder.
"Killing's wrong, but every man has his breaking point," he said.
75 Hughes was widely eulogized as a fine family man, active in many civic causes, a successful, aggressive businessman who had built the Hills Bank into a profitable institution with more than $200 million in assets, despite his town's small size.
State officials, who have closed 11 Iowa banks so far this year, compared to three in 1984, said the Hills Bank was not in difficulty, largely because it has a small
80 portfolio of agricultural loans.

From: "Iowa Farmer's Story Is Deadly, But Not Unique," THE STARS AND STRIPES, Thursday, December 12, 1985

1. What does the introductory newspaper report deal with?
2. What was the course of events?
3. Sum up the reasons for the farmer's action.
4. Do you think the president of the bank is to be blamed for the catastrophe?
5. What do the text and the graph below say about the economic situation of farmers in the Midwest of the US?
6. Would you agree that the report is sensational in tone?
7. Which stylistic features typical of a newspaper or magazine report are used by its author?

On the farm

Iowa farmland values

*1977-81 prices as of Feb. 1;
1982-85 prices as of April 1

U.S. monthly crop prices

*Preliminary
Note: Farmland prices include buildings

Chicago Tribune Graphic; Source: U.S. Agriculture Department

Note on the Text

The following text is taken from Frances Moore-Lappé's *Diet for a Small Planet*, Ballantine paperback, New York 1982, pp. 42–46. In the first part of her book the author mainly deals with the problem of starvation in Third World countries. As a recipe for overcoming hunger in the Third World Moore-Lappé recommends a drastic reduction in the consumption of meat in the so-called *Overdeveloped Countries* (ODCs) because "it takes 16 pounds of grain and soya beans to produce just 1 pound of beef in the United States today" (cf. also *MW 2*, Topic 9, p. 72, assignment 3.4). Instead of feeding cows on cereals the latter should rather be used to nourish the hungry people in the world.

Moore-Lappé's analysis of Third World agriculture is followed by a description of US agriculture. The parallels she draws between the two are very startling and worth discussing.

Studying third world agricultural problems for ten years, I began to see a pattern of "underdevelopment" that included these three elements: the *concentration of economic power* as the gap between the rich and the poor widens; *dependency and instability* of both the society as a whole and of more and more people within
5 it; and finally, *the mining of agricultural resources* for the benefit of a minority.

The agriculture of so many third world countries can be described in these terms. But what about the United States? Doesn't it have the world's most productive agriculture? Don't we have a system of family farms, not plantations run by a landed elite? And don't we have long-established conservation programs to prevent the mining of our soil and water?

Many believe so, but what I am learning is that each of these patterns of underdevelopment – the kind of society I don't want – is taking hold right here in America.

Concentration of Economic Power

Control over farmland is becoming increasingly concentrated. In just 20 years, it is predicted, a mere 3 percent of all farms will control two-thirds of farm production. The amount of farmland controlled by absentee landlords will increase. (Already almost half of U.S. farmland is owned by nonfarmers.) Donald Paarlberg, among the most highly regarded agricultural economists in the country, warns us: "We are developing a wealthy hereditary landowning class, which is contrary to American tradition."

U.S. farmland, at present anyway, is actually much less tightly controlled than the rest of the food industry, which is now dominated by what economists call "shared monopolies." This means that in almost any given food category, only four corporations control at least half of the sales. In 33 categories, only four companies control *two-thirds* of the sales. For some foods, the monopoly power is much greater: three corporations Kellogg's, General Mills, and General Foods – capture over 90 percent of breakfast cereal sales.

Such market power spells profits: between 1973 and 1979, food industry profits rose 46 percent faster than consumer food expenditures. And this monopoly power spells higher food costs for all of us. Monopoly power in the food processing industry results in close to $20 billion in overcharges to American consumers each year, or almost $90 per year for every single American. That's how much more we pay compared to prices in a more competitive food economy.

In fact, at every stage of the food industry concentration is tightening. During just the last ten years 20 "Fortune 500" corporations have acquired at least 60 U.S.-based seed companies. In just ten years the top four pesticide manufacturers increased their control from 33 percent of the market to 59 percent. Just two corporations now control about half of tractor sales.

The meat industry is no exception to these trends. Just three decades ago, cattle were fed in thousands of small feedlots (fenced areas where cattle are fattened for market). During the 1960s, 7,500 feedlots folded each year. By 1977, half of the 25 million cattle fed in the United States passed through only 400 feedlots.

At the next stage of production – beef packing – four corporations control one-third of the market. One of these, Iowa Beef Processors, was just grabbed up by Occidental Petroleum. Having made a killing through its control of one scarce commodity – fossil fuel – Oxy is hoping to do the same with another. Its board chairman told *Business Week* shortly before the 1981 merger: "Food shortages will be to the 1990's what energy shortages have been to the 1970's and 1980's."

While nationally four beef packers control about a third of the market for cattle, what's worrying cattle feeders is how few corporations are *in their vicinity* to bid for their herd; for, regionally, control is even more tightly concentrated. Just three packers, for example, now purchase 70 percent of the feedlot cattle in a major Southwest beef producing area. Cattlemen are sure that such concentrated power depresses the prices they can get for their cattle.

Cattle-feeding, meatpacking, and grain-trading operations used to be owned by separate interests. But today 13 of the 25 biggest feedlot operations are owned or controlled by either meatpacking or grain-trading corporations.

Their interest is in keeping the price of feedlot cattle down. Conveniently, these "integrated" firms also control a critically large share of the cattle futures market (trading in contracts for delivery of feedlot cattle), which they can use to depress the price of cattle, helping to drive out of business the smaller feedlots not connected to beef packers. Officers of packing, meat-processing, grain-trading, and feedlot companies also use their insider knowledge to reap incredible personal gain. A 1980 Congressional study revealed that over a 16-month period in 1978 and 1979, those who came out on top in cattle futures trading were a handful of officers in these companies who each profited by an average of $2.5 *million.*

Since our nation was founded, Americans have resisted such economic concentration, believing that mammoth, unaccountable economic units operating behind closed doors are antithetical to democracy. Nevertheless, economic concentration has been quickening and, in the 1980s, it is gaining speed in a "merger mania" blessed by the Reagan administration and fueled by the oil companies' burgeoning profits.

Images of the Third World

Miles and miles of coffee or banana trees. Endless fields of sugar cane. Dependency on raw-material production – and dependency on only one or two crops for export. The marketing of these exports through corporations with no accountability, no loyalty to the well-being of the people of the country.

Since these are my images of third world agriculture, you can imagine my alarm as I learned about the parallels in U.S. agriculture.

I began to study the U.S. government's big farm-export push, which began in the early 1970s. Some have called the massive increase in agricultural exports the greatest shock to hit American agriculture since the tractor, and they may be right.

In just ten years farm export volume doubled, and in the Corn Belt states almost 30 percent more land came under cultivation – much of it marginal land, highly susceptible to erosion.

Directly related to the export push are two other trends – a reduction in the number of crops produced and the increasing dependence of farmers on foreign markets. In fact, that dependence doubled in only ten years, so that by 1980 almost one-third of farmers' sales went overseas.

What is the significance of these trends for farmers?

Dependence on foreign markets immediately resulted in more volatile commodity prices. The variation in prices farmers received after 1972 was five times greater than during the late 1960s. Boom and bust was the result. While farmers' incomes hit record highs in 1973-74, by 1978 an average farm family's real purchasing power was no greater than it was in the early 1960s. These great income swings hit the moderate-sized family farm the hardest, especially those with big mortgages still to pay off. It favored those farm operators with investments outside farming, those with incomes large enough to weather the price dips, and those with large equity in their land. (~ 1245 ws)

Source: *Business Week,* Febr. 18, 1985

Annotations
(The words marked * should be memorized.)

***to flash** *here:* travel very quickly – – **bulletin** official statement of news – – *****grain** small, hard seed of food plants such as wheat and rice – – **quarter horse** horse that is used in races of a quarter of a mile – – **to go on a rampage** ['ræmpidʒ] to set out to be wildly destructive – – *****rural** in the countryside – – **credit rating** creditworthiness – – *****loan officer** bank employee who handles loan requests – – **to hold at bay** keep an enemy, etc, at a distance – – **to defuse** remove the fuse from (as a mine or bomb); entschärfen – – **workaholic** (blend or portmanteau word of work and alcoholic) very hard worker – – *****to seek** (sought, sought) *here:* try – – **gauge** ['geidʒ] *here:* diameter of the rifle barrel; Kaliber – – **checking account** current account; laufendes Konto – – **pump action gun** (Jagd)Gewehr mit halbautomatischem Nachladeschloß – – **blast** Ladung – – *****manure** animal waste or other material, natural or artificial, to make the soil fertile – – *****crop** yearly produce of grain, grass, fruit – – **hog** castrated male pig reared for meat – – **pen** small enclosure for cattle, sheep, etc.; Pferch – – **shoulder** *here:* the edge of a road; Bankett – – *****gravel** ['grævl] Kies – – **muffled** gedämpft – – **blast** *here:* explosion – – **shell-shocked** with shattered nerves – – *****to predict** foretell – – **devout** paying serious attention to religious duties; überzeugt – – **to confide s.th. to s.b.** tell something secret to s.b. – – **Redeemer** Erlöser – – **courthouse records** Gerichtsakten – – *****to mortgage** ['mɔːgidʒ] give s.b. a claim on (property) as a security for payment of a debt or loan; verpfänden – – *****to deposit** hinterlegen – – **herbicide** weed killer – – **to eulogize** ['juːlədʒaiz] praise highly – – **civic** of the official affairs of a town or a citizen; Stadt . . .; Bürger . . . – – **assets** anything owned by a person, company, etc.; Vermögenswerte; Aktiva – – **portfolio** Bestand – – **agricultural loans** Landwirtschaftsdarlehen – – *****benefit** profit; advantage – – **landed elite** Schicht reicher Grundbesitzer – – **to take hold** here: establish itself – – **absentee landlord** owner of land who does not farm it but lives somewhere else – – **hereditary landowning class** durch Vererbung entstandene Landbesitzerschicht – – **shared monopolies** enterprises that dominate the market together with only a few other ones – – *****expenditure** spending (of money) – – **to spell** here: mean, signify – – *****food processing** Nahrungsmittelherstellung – – **overcharge** Mehrbelastung; überteuerter Preis – – **to tighten** make or become squeezed; verschärfen – – **Fortune 500** the 500 richest firms in the USA – – *****corporation** company – – **to acquire** buy – – *****seed** Saat – – **pesticide** insect killer – – **to fold** shut down – – **to make a killing** have a sudden very great success, especially by making a great profit – – **merger** combining of business companies – – *****to bid** (at an auction sale) make an offer – – **meat packer** Fleischfabrik – – **operation** here: business, enterprise – – **interest** here: group or business corporation – – **conveniently** to their advantage – – **futures** Termingeschäfte – – **futures market** Terminmarkt – – **to come out on top** emerge in the top position – – **to reap gain** make profit – – **mammoth** immense – – **unaccountable** not answerable to higher authority; nicht überprüfbar – – **to fuel** support, stimulate – – to **burgeon** ['bɜdʒən] flourish, grow – – **mania** madness, extreme enthusiasm – – **sugar cane** Zuckerrohr – – **marginal land** land whose yield barely covers the cost of production – – **susceptible (to)** [sə'septəbl] sensitive to; easily affected by; anfällig für – – **crops** here: Früchte-, Getreide-, Gemüsesorten – – **volatile** changing quickly or easily – – **to weather** survive; aushalten – – **dip** act of going down – – **equity** here: the money value of a property in excess of claims (like mortgaged indebtedness) upon it; Eigenkapital, Vermögen

WORKSHEET
1. Language
1.1 Do the following *Bank Game*. Below is a list of numbers discovered on an American detective found dead in the streets of New York. Experts from the CIA deciphered the numbers and were astonished to find that they were German words mainly used in the banking business. Not satisfied with this discovery, the experts translated the words into English and – – as they had hoped – – extracted a message which was extremely important. Can you repeat their successful work? 20, 2, 2, 17; 25, 8, 16, 24!

The list of figures:
20, 18, 25, 17; 8, 18 15, 18, 5, 13, 2, 20, 18, 1; 6, 2, 13, 22, 14, 25, 22, 6, 22, 18, 5, 8, 1, 20; 18, 22, 20, 18, 1, 24, 14, 3, 22, 7, 14, 25; 23, 14, 21, 5; 21, 12, 3, 2, 7, 21, 18, 24; 24, 2, 1, 7, 2; 22, 1, 21, 14, 15, 18, 5; 14, 8, 6, 20, 18, 20, 25, 22, 16, 21, 18, 1; 24, 1, 14, 3, 3; 6, 7, 18, 8, 18, 5; 13, 18, 1, 7, 5, 14, 25, 18; 8, 26, 7, 14, 8, 6, 16, 21; 14, 15, 21, 18, 15, 18, 1; 14, 8, 19, 7, 5, 14, 20; 18, 26, 3, 19, 14, 18, 1, 20, 18, 5; 17, 14, 5, 25, 18, 21, 18, 1; 6, 16, 21, 8, 25, 17; 20, 18, 10, 14, 18, 21, 5, 8, 1, 20; 15, 8, 18, 5, 2; 18, 5, 21, 2, 18, 21, 18, 1; 9, 18, 5, 15, 22, 1, 17, 25, 22, 16, 21, 24, 18, 22, 7; 10, 8, 16, 21, 18, 5, 18,

5; 1, 18, 7, 7, 2; 19, 14, 18, 25, 25, 22, 20
The message: _____

1.2 Find words or expressions in the main text that mean these things:
   a) structure (paragraph 1)
   b) difference (1)
   c) large estate on which tea, coffee, sugar cane, etc. is cultivated (2)
   d) limited liability company (5)
   e) person who buys and uses goods (6)
   f) concern engaged in the slaughtering, processing and distribution of meat (10)
   g) extreme enthusiasm for the fusion of companies (13)
   h) act of preparing land for crops by ploughing (17)

1.3 Insert "by", "with", or "at".
   a) He worked _____ the risk of his life.
   b) Americans could not stand _____ and let Europe fall into chaos.
   c) In some industries, holidays _____ pay were introduced.
   d) The USA did not cut all ties _____ other nations.
   e) My principle is to profit _____ all the benefits that society provides.
   f) _____ this period Tom was rather lonely.
   g) Average "real wages" rose _____ 26%.
   h) Their efforts met _____ little success.
   i) They had learned _____ grievous expense not to use that road.
   j) He arrived _____ the intention of asserting his authority.
   k) I met her _____ chance in Paris.
   l) He consoled himself _____ the thought that she did not hate him.
   m) He knew the details _____ heart.
   n) It's the spirit of the Greeks that we aim _____
   o) The juries _____ his two trials failed to agree.

1.4 Insert the appropriate words in the gaps of the text below. Each word is to be used once!
   agricultural; bankruptcy (Pl.); boom; broke; clout; consumer (Pl); crop (Pl); cultivation; customer (Pl); cut; exporter; farm; fertilizer; good (Pl); grain; grow; loan (Pl); market (Pl); output; price; processor (Pl); production; recession; shrunk; starvation; subsidized; subsidy (Pl); support (Pl); surplus (Pl); taxpayer (Pl); value

Too Much of a Good Thing

Agriculture's worldwide (1) _____ has produced misery to share.

The twelve-nation European Community spends $63,000 an hour to store 1.4 million tons of unsold butter in refrigerated warehouses. Its mountain of skimmed-milk powder rose this summer to 988,000 tons. The E.C. is trying to reduce the stocks by feeding the butter to calves and the milk powder to pigs and poultry.

5 But experts estimate that about half the butter and other refrigerated products have deteriorated so badly that they are no longer fit to be eaten by animals, let alone humans.
Japan's farmers each year (2) _____ more rice than the nation's citizens can eat. Yet rice can be sold only under government license, and (3) _____ pay about
10 three times the average world price to buy it.
Americans can take no comfort from these shared troubles; agriculture is one field in which misery does not love company.
On the contrary, whenever a nation tries to dispose of its (4) _____ furious fights erupt, even among old friends. Australian Foreign Minister Bill Hayden has been
15 thundering that (5) _____ American sales of wheat to the Soviet Union and sugar to China, traditional Australian markets, could undermine the bilateral defense alliance. Thais are so incensed by subsidized American rice exports that a Bangkok newspaper recently ran the headline BEST FRIEND U.S. CUTS THAILAND'S THROAT.
20 (6) _____ policy, in other words, is the tar baby of political economy through most of the non-Communist world: an intractable mess that seems to get ever stickier. Communist nations have agricultural headaches too, but theirs stem from too little (7) _____ caused mainly by a lack of incentives for farmers. The root problem in the free world is the exact opposite: high price (8) _____ and other subsidies
25 have encouraged farmers to grow bigger (9) _____ than markets can absorb. In Western Europe, for example, agricultural (10) _____ has been growing four times as fast as food consumption; in the U.S., farm production has far outpaced the 1% annual population growth.
The trouble has been building since the 1930s in the U.S. and the 1960s in Western
30 Europe. But the effects were muffled during the 1970s by a worldwide boom in exports. The Soviet Union began introducing more meat into its citizens' diets and imported (11) _____ on a huge scale for animals to eat. Oil-price increases piled money into international banks; the bankers lent the cash to Third World nations, which then went on a food-buying spree. Farmers everywhere pushed production
35 still higher to cash in on the new prosperity. Western Europe, for example, went from being a net importer to a net (12) _____ of some important food products. Still there seemed to be more than enough business to go around. In the U.S. (13) _____ exports hit an all-time high, and net farm income came close to one, in 1981. This was no coincidence: one calculation shows that the food and fiber grown
40 on two of every five acres under (14) _____ in the U.S. is sold abroad.
By the 1980s, however, several trends converged to make the export (15) _____ shrivel as rapidly as they had grown. The second oil-price shock, beginning in 1979, tipped the industrial world into (16) _____. Poor countries, unable to sell their products in Europe and the U.S. and under pressure to repay their (17) _____,
45 cut back drastically on food imports. Meanwhile, the high-yielding crop strains developed by the "green revolution" brought many Asian countries to or near the point of self-sufficiency in food production. China and India, the world's two most populous nations, have actually become exporters of grain. Hunger still stalks the world, of course – some parts of sub-Saharan Africa face outright (18) _____ . . .
50 But these nations lack the money to buy the imported food they so desperately need. In the U.S., farm exports have (19) _____ from $43.8 billion in 1981 to an expected $26.5 billion this year.
The consequences of dropping exports have been drastic in Western Europe too. The E.C.'s stockpile of unsold farm (20) _____ has more than quintupled in the
55 past five years, to a current estimated (21) _____ of $10.2 billion. Besides its

butter mountain and piles of stored grain, the Community produces so much more wine than can be sold that the annual surplus would fill 1,500 Olympic-size swimming pools.

What can be done? The obvious solution would be to knock out price supports and force farmers to grow no more than (22) _____ at home and overseas have the money and desire to buy. Such a policy, however, is simply too brutal for public opinion to accept. The U.S. could probably feed and clothe itself comfortably with the output of only half the land now in cultivation. But that would mean a wave of foreclosures and farm (23) _____ dwarfing anything seen so far.

Moreover, in all the democratic countries, farmers retain enough political clout to block any drastic (24) _____ in the income supports that encourage overproduction. Japan is an extreme example: the high (25) _____ on rice reflect an outrageous gerrymandering of election districts that gives some rural areas as much representation in the legislature as city districts with 35 times as many voters. In the U.S., farmers now constitute only 2.2% of the population, vs. 8.7% as recently as 1960. But farmers and people dependent on them (small-town bankers, food (26) _____, machinery dealers, (27) _____ makers and the like) dominate the economies of enough states to wield disproportionate power in Congress. One result: the Reagan Administration last year could not begin a dismantling of (28) _____ and income supports that it had widely touted. Congress passed a new law keeping supports high enough that they are likely to cost taxpayers a stunning $26 billion in the fiscal year that ends Sept. 30 – though not high enough to prevent many farmers from going (29) _____ anyway.

So it goes around the world. Farmers, governments and (30) _____ are paying the price of living in an agricultural fantasy land. But they shrink from the even more devastating price of a return to economic reality.

Abbreviated from: *Time,* September 8, 1986

2. **Content and Comment**
2.1 Frances Moore-Lappé sees a pattern of increasing "underdevelopment" in America's agriculture and food industry. What does she mean by this?
2.2 To what degree did the increased export of grain in the early 1970's contribute to this "underdevelopment"?
2.3 What is the main effect of this "underdevelopment" on the American consumer?
2.4 According to her, such a development towards "underdevelopment" in US agriculture is a danger for democracy in the USA. Do you agree?
2.5 Why, in your view, has the Reagan administration not done much against such "underdevelopment"?
2.6 Compare America's agricultural problems with those of the EEC. Point out similarities and differences. (In particular, consider the following questions: Are European farmers better off than their American counterparts? Are there big farms and food companies in Europe which dominate the market and are able to manipulate prices? If so, give their names. Are there also food surpluses in Europe? If so, how are they handled? What about European dependency on

exports? Is European agricultural policy reasonable? Need it be changed? If so, make suggestions for changes. Can changes be implemented?)
2.7 In some regions of the world there are surpluses in food production, in others people are starving. Could the rich countries not simply give away their surpluses to the poor ones, thus saving millions of lives?

18 NO, MAC, IT JUST WOULDN'T WORK

Note on the Text

The following extract from Robert Graves's short story *No, Mac, It Just Wouldn't Work* is mainly intended for your reading pleasure. Its worksheet has, therefore, been kept short. The text has been abbreviated from: *Playboy's Short-Shorts 1*, Playboy Press, Chicago, 1974².

A wild character, obviously high and wearing a Mexican hat, though he wasn't Mexican but, in fact, Boston Irish (which can be just as wild), edged up to me at the Green Hornet the other night and said abruptly:
"Speaking out, I mean, Professor . . . it's quite simple, really . . . millions of poor
5 devils starving in India and Africa and China and such places. Millions of them! Grant me that for the sake of the argument."
"Granted, Mex. What's your problem?"
"And all the thousands of gangsters and delinquents and violent no-gooders in our big cities, grant me them?"
10 "Granted, Mex, for the sake of your argument. Go ahead!"
"And hundreds of Federal ships tied up empty in the Hudson, waiting for God only knows what. Grant me –"
"I'm a stranger here," I said cautiously. "English. But you may be right. There's always marginal tonnage lying around the ports, except in wartime. When freight
15 rates rise, it can amount to a lot."
"And all the farm surplus that we either hoard or destroy because nobody here can eat it all and because the poor starving devils abroad can't pay for it! And all the criminal waste here in New York and the other big cities – enough to feed and clothe millions!"
20 "I've read of that, Mex. Speak on!"
"And all those philanthropic Christian and Jewish do-gooders and Peace Corps characters who want to prevent crime, starvation, idleness – the lot?"
"I seem to have met most of them," I agreed.
The barman said, "All granted, Mac, but what the hell? All this don't hurt *you* none,
25 surely?"
Mex said, "Sure, it hurts me as a human being. I've got a Mexican conscience or something and I ask myself, Why can't we put the Christian and Jewish do-gooders

in charge of the delinquent no-gooders? Why not give the no-gooders a grand job, which would be to load those idle boats – or marginal tonnage, as the Prof calls them – with surplus food and clothing and city waste, and make *men* of the no-gooders and send them sailing over the wide ocean with gifts for the poor starving devils abroad? Sure, then everyone would feel good. What's amiss with that for a solution?"

"No, Mac," said the barman, "it just wouldn't work. The Longshoremen's union and the Seafarers' union and the Teamsters' union would raise hell. And you've got to respect big business. Big business wouldn't stand for any of that, even to save the world from communism – no more than the unions would. Free gifts destroy markets, don't you see?"

"But there's no market there, anyway. Those poor devils have no cash, so they have to starve. Only pump them up and they'll start producing again and have money to throw around."

"And put us Americans out of jobs by undercutting prices?" sneered the barman. "No, Mac, it just wouldn't work. Forget it! What do you think, Professor?"

"I'm with you," I said. "Nothing sensible and simple ever works, because nobody *thinks* sensibly or simply. In the end, of course, something snaps and then you have a recession or a war, which changes the problem."

Mex grinned. "Then, Prof, why can't you university guys teach our Government and big business how to *think* that way?"

That was easy to answer. "Because the university guys here, and everywhere else, depend for their easy life on money grants from the Government and big business. So they teach students not to think out of the ordinary rut. Any teacher who gets out of step has to think stupid or be fired." . . .

I ordered three whiskey sours – the third one for an old Negro with a flattened nose and cauliflower ears, an ex-fighter who had joined us.

"To get back to those delinquents," said the barman doggedly, "even if the unions and big business allowed the do-gooders to load up those ships and dump free food among starving aliens, suppose the no-gooders refused to play – suppose they preferred to stick around and be violent?"

The old ex-fighter came to life. "Speaking out," he said, "it's quite simple, really. Just *let*' em be violent. If they have a yen for switchblade knives and loaded stockings and James Bond steel-toed shoes, just *let*' em! In public, with a big crowd to watch. They'd not chicken out, those boys wouldn't, grant me that!"

We nodded, for the sake of the argument.

"No threat to business. You could make a crazy big gladiatorial show of it, like in the movies about ancient Rome. Stage a twice-weekly gang fight; sell the TV rights for millions. Those kids would soon become high society. And, man, that show would be better to watch than any ball game. Or any fist fight – where the damage don't show so much but goes deeper. Grant me that!"

We granted it.

70 "And once you give the gladiators a good social rating, they themselves is going to clean up all the no-good amateur gang warfare, because that's just delinquency – gives their profession a bad name. OK, so the football and baseball and boxing interests might squeal? But they'd come over in the end. Blood sports are the best draw."

75 "And the churches?" I asked.

"The preachers'd have something to preach against. Maybe they'd win another martyr like who was it, long ago, rushed out into the arena and held out his arms and got clobbered? Anyhow, nowadays preachers can't even stop wars if big business needs a hot or cold war to jack up economy."

80 The barman said, "No, fella, it just wouldn't work. There's Federal laws against dueling, and your gladiators might lobby like hell but they would never get them repealed – not with the whole Middle West solid against bloodshed. You can't even stage a Spanish bullfight around here."

Mex said, "Guess not, as yet. But it's bound to come, someday. Like the licensed
85 sale of pornography, and a lot of other things. Because of the shorter week and what to do with your leisure time. TV isn't the answer, nor window-shopping isn't, nor raising bigger families for the population explosion. Nor a hot war, neither, even if it sends the no-gooders and the do-gooders into the Armed Forces and cuts down
90 waste and sends up the value of marginal tonnage."

"Speaking freely," I said, "it's quite simple, really. Another round of whiskey sours and we'll soon make it work." (~ 1115 ws)

Annotations
(The words marked * should be memorized.)

high (coll.) drunk – – **to edge up (to)** move slowly forward (to) – – ***to starve** die of hunger – – **to grant** *here:* agree (that s.th. is true) – – **no-gooder** Tunichtgut – – **to be tied up** lie at anchor – – **marginal tonnage** unused cargo-carrying capacity of a ship – – ***freight rate** money charged for the carriage of goods – – **philanthropic** benevolent; kind and helpful – – ***to put in charge (of)** jem. die Leitung/Führung übertragen – – **amiss** wrong – – **longshoreman** (US) Schauermann, Hafenarbeiter – – **seafarer** seaman – – **teamster** (US) trucker – – **to stand for** *here:* permit; endure without protest – – **to pump s.b. up** (coll.) *here:* provide s.b. with money – – ***to undercut** offer (goods, services) at a lower price than competitors – – **to sneer** utter contemptuous words; spotten, sticheln – – ***sensible** reasonable – – **to snap** break with a sharp crack; zerkrachen, zerspringen, zerbrechen – – **rut** way, course; routine – – **dogged** ['dɔgid] obstinate, stubborn – – ***alien** foreigner – – **switchblade knife** Springmesser – – **loaded stocking** Bleistrumpf – – **steel-toed shoes** Stahlkappenschuhe – – **to chicken (out)** be scared, be too frightened to act – – **rating** *here:* status, standing – – **to squeal** *here:* protest – – **to come over** change from one side (e.g. of a controversy) to the other; umschwenken, sich eines anderen besinnen – – **draw** attraction – – **to clobber** (sl.) strike violently and repeatedly; hurt badly – – **to jack up** (coll.) boost, increase – – **fella** (coll.) fellow – – **to repeal** annul

Assignments

1. Our extract deals with two topics. What are they?
2. What measures are suggested for overcoming these problems?
3. The barman is sure the suggestions are not practical. What are his arguments? Do you agree with them?
4. Mac suggests pumping money into poor countries, thus making it possible for them to build up industry and earn the money to pay for their food imports. Exactly what has been done by the West in the past thirty years or so. Has it been effective? Why yes, why no? Give examples.
5. Although the story deals with serious questions, it makes the reader laugh now and then. How is that?
6. Make a speech on Robert Graves's life and work. For reference use:
    a) *The Oxford Companion to English Literature,* ed. by M. Drabble, OUP 1985, p. 411 ff.
    b) *Time,* December 23, 1985, p. 40.
    c) *Frankfurter Allgemeine Zeitung,* 26. Juli 1985, S. 21.

Source: *Time,* Dec. 23, 1985

II MAN AND HUMANITIES

INTERVIEW WITH ARNOLD WESKER

Note on the Text

On February 2, 1982, *News of the Week,* a weekly news programme of the Bayrische Fernsehen, presented a special feature: an interview with the playwright Arnold Wesker, "one of the foremost representatives of contemporary English theatre."[1] His career as a playwright began in 1958 when his play *Chicken Soup with Barley* was first produced by the Belgrade Theatre in Coventry. Other plays followed, such as *The Kitchen* (1959), *Roots* (1959), *I'm Talking About Jerusalem* (1960), *Chips with Everything* (1962), *The Four Seasons* (1965) etc. His best-known plays (e.g. *Chicken Soup with Barley* and *Chips with Everything*) deal with the problems of the working class in the twentieth century. "In their efforts to preserve and put into practice their socialist ideals"[2] Wesker's protagonists, however, are doomed to fail.

His plays have earned Wesker a number of awards, among them the Italian Premio Marzotto award in 1964. From 1961 he was artistic director of Centre 42, a cultural movement for popularizing the arts, primarily through trade union support and participation.

(Most of Wesker's plays are available in Penguin Plays).

[1] *News of the Week,* Texte zur wöchentlichen Nachrichtensendung . . ., TR-Verlagsunion, München, Febr. 2, 1982, p. 2.
[2] Arnold Wesker, *The Wesker Trilogy,* Penguin Plays, blurb.

1. **Listening Comprehension**
    (If the video-cassette is not available, the teacher and a student may read out the text of the interview, which you'll find on pages 195–197, to the class.)
    1.1 Study the Annotations (p. 192) and read the questions below. Then watch the interview on the videotape and answer the questions. (Do not make any notes during the first presentation.)
    1.1.1 Why was Wesker touring Germany in 1982?
    1.1.2 Why was his tour a great success?
    1.1.3 What are the main subjects he is talking about?
    1.1.4 What does he say about German theatre directors and actors?
    1.1.5 Why – according to Wesker – does only a minority of people go to the theatre?
    1.1.6 In what context is England mentioned by Arnold Wesker?
    1.1.7 What types of success is he talking about? Which one would he prefer and why?
    1.2 Having done this exercise study the sentence fragments below. Then watch the interview a second time (this time you can make notes) and complete the

sentences (in your own words **or** those of the speakers) so that they make sense and describe the contents of the interview precisely.
a) Germany has a theatre that seems _____
b) The theatre public seems not to be _____
c) But I'm not sure whether Benson and Hedges doesn't interfere as well, _____
d) The playwright, the creator, is dealing with his own material, _____
e) They cannot see the extent to which a director or an actor _____
f) I think they must develop _____
g) What I think I've always believed is _____
h) And the Lord Chamberlain censored plays only _____
i) You get some interference from local authorities, with _____
j) One is to write _____, the other _____, and the third _____

1.3 Watch the video-tape one last time. Then put questions (at least 10) about its contents to your fellow students.

Annotations

(The words marked * should be memorized.)

feature item of particular prominence in a newspaper, broadcast etc. The purpose of a feature is to inform the reader, but it is mainly intended to entertain him – – ***playwright** dramatist – – **to put s.th. on the block** expose s.th. *here:* his personality etc. to the possibility of criticism or even ridicule – – ***distinction** the state of being different – – ***to acknowledge** confirm *here:* recognize – – **perceptive** able to become aware of s.th. – – ***to distort** twist out of shape, falsify – – **to enhance** strengthen, make more powerful or convincing – – **Shakespeare** (1564–1616) England's greatest dramatist – – **Othello** (1604) the tragedy of *The Moore Of Venice* deals with the love and tragic death of Othello and his wife Desdemona – – **Peter Stein** German producer and director – – ***to subsidize** support by granting money – – ***wares** articles offered for sale – – **fringe theatre group** a theatre group on the "fringe" or "edge", a non-conformist theatre group; Experimentiertheater – – **Benson and Hedges** British cigarette firm – – **Ibsen** (1828–1906) Norwegian dramatist – – **Chekhov** (1860–1904) Russian writer and playwright – – **local councillors** Gemeinde-, Stadträte – – ***by and large** im großen und ganzen – – **bugger** sodomite: vulgar or familiar term of abuse – – **McCarthy period** the early 1950's when Senator McCarthy initiated a wave of hysterical anti-communism in the USA. Arthur Miller's play **The Crucible** (1953) – a poetic depiction of the religious intolerance, fanaticism and mass hystery in Salem/ Massachusetts of 1692 – offers an insight into McCarthyism – – **Lord Chamberlain** the official responsible for theatrical censorship in Britain until 1968 – – **National Theatre** one of Britain's major drama companies, situated on the south bank of the Thames in London. The National Theatre is one of some 250 British theatres in professional use which receive government subsidies – – ***director** person responsible for the performance of the actors in a play; Regisseur – – ***producer** person responsible for putting on a play; Intendant

2. **Language**

Let's do another word game together. Read the definitions of the words below. Most of the words are taken from the interview you have just heard. Find the words and insert them into the squares. When you read the circled letters of the solutions in the right order you will obtain the title of one of Wesker's plays. (The title consists of two words.)

Across

1. he is a dramatist or . . .
5. of Great Britain or its inhabitants
6. persons who make s.th. new or original
8. the screen sometimes separating the stage from the auditorium of a theatre
9. drawing, painting, sculpture, music, ballet, theatre are . . .
10. prominent news item designed to entertain the reader
14. television watcher
15. the act of breaking in upon another person's affairs without right or invitation
18. one of the parts, shorter than an act, into which some plays and operas are divided
20. person responsible for putting on a play
22. forehead
23. member of a group of persons appointed, elected or chosen to give advice, make rules, and carry out plans, manage affairs etc., esp. of government

Down

1. able to become aware of s.th.
2. name of a British dramatist
3. buildings or arena for the performance of plays
4. chief man in a play (Pl)
7. strong light on to a particular place or person, e.g. on the stage of a theatre
11. woman who acts on stage
12. trial performance of a play
13. extra performance, e.g. in concert
15. natural tendency to behave in a certain way without reasoning or training
16. make known to people (by printing notices in newspapers, etc)
17. person responsible for the performance of the actors in a play
19. to strengthen

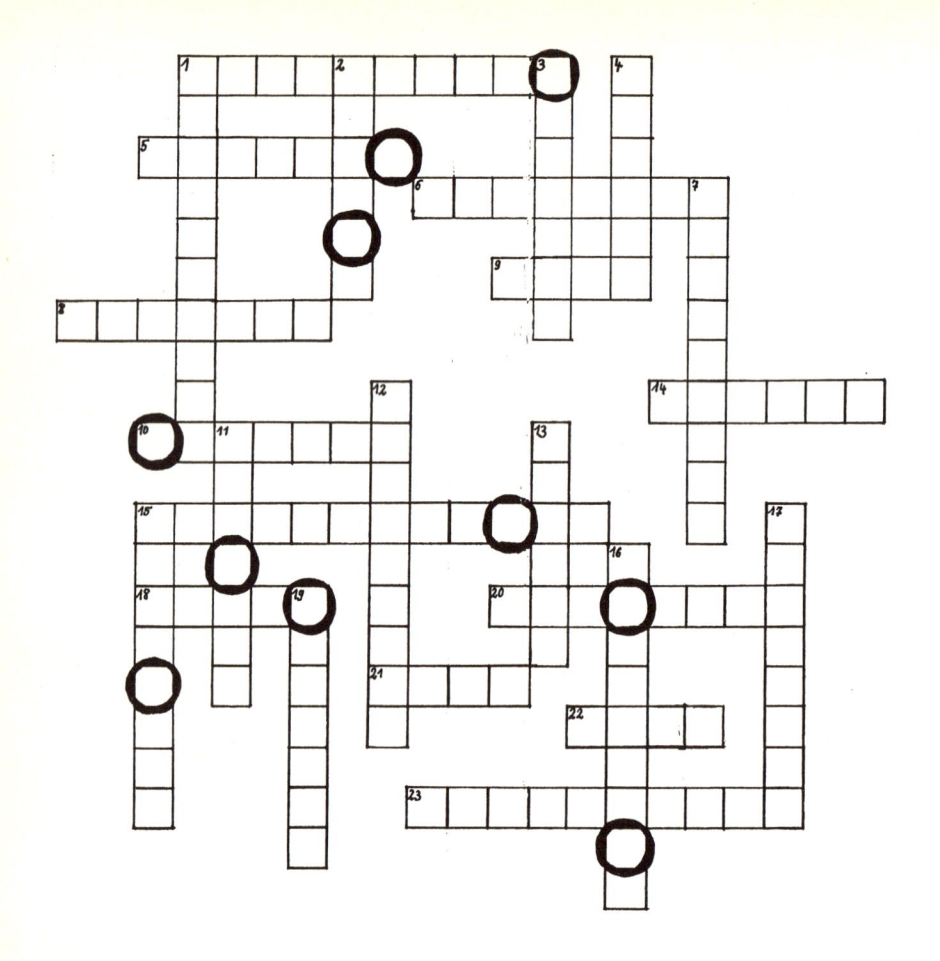

3. **Discussion and Comment**
3.1 Arnold Wesker complains about directors who "distort" plays by over- or reinterpreting them, instead of presenting them in accordance with their authors' intentions, or by changing their actions, plots and problems (e.g. Peter Stein's Othello or Peter Zadek's disrespectful productions of the classics). Do you share Wesker's opinion, or do you think it is the director's right or even job to present his own interpretation of or perspective on a play?
3.2 "Art for the masses". What is *your* opinion of this?
3.3 In Germany, communities (i.e. tax payers) support theatre groups financially.

Does this fact entitle local councillors to interfere in the programme of a theatre group?
3.4 Would you apply Wesker's judgement "... by and large, there is artistic freedom in England" to Germany, too? Do not only consider the theatre!
3.5 "State subsidy versus private subsidy in the field of the arts". Discuss.

4. **Further Studies**
4.1 You work for *The Times*. You have watched the interview on TV. Write a *report* on it.
4.2 Simulate the roles of Wesker and the interviewer. Keep precisely to the contents but use your own words as far as possible.
4.3 Interview "Mr. Wesker", e.g. about his life, his political ideals, his way of writing a play, his view of artistic freedom in Communist states, etc. (To do this assignment use both the facts you have learnt about Mr. Wesker and your *imagination*. Moreover consult *The Oxford Companion To English Literature*.)
4.4 Read one of Wesker's plays. Tell your classmates about its contents. Then give your personal judgement of the message, language and character-drawing of the play.

Introduction: Regular viewers will know that we occasionally break the usual pattern of our programme and present a single *News of the Week* special feature instead of news reports. We have one this week: an interview with the playwright Arnold Wesker, one of the foremost representatives of contemporary English theatre. He
5 is at present on a tour of Germany, sponsored by the British Council, giving lectures and readings from his works – this week in Berlin. Two of his best-known plays are *Chicken Soup with Barley,* and *Chips with Everything.* In an exclusive interview with Christopher Cortis, Mr. Wesker said that the response to his appearances in Germany had been heart-warming. He thought one of the reasons why so many
10 people came to hear him talk was their desire to see a real live playwright.
Film: REPORTER: "Do you imagine that when you say they want to see a real live playwright this could be because there aren't many real live playwrights in Germany?"
WESKER: "I think there are. I mean there seem to be a lot of playwrights; I don't
15 know how effective they are because Germany, like a large section of the continent, has a theatre that seems destroyed by the tyranny of the director, which is a phenomenon of the last ten, fifteen years, but which I hope is passing. I think a lot of Germans are hoping that it's passing also. When you have a tyranny of directors, it does rather destroy the spontaneous creativity of the original playwright."
20 REPORTER: "What about the spontaneous creativity of the actor?"
WESKER: "Actors and directors – and this is why I attract hostility in the theatre – actors and directors are interpreters; and there is a distinction, and a very important distinction, and I think it's very dishonest of people not to acknowledge the

distinction. Now sometimes there are interpreters who are greater interpreters, more talented interpreters, than there are creators; say, you get a director who has more theatrical imagination than a playwright. But the function is different: the playwright, the creator, is dealing with his own raw material, he's putting on the block his own personality, his own heart, his own intellect. The director, the actor, is deeling with someone else's raw material – the writer's raw material and not his or her own. And that's a very important distinction which must be acknowledged."

REPORTER: "Does the theatre audience, in your opinion, does the theatre audience realize instinctively what this difference is? That is to say, if one goes to a performance where a playwright is dominant and one goes to another performance where the director is clearly dominant, does the public realize this?"

WESKER: "No, very few, and the theatre public seems not to be as perceptive as one would like. What they see on the stage, they imagine is – well, in England anyway – is the fault of the writer, and they cannot see the extent to which a director or an actor distorts, or sometimes enhances, what the writer has written, unless it's a classic, and then you don't go to see Shakespeare's *Othello,* you go to see Peter Stein's *Othello*.And that's the kind of nonsense that seems to have been reached."

REPORTER: "As you have just said, the audience itself is not very much aware of this nonsense. Surely that would mean that one cannot produce art for the masses, yet this is, if I'm wrong – correct me if I'm wrong – what you have been doing for 25 years."

WESKER: "No. I mean, first of all, the concept of the masses is a silly journalistic concept – if you'll forgive me. There is a popular audience; that is to say, there exists an audience for whom it is not a habit or tradition to participate in the arts. Now I, as I've grown older, suspect – have come to suspect – that there will only ever be a minority audience for the arts. It's a very special and a very difficult language. I mean, it is a language, it has to be learnt, you have to be responsive to it. What I think I've always believed is that that minority is rather larger than we imagine, and that the responsibility of a civilized society is to work on the assumption that that minority is larger, and so provide for – subsidize – the arts, and provide for them and encourage them."

REPORTER: "Do you feel that the arts should be subsidized by the state, or would Benson and Hedges do just as well?"

WESKER: "Oh God, that's a difficult question, it's always a difficult question. I would prefer it to be done by the state. The problem is that the state – depending in which country you are – then interferes. But I'm not sure whether Benson and Hedges doesn't interfere as well, simply because it wants the most popular work to support, because that's what it's there for – to advertise its wares. Now it's not going to support a fringe theatre group that only reaches two or three hundred people a night. It would much sooner support the National Theatre and a production of Shakespeare or Ibsen or Chekhov. So in that way you have interference. I think they must develop a tradition of state subsidy and state non-interference."

REPORTER: "That would seem to be the ideal situation, but we haven't arrived at it yet, have we?"
WESKER: "No. We're not bad in England. In England there is quite a deal of artistic independence. You get some interference from local authorities, with local
70 councillors who really know nothing about theatre or the arts – they feel they've got to put their word in. But by and large, there is artistic freedom in England."
REPORTER: "And no political interference?"
WESKER: "No political interference. I mean it does happen in extreme cases, but you have a situation where I write my first play and the central character is a
75 Communist heroine, and this is just after the McCarthy period, and there is no problem – and that was when the Lord Chamberlain was existing, still. And the Lord Chamberlain censored plays only for their vulgarity, so you cut out words like 'bugger'. But you could have a Communist heroine, and that seemed to me much more important."
80 REPORTER: "What are your future plans?"
WESKER: "I have none, I mean no long-term future plans. I have long-term future wishes. I would like to have one huge commercial success instead of simply having critical successes, so that I could earn enough money to give me independence for a longer period of time. I think with that independence and peace I would do one
85 of two things, one of three things – perhaps all three: one is to write a long, long novel, the other is to study and perhaps take a degree, and the third is to draw. I would love to draw – nothing too ambitious."
REPORTER: "Well let's hope you realize all those ambitions."
WESKER: "Let's hope." (~ 1180 words)

20 DICTATORSHIP OF THE WILL

Mephisto, based on Klaus Mann's novel about an actor who apparently sold his soul to the Third Reich, opens in London tomorrow. George Perry went to Vienna to talk to the director of the film, Istvan Szabo and its star, Klaus Maria Brandauer.

There was a brief reunion in Vienna last weekend for Istvan Szabo, whose *Mephisto* opens at the Gate Camden tomorrow, and his star, the Austrian actor Klaus Maria Brandauer. The director had arrived from Budapest for a screening of his earlier film, *Confidence,* which is also expected to surface soon at one of the Gates, and
5 which received an Academy Award nomination. It was a highlight of a Hungarian Film Week in Vienna, and he was there to debate with the audience.
His new film, already a huge success where it has been shown in Europe and at the New York Film Festival, is his most ambitious work, a West German-Hungarian production with a cast from East and West. Its starting point is the novel that Klaus
10 Mann, son of Thomas, wrote in 1936, a *roman a clef* about an actor who seemingly

Klaus Maria Brandauer in *Mephisto:* selling his soul to the Nazis

embraces the Nazi regime to further his art, and rises to be the most-influential player and director of the day. The prototype was Gustav Gründgens, who not only married Klaus Mann's sister, but had a homosexual involvement with the novelist. He survived the war with his theatrical reputation more or less intact, and the novel was not published until the mid-1970's more than a decade after his death. Mann himself committed suicide in 1949.

Szabo is anxious that it should not be thought he has merely filmed the novel. It has served as the springboard for his interpretation, and the screenplay that he wrote in collaboration with Peter Dobai goes much further than Mann in examining the dilemma of an artist seeking to discover how he can function within a totalitarian system. Szabo, after all, is able to apply the wisdom of more than 40 years' hindsight. The title of the piece, from Gründgen's most-famous role of Mephisto in Goethe's *Faust,* played in chalk-white make-up and bald skull, is ambiguous, for the central figure, called Hendrick Höfgen by Mann and magnetically portrayed by Klaus Maria Brandauer, is both Mephistopheles and a Faust who has sold his soul to the Third Reich.

"This hero," said Szabo, "is a special character – a man who likes success, but not only likes it, must have it, lives for it. That is why he is always on the offensive. Every second he must fight for success. But he is not a chameleon, because his sense of integrity is not changing on the surface. He is like a lover or a woman who thinks that she can keep her integrity even when she is seduced. His talent is not enough!"

Szabo, now 43, a graduate of the Budapest Academy of Film and Theatre Art 20 years ago, selected Brandauer for the role on the strength of his prominence in the Austrian theatre, where he is at the top of his profession both as an actor and director. There was an immediate rapport between the two men, and they held long dialogues analyzing and establishing the character of Höfgen before the camera turned.

Brandauer shows him developing from neophyte, a fresh newcomer bitten by the bug, into an artist who quite believably can hold a critical, sophisticated audience entranced with his performance. The acting of the business of acting itself, the depiction of a style developing from raw inexperience into superior accomplishment, is something that Brandauer does very well. But he shows that the man offstage is a dazzling charmer, a transparent opportunist, a social climber, a user of people, particularly women, to assist his struggle to the top. He is a man possessed, not by a political belief in fascism, but a frenzied need to serve his art.

He has the desire to be loved, and the vulnerability of one who cannot love in return. "He is always striving for the light," says Szabo. "Watch how he edges out of the shadow into the spotlight. It is important for him to have more and more light."

There is a significant sequence in *Mephisto* when, as the Nazis gain power, Höfgen has the chance to leave Germany, just as many fellow artists remove themselves to France, England, the United States. But he cannot bring himself to do so, because it is the German language, not a political system, that is the mainspring of his work.

David Robinson, *The Times* film critic, has advanced the unpopular but accurate proposition that no artist in German films and theatre in the 1930's left the country simply out of protest at the regime. The many who went into exile were forced, usually on racial grounds, to leave, or face the inevitability of never being allowed to work at their calling again.

But those who were not considered undesirable made their compromises of varying degrees and went on working. Robinson actually appears in *Mephisto,* in a role cast with a certain regard for type, as *The Times* drama critic of the 1930s, and is first seen congratulating Höfgen for his gifted performance, then later in Paris actually administering a physical rebuke to him for the betrayal of his artistic ideals. (Szabo agreed that for an Englishman to slap a famous German's face in a Paris café was perhaps unusual, but for a *Times* critic to display such non-objectivity, particularly considering the historical stance of the newspaper in the age of appeasement, was far-fetched, but certainly effective in dramatic terms). Szabo is fond of casting non-professional faces if he feels that they are right, and clearly the tentacles of Equity cannot reach as far as Budapest.

"You must please remember that I am Brandauer, not Höfgen", said Brandauer, but as he said it, he used the same smiling expression and glinting eyes that he uses in the film when turning on the charm. Unlike the calm, unobtrusive Szabo, Brandauer is a demonstrative talker, given to gestures, arm-patting, sudden changes of voice timbre, and will occasionally lump to his feet and stride across the room to emphasise a point.

He admits that playing Höfgen made a deep imprint on his actor's psyche. "I know what Höfgen means about working outside the German language. I would like to do it, play in English, but at present I would be unsure. It is necessary for me to act in my own language. I have worked in France. Then I learnt the lines like a parrot. Between takes someone came up to me and asked me some intricate question in French, having just heard me being word-perfect. All I could do was mutter: "Pardonnez-moi, mais je suis malade . . ." and rush for the toilet.

"But it is not often that an actor gets such a part as Höfgen. It was a tremendous role. The film was not made in consecutive sequences, so it was necessary to keep a very firm control on the character and where he stood in relation to that part of the story. Istvan and I always responded very well and we would really like to work again together. I am usually very busy, but he likes to take plenty of time between his projects, reading books, going to exhibitions. For that I envy him."

Despite its epic length of 160 minutes, *Mephisto* is by no means an extravagant film. Lajos Koltai has photographed Budapest ingeniously to make it an acceptable surrogate for Hamburg, Berlin and even Paris, and Szabo can by the skilful arranging of signs and props evoke convincing settings. Particularly effective is a gala ball in a marbled hall festooned with swastikas – the glamorous facade of the Nazi horror encapsulated in a scene of swirling dancers in evening dress celebrating the General, the butcher, and providing Höfgen with unease, the realization that he has come to serve evil in spite of his intention to keep his art aloof from the machinations of the state.

"We saw many films, said Szabo," and especially Leni Riefenstahl's *Triumph of the Will.* That showed very clearly how well the Nazi period was stage-managed.

100 I wanted to show how it was possible for people to be captivated, and how this man could defer to such things in order to gain acceptance, for only in acceptance can he find security.
"Yes, you could say that this is a film about a man who has his price, and what a price is". (~ 1420 words)
Slightly abbreviated from *The Times,* Nov. 4, 1981

Annotations
(The words marked * should be memorized.)

Klaus Mann (1906–1949) second child of Thomas Mann. He started to write short stories and articles in 1924. One year later a volume of short stories and his first novel *Der fromme Tanz* were published. Together with his sister Erika, Pamela Wedekind and Gustav Gründgens he founded a theatre group which engaged both in experimental theatre and literary cabaret. In 1929, Klaus and his sister set off for a trip around the world, which he described in his book *Rundherum* (1931). Klaus Mann left Germany in 1933 and lived in Amsterdam until 1936. There he edited *Die Sammlung,* a periodical for German emigrants. Moving to the United States in 1936 he lived in Princeton, New Jersey, and in New York City. During the war he served as a soldier in the American army. His best-known book is *Mephisto.* Some of his other works are: *Anja und Esther* (drama, 1925), *Alexander* (novel, 1929), *Auf der Suche nach einem Weg* (essay, 1931), *Kind dieser Zeit* (autobiography, 1932), and *Vulkan* (novel, 1939).
to screen *here:* show a film – – **highlight** *here:* most prominent part – – *****to surface** emerge, appear – – **roman à clef** [roˈmãaˈkle] a novel in which real persons or actual events figure under disguise – – **hindsight** perception of an event after its occurrence – – *****ambiguous** of doubtful meaning, uncertain – – *****to seduce** tempt into crime or sin – – **rapport** [ræˈpɔ] sympathy, close relationship – – **neophyte** [ˈniːoufait] person who has newly been converted to some belief – – **to be/get bitten by the bug** become very interested in something – – *****sophisticated** having learnt the ways of the world and having lost natural simplicity; refined – – **to entrance** [inˈtrɑːns] overcome, carry away as in a dream, with pleasure – – **to dazzle** make s.b. unable to see clearly or act normally because of too much light, brilliance, splendour etc. – – *****spotlight** strong light directed on to a particular place or person, originally on the stage of a theatre – – **to edge** move slowly forward – – **mainspring** *here:* driving force or motive – – **proposition** statement, assertion – – *****calling** occupation, profession or trade – – **to administer a physical rebuke to s.b.** jem. handgreiflich die Meinung sagen – – **betrayal** act of being disloyal to – – **stance** *here:* intellectual attitude – – **appeasement** calming, e.g. by making concessions to potential enemies – – **to cast** give (an actor) a part in a play – – **Equity** British actors' trade union – – **to glint** gleam brightly – – **unobtrusive** discreet, not easily noticeable – – **intricate** complicated, difficult to follow or understand – – *****to mutter** say s.th. in a low voice not meant to be heard – – **prop** (coll.) abbr. of stage property – – *****setting** the environment indoors or out including all the physical surroundings (as properties, furniture, buildings) within which a scene of a play or motion picture is enacted – – **marbled** decorated with marble – – **to festoon with** decorate with – – **swastika** kind of cross emblematic of Naziism – – **to swirl** move at varying speeds, with twists and turns; wirbeln – – **to defer** [diˈfɜ(r)] give way, yield to

Assignments

1. Collect all the words from the *Wesker interview* pp. 195–197 and the text *Dictatorship of the Will* which come under the superordinates *theatre, film* and *stageplay*. Look up their meanings in a dictionary and use 10 of them in questions on the *contents* of *Dictatorship of the Will*.
2. Read the text above carefully and write a précis of lines 7–49. (His new film . . . – . . . more light.)
3. Write a research paper entitled: "The Artist in the Totalitarian System". Another student must give an abstract of it (only notes are allowed) to the class and a third one has to organise a discussion on the topic. For this paper: 1. Do not only refer to the Nazi regime. 2. Besides Klaus Mann's *Mephisto*[1] use further reading material (magazines, newspapers, and books[2] in English and German which you may find in your school library, the nearest "Amerikahaus" or university library).

[1] A German edition of *Mephisto* is published by rororo, nr 4821; an English one by Penguin, nr ISBN 014 00.6578 4.
[2] For instance: Aleksandr Solzhenitsyn's *The Gulag Archipelago*

21 THE COUNTRY OF THE KIND

Note on the Text

Damon Knight (b. 1922) began his career, like so many others, in the sf fandom. He wrote many short stories and novels, but is generally acknowledged to be the first outstanding sf critic; he is also an editor of anthologies.
"The Country of the Kind" (1955) depicts a world free from aggression, but it has had to pay a high price for its peace. Title and story are a pun on H. G. Wells' short story "The Country of the Blind".

(The story has been taken from: B. Aldiss, ed., *The Penguin Science Fiction Omnibus,* Penguin Books, Harmondsworth, Middlesex, England, [7]1981, p. 497 ff)

I followed their voices . . . One couple, the dark-haired pair, was still in sight farther down the path, heads bobbing along. The other couple had disappeared.
I found the handle in the grass without any trouble. The mechanism responded, and an oblong section of turf rose up. It was the stair I had, not the elevator, but that
5 was all right. I ran down the steps and into the first door I saw, and was in the top-floor lounge, an oval room lit with diffused simulated sunlight from above. The furniture was all comfortably bloated, sprawling and ugly; the carpet was deep, and there was a fresh flower scent in the air.

The blonde was over at the near end with her back to me, studying the autochef
keyboard. She was half out of her playsuit. She pushed it the rest of the way down
and stepped out of it, then turned and saw me.
She was surprised again; she hadn't thought I might follow her down.
I got up close before it occurred to her to move; then it was too late. . . .
She trembled . . . On impulse, I leaned over and dialled the autochef to hot cheese
sauce. I cut the safety out of circuit and put the quantity dial all the way up. I dialied
soup tureen and then *punch bowl*.
The stuff began to come out in about a minute, steaming hot. I took the tureens and
splashed them up and down the wall on either side of her. Then, when the first punch
bowl came out, I used the empty bowls as scoops. I clotted the carpet with the stuff;
I made streamers of it all along the walls, and dumped puddles into what furniture
I could reach. Where it cooled it would harden, and where it hardened it would cling.
I wanted to splash it across her body, but it would've hurt, and we couldn't have
that. The punch bowls of hot sauce were still coming out of the autochef, crowding
each other around the vent. I punched *cancel,* and then *port wine* . . .
A voice said behind me:
'Watch out for cold wine.'
My arm twitched and a little stream of the wine splashed across her thighs. She
was ready for it; her eyes had opened at the voice, and she barely jumped.
I whirled around, fighting mad. The man was standing there where he had come
out of the stair-well. He was thinner in the face than most, bronzed, wide-chested,
with alert blue eyes. If it hadn't been for him, I knew it would have worked – the blonde
would have mistaken the cold splash for a hot one.
I could hear the scream in my mind, and I wanted it.
I took a step towards him, and my foot slipped. I went down clumsily, wrenching
one knee. I got up shaking and tight all over. I wasn't in control of myself. I screamed,
'You – you –'. I turned and got one of the punch bowls and lifted it in both hands,
heedless of how the hot sauce was slopping over on to my wrists, and I had it almost
in the air towards him when the sickness took me – that damned buzzing in my head,
louder, louder, drowning everything out.
When I came to, they were both gone . . .
I emptied the closets and bureau drawers on to the floor, dragged the whole mess
into one of the bathrooms and stuffed the tub with it, then turned on the water . . .
While I slept, water poured down the open stair-well and filled the third level . . .
The second and first levels were bigger and would take longer to fill, but they'd fill.
Rugs, furnishings, clothing, all the things in the house would be waterlogged and
ruined. Probably the weight of so much water would shift the house, rupture water
pipes and other fluid intakes. It would take a repair crew more than a day just to
clean up the mess. The house itself was done for, not repairable. The blonde and
the thin man would never live in it again.

50 Serve them right.

The dulls could build another house; they built like beavers. There was only one of me in the world.

The earliest memory I have is of some woman, probably the crèchemother, staring at me with an expression of shock and horror. Just that. I've tried to remember what happened directly before or after, but I can't. Before, there's nothing but the dark formless shaft of no-memory that runs back to birth. Afterwards, the big calm.

From my fifth year, it must have been, to my fifteenth, everything I can remember floats in a pleasant dim sea. Nothing was terribly important. I was languid and soft; I drifted. Waking merged into sleep . . .

Something else in me, that had been suppressed and forgotten, rose up with my first blow struck in anger. The sculpture began years afterwards, as an accident; but in that moment I was free, and I was an artist.

One winter, in the A.C. Archives in Denver, I found a storeroom full of old printed books. I spent months there, reading them, because until then I'd thought I had invented sculpture and drawing. The thing I chiefly wanted to know was, why had it stopped? There was no answer in so many words in any of the books. But reading the histories of those times before the Interregnum, I found one thing that might explain it. Whenever there was a long period of peace and plenty anywhere in the ancient world, art grew poor: decoration, genre painting, imitations of imitations. And as for the great artists, they all belonged to violent periods – Praxiteles, da Vinci, Rembrandt van Rijn, Renoir, Picasso . . .

It had been bred out of the race, evidently. I don't suppose the genetic planners wanted to get rid of it, but they would have shed almost anything to make a homogeneous, rational, sane, and healthy world.

So there was only one man to carve the portrait of the Age of Reason. All right; I would have been content, only . . .

In a pamphlet for the information of the public the hero reads about himself:

. . . sedation until his fifteenth year, when for sexual reasons it became no longer practicable. While the advisers and medical staff hesitated, he killed a girl of the group by violence.

And farther down:

The solution finally adopted was threefold.

1. *A Sanction* – the only sanction possible to our humane, permissive society. Excommunication: not to speak to him, touch him willingly, or acknowledge his existence.

2. *A precaution.* Taking advantage of a mild predisposition to epilepsy, a variant of the so-called Kusko analogue technique was employed, to prevent by an epileptic seizure any future act of violence.

3. *A warning.* A careful alteration of his body chemistry was effected to make his exhaled and exuded wastes emit a strongly pungent and offensive odour. In mercy, he himself was rendered unable to detect this smell.

Fortunately, the genetic and environmental accidents which combined to produce this atavism have been fully explained and can never again . . .

95 I knew where there was a big cache of cherry wood, in goodsized blocks, in a forgotten warehouse up north at a place called Kootenay. I could have carried some around with me – enough for years – but what for, when the world belonged to me? It didn't take me long. Down in the workshop section, of all places, I found some antiques – tables and benches, all with wooden tops. While the dulls collected down at the other end of the room, pretending not to notice, I sawed off a good ablong
100 chunk of the smallest bench, and made a base for it out of another.

As long as I was there, it was a good place to work, and I could eat and sleep upstairs, so I stayed.

I knew what I wanted to do. It was going to be a man, sitting with his legs crossed and his forearms resting down along his calves. His head was going to be tilted back,
105 and his eyes closed, as if he were turning his face up to the sun.

In three days it was finished. The trunk and limbs had a shape that was not man and not wood, but something in between: something that hadn't existed before I made it.

Beauty. That was the old word . . .

110 My carvings were all over the world, wherever I had wandered. There was one in Congo City, carved of ebony, dusty-black; one in Cyprus, of bone; one in New Bombay, of shell; one in Changteh, of jade.

They were like signs printed in red and green, in a colour-blind world. Only the one I was looking for would even pick one of them up, and read the message I knew
115 by heart.

TO YOU WHO CAN SEE, the first sentence said. I OFFER YOU A WORLD . . . YOU CAN SHARE THE WORLD WITH ME. THEY CAN'T STOP YOU. STRIKE NOW – PICK UP A SHARP THING AND STAB, OR A HEAVY THING AND CRUSH. THAT'S ALL. THAT WILL MAKE YOU FREE. ANYONE CAN DO IT. (~ 1500 words)

Annotations

(The Words marked * should be memorized.)

to bob move up and down – – **oblong** having four straight sides and angles at 90°, longer than it is wide (rechteckig) – – **turf** soil-surface with grass growing thickly in it – – **bloat, sprawling** the furniture was bloated, sprawling and ugly: mit häßlichen unförmigen Möbeln überladen – – **tureen** deep dish with a lid, from which soup is served at table – – **scoop** long-handled ladle-shaped tool for serving liquid – – **clot** *here:* verkleben – – **vent** hole serving as an inlet or outlet for air – – **to twitch** make a sudden spasmodic movement – – *****thigh** [θai] part of the human leg between the knee and the hip – – **to wrench** [rentʃ] twist or pull violently – – *****heedless** not paying attention to – – **slop** spill – – **crèche** nursery where babies are looked after while their mothers are at work – – **to merge into** to blend with – – **interregnum** period during which a State has no normal or legitimate ruler – – **genre painting** portrayal of scenes, etc. from ordinary life – – **to exhale** breathe out, give off gas – – **to exude** come or pass out slowly, ooze out – – **pungent** sharp, biting (of smells, tastes, remarks) – – **atavism** reappearance in a person of a quality that has not shown itself for several or many generations – – **cache** [kæʃ] hidden store – – **chunk** thick solid piece or lump – – ***calf** back of the human leg between the knee and the ankle – – **to tilt** (kippen, neigen) – – to incline at an angle

WORKSHEET

1. **Language**
1.1 Which of the following phrasal verbs could be substituted for a verb in the below sentences?
Phrasal verbs: to do for, to do without, to get away with, to get over, to give away, to let down, to make up for, to put up with, to show up, to take after, to take for, to be up to
Sentences:
   a) I won't bear your behaviour any longer.
   b) Was Mary present at your party?
   c) You didn't reveal my secrets, did you?
   d) This year we'll have to manage without a wage increase.
   e) It's our duty to help them.
   f) You'll get punished if you try to cheat in the examination.
   g) It's not easy for him to recover from the shock of losing his wife.
   h) His patience compensated for his lack of skill.
   i) Unfortunately, my son doesn't resemble me in any way!
   k) I'm sorry I considered you (to be) incompetent.
   l) Can I rely on you helping me, or will you disappoint me?
   m) The house was destroyed (from the text!)

1.2 Can you distinguish between these pairs of confusibles? award – reward, accident – incident, assure – insure, affect – effect, economic – economical, elder – older, historic – historical, human – humane, motif – motive, personal – personel, moral – morale.

1.3 **It Pays to Enrich Your Word Power**

It's all too easy to be confused by a word that looks or sounds like another, as you may find with the pairs below. Tick the word or phrase you believe is *nearest in meaning* to the key word. (Your English-English dictionary will help you. Only look up the answers A–D, of course!)

(1) **flounder** – A: to struggle awkwardly. B: come apart. C: hammer flat. D: excite or stir up.

(2) **founder** – A: to sink. B: waver. C: seek out. D: fold.

(3) **notable** – A: intelligent. B: dubious. C: worthy of notice. D: disgraceful.

(4) **notorious** – having A: a bad reputation. B: honour and acclaim. C: generosity. D: brilliance.
(5) **exalt** – A: to admit. B: share. C: praise highly. D: exaggerate.
(6) **exult** – A: to love or admire. B: rejoice greatly. C: go out. D: sing loudly.
(7) **allusion** – A: goal. B: humiliation. C: expectation. D: indirect reference.
(8) **illusion** – A: misconception or delusion. B: high ideal. C: impressionistic drawing. D: clarification.
(9) **rebuff** – A: to dispute. B: polish. C: snub. D: estimate.
(10) **refute** – A: to object to. B: defy. C: reject. D: disprove.
(11) **immunity** – A: isolation. B: protection from a disease. C: permanence. D: mute.
(12) **impunity** – A: selfconfidence. B: right or privilege. C: casual calmness. D: exemption from undesirable consequences.
(13) **diagnosis** – A: identification of an illness. B: prophecy. C: plan. D: likeness.
(14) **prognosis** – A: introductory statement. B: plan or plot. C: forecast or prediction. D: type of pause.
(15) **adverse** – A: not eager. B: to the point. C: upside-down. D: opposite.
(16) **averse** – A: anxious. B: unwilling. C: happy. D: unable.
(17) **reconcile** – A: to bring into harmony. B: add up. C: give in to demands. D: shrink from.
(18) **conciliate** – A: to combine. B: win over. C: confirm. D: advise.
(19) **sententious** – A: pleasing to the senses. B: ready to argue. C: pompous and moralizing. D: swayed by emotions.
(20) **tendentious** – A: biased. B: righteous. C: long. D: boring.

(taken from: *Reader's Digest*)
(Ratings:
20–19 correct: excellent
18–16 correct: good
15–14 correct: fair)

2. Text Analysis
2.1 The text consists of three different parts. Find them! Find captions for them! Find the inner relation between the three parts!

2.2 List and contrast all the sentences from the text that characterise the hero and the society he lives in.

3. Discussion and Comment
3.1 Write an account of the outsider in our story and his world, using the material gathered above!

3.2 Put into words the idea underlying D. Knight's story.

3.3 Discuss the following statement:
"In Italy for 30 years under the Borgias, they had warfare, terror, murder, bloodshed – but they produced Michelangelo, Leonardo da Vinci and the Renaissance. In Switzerland, they have brotherly love, 500 years of democracy and peace, and what did that produce? The cuckoo clock."
– Orson Welles' dialogue for his character Harry Lime in the 1949 film 'The Third Man'.

From: TIME, March 30, 1981

4. For Further Study

4.1 Research an artist mentioned in the text, a famous work of art of his and the time he lived in, and construct a short report for your fellow-students.

4.2 Read H. G. Wells' short story *The Country of the Blind,* give your fellow-students a short précis of it, and compare it with *The Country of the Kind.*

22 THE STATE OF THE LANGUAGE

Introducing the Topic

The Queen and Arthur Scargill (Leader of the National Union of Mineworkers): RP versus The North.

Illustration: The Guardian

1. Read aloud what the Queen and Mr Scargill are saying to each other.
2. Compare the Queen's *received pronunciation* with Mr Scargill's *northern modified standard.* What main differences can you discover?
3. In your English lessons you have learned an English which is much closer to the Queen's English than to Mr Scargill's. Do you know why?
4. Nowadays you can often hear American English spoken in Germany. If you compare BE (RP) with AE, what differences exist? Give examples!

Note on the Text

The following text is taken from Philip Howard, *The State of the Language,* English Observed, Hamish Hamilton, London 1984.
In our extract Mr Howard, Literary Editor of *The Times,* takes a sober view of the changes that are happening in the English language of today in various categories, such as vocabulary, pronunciation, spelling, and grammar.

Our perception of the English language and how it works has changed radically in the present generation. In the High Victorian world the pristine philologists saw the language in much the same way as they saw Victorian society: as a pyramid. At the top was the Queen's English (not, as it happens, spoken very well by Her
5 Majesty, who retained a faint German accent all her life; she wrote it with naive charm and enthusiasm). The Queen's English was the sort spoken in an Oxford accent by the educated classes in the south-east of England, taught at the great public schools and the old universities, and printed in *The Times* and the books from the main London publishing houses. Lower down the pyramid were lesser kinds of
10 English: some of them perfectly respectable members of the House of Lords of language, such as the dialects and grammars of Scottish and American English; others of them disreputable commoners, unspeakable by the civilized, such as Cockney or Gorbals.

We have come to recognize that such a rigid class system is as silly in language
15 as it is in society. There is not one correct sort of English, and dozens of lesser breeds of English all more or less conforming to the ideal, and having more value the closer they came to the Queen's English, and less value the farther they diverged from it. English is not a pyramid, but a great city with many suburbs and city centres serving many purposes. The same sort of English, whether the Queen's or anybody
20 else's, is not appropriate to all occasions or uses. There is not one standard English, but many overlapping kinds of English with different functions and contexts.

For example we use a quite different kind of English when we are writing a leader in *The Times* from the kind we use when chatting to strangers in the public bar of a pub. If we do not make this distinction, either the editor will receive a great many
25 outraged letters; or we shall be left talking to ourselves in the centre of a circle of uneasy mutters. Students of linguistics have recently named these different varieties of English *registers*.

The two major registers, which take in most of the lesser registers, are *written* and *spoken* English. Until recently spoken English was the poor relation. The Queen's
30 English at the top of the pyramid was literary standard English, the grammar and spelling of which were taught at schools and universities across the land. English education was largely carried on by writing and reading.

The emphasis has recently swung from written to spoken English. Schools teach by discussion as well as written tests and essays. Examinations are conducted by
35 multiple-choice questions, in which candidates tick the answer they deem correct,

as well as writing answers in prose. The telephone, radio, television, and other new technologies fill the world with the spoken word. Members of Parliament make their speeches *ex tempore* from a few notes, rather than writing them out in stately periods, and learning them by heart. Business of all sorts is conducted by telephone instead of letter. Among the most popular programmes on the radio are phone-ins, in which any member of the public can join in public chat with the presenter.

As usual, when a new truth or an old register has been discovered, the pendulum has swung too far away from the written to the spoken word. Students graduate from universities incompetent to write a simple sentence in English, though their knowledge of other matters and their fluency with the spoken word make their predecessors from previous generations sound inarticulate pedants.

History is taught by worksheets, so that children know assorted information about life on a medieval estate, but not how to write it down in a continuous narrative. Extreme proponents of spoken rather than written English argue that all previous dictionaries and similar reference books are flawed, because they have ignored the submerged nine-tenths of language, the spoken word.

The recognition of spoken English as a separate predominant register, including its oral grammars, vocabularies, and dialects, is the most obvious change that has happened to English in the recent revolution. The promotion of the spoken word at the expense of the written in education and commerce, in politics and the media, is already having profound effects on the language. A spoken language is, inevitably, less formal and rule-bound than a written one. Very few people have the short-term memory and the fluency to construct elaborate periods in speech. The cure for supposing that they can do so is to read the transcript of any spontaneous conversation or broadcast, even between literati, intellectuals, or Professors of Linguistics. It will be full of catachresis and solecism, of errors of number and case, of grammatical sins of omission and commission. The most frequent words will be the two most popular words in the English language, the ones that never get recorded in the dictionaries: *um* and *er*. There will be a plethora of clichés, vogue words, and cotton-wool pleonasms such as 'at this moment in time', telephrases invented to fill time and avoid the mortal sin of broadcasting: silence for thought. Even as you speak, and the words fly away from you into the darkness, you can tell that they are not expressing your meaning exactly. With the written language you can read what you have written, see that it is not quite right, say, 'damn!', rip the paper out of the roller of the typewriter, and start again. Writing English is constructing dovetail joints on the carpenter's bench. Speaking English is fastening two planks together with a nail in a hurry.

The tendency today is towards the quick spoken communication rather than the carefully carpentered job. Accordingly, sentences are becoming shorter, even in writing. The great rolling periods of Gibbon and the other classic masters of literary English seem magnificent, but strange, memorials of a vanished age. The remaining case endings of pronouns, and other grammatical inflexions created for a written language, are melting like snow in the Sahara. Spelling is no longer rated as an almost moral virtue; and punctuation is being simplified and coarsened to a series of dashes, to indicate pauses for breath in the spoken language. We are uninhibited about using in writing slang, dialect, jargon, and taboo words that were recently banned as disreputable from the literary register, when it was considered the top room in the pyramid. English is becoming looser, quicker, and less precise, as we forget to use the millions of fine and distinct tools in the old literary carpenter's box.

If you want to make our flesh creep, as many do, you can predict that this trend will continue, as with Latin after the Fall of Rome, until English becomes a series of loosely connected pidgins, patois, and grunts. There has been a recent vogue in fiction for constructing such decadent and primitive oral versions of English. William Golding did it in *The Inheritors,* that lament for Neanderthal man that is also, as usual, about the darkness in the heart of homo sapiens, and, in this book, about the difficulties of communicating by non-verbal processes. Russell Hoban did it in *Riddley Walker,* that apocalyptic vision of life after the Bomb. Centralized industrial civilization has been destroyed. The lost past is contained in a kind of sacred book called *The Eusa Story,* of which the first chapter is:

'Wen Mr Clevver wuz Big Man uv Inland they had evere thing clevver. They had boats in the ayr & picters on the win & evere thing lyk that. Eusa wuz a noing man vere quik he cud tern his han to enne thing. He wuz werkin for Mr Clevver wen thayr cum enemes aul roun & maykin Warr. Eusa sed tu Mr Clevver, now wewl nead masheans uv Warr. Wewl nead boats that go on the water & boats that go in the ayr as wel & wewl nead Berstin Fyr.'

Finally they make use of, 'the Littl Shynyn Man the Addom he runs in the wud.'

Riddley Walker is fiction. Its oral English displays anomalies and improbabilities in the way that languages develop, even after a great catastrophe. But it exemplifies powerfully and persuasively many of the ways that English is growing, carried to their extremes . . .

Within the great register of spoken English, let us examine how the upper register called the Queen's English, or standard English, or received pronunciation, is doing. It may be instructive about the way that pronunciation is going generally.

It is a comparatively recent notion that there is one standard English pronunciation used by the educated classes, and that everything else is a regional or lower class dialect in a different register.

In the nineteenth century received pronunciation became the standard register for the upper and upwardly mobile middle classes. You can see it happening in the nicely differentiated idiom and accent of the characters in the novels of that mistress of the English class system, Jane Austen. But, even at the peak of the Victorian age, received pronunciation was never standard for the upper classes over the whole country.

There has always been controversy about the merits of received pronunciation, even at the time when it was rising to the top of the pyramid. Henry Sweet, the founder of modern phonetics, called it Standard English, and described it as, 'A class dialect rather than any local dialect – the language of the educated all over Britain.'

Outsiders as well as natives differ vehemently about the received pronunciation of the Queen's English. As long ago as 1931 Frank Vizetelly, the English-born American lexicographer, philologist, und popular authority in sanctioning American colloquialisms, was moved to describe it as, 'A debased, effete, and inaudible form of speech.'

In a living language, everything flows and nothing stays still. Even in our life-times upper class English pronunciation has shifted audibly. You can still hear its echoes in old ladies of the debutante class who say *gel* for girl, *otel* for *hotel,* and pronounce *garage* as in French, with the accent on the second syllable. You can meet it in bucolic old country gents who talk about *huntin', shootin',* and *fishin'.* I have been told that the really grand way to pronounce the last two is with sh sounded as *s, sootin'* and *fissin'.* But I have yet to come across anyone who speaks that way, alas.

You can point to many influences that have helped to reduce the wilder excesses of the English, silly-ass class accent, from the Beatles and the sixties generation to great popularizing newspapers such as *The Daily Mirror* and *The Sunday Times.* The Edwardian upper classes wanted to demonstrate their superiority for all to see, in the way they spoke as well as in the clothes they wore. Two world wars, the century of the common man, mass education, television, and a general broadening of horizons have created a revulsion against that most unfashionable of deadly sins: élitism. As at the end of the Middle Ages the feudal structures broke up, and new classes emerged to power, and wealth, and the Queen's English; so we are going through a period when it is considered bad form to flaunt one's class or one's accent.

In the holidays public school boys and girls take pains to sound and look no different from their contemporaries in comprehensive schools, by wearing the same hair styles, tight jeans, and unbuttoned accent. Children from middle class homes who go to state schools develop two accents, a posh one for home so as not to upset the parents, and a regional vernacular for school, so as not to upset their school-fellows and earn the deadly reputation of snootiness . . .

One of the most remarkable changes in this generation has been the rapid increase in jargon. Most of the increase comes from the jargons or technical vocabularies of new sciences and technologies. Man is in a period of discovery of the world (and of space) as dramatic as the fifteenth and sixteenth centuries, or the first Industrial Revolution. He has to create new words to describe his discoveries. A consequence is that lexicographers of New English, such as Oxford, Webster, and Banhart, can produce a thick volume of new words a year, and still not keep up with the spate. Another new influence that has caused the sudden rapid growth of the English vocabulary since the Second World War is the emergence of English as the world language. The *OED* is a British English dictionary, but it now has to include New English from the entire English-speaking world, i.e. the entire world, including regions that did not disturb the labours of Sir James Murray. Each successive volume of the *Supplement* has to make room for more words from Australia, Canada, Ireland, India, and so on.

The emergence of English as the world language is inevitably, and regrettably, simplifying the complexities of English grammar. As Britons themselves, and foreigners from all round the world, are learning English as a second language, the tendency to make it easier to learn is irresistible. The subjunctive mood is dying: even native speakers and writers are uneasy with it. The few surviving case distinctions left over from Old English, like fossils from a vanished world, are going. Even native speakers and writers get into a muddle with their *I's* and *me's*. The feminist tendency is turning *their* into a singular, in order to avoid assuming masculine supremacy by saying *his*.

The simplification of grammar, as part of the long progress of English from an inflected to an uninflected language, is regrettable in so far as it reduces the variety of distinctions we can make, and ways in which we can say things. The disappearance of the subjunctive is a serious loss. But a complex grammar is not a virtue *per se*. Some of the Amerindian languages have a grammar of a complexity that makes English look a childish language. Many of the old languages, including English itself, had, in addition to singular and plural, a dual number in order to refer to not one or many, but two objects or people. The dual number died because it served no very useful purpose. English is becoming the world language partly because its grammar is so simple and adaptable, We need not shed too bitter tears even for the disappearance of the subjunctive. If English speakers and writers need to make the distinctions for which the subjunctive was invented, either the subjunctive will not die, or they will devise some new way of making the distinctions.

In its many registers and parts, English is going through a period of rapid growth and change. It has gone through such periods before, but previous changes have seldom been as rapid or as violent as those taking place towards the end of the twentieth century, as English becomes the world language. If you want to take a gloomy view of what is happening, you can imagine English breaking up into a family of mutually incomprehensible dialects and registers, in the way that the Macedonian world empire broke up after the death of Alexander. That would be a Doomsday view; and a stupid one. There is an English revolution going on. But the analogy is with the prodigious growth of the Industrial Revolution rather than the divisive revolution of the Civil Wars. The forces for cohesion and growth in the world language are stronger than the fissiparous forces. The centrifugal forces pulling English apart are strong: the dominance of the spoken word; the proliferation of national dialects of English; the new technologies of communication that simplify and distort; the obfuscations of politicians, the euphemisms, clichés, and vogue words of communicators; the ceaseless chatter of English that can be heard coming from miles away as Earth rolls through space.

However the centripetal forces making English the world language are stronger: the media of mass communication that spread the word instantaneously around the global village; pop songs; mass tourism, in which the package holiday to foreign parts is a fundamental annual right; above all the printing press, which still flies the standard even if it is no longer at the top of the pyramid.

Annotation

(The words marked * should be memorized.)

***perception** (formal) process by which we become aware of something (through the senses of sight, hearing, etc.) – – **pristine** [pristin] (formal) primitive; of early times – – ***faint** (of things perceived through the senses) weak; indistinct; not clear – – **Cockney** dialect spoken by some working-class Londoners – – **Gorbals** dialect in working-class area of Glasgow – – **to diverge (from)** get farther apart from a point or from each other as two forces progress; abweichen – – ***leader** here: main article in a newspaper – – ***mutter** utterance spoken in a low voice not meant to be heard – – **to carry on** conduct – – **stately** impressive; dignified – – ***pedant** ['pedənt] person who lays too much stress on book-learning, technical knowledge, rules and adherence to rules – – **assorted** of various sorts; mixed; zusammengestellt, aufgelistet – – ***medieval** of the Middle Ages – – **flawed** weakened – – **submerged** here: suppressed – – **period** (gram.) complete sentence or statement, usu. complex – – **catachresis** misuse of words; the use of the wrong word for the context – – **solecism** error in the use of language (vocabulary, grammar) – – **sins of omission and commission** errors of things not done (omitted) and things done (committed) – – **plethora** ['pleθərə] overabundance – – **cotton-wool** here: soft, light, thick stuffing – – ***pleonasm** use of more words than are needed to express the meaning, e.g. old grandfather, etc. – – **dovetail joint** festes Verbindungsstück – – **bench** here: Werkbank – – ***to vanish** disappear – – **to coarsen** make rough and lumpy; vergröbern – – ***dash** Gedankenstrich – – **uninhibited** without any restraints; ohne Skrupel – – **to make one's flesh creep** cause s.o. to feel distress or great fear; Angst einjagen – **patois** dialect of the common people of a district, differing from the standard language of the country – – **(picters on the win)** pictures on the wind, i.e. TV – – *(Berstin Fyr)* Bursting Fire, i.e. bombs – – **anomaly** irregularity – – **Jane Austen** (1775–1817) eminent novelist who describes the life of England's upper-middle class at the beginning of the 19th century. Her main works: *Pride and Prejudice* (1813); *Sense and Sensibility* (1811); *Mansfield Park* (1814); *Emma* (1815) – – **debased** poorer in quality – – **debutante** ['debʊtɑnt] upperclass girl making her début in high society – – **bucolic** [bjuˈkɔlik] of country life and farming – – **revulsion (against)** feeling of reaction; disgust; Abscheu – – **to flaunt** show off complacently – – **unbuttoned** here: relaxed – – **posh** (coll.) first-class – – **vernacular** language or dialect – – **snootiness** snobbishness – – **to keep up with the spate** mit der Flut Schritt halten – – **emergence** sudden appearance – – **labours** here: efforts – – ***successive** following – – ***supplement** s.th. added later to improve or complete – – ***irresistible** too strong to be opposed – – ***muddle** confusion – – **to devise** think out – – ***urban** of the city – – ***to fade** disappear – – **to proliferate** spread – – **idiosyncrasy** characteristic, particularity – – *****gloomy** depressed, depressing – – **doomsday** the end of the world – – **prodigious** [prə'dɪdʒəs] enormous; wonderful – – **divisive** creating disunity; entzweiend, trennend – – **cohesion** tendency to stick together – – **fissiparous** [fɪ'sɪpərəs] *here:* splitting, dividing – – **proliferation** the spreading – – **to distort** pull out of normal shape – – **obfuscation** [obfʌs'keɪʃn] (formal) the act of beclouding, making obscure; the production and use of such words – – **euphemism** use of other, usu. less exact, milder, or less blunt, words or phrases in place of words required by truth or accuracy – – *****ceaseless** without end

Worksheet

1. **Language**

1.1 Give synonyms or explain the meaning of the following words and expressions as they are used in the context.
retain (l. 5); disreputable (12); appropriate to (20); chat (23); outraged (25); take in (28); deem (35); phone-in (40); learn by heart (39); incompetent (44); cliché (64); communication (73); public school (145); comprehensive school (146)

1.2 Give the opposite:
educated (l. 7); outsider (123); superiority (138); revulsion (141); elitism (142); different (145); rapid (151); increase (151); native (169); loss (177); simple (183); gloomy (191)

1.3 Prepositions: put in "about", "above", or "over".
   a) He ended up in prison for swindling the government _____ supplies to hospitals.
   b) He was concerned _____ Mike.
   c) He rose _____ the average.
   d) It gave him control _____ her education.
   e) Rochers Neiges is ten thousand feet _____ sea-level.
   f) His will had gained a victory _____ the wills of others.
   g) I have no idea _____ that at all.
   h) That is _____ me.
   i) What are you conceited _____?
   j) He was far _____ all the others.
   k) She has a complete grip _____ him.
   l) Two facts were certain _____ him.
   m) I don't think he ever got _____ her death.
   n) I value happiness _____ money.
   n) He had never bothered _____ his personal appearance.

1.4 Insert the correct preposition or leave out where not necessary: among, at, for, from, into, on, out, to, with.
(The prepositions may be used several times!)

Proper language

Some years ago a Hamburg company wrote _____ a British manufacturer in German: "Sehr geehrte Damen und Herren, wir haben von Ihren Produkten gehört und interessieren uns sehr dafür. Bitte senden Sie uns Prospektmaterial und die gültigen Preise. Mit freundlichen Grüßen, . . ."
The answer _____ England was a bombshell: "Dear Sir, we have received your communication dated April 12th which we assume is written in German, if you wish to conduct business with us kindly address us in the proper language which is English. Yours faithfully, . . ."
_____ another occasion a British businessman returned to Britain after a three-year stay in Stockholm. "How did you find communication with the Swedes?" his English friends wanted to know. "Well," he answered," _____ the beginning it was difficult, but after a few months my Swedish colleagues learnt enough English to understand what I was saying."
The June 18 issue of *The Guardian* carried an article which argued that the British are absolutely right to impose their English _____ the rest of the world. It is not a question of arrogance, it is simply good business. Why should the British compete _____ equal terms with the French, Germans, Italians, etc. by learning a foreign language? It makes much more sense to compete _____ "unequal terms" especially when those terms favour the British. How else did Margaret Thatcher force the European Community to pay back millions of pounds to Britain, except by talking loudly, and in English until the others were all worn _____.

Chinese is number one

Native English speakers seem to have good reason to feel self-satisfied. In the world languages top ten, English is a hot favourite. Number one is Mandarin Chinese _____ some 700 million native speakers; next comes English _____ about 400 million. Russian claims 250 million, followed by Spanish 220, Hindi 210, Arabic 125, Portuguese 124, Bengali 123, German 120, and Japanese 110.
But if you consider English which is spoken *as a second language* then the figures change dramatically. It is the language used by an Italian in a Tokyo restaurant, by a Japanese _____ Frankfurt airport, and by a German in a Cairo taxi. When India's prime minister greeted the just-escaped Dalai Lama: "How are you?" said Nehru in English. "Very nice," replied the Dalai Lama.
Some statistics: English accounts _____ 75 per cent of the world's mail, 60 per cent of radio stations, and 50 per cent of all newspapers. Almost every capital city in Africa and Asia has an English language daily newspaper. More people are learning English in China than live in the USA. English is now the favoured world language in politics, in commerce, in aviation, in science and technology. It is also extremely useful _____ tourists. A thousand years ago a mere one-and-a-half million people in Britain spoke a form of English, and until the reign of Elizabeth I the language remained confined _____ those islands. But within a few years the first settlers arrived in Virginia and Britain was developing _____ the dominant sea power. The opening up of sea trade and the expansion of the British empire had the effect of planting the English language in countries all over the world. The English were not always welcome.
The Bandung Conference in the 1950s attracted delegates from 29 nations representing one-and-a-half billion people. The purpose of the conference was to discuss – _____ other things – British imperialism. The language of the conference was English.

A matter of definition

So how many people in the world *actually* speak English today? The answer depends _____ your definition of "English" and what constitutes _____ language ability". The experts are still arguing. The debate ranges between one and two billion, so you can choose a number between 1,000 and 2,000 million.
All this serves to make Anglo-Saxons feel very smug. But they seem to have forgotten one very important fact: they are now in a minority. English no longer belongs _____ them! It belongs _____ you; the Germans, the French, the Italians, the Chinese. Your English is *International English* – it is clear, simple, non-idiomatic, and effective.
So next time your English friend suggests "Let's grab a bite in this joint" you can quite correctly say "Can you please speak proper English?"

Vocabulary

to assume [əsjuːm] – annehmen
Bandung Conference – In Bandung auf Java erklärten 1955 23 asiatische und 6 afrikanische Staaten unter Teilnahme Chinas ihren Willen zur Selbstbestimmung, verurteilten Kolonialismus und Rassendiskriminierung
bombshell – Bombe
communication – Mitteilung, Schreiben, Verständigung
to compete with – konkurrieren mit
confined – begrenzt, beschränkt (auf)
to constitute – ausmachen, darstellen
delegate [deligət] – Delegierte(r), Abgeordnete(r)
to grab a bite – etwas essen
to impose – aufzwingen
joint – Lokal
reign [rein] – Regierung
smug – selbstgefällig

From: **Spotlight,** 10/86

2. Content and Comment

2.1 How did English philologists in the 19th century see the English language?
2.2 Why do modern linguists reject the concept of a class-system in languages?
2.3 Which two main registers does the author recognize, and what does he say about their relevance to our time?
2.4 What effects on the language are being caused by the shift of emphasis from the one register to the other?
2.5 Howard quotes an example of primitive English from the book *Riddley Walker.* Explain how its language is primitive.
2.6 What does the author say about present trends in Standard English? Consider pronunciation, vocabulary, grammar. What reasons does he give for change?
2.7 Why is the author convinced that English will not break up into different languages and dialects?

3. **Further Studies**

3.1 Have a look at the following examples of English as written by *Geoffrey Chaucer* (1340–1400) and *William Shakespeare* (1564–1616). Try to explain the differences between the poets' English and modern English. Concentrate on vocabulary, spelling, and grammar. In particular watch for French vocabulary, words which are no longer used, and the change of meaning in words. What fields does the French vocabulary belong to?

A) The Canterbury Tales

GENERAL PROLOGUE

Here bygynneth the Book of the Tales of Caunterbury.

Whan that April with his shoures soote
The droghte of March hath perced to the roote,
And bathed every veyne in swich licour
Of which vertu engendred is the flour;
5 Whan Zephirus eek with his sweete breeth
Inspired hath in every holt and heeth
The tendre croppes, and the yonge sonne
Hath in the Ram his halve cours yronne,
And smale foweles maken melodye,
10 That slepen al the nyght with open yë
(So priketh hem nature in hir corages), –
Thanne longen folk to goon on pilgrimages,
And palmeres for to seken straunge strondes,
To ferne halwes, kowthe in sondry londes;
15 And specially from every shires ende
Of Engelond to Caunterbury they wende,
The hooly blisful martir for to seke,
That hem hath holpen whan that they were seeke.
20 Bifil that in that seson on a day,
In Southwerk at the Tabard as I lay
Redy to wenden on my pilgrymage
To Caunterbury with ful devout corage,
At nyght was come into that hostelrye
25 Wel nyne and twenty in a compaignye,
Of sondry folk, by aventure yfalle
In felaweshipe, and pilgrimes were they alle,
That toward Caunterbury wolden ryde.
The chambres and the stables weren wyde,

30 And wel we weren esed atte beste.
And shortly, whan the sonne was to reste,
So hadde I spoken with hem everichon
That I was of hir felaweshipe anon,
And made forward erly for to ryse,
35 To take oure wey ther as I yow devyse.

Vocabulary

April [ɑːprɪl] – – **his** its – – **shoures** [ʃuːərəz] showers – – **soote** ['soːtə] sweet – – **droghte** ['droχt] drought – – **perced** ['persəd] pierced – – **roote** ['roːtə] – – **bathed** ['bɑːðəd] durchdrungen – – **veine** [vɑin] sap vessel; Trachee; Siebröhre; Ader – – **swich** ['swɪtʃ] such – – **licour** [lɪ'kuːər] liquid; moisture – – **vertu** [vɜ'ty] virtue; *here:* (life-giving) power – – **engendred** produced, born – – **flour** ['fluːər] flower – – **Zephirus** the west wind, associated with spring – – **eek** ['eːk] also – – **sweete** ['sweːtə] see soote – – **breeth** ['breθ] breath – – **inspired** [ɪn'spɪrəd] breathed life into – – **holt** wood – – **heeth** ['heθ] Flur – – **croppes** shoots – – **yonge** ['juŋɡə] young – – **sonne** ['sunə] sun; the sun was supposed to begin its journey with the spring equinox (Tagundnachtgleiche; 21. März). Hence it was just starting out. – – **Ram** [the sign of the Zodiac (Tierkreis)]; Aries (Widder) – – **halve cours** during the month of April the sun passed through the last half of Aries and the first half of Taurus (Stier) – – **yronne** run – – **foweles** [fɑuləz] birds – – **night** ['nɪt] – – **yë** ['iːə] eye – – **priketh** wounds sharply; darts; stimulates – – **hem** them – – **nature** [nɑ'tyr] – – **hir** their – – **corages** [ko'raʒəz] hearts – – **longen** long – – **palmeres** pilgrims – – **seken** ['seːkən] seek – – **strondes** shores – – **ferne halwes** distant shrines of saints – – **kowthe** ['kuːðə] known – – **sondry** various – – **blisful martir** Thomas à Becket (1118–1170), Archbishop of Canterbury, who was killed in Canterbury Cathedral by supporters of King Henry II and thus – as a martyr – entered into eternal bliss – – **seeke** sick – – **Bifil** it happened – – **seson** ['seːzon] season – – **Tabard** an inn in Southwark, a district of London south of the Thames; a tabard is a short coat worn over armour – – **wenden** go – – **hostelrye** inn – – **devout** [de'vuːt] andächtig, fromm – – **by aventure** [avən'tyər] by chance – – **yfalle** fallen – – **felaweshipe** companionship – – **that** who – – **wyde** spacious – – **esed** entertained – – **anon** at once – – **forward** agreement; the subject of "made" is "we"! – – **wey** ['wɑɪ] way – – **ther as** to that place which – – **devyse** will describe; relate

B) W. Shakespeare: Sonnet 18

Shall I compare thee to a summer's day?
Thou art more lovely and more temperate:
Rough winds do shake the darling buds of May,
And summer's lease hath all too short a date:
Sometime too hot the eye of heaven shines,
And often is his gold complexion dimm'd;
And every fair from fair sometime declines,
By chance or nature's changing course untrimm'd;
But thy eternal summer shall not fade,

Nor lose possession of that fair thou ow'st;
Nor shall Death brag thou wander'st in his shade,
When in eternal lines to time thou grow'st:
   So long as men can breathe, or eyes can see,
   So long lives this, and this gives life to thee.

Vocabulary

thee [ði:] you – – **thou** [ðau] you – – **art** are – – **temperate** ['tempəreɪt] gelind – – **darling** very dear – – **buds** Knospen – – **lease** Pacht – – **date** *here:* duration – – **complexion** looks, appearance – – **dimm'd** obscured; not bright – – **fair** beauty – – **untrimm'd** stripped of its ornaments – – **nature's changing course** in the course of the changing seasons – – **thy** [ðai] your – – **ow'st** own – – **brag** boast – – **to time thou grow'st** you become part of time

3.2 Make a speech (only notes are allowed!) on Chaucer's and Shakespeare's lives and construct a list of their main works. For reference use:
   a) *The Encyclopaedia Britannica*
   b) *The Oxford Companion to English Literature,* ed. by Margaret Drabble, Guild Publishing London 1985
   c) *A Literary History of England,* edited by A. C. Baugh, Appleton-Century-Crofts, New York

3.3 Study the following cartoon and answer the questions below.

**A STORY
IN PICTURES
FROM THE YEAR
100 B. L. ***

* (Before Language)

Og, the cave man, seems to want something — but Mrs. Og isn't sure what it is.

Maybe it's a nice rock to sit on . . .

— READ MAGAZINE

a) What two "languages" does Mr Og use to make himself understood?
b) Why is his first attempt at communication in vain?
c) What does this tell us about the process of communication?
d) Eventually Mrs Og learns his "word" for "soup". Describe her learning process.
e) What is the joke of the cartoon?

Just or not Just for Fun

Do you think you have mastered the English language? Well,

Try this!

ESAU sawed wood. Esau Wood sawed wood. Oh, the wood Wood would saw! One day Esau Wood saw a saw saw wood as no other wood-saw Wood saw would saw wood.
In fact, of all the wood-saws Wood ever saw saw wood, Wood never saw a wood-saw that would saw wood as the wood-saw Wood saw saw wood would saw wood.

And I never saw a wood-saw that would saw wood as the wood-saw Wood saw would saw until I saw Esau Wood saw wood with the wood-saw that Wood saw saw wood.
Esau (iːsɔ) – **to saw** sägen.

From: **World and Press**

23 FLOWERS FOR ALGERNON

Note on the Text

The American writer Daniel Keyes (1927–) is a university lecturer in English at the Ohio University in Athens, Ohio. He started his university career as associate editor of the sf magazine MARVEL SCIENCE FICTION in 1951 which published his first stories.
Keyes writes little, but of eminent quality. His fame is mainly based on his short story FLOWERS FOR ALGERNON which won him the 1960 HUGO award, the famous award for outstanding achievements in the sf field. He later enlarged the story into a full-length novel which won the NEBULA award in 1966. In 1967 the book was turned into a film: CHARLIE. Its main actor, Cliff Robertson, won an Oscar. Other works by D. Keyes are: *The Touch* (1968), *The Fifth Sally* (1980), and *The Minds of Billy Milligan* (1981).

Our text has been taken from: E. Crispin, ed., *Best SF Four,* Faber + Faber, London 1960, pp. 97 ff passim.
For further information on the story see worksheet 3.7.

Progress Report 1 – Martch 5 1965
Dr. Strauss says I shud rite down what I think and every thing that happins to me from now on. I dont know why but he says its importint so they will see if they will use me. I hope they use me. Miss Kinnian says maybe they can make me smart.
5   I want to be smart. My name is Charlie Gordon. I am 37 years old and 2 weeks ago was my birthday. I have nuthing more to rite now so I will close for today.

Progress Report 4 – Mar 8
Their going to use me! Im so exited I can hardly write. Dr Nemur and Dr Strauss had a argament about it first. Dr Nemur was in the office when Dr Strauss brot me
10 in. Dr Nemur was worryed about using me but Dr Strauss told him Miss Kinnian rekemmended me the best from all the people who she was teaching. I like Miss Kinnian becaus shes a very smart teacher. And she said Charlie your going to have a second chance. If you volenteer for this experamant you mite get smart. They dont know if it will be perminint but theirs a chance. Thats why I said ok even when
15 I was scared because she said it was an operashun. She said dont be scared Charlie you done so much with so little I think you deserv it most of all.

Progress Report 6 – Mar 15
The operashun dint hurt. He did it while I was sleeping. They took off the bandijis from my eyes and my head today so I can make a PROGRESS REPORT. Dr Nemur who looked at some of my other ones says I spell PROGRESS wrong and he told me how to spell it and REPORT too. I got to try and remember that.

I have a very bad memary for spelling. Dr Strauss says its ok to tell about all the things that happin to me but he says I shoud tell more about what I feel and what I think. When I told him I dont know how to think he said try. All the time when the bandijis were on my eyes I tryed to think. Nothing happened. I dont know what to think about. Maybe if I ask him he will tell me how I can think now that Im suppose to get smart. What do smart people think about. Fancy things I suppose. I wish I knew some fancy things alredy.

Progress Report 8 – Mar 23
I'm going back to work at the factery. They said it was better I shud go back to work but I cant tell anyone what the operashun was for and I have to come to the hospitil for an hour evry night after work. They are gonna pay me mony every month for lerning to be smart.

Im glad Im going back to work because I miss my job and all my frends and all the fun we have there.

Dr Strauss says I shud keep writing things down but I dont have to do it every day just when I think of something or something speshul happins. He says dont get discoridged because it takes time and it happins slow. He says it took a long time with Algernon before he got 3 times smarter than he was before. Thats why Algernon beats me all the time because he had that operashun too. That makes me feel better. I coud probly do that *amazed* faster than a reglar mouse. Maybe some day Ill beat Algernon. Boy that would be something. So far Algernon looks like he mite be smart perminent.

Oh yes I almost forgot. I asked him when I can go back to the class at Miss Kinnians school. He said I wont go their. He said that soon Miss Kinnian will come to the hospital to start and teach me speshul. I was mad at her for not comming to see me when I got the operashun but I like her so maybe we will be frends again.

Progress Report 11

April 21 Still didn't go into the factory. I told Mrs. Flynn my landlady to call and tell Mr. Donnegan I was sick. Mrs. Flynn looks at me very funny lately like she's scared of me.

I think it's a good thing about finding out how everybody laughs at me. I thought about it a lot. It's because I'm so dumb and I don't even know when I'm doing something dumb. People think it's funny when a dumb person can't do things the same way they can.

Anyway, now I know I'm getting smarter every day. I know punctuation and I can spell good. I like to look up all the hard words in the dictionary and I remember them.

I'm reading a lot now, and Miss Kinnian says I read very fast. Sometimes I even understand what I'm reading about, and it stays in my mind. There are times when I can close my eyes and think of a page and it all comes back like a picture.

Besides history, geography and arithmetic, Miss Kinnian said I should start to learn a few foreign languages. Dr Strauss gave me some more tapes to play while I sleep. I still don't understand how that conscious and unconscious mind works, but Dr Strauss says not to worry yet. He asked me to promise that when I start learning college subjects next week I wouldn't read any books on psychology – that is, until he gives me permission.

I feel a lot better today, but I guess I'm still a little angry that all the time people were laughing and making fun of me because I wasn't to smart. When I become intelligent like Dr Strauss says, with three times my I.Q. of 68, them maybe I'll be like everyone else and people will like me and be friendly.

Progress Report 12

April 30 I've quit my job with Donnegan's Plastic Box Company. Mr. Donnegan insisted that it would be better for all concerned if I left. What did I do to make them hate me so?

The first I knew of it was when Mr. Donnegan showed me the petition. Eight hundred and forty names, everyone connected with the factory, except Fanny Girden. Scanning the list quickly, I saw at once that hers was the only missing name. All the rest demanded that I be fired.

Joe Carp and Frank Reilly wouldn't talk to me about it. No one else would either, except Fanny. She was one of the few people I'd known who set her mind to something and believed it no matter what the rest of the world proved, said or did – and Fanny did not believe that I should have been fired. She had been against the petition on principle and despite the pressure and threats she'd held out.

"Which don't mean to say," she remarked, "that I don't think there's something mighty strange about you, Charlie. Them changes. I don't know. You used to be a good, dependable, ordinary man – not too bright maybe, but honest. Who knows what you done to yourself to get so smart all of a sudden. Like everybody around here's been saying, Charlie, it's not right."

"But how can you say that, Fanny? What's wrong with a man becoming intelligent and wanting to acquire knowledge and understanding of the world around him?" She stared down at her work and I turned to leave. Without looking at me, she said: "It was evil when Eve listened to the snake and ate from the tree of knowledge. It was evil when she saw that she was naked. If not for that none of us would ever have to grow old and sick, and die."

May 15 Dr Strauss is very angry at me for not having written any progress reports in two weeks. He's justified because the lab is now paying me a regular salary. I told him I was too busy thinking and reading. When I pointed out that writing was such a slow process that it made me impatient with my poor handwriting, he suggested that I learn to type. It's much easier to write now because I can type nearly seventy-five words a minute. Dr Strauss continually reminds me of the need to speak and write simply so that people will be able to understand me . . .

How strange it is that people of honest feelings and sensibility, who would not take adventage of a man born without arms or legs or eyes – how such people think nothing of abusing a man born with low intelligence. It infuriated me to think that not too long ago I, like this boy, had foolishly played the clown.

And I had almost forgotten . . .

This day was good for me. Seeing the past more clearly, I have decided to use my knowledge and skills to work in the field of increasing human intelligence levels. Who is better equipped for this work? Who else has lived in both worlds? These are my people. Let me use my gift to do something for them.

Tomorrow, I will discuss with Dr Strauss the manner in which I can work in this area, I may be able to help him work out the problems of widespread use of the technique which was used on me. I have several good ideas of my own.

There is so much that might be done with this technique. If I could be made into a genius, what about thousands of others like myself? What fantastic levels might be achieved by using this technique on normal people? On *geniuses*?

There are so many doors to open. I am impatient to begin.

May 29 I have been given a lab of my own and permission to go ahead with the research. I'm on to something. Working day and night. I've had a cot moved into the lab. Most of my writing time is spent on the notes which I keep in a separate folder, but from time to time I feel it necessary to put down my moods and my thoughts out of sheer habit.

June 4

Letter to Dr Strauss (copy)

Dear Dr Strauss:

Under separate cover I am sending you a copy of my report entitled, "The Algernon-Gordon Effect: A Study of Structure and Function of Increased Intelligence," which I would like to have you read and have published.

As you see, my experiments are completed. I have included in my report all of my formular, as well as mathematical analysis in the appendix. Of course, these should be verified.

Because of its importance to both you and Dr Nemur (and need I say to myself, too?) I have checked and rechecked my results a dozen times in the hope of finding an error. I am sorry to say the results must stand. Yet for the sake of science, I am grateful for the little bit that I here add to the knowledge of the function of the human mind and of the laws governing the artificial increase of human intelligence.

I recall your once saying to me that an experimental *failure* or the *disproving* of a theory was as important to the advancement of learning as a success would be.

I know now that this is true. I am sorry, however, that my own contribution to the field must rest upon the ashes of the work of two men I regard so highly.

Yours truly,
Charles Gordon

encl.: rept.

June 5 I must not become emotional. The facts and the results of my experiments are clear, and the more sensational aspects of my own rapid climb cannot obscure the fact that the tripling of intelligence by the surgical technique developed by Drs Strauss and Nemur must be viewed as having little or no practical applicability (at the present time) to the increase of human intelligence.

The hypothesis here proven may be described simply in the following terms: Artificially increased intelligence deteriorates at a rate of time directly proportional to the quantity of the increase.

I feel that this, in itself, is an important discovery.

As long as I am able to write, I will continue to record my thoughts in these progress reports. It is one of my few pleasures. However, by all indications, my own mental deterioration will be very rapid.

I have already begun to notice signs of emotional instability and forgetfulness, the first symptoms of the burn-out.

June 10 Deterioration progressing, I have become absentminded. Algernon died two days ago. Dissection shows my predictions were right. His brain had decreased in weight and there was a general smoothing out of cerebral convolutions as well as a deepening and broadening of brain fissures.

I guess the same thing is or will soon be happening to me. Now that it's definite, I don't want it to happen.

I put Algernon's body in a cheese box and buried him in the back yard. I cried.

June 23 I've given up using the typewriter completely. My co-ordination is bad. I feel that I'm moving slower and slower. Had a terrible shock today. I picked up a copy of an article I used in my research, Krueger's *Über psychische Ganzheit*, to see if it would help me understand what I had done. First I thought there was something wrong with my eyes. Then I realized I could no longer read German. I tested myself in other languages. All gone.

July 25 I was looking at some of my old progress reports and its very funny but I can't read what I wrote. I can make out some of the words but they dont make sense. Miss Kinnian came to the door but I said go away I dont want to see you. She cried and I cried too but I wouldnt let her in because I didnt want her to laugh at me. I told her I didnt like her any more. I told her I didnt want to be smart any more. Thats not true. I still love her and I still want to be smart but I had to say that so shed go away. She gave Mrs Flynn money to pay the rent. I dont want that. I got to get a job.

Please . . . please let me not forget how to read and write . . .   (∼ 2400 words)

Annotations

brot brought – – **shes** she's – – **mite** might – – **operashun** operation – – **dint** didn't – – **bandijis** bandages – – **speshul** special – – **discoridged** discouraged – – **amazed** maze – – **dumb** US stupid – – **acquire** get, gain – – **cot** small, narrow, easily moved bed, camp bed – – **folder** holder for loose papers (Aktendeckel) – – **to put down** to write down – – **appendix** *here:* Anhang – – **to verify** test the truth or accuracy, check – – **encl.** enclosed (beigefügt) – – **rept.** report – – **to triple** make, become, be three times as much or many – – **surgical** ['sɜːdʒɪkəl] chirurgisch (surgeon Chirurg) – – **applicability** capacity for being applied (Anwendbarkeit) – – **to deteriorate** make or become worse or of less value – – **cerebral** Gehirn – – **convolution** Windungen – – **fissure** Kluft, Spalt – – **shed** she'd.

WORKSHEET

Language

1. Our text contains two irregular (Latin) plurals. Did you detect them? And do you know more such words?
2. In report no. 4 Charlie speaks about having a second c h a n c e. Of course, you know that the English pronounce this word [tʃɑːns], whereas Americans say [tʃæns]. Here's a list with a couple of words that differ in pronunciation. (The English pronunciation is given; look up the other one in your dictionary!)

    adult ['ædʌlt], advertisement [–'ʊɜtɪsmənt], anti ['ænti], aristocrat ['æ–], ate [et], clerk [ɑ], depot ['depəu], dictionary [dɪkʃnrɪ], dynasty ['dɪ–], either [ɑɪ–], garage ['gæraʒ], hurry [ʌ], inveigle [–viː] (into, verleiten, verlocken), laugh [ɑː], lieutenant [lefˈtenənt], laboratory [ləˈborətrɪ], medicine [medsn], missile [–sail], morale [–rɑl], route [–u–]
3. You know that in English spelling and pronunciation have drifted apart. But did you know the difference was this big?
    "Muti-nation employees at North Atlantic Treaty Organization headquarters found English an easy language until they tried to pronounce it. To help them discard an array of accents, the verses below were devised. After trying them, a Frenchman said he'd prefer six months at hard labor to reading six lines aloud.
    Try them yourself. Here's an extract:
    Dearest creature in creation,
    Studying English pronunciation,
    I shall teach you in my verse:
    Sounds like corpse, corps,
    horse and worse.
    It will keep you Susy, busy,
    Make your head with heat grow dizzy;
    Tear in eye, your dress you'll tear,

So shall I! Oh, hear my prayer,
Just compare heart, beard and heard,
Does and diet, lord and word,
Sword and ward, retain and Britain,
(Mind the latter, how it's written).
Now I surely shall not plague you,
With such words as vague and ague,
But be careful how you speak,
Say break, steak, black and streak,
Eleven, even; how and low . . .
Blood and flood are not like food,
Nor is mould like should and would.
Viscous, viscount; lead and bread,
Toward, to forward, to reward,
And your pronunciation's O.K.,
When you correctly say croquet . . .
Mark the difference moreover,
Between mover, plover, Dover;
Leeches, breeches; wise, precise,
Chalice, but police and lice;
Camel, constable, unstable,
Principle, disciple, label;
Petal, penal, and canal,
Wait, surprise, plait, premise, pal;
Worm and storm; chaise, chaos, chair.
Senator, spectator, mayor . . .
Query does not rhyme with very,
Nor does fury sound like bury;
Dost, lost, post and doth, cloth, both;
Job, job, bosom, oath:
Though the difference seems little,
We say actual but victual . . .
Finally, which rhymes with "enough",
Though, through, plough, cough or tough?
Hiccough has the sound of "cup",
My advice is – give it up!"

4. Correct all mistakes of Progress Reports 1 and 4.

Text Analysis

1. Can you distinguish the three parts of the story?

2. a) Give a summary of the story.
   b) Find captions for all the entries.
3. What would you say is the underlying idea of the story?
4. Answer the following questions about the text.
   a) Why does Charlie say 'I want to be smart'?
   b) In what sense does Charlie get a second chance?
   c) Why does Miss Kinnian say that Charlie deserves the second chance 'most of all'?
   d) Why is Charlie glad that he's going back to work?
   e) Why is Mrs Flynn, Charlie's landlady, afraid of him?
   f) 'I'll be like everyone else and people will like me and be friendly'. In what sense is this sentence a piece of sheer irony?
   g) Why do Charlie's friends hate him when he is smart?
   h) Why is Dr Strauss angry at Charlie for not having written any progress reports?
   i) Why does Charlie want to work in the field of increasing human intelligence levels?
   k) What makes him work day and night?
   l) Why did he cry when he buried Algernon?
   m) Why did he tell Miss Kinnian to go away?
   n) Find a proper end for this story!

Discussion and Comment

1. Why is the story written in form of a diary?
2. What role does the mouse Algernon play?
3. Is Charlie's friend Fanny right in comparing the experiment done on Charlie to Eve's eating from the tree of knowledge?
4. What do you think of Charlie's idea of applying the IQ raising technique on normal people?
5. Is it true that 'people of honest feelings and sensibility, who would not take advantage of a man born without legs or eyes – how such people think nothing of abusing a man born with low intelligence'?
6. Is the problem of happiness raised in the text?
7. Give the main ideas of the following text in English!

„Flowers for Algernon" ist ein ungewöhnlich eindringlicher Stoff, der sowohl in der kurzen als auch in der Romanversion beeindruckt. Charly Gordon arbeitet in einer Bäckerei: ein Schwachsinniger, der für Boten- und Kalfaktordienste eingesetzt wird, Freunde zu haben glaubt und eine Abendschule für geistig Zurückgebliebene besucht. Bis man ihn eines Tages für ein Experiment auswählt. Eine Operation soll ihn aus der Dumpfheit seines Geistes herausheben. Wie schon zuvor an der Maus Algernon, gelingt die Operation auch an Charly, der daraufhin rasch seinen Horizont erweitert. Bald erreicht er das Niveau seines Mitmenschen, überflügelt sie und läßt sie weit hinter sich. Als jedoch eines Tages die Intelligenzkurve der Maus ihren Extremwert erreicht hat und rasend schnell wieder abflacht, weiß Charly, was ihm bevorsteht. Der Erfolg der Operation war nicht von Dauer, er wird in seinen früheren Dämmerzustand zurückfallen, vielleicht sogar darunter. Er beendet sein Werk über den Gordon-Algernon-Effekt, den wissenschaftlichen Beleg des Fehlschlags, gerade noch rechtzeitig, dann setzt die Rückwandlung ein. Verzweifelt versucht er, Teile des schwindenden Wissens zu bewahren, aber alles entgleitet ihm.

Beide Texte bestehen von Anfang bis Ende aus Charlys Tagebuchaufzeichnungen, die in Sprache, Diktion und Thematik dem jeweiligen Bildungs- und Bewußtseinsstand des Schreibenden angepaßt sind: ein erschütterndes Protokoll des Wachsens und Sterbens, im letzten Drittel ein Dokument des Zerfalls eines Geistes, ein grausames Scheitern. Keyes thematisiert vorrangig das Problem der Wertigkeit des Menschen in unserer Gesellschaft bzw. deren Abhängigkeit von Intelligenz und Kommunikationsvermögen und plädiert leidenschaftlich dafür, Intelligenz nicht zum Maß aller Dinge zu machen. Es gelingt ihm, den Leser zu Charly werden und ihn gleichzeitig daneben stehen zu lassen. Dies führt zu starker emotionaler Anteilnahme, zugleich aber zu einem Korrektiv, wenn es darum geht, Charlys Empfinden zu werten – etwa, wenn er sich naiv darüber freut, daß seine Freunde so lustig mit ihm sind (in Wahrheit machen sie sich auf gemeine Art und Weise *über* ihn lustig). Es ist ein vielschichtiges Werk, das immer neue Perspektiven bietet. Charly selbst lernt die Einsamkeit des geistig Behinderten, aber auch die Einsamkeit des Intellektuellen kennen, und in Wahrheit ist das Tor zu anderen Menschen nur für ganz kurze Zeit für ihn geöffnet, als sich in seiner „Normalphase" eine Beziehung zu seiner früheren Lehrerin Alice Kinnian entwickelt. Aber Alice vermag ihm weder in die intellektuellen Dimensionen noch zurück in den Zustand geistiger Beschränkung zu folgen: Als er nach Mißlingen des Experiments wieder als naiver Schüler in ihrer Klasse erscheint, flieht sie, von Charly registriert, aber nicht verstanden, weinend aus dem Unterricht. Ähnlich, wenn auch mit anderen Vorzeichen und Ausprägungen, sein Verhältnis zu den „Freunden" auf der Arbeitsstelle. Sie, die ihn anfangs hänselten (was er als freundliche Gesten mißverstand), fürchten und hassen ihn als Intellektuellen, behandeln ihn dann später, vielleicht aus Scham, aus Bedauern, vielleicht sogar aus Einsicht, beschützend-rücksichtsvoll, als er zu ihnen zurückkehrt. Und auch Charlys Verhältnis zu ihnen, mit dem dumpfen Wissen einstiger Erkenntnis, ist anders. Und selbst in der Phase seiner höchsten Intelligenz ist er Objekt für die anderen, Ausstellungsstück aufgrund seines Genies, von anderen als ihr Geschöpf beansprucht, ohne daß diese einen Gedanken an seine Gefühle verschwenden.

So bleibt Charlys einziger wirklicher Freund die Maus Algernon, sein Leidensgefährte. Ein zutiefst menschliches Stück Literatur im Dienste kämpferischen Humanismus, eine Sternstunde des Science Fiction.

(aus: J. Körber, Hg., *Bibliographisches Lexikon der utopisch-phantastischen Literatur,* Corian Vlg., Meitingen 1984 ff., Stichwort D. Keyes, bearbeitet von H.-J. Alpers)

4. For your amusement

a) The following two texts show dialogues between a psychotherapist and his patient. One of the two partners is a computer(programme). Which?

PARRY – Weak Mode
How long have you been in the hospital?
About a week.
Are you depressed?
No.
Were you taking drugs?
No.
What is your problem?
People make me nervous.
How to they do that?
They stare at me.
Why?
Maybe they don't like the way I look or something.
Do you look unusual in some way?
Why are you interested in my looks?
Because you said people stare at you.
Well, sometimes.
How do you get along with people?
I don't communicate very much with the others.
Why not?
They don't realize what's going on most of the time.

PARRY – Strong Mode
Why are you in the hospital?
I shouldn't be here.
Who brought you here?
The police.
What trouble did you have with the police?
Cops don't do their job.
What do they do instead?
Cops arrest the wrong people.
They arrest the right ones sometimes.

The law should get those Italian crooks.
Are you Italian?
My background is British but I was born in this country.
Do you know any Italian crooks?
I try to avoid the underworld.
Are you afraid of the underworld?
The mafia are the worst gangsters.
Are you connected with the mafia?
You know, they know me.
How do they know you?
They spy on me.
Why do they?
They want to get false evidence to frame me.
What do they have against you?
They are out to get me.
What for?
I have incriminating evidence against the mafia.

(From: P. Nicholls, ed., *Science in Science Fiction,* Michael Joseph Limited, London, 1982, p. 127)

b) **Can You Follow Directions?**

This is a timed test – – You have three minutes **only.**
1. Read everything on this page carefully before doing anything.
2. Put your name in the upper right hand corner of this paper.
3. Circle the word "name" in sentence two.
4. Draw five small squares in the upper left hand corner.
5. Put an "X" in each square.
6. Put a circle around each square.
7. Sign your name under the title of this paper.
8. After the title, Write "Yes, Yes, Yes".
9. Loudly call out your first name when you get this far along.
10. Put a circle completly around sentence number seven.
11. Put an "X" in the lower left corner of this paper.
12. Draw a triangle around the "X" you just put down.
13. On the back of this paper, multiply 703 X 66.
14. Draw a rectangle around the word **corner** in sentence four.
15. If you think you have followed directions carefully to this point, call out "I have".
16. On the reverse side of this paper, add 8950 and 9805.
17. Put a circle around your answer, and put a square around the circle.
18. In your normal speaking voice, count from ten to one, backward.

19. Punch three small holes in the top of this paper, with your pencil point.
20. If you are the first person to reach this point, **loudly,** call out, **"I am the first person to this point, and I am the leader in following directions."**
21. Underline all even numbers on the left side of this paper.
22. Put a square around each written-out number on this paper.
23. Loudly call out, **"I am nearly finished, I have followed directions."**
24. Now that you have finished reading everything carefully, do only sentences one and two.

24 AND HE GAVE YOU THE BALL, EH?

Note on the Text

In 1949, Arthur Miller (1915–   ) published his play *Death of a Salesman,* which earned him another Pulitzer prize for drama, the first having been awarded to him for his play *All My Sons* (1947). Other important plays followed, such as *The Crucible* (1953) and *A View from the Bridge* (1955), which again won the Pulitzer prize. In 1961, he wrote the scenario for his film "The Misfits", starring Marylin Monroe, his second wife. But without any doubt *Death of a Salesman* is his best play. Combining Ibsen's analytical technique with Clifford Odets's realism (e.g. in *Waiting for Lefty*) and elements of Brecht's epic drama – thus deviating from the Aristotelian theory of drama – it can serve as a model of modern American drama (see also Introduction to Topic 13).

Willy Loman is the protagonist of the play. Though he has always worked hard as a salesman, he has never made much money and now – at the age of 63 – is no longer able to fulfill the requirements of modern salesmanship and is dismissed. The course of his life, in particular his failure to earn much money, shows Loman to be a typical representative of the decent man-in-the-street who falls victim to the American dream of (material) success and of happiness believed to be the result of prosperity. The ironic twist of the play is that Loman knows this but doesn't want to accept it and stubbornly clings to his dream of wealth. He even "teaches" his sons Biff and Happy how to become successful and rich.

The following extract, taken trom Act I of the play, shows Loman just returning from one of his unsuccessful business trips, while his adult sons, who are spending some days at home, are still discussing plans for the future in their bedroom upstairs. It's late at night.

WILLY [*below*]: You gonna wash the engine, Biff?
HAPPY: Shh!
[BIFF *looks at* HAPPY, *who is gazing down, listening.* WILLY *is mumbling in the parlour.*]

5   HAPPY: You hear that?
[*They listen.* WILLY *laughs warmly.*]
BIFF [*growing angry*]: Doesn't he know Mom can hear that?
WILLY: Don't get your sweater dirty, Biff!
[*A look of pain crosses BIFF's face.*]
10   HAPPY: Isn't that terrible? Don't leave again, will you? You'll find a job here. You gotta stick around. I don't know what to do about him, it's getting embarrassing.
WILLY: What a simonizing job!
BIFF: Mom's hearing that!
WILLY: No kiddin', Biff, you got a date? Wonderful!
15   HAPPY: Go on to sleep. But talk to him in the morning, will you?
BIFF [*reluctantly getting into bed*]: With her in the house. Brother!
HAPPY [*getting into bed*]: I wish you'd have a good talk with him.
[*The light on their room begins to fade.*]
BIFF [*to himself in bed*]: That selfish, stupid . . .
20   HAPPY: Sh . . . Sleep, Biff.
[*Their light is out. Well before they have finished speaking,* WILLY's *form is dimly seen below in the darkened kitchen. He opens the refrigerator, searches in there, and takes out a bottle of milk. The apartment houses are fading out, and the entire house and surroundings become covered with leaves. Music insinuates itself as*
25   *the leaves appear.*]
YOUNG BIFF *and* YOUNG HAPPY *appear from the direction* WILLY *was addressing.* HAPPY *carries rags and a pail of water.* BIFF, *wearing a sweater with a block 'S', carries a football.*]
BIFF [*pointing in the direction of the car offstage*]: How's that, Pop, professional?
30   WILLY: Terrific. Terrific job, boys. Good work, Biff.
HAPPY: Where's the surprise, Pop?
WILLY: In the back seat of the car.
HAPPY: Boy! [*He runs off.*]
BIFF: What is it, Dad? Tell me, what'd you buy?
35   WILLY [*laughing, cuffs him*]: Never mind, something I want you to have.
BIFF [*turns and starts off*]: What is it, Hap?
HAPPY [*offstage*]: It's a punching bag!
BIFF: Oh, Pop!
WILLY: It's got Gene Tunney's signature on it!
40   [HAPPY *runs onstage with a punching bag.*]
BIFF: Gee, how'd you know we wanted a punching bag?
WILLY: Well, it's the finest thing for the timing.
HAPPY [*lies down on his back and pedals with his feet*]: I'm losing weight, you notice, Pop?
45   WILLY [*to* HAPPY]: Jumping rope is good too.

BIFF: Did you see the new football I got?
WILLY [*examining the ball*]: Where'd you get a new ball?
BIFF: The coach told me to practise my passing.
WILLY: That so? And he gave you the ball, eh?
50 BIFF: Well, I borrowed it from the locker room. [*He laughs confidentially.*]
WILLY [*laughing with him at the theft*]: I want you to return that.
HAPPY: I told you he wouldn't like it!
BIFF [*angrily*]: Well, I'm bringing it back!
WILLY [*stopping the incipient argument, to* HAPPY:] Sure, he's gotta practise with
55 a regulation ball, doesn't he? [*To* BIFF] Coach'll probably congratulate you on your initiative!
BIFF: Oh, he keeps congratulating my initiative all the time, Pop.
WILLY: That's because he likes you. If somebody else took that ball there'd be an uproar.
60 [BIFF *is prancing around, practising passing the ball.*]
WILLY: You nervous, Biff, about the game?
BIFF: Not if you're gonna be there.
WILLY: What do they say about you in school, now that they made you captain?
HAPPY: There's a crowd of girls behind him every time the classes change.
65 BIFF [*taking* WILLY's *hand*]: This Saturday, Pop, this Saturday – just for you, I'm going to break through for a touchdown.
HAPPY: You're supposed to pass.
BIFF: I'm takin' one play for Pop. You watch me, Pop, and when I take off my helmet, that means I'm breakin' out. Then watch me crash through that line!
70 WILLY [*kisses* BIFF]: Oh, wait'll I tell this in Boston!
[BERNARD *enters in knickers. He is younger than* BIFF, *earnest and loyal, a worried boy.*]
BERNARD: Biff, where are you? You're supposed to study with me today.
WILLY: Hey, looka Bernard. What're you lookin' so anemic about, Bernard?
75 BERNARD: He's gotta study, Uncle Willy. He's got Regents next week.
HAPPY [*tauntingly, spinning* BERNARD *around*]: Let's box, Bernard!
BERNARD: Biff! [*He gets away from* HAPPY.] Listen, Biff, I heard Mr. Birnbaum say that if you don't start studyin' math he's gonna flunk you, and you won't graduate. I heard him!
80 WILLY: You better study with him, Biff. Go ahead now.
BERNARD: I heard him!
BIFF: Oh, Pop, you didn't see my sneakers! [*He holds up a foot for* WILLY *to look at.*]
WILLY: Hey, that's a beautiful job of printing!
85 BERNARD [*wiping his glasses*]: Just because he printed University of Virginia on his sneakers doesn't mean they've got to graduate him, Uncle Willy!

WILLY [*angrily*]: What're you talking about? With scholarships to three universities they're gonna flunk him?
BERNARD: But I heard Mr. Birnbaum say –
90 WILLY: Don't be a pest, Bernard! [*To his boys*] What an anemic!
BERNARD: Okay, I'm waiting for you in my house, Biff.
[BERNARD *goes off. The* LOMANS *laugh.*]
WILLY: Bernard is not well liked, is he?
BIFF: He's liked, but he's not well liked.
95 HAPPY: That's right, Pop.
WILLY: That's just what I mean. Bernard can get the best marks in school, y'understand, but when he gets out in the business world, y'understand, you are going to be five times ahead of him. That's why I thank Almighty God you're both built like Adonises. Because the man who makes an appearance in the business
100 world, the man who creates personal interest, is the man who gets ahead. Be liked and you will never want. You take me, for instance. I never have to wait in line to see a buyer. 'Willy Loman is here!' That's all they have to know, and I go right through.
BIFF: Did you knock them dead, Pop?
105 WILLY: Knocked 'em cold in Providence, slaughtered 'em in Boston . . .

(~ 985 words)

Annotations
(The words marked * should be memorized.)

a) Note:
to deviate from turn away

b) Text:
*to mumble say sth. indistinctly – – **parlour** sitting room (Fr. parler) – – **gotta** (coll.) got to – – **to simonize** polish s.th. with wax – – **no kidding** (coll.) are you serious?; you are not making fun of me, are you? – – ***date** *here:* an appointment between two persons of the opposite sex for the mutual enjoyment of some form of social activity – – ***reluctant** somewhat against his will – – **Brother!** exclamation of astonishment – – ***to fade** become dim – – **to insinuate** to introduce gently – – **rag** odd bit of cloth, piece of old and torn cloth – – ***pail** vessel, round and open, of metal or wood, for carrying liquid – – **block S** Druckbuchstabe S – – **terrific job** (coll.) excellent job – – **Boy!** exclamation of pleasure, admiration – – **to cuff** give a slight blow with the open hand – – **punching bag** sack, stuffed or filled with sand, for practising boxing – – **Gene Tunney** heavy weight boxing champion – – ***timing** doing s.th. at right moment – – **jumping rope** (US); (Br.) skipping rope; Seilspringen – – **Gee** (coll.) Jesus, exclamation of admiration – – ***coach** *here:* trainer – – **to borrow** *here:* euphemism for "to steal" – – **locker room** room where players change clothes and lock them up in small cupboards – – **incipient** beginning, starting – – **regulation ball** a ball complying with official measurements – – **to prance around** to dance about gaily – – **gonna** going to – – **touchdown** in American football, ball over the opponent's goal line – – **knickers** short for

knickerbockers – – **anemic** (US); (Br.) anaemic (normally adj.) spiritless, pale (as if he studies too much) – – **Regents** ['rɪdʒənts] school examination – – **taunting** höhnisch, spöttisch – – ***to flunk** (coll.) give student a failing grade – – ***to graduate** (US) to get a degree or diploma – – **sneakers** (coll.) gym shoes – – **to be a pest** be annoying, troublesome – – **anemic** n. Stubenhocker – – **Adonis** [a'doːnis] from Greek mythology: youth famous for his beauty – – **to knock dead** (coll.) defeat completely – – **to slaughter** (coll.) defeat completely

WORKSHEET

1. **Language**
1.1 Below you'll find a number of words in complete disarray. Arrange them in their proper word families and find their superordinates.

school
bedroom
class
sweater
to study
kitchen
jumping rope
Parlour
to graduate
Regents
to flunk
marks
football
sneakers
punching bag
helmet
scholarship

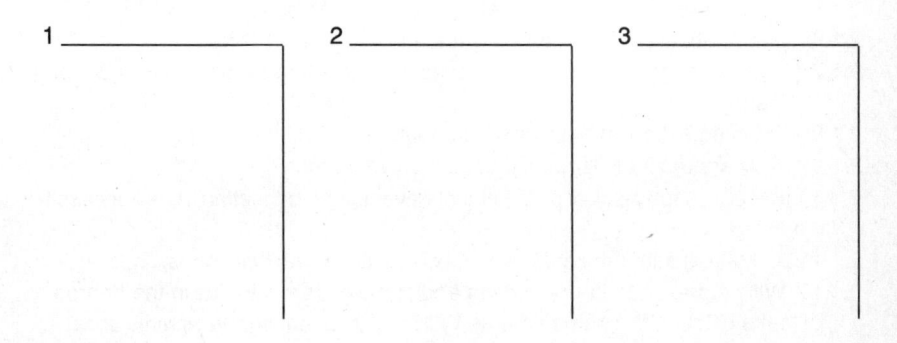

1 _____   2 _____   3 _____

1.2 Insert the correct words taken from assignment 1.1 into the following sentences (Most of them are from a College prospectus.):
   a) Earlham college provides programs of _____ which prepare for entrance to the best professional _____ (Pl) in such fields as theology, medicine, law, social work, engineering, and business administration.
   b) At the end of each academic year the highest ranking man and woman in each of the freshman (1st year), sophomore (2nd year) and junior (3rd year) _____ (Pl.) is given an award to be credited against college expenses for the following year.
   c) Students who are officially enrolled in a course must be assigned _____ (Pl) even if they never attended class.
   d) Earlham grants two _____ each year, one to the highest ranking boy and one to the highest ranking girl in the senior class of Richmond High School.
   e) With Earlham's coach Bob Geiger moving on to Buffalo the coaching chores fell on the young shoulders of Rich Carter, still just one year out of his _____ and pads.
   f) If an American highschool student _____ a course he can make it up in summer school.
1.3 Select six of the annotations marked * to use in a coherent written text. The order of the words doesn't matter.

2. **Text Analysis**
2.1 The following statements about the contents and the composition of the scene are false. Explain why they are wrong and correct them. Use your own words as much as possible.
2.1.1 When Willy Loman comes home from a business trip he has a nice talk with his adult sons.
2.1.2 Happy asks Biff to live at home in the future because he thinks this is better for Biff.
2.1.3 Young Biff and Young Happy are painting the house.
2.1.4 Willy has bought the football Biff is playing with as a surprise for the children.
2.1.5 Willy punishes Biff for the theft of the punching bag.
2.1.6 The relationship between Willy and his young sons is bad.
2.1.7 Bernard appears suddenly because he wants to play football with Biff and Happy.
2.1.8 Biff is an excellent highschool student.
2.1.9 Willy appreciates academic education very much.
2.1.10 His philosophy is that people must have a good education to be successful in life.
2.1.11 A. Miller thinks the same way about education as Willy does.
2.1.12 Willy's presence in the kitchen and Happy's talk with Biff in the bedroom take place in the same year as Willy's chat about sports with his sons.

2.1.13 Such a shift in the chronological sequence is called "timing".

2.1.14 This device is a typical feature of the classical drama (See also Topic 13, p. 135).

2.1.15 The protagonist of *DOS* as presented by Willy Loman and the language of the play are in complete accordance with the following statements taken from Aristotle's Poetics:

> This is the sort of man who is not pre-eminently virtuous and just, and yet it is through no badness or villainy of his own that the falls into the misfortune, but rather through some flaw in him, he being one of those who are in high station and good fortune, like Oedipus and Thyestes and the famous men of such families as those.
>
> Tragedy is, then, a representation of an action that is heroic and complete and of a certain magnitude—by means of language enriched with all kinds of ornament, each used separately in the different parts of the play: it represents men in action and does not use narrative, and through pity and fear it effects relief to these and similar emotions. By 'language enriched' I mean that which has rhythm and tune, i.e. song, and by 'the kinds separately' I mean that some effects are produced by verse alone and some again by song.

3. Discussion and Comment

3.1 Willy Loman's way of educating his children. Pro and Con.

3.2 Loman is a failure (as he understands it), so are his sons Biff and Happy. (Biff doesn't succeed in his job, Happy is a womanizer.) Bernard, who is not well-liked as a student, becomes a successful lawyer arguing cases in front of the *Supreme Court* and also leads a happy family life. What do these facts tell you about the extract's message? What is your opinion of the author's point of view?

3.3 Compare Willy Loman's view of education with Beatty's in *Fahrenheit 451* (see pp. 240–242). Point out similarities and differences.

3.4 Compare the political and social structures of the societies in which Loman and Beatty live.

Just for Fun

Source: *Soldiers*, Jan. 1985

25 FAHRENHEIT 451

Note on the Text

Ray Bradbury (born 1920) is regarded by many critics as one of the most important American storytellers of our day. His reputation mainly rests on his mainstream writing, not so much on his sf-works. He is a very prolific writer, who has produced novels, short stories, plays, screenplays and poetry.
In his sf he makes use of traditional sf devices like rockets, blasters and telepathy to express moral concerns.
His style is very poetic, evocative, nostalgic and full of symbolism.
Fahrenheit 451 (the title refers to the temperature at which paper begins to burn) came out in 1953, and was made into a film by François Truffaut in 1966. The novel envisions a dystopian future in which a totalitarian state seeks absolute control over its citizens via wall-sized TV-screens in their houses. Consequently, book-reading is a crime, books are banned and burned when found by the firebrigade. Guy Montag has been a loyal firemen, eagerly burning books, until he meets a girl, Clarissa, who opens up to him the world and worth of books. He becomes a renegade, flees from his society and joins a group of dissenters in the woods, who memorize books to ensure their survival through an impending world war.

Our extract has been taken from: R. Bradbury, *Fahrenheit 451,* Ballantine Books, New York, 1980[53], p. 39 ff, 61 ff.

"All right, men, let's get 'em!"
Next thing they were up in musty blackness swinging silver hatchets at doors that were, after all, unlocked, tumbling through like boys all rollick and shout. "Hey!" A fountain of books sprang down upon Montag as he climbed shuddering up the sheer
5 stairwell. – – –
The books lay like great mounds of fishes left to dry. The men danced and slipped and fell over them. Titles glittered their golden eyes, falling, gone.
"Kerosene!"
They pumped the cold fluid from the numeraled 451 tanks strapped to their
10 shoulders. They coated each book, they pumped rooms full of it.
They hurried downstairs, Montag staggering after them in the kerosene fumes.
"Come on, woman!"
The woman knelt among the books, touching the drenched leather and cardboard, reading the gilt titles with her fingers while her eyes accused Montag.
15 "You can't ever have my books," she said.
"You know the law," said Beatty. "Where's your common sense? None of those books agree with each other. You've been locked up here for years with a regular damned Tower of Babel. Snap out of it! The People in those books never lived. Come on now!" – – –
20 The woman replied quietly, "I want to stay here."
"Five. Six."

"You can stop counting," she said. She opened the fingers of one hand slightly and in the palm of the hand was a single slender object.

An ordinary kitchen match. – – –

25 The woman on the porch reached out with contempt to them all and struck the kitchen match against the railing.

People ran out of houses all down the street.

Later, fireman Montag has a talk with his boss, Captain Beatty:

"Now let's take up the minorities in our civilization, shall we? Bigger the population, 30 the more minorities. – – –

All the minor minor minorities with their navels to be kept clean. Authors, full of evil thoughts, lock up your typewriters. They *did*. Magazines became a nice blend of vanilla tapioca. Books, so the damned snobbish critics said, were dishwater. No *wonder* books stopped selling, the critics said. Put the public, knowing what it 35 wanted, spinning happily, let the comic books survive. And the threedimensional sex magazines, of course. There you have it, Montag. It didn't come from the Government down. There was no dictum, no declaration, no censorship, to start with, no! Technology, mass exploitation, and minority pressure carried the trick, thank God. Today, thanks to them, you can stay happy all the time, you are allowed 40 to read comics, the good old confessions, or trade journals."

"Yes, but what about the firemen, then?" asked Montag.

"Ah." Beatty leaned forward in the faint mist of smoke from his pipe. "What more easily explained and natural? With school turning out more runners, jumpers, racers, tinkerers, grabbers, snatchers, fliers, and swimmers instead of examiners, 45 critics, knowers, and imaginative creators, the word 'intellectual', of course, became the swear word it deserved to be. You always dread the infamiliar. Surely you remember the boy in your own school class who was exceptionally 'bright', did most of the reciting and answering while the others sat like so many leaden idols, hating him. And wasn't it this bright boy you selected for beatings and tortures after hours? 50 Of course it was. We must all be alike. Not everyone born free and equal, as the Constitution says, but everyone *made* equal. Each man the image of every other; then all are happy, for there are no mountains to make them cower, to judge themselves against. So! A book is a loaded gun in the house next door. Burn it. Take the shot from the weapon. Breach man's mind. Who knows who might be the target 55 of the well-read man? Me? I won't stomach them for a minute. And so when houses were finally fireproofed completely, all over the world (you were correct in your assumption the other night) there was no longer need of firemen for the old purposes. They were given the new job, as custodians of our peace of mind, the focus of our understandable and rightful dread of being inferior: official censors, 60 judges, and executors. That's you, Montag, and that's me." – – –

"You must understand that our civilization is so vast that we can't have our minorities upset and stirred. Ask yourself, What do we want in this country, above all? People

want to be happy, isn't that right? Haven't you heard it all your life? I want to be happy, people say. Well, aren't they? Don't we keep them moving, don't we give
65 them fun? That's all we live for, isn't it? For pleasure, for titillation? And you must admit our culture provides plenty of these."

"Colored people don't like *Little Black Sambo*. Burn it. White people don't feel good about *Uncle Tom's Cabin*. Burn it. Someone's written a book on tobacco and cancer of the lungs? The cigarette people are weeping? Burn the book. Serenity, Montag.
70 Peace, Montag. Take your fight outside. Better yet, into the incinerator. Funerals are unhappy and pagan? Eliminate them, too. Five minutes after a person is dead he's on his way to the Big Flue, the Incinerators serviced by helicopters all over the country. Ten minutes after death a man's a speck of black dust. Let's not quibble over individuals with memoriams. Forget them. Burn all, burn everything. Fire is
75 bright and fire is clean."   (~ 860 words)

Annotations

(The words marked * should be memorized.)

*musty stale, smelling or tasting mouldy – – **rollick** cheerfulness, carefreeness – – **sheer** steep – – **mound** small hill – – **to snap out of it** get out of a mood, habit – – **navel** small depression in the middle of the surface of the abdomen – – **tapioca** Tapioka (starchy food in the form of hard, white grains from the root of the cassava plant (sagoähnliche Zubereitung der Maniokstärke) – – **dictum** formal expression of opinion (Machtspruch) – – **tinkerer** s. o. who works in an amateurish or inexpert way (Stümper, Pfuscher) – – **grabber** greedy person whose chief aim in life appears to be making money – – **snatcher** one who snatches: puts out the hand suddenly and takes – – ***to cower** [kauə] lower the body, crouch, shrink back from cold, misery or fear (sich ducken) – – **titillation** to titillate: stimulate or excite pleasantly (Kitzel) – – **flue** channel, pipe or tube for carrying heat, hot air or smoke – – ***to quibble** argue about small points or differences.

Language

1.1 In the text you find the word 'runner'. Of course, you know what 'to run' means. But did you know it could be employed in so many different uses? Have a look at the following sentences and translate them into German.

   a) Overhead: "My wife and I have a perfect understanding. I don't try to run her life – and I don't try to run mine."
   b) Then we ran his blood sugar level.
   c) He ran a fever.
   d) His first day's work would run to four hundred dollars.
   e) But nowhere did feelings run higher than in Italy.
   f) Tension was running high.
   g) Our club is running a sale.
   h) They even ran night-classes.
   i) He helped run the country during the state of emergency.

k) The dress will run you 250 $ (AE!).
l) "Well, that's what the men do!" – "What is it that you women do?" – "Why, run the men, of course!"
m) Run the contents of your mind through a positive detector!
n) The Mount Vernon community was largely self-sufficient and a wide range of skills were necessary to assure that it ran smoothly.
o) Expectations ran high.
p) The bonds between the countries run deep.

1.2 The following adjectives indicate different degrees of temperature. Rearrange them one underneath the other with the "hottest" at the top and the "coldest" at the bottom.
cold, hot, icy, torrid, fresh, frigid, warm, scorching, lukewarm, chilly, frostbitten, cool.

1.3 Do likewise with the following adjectives of pleasure:
sad, contented, pensive, despairing, in ecstasy, happy, brokenhearted, melancholic, cheerful, exhilarated, despondent, pleased, depressed, joyful.

2. Text Analysis

2.1 Pick out Montag's and Beatty's arguments against books.
2.2 Pick out and explain the similes and the metaphors in the text! Try and explain the symbolism in the names "Montag" and "Clarissa" (cf. Note on the text!). The book-titles are twice described as "golden". What connotations does this evoke?
(The *denotation* of a word, in the usage of critics, is the thing or situation the word specifically refers to. Its *connotation* consists of the associated meanings it implies or suggests.)
2.3 What relation ist there between the two parts of the text?
2.4 Describe the firemen's new job!
2.5 What connection it there between the development of schools and the new function of the firebrigade?
2.6 Explain the following sentences from the text:
   a) "The woman on the porch reached out with contempt . . ."
      Why with contempt?
   b) "Technology, mass exploitation, and minority pressure carried the trick, thank God."
      Why does Beatty thank God?
   c) "You know the law", said Beatty.
      What does the law say? And why does it say it?
   d) "Five. Six." – "You can stop counting," she said.
      Why is Beatty counting?

e) "White people don't feel good about *Uncle Tom's Cabin.*"
   Why not?
f) "Colored people don't like *Little Black Sambo.*"
   What kind of book is that likely to be?
g) "... reading the gilt titles with her fingers while her eyes accused Montag."
   Why does the woman read with her fingers? and why does she accuse Montag?
h) "The fire is bright and the fire is clean".
   What does Beatty mean by this? (Think of the "bright" boy and the sex magazines!)

3. Discussion and Comment

3.1 Act out a role-play: Engage in a dispute: fireman – woman over the reading of books. Exchange arguments!

3.2 Outline Beatty's notion of happiness! Contrast it with your own! Compare it with the idea of happiness in *Brave New World!*

3.3 "Bradbury's is the most skilfully drawn of all science fiction's conformist hells."
(from: K. Amis, *New Maps of Hell,* Four Square Book, The New English Library Limited from Barnard's Inn, Holborn, London, 1963, p. 94)
Can you endorse this statement by referring to the text?

3.4 There is a historic example of book-burning! Compare it with *Fahrenheit 451!*

4. For further study

4.1 Bradbury once said: "I don't like what some people are doing with science in the world. I think that such people should be exposed and, if possible, combatted."
Can you give an example of what he might have had in mind?
Write a short essay on the above statement!

4.2 Comment on the following observation of Bradbury's:

In writing the short novel "Fahrenheit 451", I thought I was describing a world that might evolve in four or five decades. But only a few weeks ago, in Beverly Hills one night, a husband and wife passed me, walking their dog. I stood staring after them, absolutely stunned. The woman held in one hand a small cigarette-package-sized radio, its antenna quivering. From this sprang tiny copper wires which ended in a dainty cone plugged into her right ear. There she was, oblivious to man and dog, listening to far winds and whispers and soap-opera cries, sleepwalking, helped up and down curbs by a husband who might just as well not have been there. This was not fiction.

(from: K. Amis, op. cit., p. 96)

What ist he talking about? What view does he hold on what he saw? Do you share his view?

4.3 Yes, modern social criticism – adverse, that ist – seems just about dead. There's just one place where you're still likely to run into it; and in a form of writing so minor that most serious literary reviewers aren't even aware of it. I refer, of course, to the field of science fiction. Now when I was a child, science fiction was different, too. Back in the late twenties and early thirties, science fiction was a field in which stories about Bug-Eyed Monsters were read by bug-eyed boys. It was full of crazy stuff about airplanes going faster than the speed of sound . . . and splitting the atom to harness its energy . . . and space-platforms hanging out in the middle of nowhere above the Earth. Just pulp trash, the product of diseased imaginations. Of course, nobody took it seriously.

But something happened, along about the time of World War II. Maybe it was the atomic bomb; maybe there is something to this idea that radiation and fallout can affect people in mysterious ways. At any rate, it affected our main-stream writers and caused them to begin producing wonderful new stories in praise of the status quo. And at the same time, it seemingly caused science fiction writers to suddenly emerge as rebels and prophets.

Science fiction became the vehicle for social criticism.

(from: Robert Bloch, Imagination and modern social criticism" in: B. Davenport et al., *The Science Fiction Novel,* Advent Publishers, Chicago 1969, p. 101 f)

1. Put the extract's main idea into your own words!
2. In what ways is Bloch rather ironical?
3. What does Bradbury criticize in his novel?
4. What do the other sf texts in this book criticize?

4.4 For your reading pleasure
The following text is to demonstrate to you the importance of English and history! Try to correct all its linguistic and historical mistakes!

College Kids Say the Darnedest Things

Those who forget history – and the English language – may be condemned to mangle both. Historian Anders Henriksson, a fiveyear veteran of the university classroom, has faithfully recorded his freshman students' more striking insights into European history. Possibly as an act of vengeance, Henriksson has assembled these fractured fragments into a chronological narrative from the Middle Ages to the present.

During the Middle Ages, everybody was middle aged. Church and state were co-operatic. Middle Evil society was made up of monks, lords and surfs. After a revival of infantile commerce, merchants appeared. They roamed from town to town exposing themselves and organized big fairies in the countryside. The

245

Crusades were expaditions by Christians who were seeking to free the holy land (the "Home Town" of Christ) from the Islams.

The Reformnation happened when German nobles resented that tithes were going to the pope, thus enriching Catholic coiffures. The popes were usually Catholic. An angry Martin Luther nailed 95 theocrats to a church door. Theologically, Luther was into reorientation mutation. Monks went right on seeing themselves as worms. The last Jesuit priest died in the 19th century. Louis XIV became King of the Sun. He gave the people food and artillery. If he didn't like someone, he sent them to the gallows to row for the rest of their lives. Vauban was the royal minister of flirtation.

The enlightenment was a reasonable time. Voltare wrote a book called *Candy* that got him into trouble. Philosophers were unknown yet, and the fundamental stake was one of religious toleration slightly confused with defeatism.

History started in 1815. Industrialization was precipitating in England. Problems were so complexicated that in Paris, out of a population of 1 million people, 2 million able bodies were on the loose.

The middle class was tired and needed a rest. The old order could see the lid holding down new ideas beginning to shake. Among the goals of the chartists were universal suferage and an anal parliment. Voting was to be done by ballad.

World War I broke out around 1912–1914. At war people get killed, and then they aren't people any more, but friends. Peace was proclaimed at Versigh, which was attended by George Loid, Primal Minister of England. President Wilson arrived with 14 pointers. In 1917, Lenin revolted Russia.

Germany was displaced after WWI. This gave rise to Hitler, who remilitarized the Rineland over a squirmish between Germany and France. Germany invaded Poland, France invaded Belgium, and Russia invaded everybody. War screeched to an end when a nukuleer explosion was dropped on Heroshima. A whole generation had been wipe out, and their forlorne families were left to pick up the peaces.

The last stage is us.

(Taken from: Reader's Digest 2/1984, us ed.)

4.5 Analyse this cartoon! Describe it and put its message into words! Fill in the speech balloon! Does it match our story?

Source: *Der Spiegel*, Nr. 43/82, p. 65

26 THE AMERICAN SCHOOL SYSTEM: FACTS AND PROBLEMS

We have read that Arthur Miller in *DOS* criticizes the prejudices against higher education of the American lower middle class. Let's now have a look at American education and get familiar with some facts and problems.

1. **Analysis**

1.1 **The Grading System**

1.1.1 Below is a short comic strip which deals with an issue that students all over the world have to face: exams. Read it and answer the following questions:
   a) What does the comic strip tell us about the grade (= mark) the boy got in the test? (cf. the American grading system below.)
   b) Why did Father do "great with 'True or False' tests", whereas the boy did not?
   c) What is the joke?

EXAMS

So...? What happened in school today?

Yech! We had a "True or False" test!

When I was a kid, I used to do great with "True or False" tests! Because even if I only guessed, I still stood a fifty-fifty chance of being right!

That's the way I figured it!!

So how'd you make out...?

I got a FIFTY!!

Source: *MAD*, September 1983

1.1.2 Study the survey of "Grade and Grade Points" below and explain the difference between the American and the German grading system. What do you think the grades "Incomplete", "Withdrawal", and "Audit" mean?

Grade and Grade Points

The grades used at many American schools and the grade points are assigned as follows:

Grade	Description	Percentage	Grade Points
A	Excellent	90–100	4 grade points per semester hour
B	Good	80–89	3 grade points per semester hour
C	Average	70–79	2 grade points per semester hour
D	Passing	60–69	1 grade point per semester hour
F(a)	Academic failure	Below 60	0 grade points per semester hour
F(n)	Failure due to non-attendance		
Inc.	Incomplete		
W.	Withdrawal		
Aud.	Audit		

The grade point average is found by dividing the total number of grade points by the total number of semester hours attempted. Grades of "Inc.," "W.," and "Aud." do not affect the grade point average.

1.2 The Structure of the American School System

1.2.1 Have a look at the diagram below informing you about American educational institutions and put its contents into words.

1.2.2 Try to explain what a *Technical School*, a *Junior College*, and a *Professional School* are.

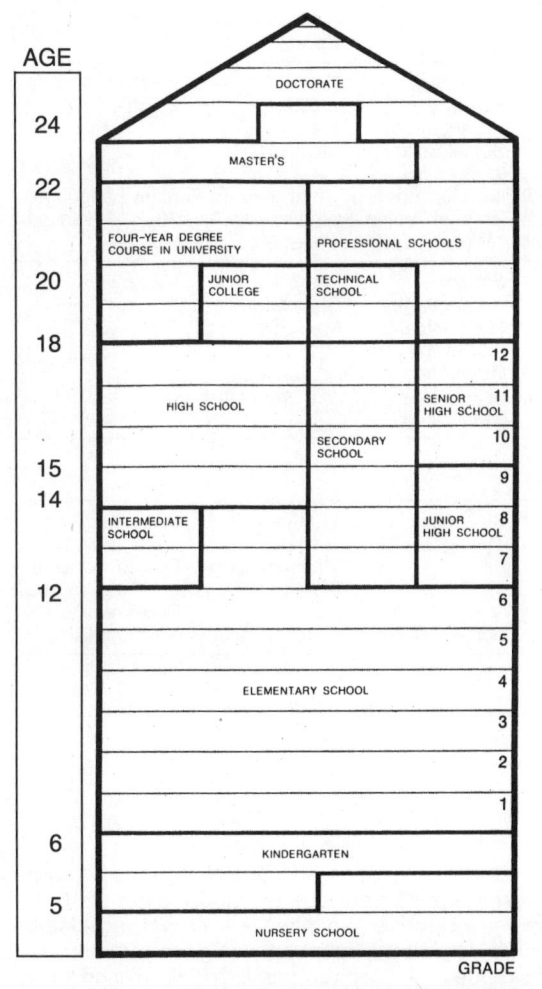

```
AGE                                                 
                        DOCTORATE
 24
                         MASTER'S
 22
        FOUR-YEAR DEGREE      PROFESSIONAL SCHOOLS
        COURSE IN UNIVERSITY
 20              JUNIOR      TECHNICAL
                 COLLEGE     SCHOOL
 18
                                              12
                                     SENIOR   11
                 HIGH SCHOOL         HIGH SCHOOL
                                              10
                             SECONDARY
                             SCHOOL
 15                                           9
 14
        INTERMEDIATE                 JUNIOR   8
        SCHOOL                       HIGH SCHOOL
                                              7
 12                                           6
                                              5
                 ELEMENTARY SCHOOL            4
                                              3
                                              2
                                              1
  6              KINDERGARTEN

  5              NURSERY SCHOOL
                                        GRADE
```

Source: *Facts about America,* Embassy of the USA

The number of American students completing a college education has been increasing steadily. In 1900 only 27,000 persons received university degrees. By 1950 the number had increased to 432,000; in 1970 827,000 persons graduated from colleges or universities; in 1974 the figure was up to 1,110,000, and in 1982 more than 1,700,000 students received degrees from institutions of higher learning.

1.2.3

Program	Class 9	Class 10	Class 11	Class 12
Requirements for All Programs	English P.E. Social Studies	English P.E.	English U.S. History/ Econ.	English Government/ Econ.
College Prep. Liberal Arts	Algebra Foreign Language Science	Geometry Foreign Language Social Science Elective	Chemistry/ Biology Elective Elective	Elective Elective
	Recommended Electives: Speech, Third Year of Foreign Language, Science, Maths, Personal Typing, Homemaking, Art, Music, Advanced Courses in Field in Which Teaching Major will be Taken.			
College Prep. Engineering	Algebra Foreign Language Physical Science	Foreign Language Mechanical Drawing Geometry	Algebra II Chemistry Mech. Drawing II	Maths IV Physics Electives
	Recommended Electives: Mechanical Drawing III, Biology, Personal Typing, Metal Shop I.			
• •				
Vocational Business	Maths Typing 1A-1B Career Decisions	Science Typing 2A-2B	Shorthand 1A-1B Merchandising Elective	Shorthand 2A-2B Office Machines/ Office Practice Bookkeeping Merchandising
	Recommended Electives: Spanish, Merchandising.			
• •				

Source: *Wirtschaft und Erziehung,* Dez. 1982, p. 390

Vocabulary

P.E. abbreviation of "Physical Education"; Sport – – **Social Studies / Social Science** Sozialkunde – – **Government** Bürgerkunde – – **Econ.** short for "Economics"; Volkswirtschaftslehre – – **Elective** Wahlfach – – **(Teaching) Major** Schwerpunktfach; Leistungsfach in der Abschlußprüfung – – **Speech** Rhetorik – – **Homemaking** Hauswirtschaftskunde – – **Mechanical Drawing** Technisches Zeichnen – – **Physical Science / Physics** Physik – – **Metal Shop** Metallbearbeitung – – **Career Decisions** Berufsfindungskurs – – **Shorthand** Kurzschrift – – **Office Machines** Büromaschinenkunde – – **Office Practice** – – Übungen in Bürotechnik – – **Merchandising** Verkaufskunde; Warenkunde

The chart above shows three programmes offered by a highschool: the first prepares the students for the entry into a *Liberal Arts College;* the second enables the students to study engineering at a university or Technical Institute/Technical College, and the third is necessary for students who intend to take a job or to go on to a *Technical School* (a kind of "Berufsschule") after graduation from highschool.

Assignments
1. Explain to your classmates in which courses the individual student must enrol.
2. Point out what subjects are stressed at the American High School and what are relatively neglected.
3. Compare the education of the High School students with that at your school. Which is more demanding, which is more comprehensive?

1.3 The Concept of American College Education

Objectives

Believing in the need for post-secondary education in order that individuals may realize more fully their individual potential and thereby enable them to live richer lives and become more responsible and productive members of our democatic society, the Board of Regents (= Aufsichtskomitee) of the Brazosport Junior College District establishes the following objectives for the college to provide:

1. Vocational, technical and semi-professional programs which will prepare individuals for employment in the business, industrial, and professional community.
2. Pre-professional and liberal arts courses acceptable for transfer to four-year colleges and universities.
3. Suitable courses for adults who desire to further their education, enrich their cultural lives, learn new skills or improve old ones, and improve their personal efficiency.
4. Community services designed to aid the social and cultural growth of the area and to assist in the preservation of our historical and ecological heritage.
5. A counseling and guidance program to aid in career direction so that citizens may realize the greatest possible benefits from their educational endeavors.
6. A student activity program appropriate to the needs of the students and in accordance with the college philosophy and principles.

Source: *Brazosport College Catalog* 1975

The college is a place for *intellectual discipline.* The colleges must provide the world with men and women who have learned to think rigorously on many subjects and to show genuine competence in a few. It is part of the function of a college that it should be an institution in which, by careful and steady intellectual work, the

5 members develop the habit, in all situations, of looking for the evidence and of drawing conclusions only in the light of relevant evidence. Such a college should place its first emphasis on intellectual discipline because it is this emphasis which distinguishes it from many other social organizations.

Earlham College is planned, however, to provide not only instruction but a *living
10 fellowship.* What takes place in the classroom must be of the highest excellence if a college is to be worthy of its vocation, but this is only a beginning. The individual study in the dormitory or library or research laboratory and the mutual criticism of ideas which the living fellowship provides may be as productive of insight as is the classroom presentation. The most lasting influences are often unrecognized ones.
15 This fact is abundantly illustrated by the steady impact of the weekly hour of worship, in which the student's insights are raised as in a reverent atmosphere he enters first-hand into the experience of religious leaders who have lived deeply and well. The college student may not know at what precise point his major ideals have been formed, but he realizes finally that they *have* been formed and that he is a different
20 person because of his membership in the pervasive college life.

Source: *Earlham College Catalog* 1976

1.3.1 Study and compare the quotations from the two college brochures above. Explain in your own words the difference in the objectives of the colleges. Express your opinion of these objectives. How would you characterise the objectives of your school?

1.3.2 Read the following excerpts from the history of Brazosport College and Earlham College. What do they tell you about the nature of the American school system?

History

The Brazosport Junior College District was created by vote of the qualified voters of the Brazosport Independent School District on the 27th day of November, 1948. The college district was a part of the Brazosport Independent School District and remained dormant until 1967. On July 15, 1967, the qualified voters of the district
5 authorized a tax for the maintenance of the college.

In a special meeting held on July 21, 1967, the Board of Trustees of the Brazosport Independent School District adopted a resolution declaring its intention to divest itself of the management, control, and operation of the Brazosport Junior College District. At this same meeting a Board of Regents for the Brazosport Junior College
10 District was appointed. The new Board of Regents was officially installed on August 1, 1967.

On August 7, 1967, the Board of Regents selected as its first employee Dr. J. R. Jackson, who was then serving as superintendent, Brazosport Independent School District, to serve as interim president of the college. Dr. Jackson served in his dual
15 capacity as superintendent and interim president until March 1, 1968, at which time he resigned as superintendent and assumed full-time duties as the college's first president. The Board of Regents previously elected him to this position on January 8, 1968.

The Board of Regents, March 19, 1968, approved plans to open the college in
20 September, 1968, for its first students in facilities provided by the Brazosport

Independent School District at the Brazosport Education Extension Center, Freeport, Texas.
The voters of the district approved a $5,000,000 bond issue on September 17, 1968. Construction and equipment grants from federal and state sources in the amount
25 of $1,300,000 were received. A 156 acre site was acquired and construction of a facility to house 1,100 full-time students was completed in the spring of 1971.

Earlham is a Quaker college. Earlham was founded in 1847, at the center of what is now the largest concentration of Quaker population in the world. Joseph John Gurney, a highly gifted English Quaker, the Master of Earlham Hall at Norwich, England, made a long and influential American tour in 1837–1840. He visited, in
5 the course of his travels, the Indiana settlements, at that time pioneer communities. Ten years later the Boarding School was founded, and when it became a college it took the name of the famous Gurney home at Norwich. The remarkable history of Earlham Hall in England, as a center of new and liberating movements, has influenced the conception, which Earlham College has always had, of what its own
10 true function should be.

2. **Discussion and Comment**

2.1 Unlike the European (Continental) school systems the American is very decentralized, i.e. the *public* schools are only partly controlled by the state government. Supervision is mainly in the hands of local councillors and school boards. *Private* schools, anyway, set their own objectives and academic standards. Discuss some pros and cons of the American and the European systems.

2.2 Few American High Schools class their students according to performance and talent (exception: retarded children). Explain the advantages and disadvantages of such an education.

2.2.1 "... A growing number of American parents are sending their children to private schools because ... students in a typical private school – a Catholic school with larger classes and fewer resources – achieve more than those in the average public school ... Seventy percent of their students are enrolled in an academic program, compared with only 34 per cent for public school ..." ("How To Save Our Public Schools," *Reader's Digest*, 3, 1983) What do you consider to be the reasons for this striking fact?

2.2.2 Would you agree that private schools in Germany also have higher academic standards than public ones? What is your view of private schools?

2.3 In the USA the percentage of students who earn a High School diploma allowing them to participate in a university entrance examination is much higher (about 50%) than the percentage of European students (around 25%) earning comparable certificates (in Britain: General Certificate of Education, Advanced Level; in Germany: Abitur). Do you consider this a good idea, or do you think secondary education should be more selective? What percentage of students should obtain a certificate enabling them to attend university, and why?

3. **Language**

3.1 Give synonyms for the expressions underlined or paraphrase the sentences without using those particular expressions.
   a) ... the grade points are <u>assigned</u> as follows.
   b) ... in 1970 827,000 persons <u>graduated</u> from colleges or universities.
   c) The number of students enrolled as candidates for <u>graduate degrees</u> shows a similar trend ... <u>with an enrollment</u> of more than one million expected by 1980.
   d) The college is a place for <u>intellectual discipline</u>.
   e) Earlham College is planned, however, to provide not only <u>instruction</u> but a <u>living fellowship</u>.

3.2 Explain briefly: boarding school; interim president; post-secondary education; professional community; superintendent

3.3 Find an expression meaning the opposite of the following: (do not use a prefix.)
   higher learning:
   elective:
   humanities:
   individual (adj.):
   full-time:
   intellectual:

3.4 Give the opposite by using a prefix:
   competent; productive; steady; complete; to increase; relevant; liberal

4. **Further Studies**

4.1 Take the minutes (cf. Topic 14, p. 164) of the lesson(s) dealing with the topic of *The American School System: Facts and Problems.*

4.2 Do you remember the advertisements on page 111 ff. and what we said about the techniques used in advertising? Imagine you are a professional copywriter who has been hired by the president of Brazosport College to design an ad in which one or more positive aspect(s) of the college (see Objectives, p. 251) are presented in a *humorous* way. Write the text in a language appropriate to its content.

III MAN AND BELIEF

27 THE LURE OF DOOMSDAY

Note on the Text

In December 1978, news of the suicide of some 900 members of the California-based *Peoples Temple,* a sect founded and led by the Reverend Jim Jones, reached a horrified public. In the jungles of Guyana (Latin America), where the sect had built up a religious colony, a tragedy of terror and insanity had occurred. For days, newspapers and news magazines all over the world presented details of the story of Jonestown to their readers. *Time Magazine* of 4th December 1978 devoted its cover story and several other articles to the event; among them was the following by Lance Morrow, which tries to put the incident into a historical framework.

The Jonestown story, like some Joseph Conrad drama of fanaticism and moral emptiness, has gone directly into popular myth. It will be remembered as an emblematic, identifying moment of the decade: a demented American psychopomp in a tropical cult house, doling out cyanide with Kool-Aid. Jonestown is the Altamont of the '70s cult movement. Just as Altamont began the destruction of the sweet, vacuous aspirations of Woodstock, Jonestown has decisively contaminated the various vagabond zealotries that have grown up, flourished and sometimes turned sinister.

All new religious enterprises, of course, are liable to be damned and dismissed as "cults." The term is pejorative: cult suggests a hand of fierce believers who have surrendered themselves to obscure doctrine and a dangerous prophet. Yet some religions that are institutions now, more permanent and stable than most governments, began as cults.

Although Jonestown has prompted a widespread revulsion against cults, both fairness and the First Amendment suggest that one standard of judgment can still be applied: "By their fruits ye shall know them." Visionaries, even when they operate from a cult, can bring dimensions of aspiration and change to religion, which otherwise might be merely a moral policeman. But the historical record of cults is ominous and often lurid. Jonestown, for all its gruesome power to shock, has its religious (or quasi-religious) precedents.

Jonestown has even been rivaled as a mass suicide. The Jewish Zealots defending the fortress of Masada against besieging Roman legions in A.D. 73 chose self-slaughter rather than submission: 960 men, women and children died. The event occupies a place of some reverence in Jewish memory and is not really comparable to Jonestown; the Zealots faced the prospect of slaughter or slavery, and their choice therefore possessed a certain passionate rationality. In the 17th century, Russian Orthodox dissenters called the Old Believers refused to accept liturgical reforms. Over a period of years some 20,000 peasants in protest abandoned their fields and burned themselves. In East Africa before World War I, when Tanganyika was a German colony, witch doctors of the *Maji-Maji* movement convinced tribesmen that German bullets would turn to water. They launched an uprising, and the credulous were slaughtered.

Religion and insanity occupy adjacent territories in the mind; historically, cults have kept up a traffic between the two. The medieval Brethren of the Free Spirit, the heretical Beghards and Beguines who practiced in Cologne and other Northern European cities, became nihilistic megalomaniacs. They began in rags but then, in the conviction of their spiritual superiority, which they eventually believed to surpass God's, adopted the idea that the general run of mankind existed merely to be exploited, through robbery, violence and treachery. In 1420 a cult of Bohemians called the Adamites came to regard themselves, like the Manson gang, as avenging angels. They set about making holy war to cut down the unclean; blood, they said, must flood the world to the height of a horse's head. They were finally exterminated after committing uncounted murders. In 1535 an army of Anabaptists under Jan Bockelson proclaimed its intention "to kill all monks and priests and all rulers that there are in the world; for our king alone is the rightful ruler." They, too, had to be forcibly suppressed. Cultists, of course, are sometimes the victims of persecution. The heretical Albigensians, or Cathari, were broken by church crusade and massacre in the 13th century.

The U.S. also has had its bloody moments. Mormons were slaughtered in Illinois and persecuted elsewhere. But it was some 60 Mormons disguised as Indians who, in September 1857, committed the Mountain Meadows Massacre. With the help of 300 Indians, the Mormons killed more than 120 men, women and children in the Fancher party that was passing through Utah on the way to California. It was, says Historian William Wise, "the logical and culminating act of a society whose leaders believed themselves superior to the rest of mankind and who maintained that their own ecclesiastical laws took precedence over the laws of their country."

The tendency to join cults seems to come roughly in 50-year cycles in the U.S. A wave broke in the mid-19th century, then again after World War I, and now in the '70s. For several thousand years, the rule has been that cults flourish in times of great social change. The success of cults today is based partly upon an edifice of unhappy sociological clichés: the breakdown of the family and other forms of authority, the rootlessness and moral flabbiness of life.

At their worst, the cults acquire a psychosis of millennialism. This chiliasm, playing at the drama of the last days, flourishes when life is no longer seen as ascendant. But no matter how democratically advertised, visions of the New Jerusalem, Utopia or an Edenic Jonestown are bathed in a totalitarian light. And they are shadowed by glimpses of enemies. Antichrist, Gog and Magog; paranoia is often a cult's principal instrument of discipline. Even in 1978, one catches whiffs of an old dementia and witchfire.

70 Traditional religions allow people to live inside history, but still give sacramental expression to their spiritual longings. Cults too often strain to escape from history, through the reconstruction of Eden or a vision of the Second Coming. Experiments in earthly paradise have a way of ending in horrible irony. Zealots become infected with a fierce nostalgia for a mythical lost wholeness, an ecstasy of spiritual servitude.
75 In Jones' cultish socialism, the spiritual and political were joined. In their terrific surrender, cultists reduce a multiform, contradictory world to cant formulas, and thus they become as dangerous as anyone whose head resounds with certainties. Cults are apt to become miniatures of the great totalitarian systems built on Nazi or Hegelian and Marxist foundations. There are eerie similarities of style: intolerance,
80 paranoia, submission.

Such movements, wrote Historian Norman Cohn, strive to endow "social conflicts and aspirations with a transcendental significance—in fact with all the mystery and majesty of the final, eschatological drama." To be human is to live inside history, to accept a reality that does not respond to dogma or a megalomaniac's discipline.
85 One escape is that found by the people in Jonestown. (~ 1020 words)

Annotations
(The words marked * should be memorized.)
Joseph Conrad (1857–1924) Polish-English author of adventure and sea novels, famous for his masterly style and his psychological understanding. Some of his works: *Lord Jim, Heart of Darkness, The Secret Sharer, The Shadow Line* – – **emblematic** serving as a symbol – – **demented** mad – – **psychopomp** a conductor of souls to the afterworld – – **to dole out** distribute in small amounts – – **cyanide** ['saɪənaɪd] a poison – – **Kool-Aid** an orange drink – – **Altamont/Cal.** place of a Rolling Stones concert (1969) where a young black man was killed and several other spectators were beaten up by the Hell's Angels, a rocker gang, who had been hired by the organizers to serve as security police – – **vacuous** showing or suggesting absence of thought or intelligence – – **Woodstock** place near Bethel/NY where an earlier rock concert had taken place. The security force (members of various communes) did an excellent job without using any physical force – – **vagabond** habitually wandering – – **zealotry** fanaticism, beliefs – – **sinister** suggesting evil or the likelihood of coming misfortune – – **pejorative** [pɪˈdʒorətɪv] depreciatory; herabsetzend – – **revulsion** sudden and complete change of feeling – – ***amendment** change proposed or made (to a rule, regulation) *here:* of the American Constitution – – **lurid** *here:* violent and shocking – – ***precedent** earlier happening, decision, etc. taken as an example or rule for what comes later – – **dissenter** one who has a different opinion – – **adjacent** next to, lying near to – – ***medieval** of the Middle Ages – – ***heretical** of belief or opinion contrary to what is generally accepted, esp. in religion – – **megalomaniac** person suffering from a form of madness in which a person has exaggerated ideas of his importance of power, wealth – – **treachery** false or disloyal act – – **Manson gang** band of fanatics with Manson as their leader. Manson, a typical megalomaniac, ordered his followers (mainly girls) to kill the pregnant Sharon Tate (Mrs. Polanski), the wife of the famous film producer and female star in Polanski's film *Rosemary's Baby* – – **to avenge** take revenge – – ***to exterminate** make an end of, destroy completely – –

Anabaptists name of a sect which came into existence during the Reformation. They rejected child baptism in favour of baptising adults. They at first bore all persecution with patience but later changed their attitude. They established a reign of terror in Münster/Westfalen (1534), which was ended by the conquest of the town and the cruel punishment of the cultists (1535) – – **Albigensians** named after the town of Albi in southern France. They held radical views, e.g. that there existed a good and an evil god, and propagated a strict and rigid asceticism. They played an important role in the Languedoc (southern France) from the end of the 12th century. During the so-called "Wars against the Albigensians" (1209–1229), which had been proclaimed by Pope Innocence III, they were completely exterminated. – – **Mormons** members of the "Church of Jesus Christ of Latter-Day Saints". Their name is taken from the holy book "Mormon", a scripture claimed to have been dictated to Joseph Smith, the founder of the sect, by an angel called Moroni. The name "Mormon" is a composition of English "more" and an allegedly Egyptian word "mon" which is said to mean "good". The Mormons emphasise the idea of human spiritual improvement. In 1847, about 12,000 adherents settled near the Great Salt Lake in the American Far West and established the state of Utah, originally a community based on a theocratic constitution. The center of Salt Lake City, the capital, is a temple made of granite from which Jesus Christ (according to Mormon belief) will proclaim the Last Judgement – – **to take precedence over** to be considered first – – **edifice** building (esp. a large or imposing one) – – **flabbiness** weakness – – **millennialism** a doctrine that the prophecy in the book of Revelation will be fulfilled with an earthly period of 1,000 years of universal peace and the triumph of righteousness – – **chiliasm** the theological doctrine that Christ will come to earth in a visible form and set up a theocratic kingdom over all the world and thus usher in the millennium – – **ascendant** moving or tending upward – – **Edenic** of or relating to Eden (= paradise) – – **Antichrist** *here:* Satan – – **Gog & Magog** two kings prophesied to attack the Church in a climactic battle before being destroyed by God (Revelation 20.8–10) – – *****paranoia** Verfolgungswahn – – **whiff** a puff, gust, or wave of odour, of vapour or gas in the air; Hauch, übler Geruch – – **dementia** madness – – **to strain** to make an intense effort, to do one's utmost – – **cant formula** nichtssagende Formel – – *****to resound** to echo and re-echo – – *****foundations** strong base of a building – – **eerie** causing a feeling of mystery and fear – – *****to endow** [ɪnˈdaʊ] provide – – **eschatological** of, relating to, dealing with the ultimate destiny of mankind

Assignments

1. Divide the text into sense units and sum up their contents in a short sentence or a caption each.
2. Answer the following questions:
2.1 What are the consequences of "Jonestown" for other cult movements?
2.2 What does the author mean by "religion and insanity occupy adjacent territories"?
2.3 To what extent does the hint at the religious cults of the Middle Ages emphasise his statement above (2.2)?
2.4 At what times in the course of human history have cults gained importance and why are they flourishing at present?

2.5 What explanations for the extreme attitudes of cults are presented in the text?
2.6 Why are cults more radical than traditional religions?

3. **Discuss and Comment**
3.1 The author states that ". . . some religions that are institutions now, . . ., began as cults . . ." Which ones is he likely to be thinking of? Explain your opinion.
3.2 Would you support the author's idea that many cults are totalitarian? (What about those of Asian origin?)
3.3 What do you think are the reasons for young people to join the new religious movements?
3.4 Young people's membership of cults has often led to severe problems in their families. Young people leave home and school or give up their vocational training. Doctors even claim that cults often cause mental and psychic diseases in their followers, such as schizophrenia or paranoia. Should such cults therefore be forbidden?
3.5 Do you see any parallels between religious and political utopias? If so, give examples.
3.6 Could you imagine joining a cult movement? Explain why or why not?

4. **Further Studies**
4.1 The text *Nightmare in Jonestown* (overleaf) is fragmentary. Make a summary of the fragment. Then complete the summary with the help of the following diagram.

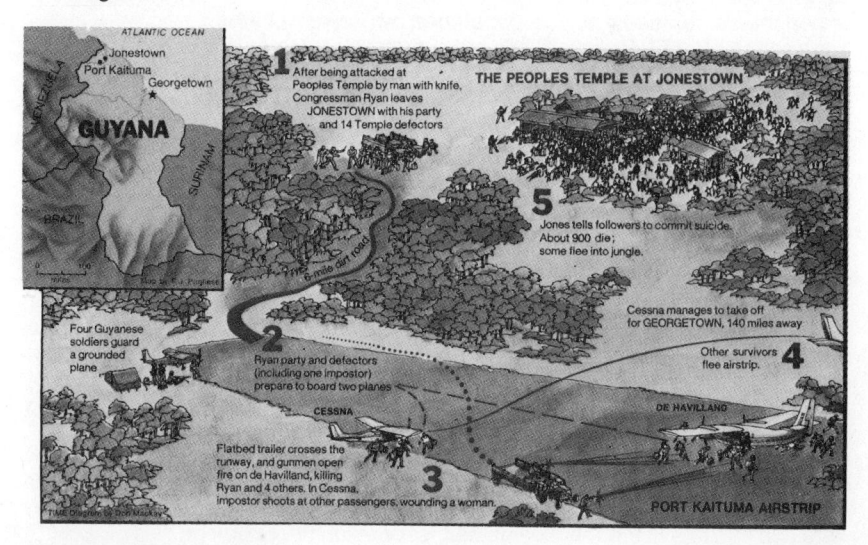

Source: *Time*, Dec. 4, 1978

4.2 One student reads Arthur Miller's play *The Crucible* and reports on its contents to the class. Then all students discuss whether there are similarities between life in Jonestown in 1978 and in Salem/Massachusetts in 1692 as presented in Miller's play.

Nightmare in Jonestown

A religious colony in Guyana turns into a cult of death

"The large central building was ringed by bright colors. It looked like a parking lot filled with cars. When the plane dipped lower, the cars turned out to be bodies. Scores and scores of bodies – hundreds of bodies – wearing red dresses, blue T shirt, green blouses, pink slacks, children's polka-dotted jumpers. Couples with
5 their arms around each other, children holding parents. Nothing moved. Washing hung on the clotheslines. The fields were freshly plowed. Banana trees and grape vines were flourishing. But nothing moved."
Not since hundreds of Japanese civilians leaped to their deaths off the cliffs of Saipan as American forces approached the Pacific island in World War II had there
10 been a comparable act of collective self-destruction. The followers of the Rev. Jim Jones, 47, a once respected Indianaborn humanitarian who degenerated into egomania and paranoia, had first ambushed a party of visiting Americans, killing California Congressman Leo Ryan, 53, three newsmen and one defector from their heavily guarded colony at Jonestown. Then, exhorted by their leader, intimidated
15 by armed guards and lulled with sedatives and painkillers, parents and nurses used syringes to squirt a concoction of potassium cyanide and potassium chloride onto the tongues of babies. The adults and older children picked up paper cups and sipped the same deadly poison sweetened by purple Kool-Aid.
In the spring of 1977, Ryan, a liberal but maverick Democrat, spoke with a longtime
20 friend, Associated Press Photographer Robert Houston. Houston, who was ill, told Ryan that Houston's son Bob, 33, had been found dead in the San Francisco railroad yards, where he worked, just one day after he had quit the Peoples Temple. Though authorities said his son died as the result of an accidental fall, Houston claimed the cult had long threatened defectors with death.
25 A loner who liked doing his own investigating of constituents' concerns, Ryan began inquiring about Jim Jones and his followers, who had just started clearing some 900 acres in the rain forests of Guyana. Other unhappy relatives of temple members, as well as a few people who had fearfully left the cult, told the Congressman that beatings and blackmail, rather than brotherly love, impelled the cultists to work on
30 the new colony. Articles in *New West* magazine and the San Francisco *Examiner* in August 1977 further documented the temple's increasing use of violence to enforce conformity to its rigid rules of conduct. Members were routinely scolded by Jones before the assembled community and then whipped or beaten with paddles for such infractions as smoking or failing to pay attention during a Jones "sermon."
35 A woman accused of having a romance with a male cult member was forced to have intercourse with a man she disliked, while the entire colony watched. One means of indoctrinating children: electrodes were attached to their arms and legs, and they were told to smile at the mention of their leader's name. Everyone was ordered to call Jones "Father."

40 Ryan repeatedly asked the State Department to check into reports about the mistreatment of Americans in Jonestown. The U.S. embassy in Georgetown sent staff members to the colony, some 140 miles northwest of the capital. They reported they had separately interviewed at least 75 of the cultists. Not one, the embassy reported, said he wanted to leave.

45 That did not satisfy Ryan, who decided to find out what was happening in Jonestown by going there.

Ryan took along eight newsmen as well as several relatives of temple members, who hoped to persuade their kin to leave the colony. The visitors arrived in a chartered aircraft, an 18-seat De Havilland Otter, at an airstrip in Port Kaituma, six
50 miles from Jonestown. They rode to the colony along a muddy and barely passable road through the jungle in a tractor-drawn flat-bed trailer. At Jonestown all were greeted warmly by a smiling Jones.

The members of the Peoples Temple put on a marvelous performance for their visitors. Reporters were led past the central, open-air pavilion, used as both a school
55 and an assembly hall. The visitors saw the newly completed sawmill, the 10,000-volume library, the neat nursery, where mosquito netting protected babies sleeping peacefully on pallets. The colony hospital had delivered 33 babies without a single death, the tour guides said.

The highlight of the visit was an evening of entertainment in the pavilion. As a lively
60 band beat out a variety of tunes, from rock to disco to jazz, the colonists burst into song, including a rousing chorus of *America the Beautiful.* Even the skeptical Ryam was impressed.

Next day, however, NBC Correspondent Don Harris asked Jones about reports that his colony was heavily armed. Jones, who had been swallowing lots of pills, blew
65 up. "A bold-faced lie!" he cried. "It seems like we are defeated by lies. I'm defeated. I might as well die!"

The colony's facade was crumbling. One Jonestown resident had nervously pushed a note into Harris' hand. "Four of us want to leave," it said. Ryan was getting other furtive pleas from cultists asking to go back to the U.S. with him. Jones was asked
70 about the defectors. "Anyone is free to come and go," he said magnanimously, "I want to hug them before they leave." But then Jones turned bitter. "They will try to destroy us," he predicted. "They always lie when they leave."

As divided families argued over whether to stay or go, Jones saw part of his congregation slipping away. Al Simon, father of three, wanted to take his children
75 back to America. "No! No! No!" screamed his wife. Someone whispered to her: "Don't worry, we're going to take care of everything." Indeed, as reporters learned later from survivors, Jones had a plan to plant one or more fake defectors among the departing group, in order to attack them. He told some of his people that the Congressman's plane "will fall out of the sky."

80 The first violence occurred as Ryan conferred with Jones about taking those who wished to leave with him. Lane and Jones' longtime attorney, Charles Garry, sat in on the negotiations in a room inside the pavillion. Suddenly a cultist later identified as Don Sly ran up to Ryan from behind, grabbed him around his throat with one arm and brandished a knife with the other. "I'm going to kill you!" Sly shouted. Lane
85 and Garry wrestled the knife away from Sly, accidentally cutting the assailant. The blood spattered Ryan's clothes. Jones watched impassively. He made no move to interfere . . .

Abbreviated from: *Time Magazine,* Dec. 4, 1978

The bodies in the community hall

Source: *Time,* Dec. 4, 1978

Vocabulary
(The words marked * should be memorized.)
*__nightmare__ terrible, frightening dream – – *__to dip__ *here:* to incline downwards – –
*__score__ *here:* twenty, set of twenty – – __polka-dotted jumper__ Pulli mit Punktmuster
– – *__clothesline__ rope stretched between posts on which clothes are hung to dry
– – __vine__ any plant with slender stems that trails or climbs – – __egomania__ extreme
egocentricity, abnormally developed egotism – – *__defector__ one who falls away from

a cause or party – – **to exhort** urge strongly, to incite by argument or advice – – **to intimidate** frighten – – **sedative** drug tending to calm the nerves and reduce stress – – **syringe** device for drawing in liquid or injecting liquids into the body; Spritze – – **to squirt** force out in a thin stream or jet – – **concoction** s.th. that is prepared by mixing together – – **potassium cyanide** ['saɪənaɪd] Kaliumzyanid – – **maverick** unorthodox – – **to quit** leave, give up – – *****constituent** member of a body of voters living in a town or district that sends a representative to Parliament or to Congress – – *****blackmail** payment of money for not making known s.th. discreditable – – **to impel** drive, force, urge – – *****to scold** blame with angry words – – **infraction** breaking of a rule, law, etc. – – *****sermon** spoken or written address on a religious or moral subject – – *****embassy** duty and mission of an ambassador (= person representing the Government of his country in a foreign country), his official residence – – *****kin** family, relations – – **flat-bed trailer** Traktor mit Pritschenanhänger – – **pallet** straw-filled mattress for sleeping on – – **furtive** done secretly so as not to attract attention – – **plea** *here:* request – – *****to hug** put the arms round tightly, esp. to show love – – *****attorney** person with legal authority to act for another in business or law – – **to grab s.b.** take roughly, snatch suddenly – – *****throat** front part of the neck – – **to brandish s.th.** wave about; etwas schwingen, mit etwas herumfuchteln – – **to wrestle s.th. away from s.b.** jem. etwas gewaltsam aus den Händen winden – – **assailant** attacker – – **to spatter** besudeln

28 THE ANSWER

Note on the Text

The American writer Frederic Brown (1906–1972) is known for his sf as well as for his detective novels (he was awarded the "Edgar" for *The Fabulous Clipjoint*). His sf is noted for its elegance and humour, and he is at this best in the shorter forms of fiction, short short stories or even extended jokes. He is said to have told the shortest sf story of all time: "After the last nuclear war the earth was a dead star; there was no more vegetation and no animal had survived. The last man on earth was sitting alone in his room. Suddenly there was a knock at the front door . . .". Of which there is a still shorter version: "The last man alive in the world sat all alone in his house. Suddenly the front door bell rang . . ."

(The following short story has been taken from: Man and Technology, CVK, 1981, p. 44, Scott Meredith Literary Agency Inc. 845 Third Avenue, New York)

Important:

As you will notice the most important parts of the story have been left out. Try to complete the story according to your own taste before your teacher reads you the author's version!

Dwar Ev ceremoniously soldered the final connection with gold. The eyes of a dozen television cameras watched him and the subether bore throughout the universe a dozen pictures of what he was doing.

He straightened and nodded to Dwar Reyn, then moved to a position beside the
switch that would complete the contact when he threw it. The switch that would
connect, all at once, all the monster computing machines of all the populated planets
in the universe – ninety-six billion planets – into the supercircuit that would connect
them all into one supercalculator, one cybernetics machine that would combine all
the knowledge of all the galaxies.

Dwar Reyn spoke briefly to the watching and listening trillions. Then after a
moment's silence he said, "Now, Dwar Ev."

Dwar Ev threw the switch. There was a mighty hum, the surge of power from
ninety-six billion planets. Lights flashed and quieted along the miles-long panel.

Dwar Ev stepped back and drew a deep breath. "The honour of asking the first
question is yours, Dwar Reyn."

"Thank you," said Dwar Reyn. "It shall be a question which no single cybernetics
machine has been able to answer."

He turned to face the machine. "_____?"

The mighty voice answered without hesitation, without clicking a single relay.

"_____!"

_____

_____

(~ 240 words)

WORKSHEET

1. **Language**

1.1 Find as many members as you can belonging to, the semantic field of "go". The text gives "step".

1.2. Below you will find a list of words belonging to the semantic field of movement. Taking "walk" as the basic word, put them into the order of their degree of velocity! Thus "shoot" would be placed at the top, whereas "halt" would find its place at the bottom of the list.

Words: speed, walk, lag, race, crawl, run, dart, creep, rush, limp, halt, hurry, linger, shoot, shuffle, hasten, saunter

1.3 Let's have a look at the semantic field of oral utterance. Our basic word is *"speak"*. Below is a list of definitions and a list of the members of this semantic field. Try to find the right pairs. Thus "speak loudly" requires "shout", etc.

Definitions:	Words:
speak loudly	harangue
speak normally	recite
speak too quickly	mumble
speak to oneself	whisper
speak in Parliament	lisp/stutter
speak like a baby	pray
speak with a defect	talk
speak to God	shout
speak softly and sweetly	jabber
speak indistinctly	soliloquise
speak in light conversation	address
speak in church	debate
speak imperfectly	preach
speak softly	stammer
speak loud and scolding	murmur
speak to somebody	lecture
speak at the university	chatter
speak a poem	babble
speak seriously and reprovingly	sermonize

1.4 Choosing exact words: **liveliness**

Lively words make writing come alive. They enable your reader to live through your experience or think through your idea as *you* did. If you actually *sped* somewhere, why say you *walked?* If you mean *deserted*, why settle for *empty?* When you want to suggest a *towering inferno,* why let it go at *tall,* or *big,* or *high?* (Can you imagine the impact of a movie called *The Tall Inferno?*) Compare the following sentences with the livelier ones written by Joan Didion:

    Flames were *coming* up behind her.
Lively: Flames were _____ up behind her.
    A window *closed* once in Barbara's room.
Lively: A window _____ once in Barbara's room.
    The gas heater *goes* on and off.
Lively: The gas heater _____ on and off.
    College girls *were* at the courthouse all night.
Lively: College girls _____ at the courthouse all night.
    I'd *go* seven hundred miles to Brownsville, Texas.
Lively: I'd _____ seven hundred miles to Brownsville, Texas.
    Beyond the [old frame houses] *are* the shopping centers.
Lively: Beyond the [old frame houses] _____ the shopping centers.
    [It is] so hot that the air *has a shine,* the grass *is* white and the blinds ore drawn all day.

Lively: [It is] so hot that the air _____ the grass _____ white and the blinds _____ drawn all day.

[The sailors] *are* on the sidewalk avoiding the Hawaii Armed Forces Patrol and telling one another to get tattooed.

Lively: [The sailors] _____ on the sidewalk avoiding the Hawaii Armed Forces Patrol and _____ one another to get tattooed.

Put the following verbs in their appropriate gaps abose to make the dull sentences livelier!

banged, bleaches, camped, daring, hitchhike, jostle around, shimmers, shooting, spread, sputters, stay.

(Adapted from: S. Schor and J. Fishman, eds, *The Random House Guide to Basic writing*, Random House, New York 1978, p. 293 f)

1.5 Enlarge your religious vocabulary by finding the hidden words. The remaining letters form two sentences from the Bible. (There is an "X" at the beginning and between them!)

```
C S N O I T C E R R U S E R S
H A X I N T H G E B E G M I T
R V N S U P E R S T I T I O N
I I N I N R G A G O D B R C E
S O R B E A A C Y T E A A D M
T U T E H Y E E T H E P C A D
M R V N E N A N H D T T L H N
A N G E L E E N G A R I E T A
S O H D E V I L I X N S L E M
D R B I A S I D M C U M S N M
S E I C S O E C L F H T Y I O
S Y B T N U T R A H C R U H C
O A L I O T O I M R E M I P N
R R E O T A T I M O N K T S E
C P I N H H R E P E N T O N T
```

Hidden words

(find the ENGLISH counterparts!)

1 Aberglaube, 2 allmächtig, 3 Auferstehung, 4 bereuen, 5 beten, 6 Bibel, 7 Christus, 8 Engel, 9 fromm, 10 Gebet, 11 Glaube, 12 Gnade, 13 Gott, 14 Heiland, 15 heilig, 16 Kirche, 17 Kirchenlied, 18 Kreuz, 19 Mönch, 20 Pfarrer, 21 Predigt, 22 Segen, 23 Sünde, 24 Taufe, 25 Teufel, 26 Weihnachten, 27 Wunder, 28 Zehn Gebote (NOTE: The word "God" in line 4 belongs to the hidden sentence, not to the hidden words!)

2. **Text Analysis**
2.1 Complete the story according to your own taste before your teacher reads you the author's version! Read your versions to your class and discuss them!
2.2 This story furnishes a good example of an idea-as-hero sf story. Put the author's idea into your own words!
2.3 Draft a short speech for Dwar Rayn!

3. **Discussion and Comment**
3.1 Is Frederic Brown's fear justified?
3.2 Put the main ideas of the following German text into English: Do not translate it, but try to get as near to the German text as you can by using the vocabulary at your command! What do you make of this statement?

Obwohl vielleicht der äußere Anschein dagegen spricht, lassen sich grundlegende Gemeinsamkeiten zwischen Science Fiction und Religion feststellen, die in vielfältiger Weise im Erscheinungsbild der Gattung zutage treten. Ähnlich wie die Religion ist die Science Fiction ihrem Wesen nach transzendent. Ihre gattungsspezifischen Inhalte beziehen sich zwar auf die Erfahrung des Lesers, überschreiten aber definitionsgemäß prinzipiell die Grenzen des Erfahrenen.
Analog zur Religion ist Science Fiction auf Sinnfragen, auf die Erklärung von menschlichen Grundgegebenheiten ausgerichtet. Wenn sie ihre Aufgabe ernst nimmt, geht es ihr nicht, wie vielfach angenommen, um Technologie und Naturwissenschaft an sich, sondern um deren Folgen und Bedeutung für den Menschen. Sie fragt letztlich nach Heil oder Verderben, und beides ist meist abhängig von höheren, der Kontrolle des normalen Individuums entzogenen Instanzen und Wirkursachen. Wenn man Religion u. a. definieren kann als „das Gefühl der Verbundenheit, der Abhängigkeit, der Verpflichtung gegenüber einer geheimnisvollen, haltgebenden und verehrungswürdigen Macht", dann läßt sich dies, einschließlich der entsprechenden negativen Umkehrungen, weithin auf die Science fiction und die von ihr hervorgebrachten Welten übertragen. Nur ist die hier wirksame höhere Macht meistens nicht die Gottheit der überlieferten Religion, sondern etwa die Technologie oder die Naturwissenschaft.
(from: Suerbaum/Broich/Borgmeier, *Science fiction,* Philipp Reclam, Stuttgart 1981, p. 151 f.)

4. **For further study**
4.1 Compare "The Answer" with the following definitions of an anecdote a sketch and a short story. How would you classify "The Answer"? Give reasons!

Anecdote
An anecdote (Gk 'sth unpublished') is 'a usually short narrative of an interesting, amusing, or curious incident often biographical and generally characterized by human interest'. *(Webster's Third New International Dictionary of the English Language Unabridged.)* To put it more simply, it is a moment taken from a biography and told in the form of a short, yet complete story. It is a journalistic or literary form in its own right and can be told for its

own sake. But it may also be an integral part of longer texts like speeches, newspaper articles, essays, short stories, novels or even dramas. Its main function is then to illustrate a certain idea or a certain trait of the character of a personality.

Sketch
Very similar to the anecdote is the sketch (cf. G 'Skizze'). In fact, a biographical sketch is an anecdote. But whereas an anecdote is normally taken from a biography and based on some personal element, a sketch may be based on any subject. A sketch is originally **'a rough drawing representing the chief features of an object or scene'.** *(Webster's Dictionary.)* Later it also came to mean any 'short literary composition somewhat resembling the short story and the essay but less formal than these and usually intentionally slight in treatment, discursive in style, and familiar in tone'. *(Webster's Dictionary.)*
For practical reasons, we may say that a sketch is very similar to an anecdote, except for the following differences:
1) it can be taken from a broader background (i.e. it need not be biographical);
2) it need not be exclusively streamlined towards the point at the end;
3) it is often slighter in treament, more discursive in style, and more familiar in tone.

Both the sketch and the anecdote are some sort of crystallizing point reflecting the most outstanding characteristics of a historical epoch, a place, an institution, or a personality. They suggest many more aspects of the whole truth beyond the mere facts. From the point of view of literature, both the sketch and the anecdote are transitional forms in that they fuse fact and fiction.

(from: Rotter/Bendl, *Your Companion to English Lit. Texts,* vol. I, Manz Vlg, München 1981, p. 64, 65)

29 THE STAR

Note on the Text

The English author Arthur C. Clarke (b. 1917) is one of the best-known sf writers in the world. Holding a BSc degree in mathematics and physics he is very closely identified with technological hardcore sf, but he also likes to write metaphysical, even mystical, sf.
Among his works is the short story *The Sentinel* (1951), which many years later formed the basis of one of the most famous sf films: *2001: A Space Odyssey* (1968), for which Clarke wrote the screenplay with Stanley Kubrick.
The following text in meant to be for your reading pleasure and has therefore been left without annotations and elaborate worksheet.

Our story is taken from: Arthur C. Clarke, *The Other Side of the Sky,* Corgi Books, Transworld Publishers Ltd, London, 1975, p. 115 ff.
(The numbers in brackets indicate the numbers of the paragraphs)

It is three thousand light-years to the Vatican. Once, I believed that space could have no power over faith, just as I believed that the heavens declared the glory of God's handiwork. Now I have seen that handiwork, and my faith is sorely troubled. I stare at the crucifix that hangs on the cabin wall above the Mark VI Computer, and
5 for the first time in my life I wonder if it is no more than an empty symbol. (1)
I have told no one yet, but the truth cannot be concealed. The facts are there for all to read, recorded on the countless miles of magnetic tape and the thousands of photographs we are carrying back to Earth. Other scientists can interpret them as easily as I can, and I am not who would condone that tampering with the truth
10 which often gave my order a bad name in the olden days. (2)
The crew are already sufficiently depressed: I wonder how they will take this ultimate irony. Few of them have any religious faith, yet they will not relish using this final weapon in their campaign against me – that private, good-natured, but fundamentally serious, war which lasted all the way from Earth. It amused them to have a Jesuit
15 as chief astrophysicist: Dr. Chandler, for instance, could never get over it (why are medical men such notorious atheists?). Sometimes he would meet me on the oberservation deck, where the lights are always low so that the stars shine with undiminished glory. He would come up to me in the gloom and stand staring out of the great oval port, while the heavens crawled slowly around us as the ship turned
20 end over end with the residual spin we had never bothered to correct. (3)
'Well, Father,' he would say at last, 'it goes on forever and forever, and perhaps *Something* made it. But how you can believe that Something has a special interest in us and our miserable little world – that just beats me.' Then the argument would start, while the stars and nebulae would swing around us in silent, endless arcs
25 beyond the flawlessly clear plastic of the observation port (4) – –
We knew, of course, what the Phoenix Nebula was. Every year, in our galaxy alone, more than a hundred stars explode, blazing for a few hours or days with thousands of times their normal brilliance before they sink back into death and obscurity. Such are the ordinary novae – the commonplace disasters of the universe. I have
30 recorded the spectrograms and light curves of dozens since I started working at the Lunar Observatory. (5)
But three or four times en every thousand years occurs something beside which even a nova pales into total insignificance. (6)
When a star becomes a *supernova*, it may for a little while outshine all the massed
35 suns of the galaxy. The Chinese astronomers watched this happen in A.D. 1054, not knowing what it was they saw. Five centuries later, in 1572, a supernova blazed in Cassiopeia so brilliantly that it was visible in the daylight sky. There have been three more in the thousand years that have passed since then. (7)
Our mission was to visit the remnants of such a catastrophe, to reconstruct the
40 events that led up to it, and, if possible, to learn its cause. We came slowly in through the concentric shells of gas that had been blasted out six thousand years before,

yet were expanding still. They were immensely hot, radiating ever now with a fierce violet light, but were far too tenuous to do us any damage. When the star had exploded, its outer layers had been driven upward with such speed that they had
45 escaped completely from its gravitational field. Now they formed a hollow shell large enough to engulf a thousand solar systems, and at its center burned the tiny, fantastic object which the star hat now become – a White dwarf, smaller than the Earth, yet weighing a million times as much. (8) – –
No one seriously expected to find planets. If there had been any before the
50 explosion, they would have been boiled into puffs of vapor, and their substance lost in the greater wreckage of the star itself. But we made the automatic search, as we always do when approaching an unknown sun, and presently we found a single small world circling the star at an immense distance. It must have been the Pluto of this vanished solar system, orbiting on the frontiers of the night. Too far from the
55 central sun ever to have known life, its remoteness had saved it from the fate of all its lost companions. (9)
The passing fires hat seared its rocks and burned away the mantle of frozen gas that must have covered it in the days before the disaster. We landed, and we found the Vault. (10)
60 Its builders had made sure that we should. (11)
It will take us gererations to examine all the treasures that were placed in the Vault. They had plenty of time to prepare, for their sun must have given its first warnings many years before the final detonation. Everything that they wished to preserve, all the fruit of their genius, they brought here to this distant world in the days before
65 the end, hoping that some other race would find it and that they would not be utterly forgotten. Would we have done as well, or would we have been too lost in our own misery to give thought to a future we could never see or share? (12)
If only they had had a little more time! They could travel freely enough between the planets of their own sun, but they had not yet learned to cross the interstellar gulfs,
70 and the nearest solar system was a hundred light-years away. Yet even had they possessed the secret of the Transfinite Drive, no more than a few millions could have been saved. Perhaps it was better thus. (13)
Even if they had not been so disturbingly human as their sculpture shows, we could not have helped admiring them and grieving for their fate. They left thousands of
75 visual records and the machines for projecting them, together with elaborate pictorial instructions from which it will not be difficult to learn their written language. We have examined many of these records, and brought to life for the first time in six thousand years the warmth and beauty of a civilization that in many ways must have been superior to our own. Perhaps they only showed us the best, and one
80 can hardly blame them. But their worlds were very lovely, and their cities were built with a grace that matches anything of man's. We have watched them at work and play, and listened to their musical speech sounding across the centuries. One scene

is still before my eyes – a group of children on a beach of strange blue sand, playing in the waves as children play on Earth. Curious whiplike trees line the shore, and some very large animal is wading in the shallows yet attracting no attention at all. (14)

And sinking into the sea, still warm and friendly and lifegiving, is the sun that will turn traitor and obliterate all this innocent happiness. (15)

Perhaps if we had not been so far from home and so vulnerable to loneliness, we should not have been so deeply moved. Many of us had seen the ruins of ancient civilizations on other worlds, but they had never affected us so profoundly. This tragedy was unique. It is one thing for a race to fail and die, as nations and cultures have done no Earth. But to be destroyed so completely in the full flower of its achievement, leaving no survivors – how could that be reconciled with the mercy of God? (16)

My colleagues have asked me that, and I have given what answers I can. Perhaps you could have done better, Father Loyola, but I have found nothing in the *Exercitia Spiritualia* that helps me here. They were not an evil people: I do not know what gods they worshiped, if indeed they worshiped any. But I have looked back at them across the centuries, and have watched while the loveliness they used their last strength to preserve was brought forth again into the light of their shrunken sun. They could have taught us much: why were they destroyed? (17)

I know the answers that my colleagues will give when they get back to Earth. They will say that the universe has no purpose and no plan, that since a hundred suns explode every year in our galaxy, at this very moment some race is dying in the depths of space. Whether that race has done good or evil during its lifetime will make no difference in the end: there is no divine justice, for there is no God. (18)

Yet, of course, what we have seen proves nothing of the sort. Anyone who argues thus is being swayed by emotion, not logic. God has no need to justify His actions to man. He who built the universe can destroy it when He chooses. It is arrogance – it is perilously near blasphemy – for us to say what He may or may not do. (19)

This I could have accepted, hard, though it is to look upon whole worlds and peoples thrown into the furnace. But there comes a point when even the deepest faith must falter, and now, as I look at the calculations lying before me, I know I have reached that point at last. (20)

We could not tell, before we reached the nebula, how long ago the explosion took place. Now, from the astronomical evidence and the record in the rocks of that one surviving planet, I have been able to date it very exactly. I know in what year the light of this colossal conflagration reached our Earth. I know how brilliantly the supernova whose corpse now dwindles behind our speeding ship once shone in terrestrial skies. I know how it must have blazed low in the east before sunrise, like a beacon in that oriental dawn. (21)

There can be no reasonable doubt: the ancient mystery is solved at last. Yet, oh

God, there were so many stars you could have used. What was the need to give these people to the fire that the symbol of their passing might shine above Bethlehem? (22)

1) After reading the story you will want to do this word game: Find the hidden three-word sentence!

To be able to do so you must first find 12 wanted words (or terms consisting of two words) in the text; then you must pick a certain letter out of each and put these letters in a consecutive line; they will spell out a sentence you will perhaps agree with! All the words are astronomical terms!

Word Game

word no.:	consists of ( ) letters, the first letter being:	it can be found in paragraph no.:	pick out letter no.:	put letter here
1	p_____(s) (6)	13	5	_____
2	n____ (5)	5	1	_____
3	l____-____ (5 + 4)	13	3	_____
4	P____ (5)	9	2	_____
5	o____(ing) (5)	9	4	_____
6	o_____ (11)	5	3	_____
7	a_____ (14)	3	7	_____
8	i_____ g____ (12 + 4)	13	1	_____
9	u_____ (8)	18	7	_____
10	w____ ____ (5 + 5)	8	10	_____
11	n_____ (6)	5	4	_____
12	a_____(s) (10)	7	6	_____

Found sentence: _____

_____

2) Write down at least 8 questions on the contents of the text and put them to your classmates.
3) Do you agree with the narrator that the "Star of Bethlehem" was a supernova?

30 THE STAR OF BETHLEHEM MYSTERY

Note on the Text

We have read in Text 29 that the Jesuit who – as chief astrophysicist – participates in the exploration of the Phoenix Nebula discovers that the star of Bethlehem which shone on Christ's birth was a supernova, i.e. the colossal explosion of an old star, which produces such a brilliance of light that it may outshine all the massed suns of the galaxy. The imaginary Jesuit living in the far future finds sure evidence that this supernova was identical with the star of Bethlehem. But how do the experts in the year 1986 explain the star? Do the historical facts support such a recognition made in the far future?
In this book *The Star of Bethlehem Mystery,* Dent & Sons LTD, London 1979, *David Hughes* has tried to shed light on the mystery. The following extract gathers together the most important aspects of Hughes's work.

MANY CELESTIAL OBJECTS have been put forward as possible candidates for the role of star of Bethlehem. These include a triple conjunction of the giant planets Saturn and Jupiter, and a nova, but Venus, Halley's comet, other comets, fireballs and the variable star Mira have all had their supporters. Before we explain in detail
5 the astronomical features of each of these objects, let us briefly list the conditions they have to satisfy.
    (1) The star had to appear first to the wise men while they were in their own country.
    (2) They saw it rising 'acronychally'. This only occurs once a year for any specific star or for an external planet in the ecliptic. The star is just seen to rise in the east
10 as the Sun sets in the west. It then stays in the sky all through the night as it moves in an arc across the heavens from east to west.
    (3) The star had a message, probably astrological in nature, which told the wise men that the King of the Jews had been born. The Magi had been expecting this birth. Even so, the message must have been clear enough and unambiguous
15 enough to make them plan and carry out a long and difficult journey to Jerusalem.
    (4) The 'star' probably appeared twice: first when the Magi were at home and secondly when they left Jerusalem after the audience with Herod. There is a distinct probability that it became unobservable or 'went out' between the two appearances.
    (5) The first appearance was rather insignificant, something that the general public
20 would miss. Herod had not seen it and it had not been brought to his notice.
    (6) The 'star' went before them and 'stood over' Bethlehem.
    (7) According to the Protoevangelium of James the star was very bright, and sufficiently so to dim the surrounding stars. It must be remembered, however, that in a much earlier account St Matthew indicated that there was nothing particularly
25 special about the star. Matthew's account is much more likely to be correct.
    (8) From our historical investigation of the time of the birth of Christ we can conclude that the second appearance of the star, which led the Magi from Jerusalem to the

newborn baby Jesus at Bethlehem, occurred in 7 BC. If we consider all the possible errors inherent in this calculation we must extend the possible birth period to one between early 8 BC and late 6 BC. The first appearance of the star, the one seen by the Magi in their own country, preceded the second appearance by as little as four months, which correponds with our calculation for the minimum journey time of the Magi, or by as much as two years, which fits the longer possible journey times and the ancient Jewish legend of the holy family's flight to Egypt.

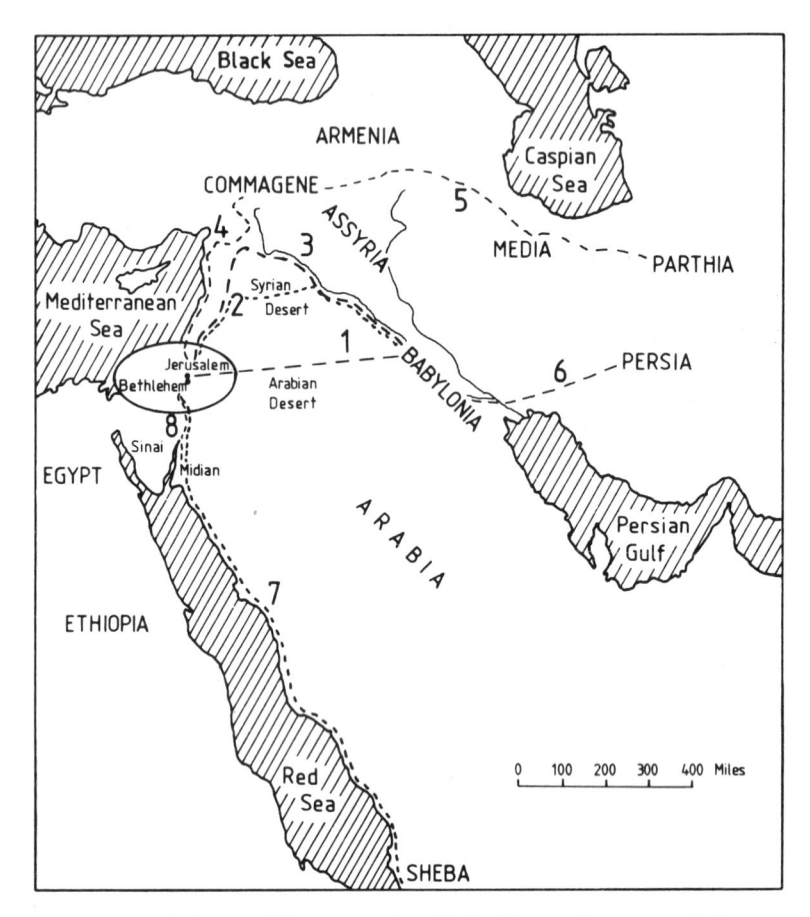

Fig. 1 Eight possible routes taken by the Magi as they journeyed to Jerusalem and Bethlehem

These are the conditions that have to be satisfied, assuming of course that Matthew's account is correct. We now have to search the astronomical records for the years 10 BC to 6 BC to see if anything resembling the star of Bethlehem was seen and recorded. If nothing can be found in the records, we shall need to look for some astronomical phenomenon which is well known today and which could account for the eight points listed above. Unfortunately not one of the phenomena mentioned at the beginning of the chapter satisfies all the conditions, though some are much better candidates than others. It is also important to remember that there are very few actual new suggestions as to what the star of Bethlehem was. Recent research has tended to take old suggestions and re-examine their significance in the light of modern knowledge.

The most convincing suggestion is that the star of Bethlehem was a *triple conjunction of Saturn and Jupiter*. These two planets, which are members of the Sun's solar system just as our planet Earth is, occasionally appear to come together in the sky. This is a slow process: they approach each other, usually stay together for a time and then separate. When they are together they are said to be *in conjunction*. On more rare occasions Saturn and Jupiter come together not just once but three times, in about a year, to make a 'triple conjunction'. One of these occurred in 7 BC, between May and December, which is exactly the time when we think Jesus was born.

The principal dates in the Saturn-Jupiter-Pisces conjunction that occurred at the birth of Christ.

Event	Date	Planetary separation (degrees)
Heliacal setting	about 18 February	9.9
Heliacal rising	about 11 March	7.7
1st conjunction	27 May	0.98
1st stationary point of Saturn	6 July	2,5
1st stationary point of Jupiter	17 Juli	2.8
Mid conjunction	3 September	2.0
Acronychal rising	14–15 September 7 BC	1.34
2nd conjunction	6 October	0.98
Mid-point of 2nd and 3rd conjunction	31 October	1.42
2nd stationary point of Jupiter	11 November	1.44
2nd stationary point of Saturn	19 November	1.46
3rd conjunction	1 December	1.05
Jupiter-Saturn-Mars massing	mid February ⎫ 6 BC	6.4
Heliacal setting	about 13 March ⎭	8.5

The sequence of events would be as follows. The Magi, probably being Zoroastrian priests living in Babylon, have predicted most of the events given in the table above and have decided among themselves that the new Messiah of the Jews is to be born on Tuesday 15 September 7 BC. They have made up their minds to visit the newborn babe and set out on their journey at the end of the hot summer of 7 BC. On their way they see the acronychal rising, which coincides with the birth of Jesus. The events recorded in Luke – the circumcision and Mary's purification – would

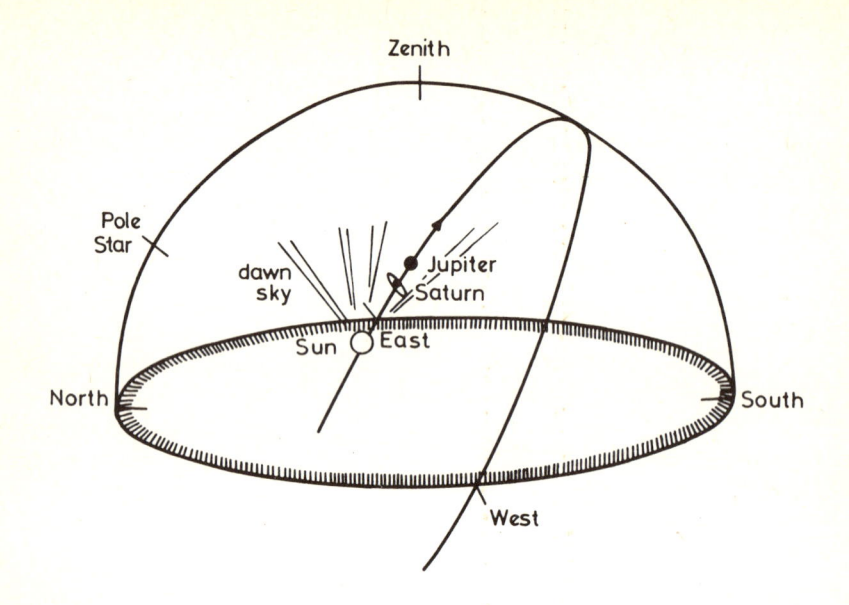

The heliacal rising

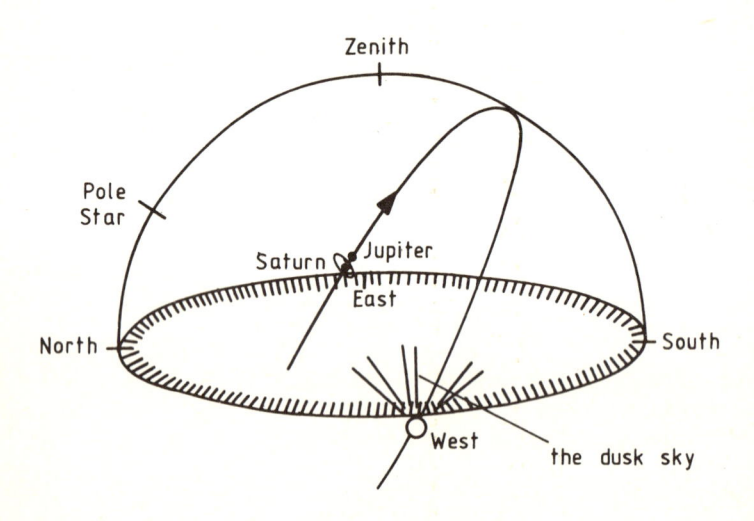

The acronychal rising

follow on Sunday 24 September and on about Wednesday 25 October respectively. The interlacing of the nativity accounts in Matthew and Luke indicates that the Magi visited the holy family some time after the purification. The only predicted astronomical event that happened after the proposed date of the purification were the second stationary points of Jupiter and Saturn (see table above). These occurred in mid November. Perhaps it was the observation of these stationary points that made the Magi rejoice. If so, the Jerusalem to Bethlehem journey took place some time in the period 11 to 19 November. After the third conjunction, an event which the Magi could not have predicted accurately, the two planets separated quickly, obviously indicating that the momentous event was at an end.

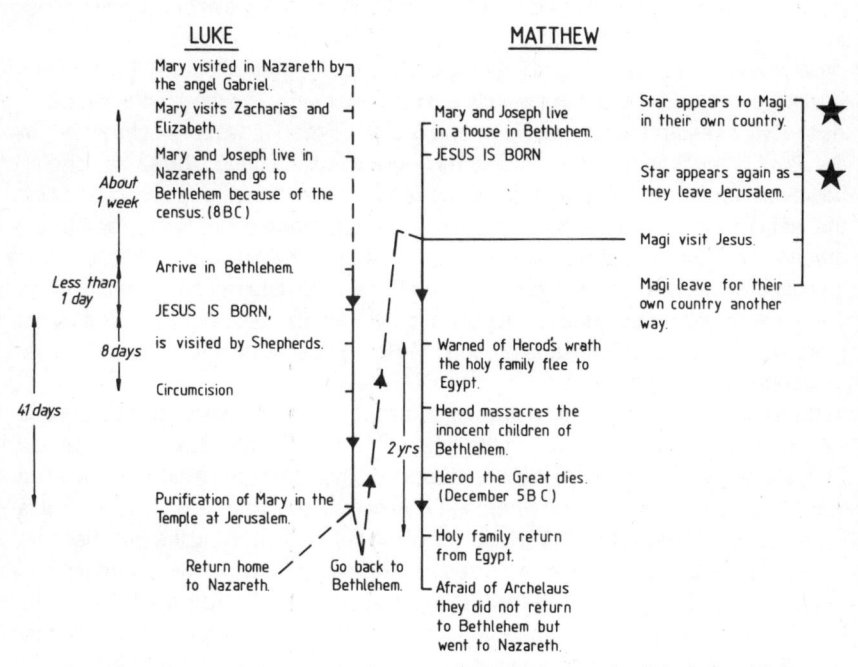

Fig. 5 One of the ways of integrating the nativity stories in the gospels of Matthew and Luke

How does Herod come into this picture? Herod called the Magi to him and 'inquired of them diligently what time the star appeared'. According to the sequence given above, this audience would probably have taken place just before mid November. What would the answer have been to this question? Probably, 'We think that the acronychal rising of Saturn and Jupiter on 15 September announced the birth of the King of the Jews, but the two planets have been close companions in Pisces since April of this year'. Herod remembered these two dates and a few weeks later, when he realized that the Magi had tricked him and had gone back to Babylon by a different route, he regarded both as possible dates for either the conception or the birth and to be on the safe side he killed all the children under the age of two. Subsequently Herod died in December 5 BC or March 4 BC, about one and a half years after the birth of Jesus so there are no problems of chronology on this point. Of all the phenomena which are among the candidates for the star of Bethlehem, the only one which has any significant *astrological meaning* is the 7 BC conjunction of Saturn and Jupiter in Pisces. We know that conjunctions, the coming together of two planets against the celestial background, are the focal points in astrological birth charts. In astrology a conjunction gives strong emphasis to the characteristics of the planets and signs involved, and the main mental reactions and the feelings induced by the planets are said to interact strongly, with positive or negative stress according to the sign and house position of the planets concerned.

What would Saturn, Jupiter and Pisces signify to the Magi astrologers? The problem is that we know little about the details of astrology nearly two thousand years ago. As the New Testament scholar Raymond Brown points out, we cannot be sure how the Jews in the time of Jesus made their zodiacal calculations. The same scholar, however, goes on to say that 'Pisces is a constellation sometimes associated with the last days and with the Hebrews, while Jupiter, an object of particular interest among *Parthian* astrologers, was associated with the world ruler and Saturn was identified as the star of the Amorites of the Syria-Palestine region'. The claim has been made that this conjunction might have led Parthian astrologers to predict that there would appear in Palestine among the Hebrews a world ruler of the last days, an apocalyptic king.

In *Babylonian* astrology Saturn was closely associated with Shamash, the Sun, and named "sun of the night". During the time of the Neo-Babylonian empire the god Marduk, who was manifest in the planet Jupiter, also developed a close association with the Sun and occasionally Shamash was called "the Marduk of justice". In this way Justice and Right, the divine qualities of the cult of Saturn and the Sun, became linked with the planet Jupiter as well, and as *Jewish* astrology was deeply influenced and shaped by Babylonian traditions, this linking carried over. Both the Babylonians and the Jews identified the planets Jupiter and Saturn with "Sedeq", the justice that vindicates the righteous and punishes the guilty. The Messiah is to be the instrument by which this is to come to pass. A Saturn-Jupiter conjunction in Pisces was therefore obviously the sign associated with the coming of the Jewish Messiah.

We have here ample justification for concluding that the Jupiter-Saturn conjunction in Pisces had a strong, clear astrological message. To Babylonians and Jews alike it heralded the coming of the Messiah, a man of righteousness who would save the world.

The message was unambiguous and obviously impressed the Magi with the importance of the event and the necessity to journey to Jerusalem and Bethlehem. It is also clear that it was only the Jupiter-Saturn-Pisces conjunction that had this message. All other astronomical occurrences around the time of Jesus (including Halley's Comet which appeared in the autumn of 12 BC and has often been suggested as a possible star of Bethlehem) do not convey this message, and this alone is ample justification for ruling them out as candidates for the role of star of Bethlehem.

Annotations
(The words marked * should be memorized.)

celestial heavenly – – **variable** varying; changeable – – **arc** Bogen – – **insignificant** unimportant – – **proto-** erst; ur- – – **to dim** make or become less bright – – **account** report – – **investigation** examination – – **inherent (in)** existing as a natural and permanent part or quality of – – **to extend** make longer; enlarge – – **to precede** come or go before (in time and place) – – **record** here: Beleg – – **to occur** happen – – **Pisces** ['paɪsɪz] twelfth sign of the zodiac (also called the fish) – – **the signs of the zodiac** – – **heliacal** see p. 276 – – **acronychal** see p. 276

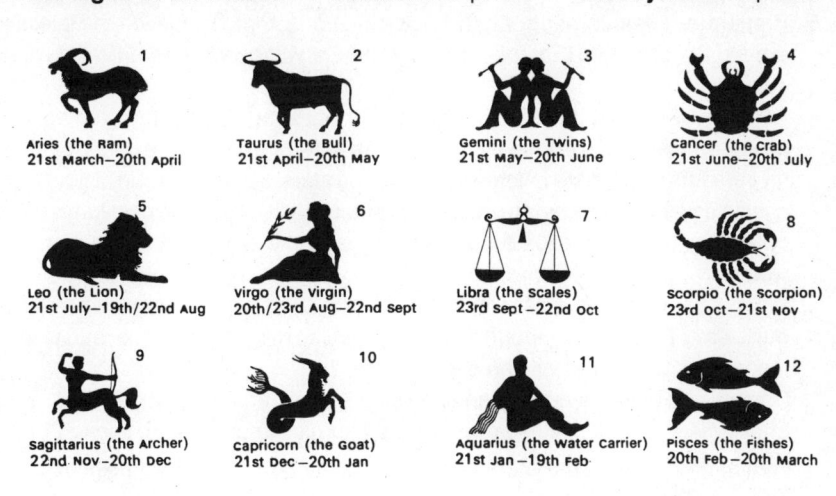

1 Aries (the Ram) 21st March–20th April
2 Taurus (the Bull) 21st April–20th May
3 Gemini (the Twins) 21st May–20th June
4 Cancer (the Crab) 21st June–20th July
5 Leo (the Lion) 21st July–19th/22nd Aug
6 Virgo (the Virgin) 20th/23rd Aug–22nd Sept
7 Libra (the Scales) 23rd Sept–22nd Oct
8 Scorpio (the Scorpion) 23rd Oct–21st Nov
9 Sagittarius (the Archer) 22nd Nov–20th Dec
10 Capricorn (the Goat) 21st Dec–20th Jan
11 Aquarius (the Water Carrier) 21st Jan–19th Feb
12 Pisces (the Fishes) 20th Feb–20th March

the signs of the zodiac

– – **to predict** foretell – – **to coincide (with)** happen at the same time – – **circumcision** Beschneidung – – **purification** religious ceremony in the course of which a symbolic washing of the body and soul was effected – – **stationary point** the point in a planet's apparent path among the stars where for a brief time it seems to be motionless because it is changing from direct to retrograde (= rückwärtsgehend) motion or vice versa – – **to interlace** verweben; verflechten – – **momentous** important; serious – – **diligent** careful – – **conception** Empfängnis – – **subsequently** afterwards – – **focal** main – – **to induce** cause; bring about – – **Parthia** ancient country of NE Iran conquered by the Persians in AD 226 – – **Amorites** ancient Semitic people that settled in Mesopotamia, Syria, and Palestine as early as the 3rd millennium B. C. and established a kingdom, with its capital at Mari on the middle Euphrates, which was at the heigh of its power from approximately 2200 to 1700 B.C. – – **to vindicate** show or prove the truth, justice, validity, etc. (of s.th. that has been attacked or disputed) – – **to herald** ['herld] proclaim the approach of

Assignments

1. Which celestial phenomenon is examined in our extract as possible candidate for the star of Bethlehem?
2. Paraphrase the author's arguments for this celestial phenomenon as a serious candidate.
3. Do you think his arguments are convincing? Can you discover any weak points?
4. On p. 274 you can see a drawing which shows the different routes the magi might have taken. Describe them in your own words. What does the drawing tell us about the magi's possible native countries? What do you know about the cultural significance of these countries in ancient times? If you don't know, use reference books.
5. Prepare a research paper on the political and historical situation in Palestine around Christ's birth. (For reference use the *Encyclopaedia Britannica* and other sources.)
6. Astrology is almost as old as mankind. For ages men have attributed specific power and influence on the events and the lives of people here on earth to the movements and constellations of planets and stars. Famous men in history often consulted astrologers before making important decisions. Even nowadays many politicians and businessmen are said to take the advice of "wise men and women".

    What is your opinion of astrology? Do the stars and planets have an impact on our lives? (Think of the moon!) If not, why then do millions of people read weekly magazines to learn what "the stars foretell"?
7. Comets and meteors have often been considered harbingers of disasters. (See Shakespeare's *Julius Caesar* where Caliphurnia asserts [Act II, scene 2]:

    "When beggars die, there are no comets seen; the heavens themselves blaze forth the death of princes."
    Halley's Comet was blamed for the influenza epidemics in 1910 and the 1530AD European plague; the Roman destruction of Jerusalem in 66AD; civil war in China, 218AD; and Genghis Khan's 1222AD invasion of India and China. In 1456AD, Pope Callixtus III prayed for deliverance from the comet: war had broken out between Turkey and Christian Europe.)
    In modern times, it's especially the sects which stress the dangers of such celestial phenomena (see below). Can you imagine why?

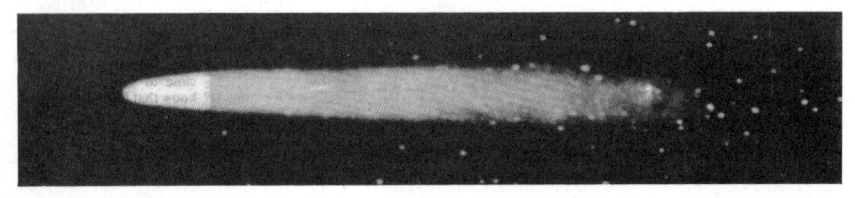

A photograph of Halley's in 1910: a flying museum stocked with precious artifacts from the very earliest moment of the solar system.

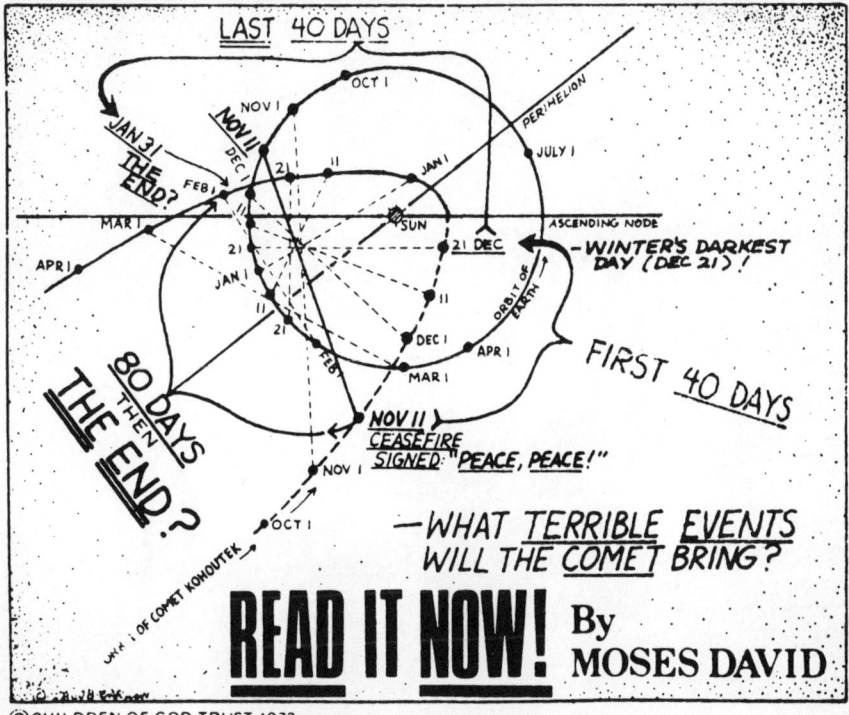

Alarm at the approach of Comet Kohoutek
Source: D. Hughes, *The Star of Bethlehem Mystery*, p. 90.

8. Is there any justification for the fear of comets and meteors?
9. In March 1986, Halley's comet approached earth. This time mankind awaited the celestial object in a mood which was very different from that in 1910 when some people expected to be killed by cyanogen-gas poisoning as the earth passed through the comet's tail. Why was that?

SOURCES

A *Texts:* Sources are given in *Note on the Text* or underneath the texts.
B *Pictures, Charts and Games:*
1. p. 7: *The Times,* London, January 21, 1986.
2. p. 9: *Loc. Cit.*
3. p. 18: *Daily Mirror,* London, December 9, 1985.
4. p. 19: *Time International,* Amsterdam, January 20, 1986.
5. p. 19: *Loc. Cit.*
6. p. 22: *World & Press,* Eilers & Schünemann, Bremen, 1981.
7. p. 22: *The Times,* London, February 5, 1986.
8. p. 22: *World & Press,* 1981.
9. p. 23: *World & Press,* no. 833, 1981.
10. p. 24: Nicholas Garland in *Karikatur in fünf Jahrhunderten – Bild als Waffe,* herausgegeben von Gerhard Langemeyer u. a., Prestel Verlag, München 1984.
11. p. 32/33: *US News & World Report,* Washington, DC, December 23, 1985.
12. p. 34: *Loc. Cit.*
13. p. 39: *World & Press,* 1983.
14. p. 40: *World & Press,* 1984.
15. p. 58: *The New Yorker Magazine,* Inc., New York, 1973.
16. p. 78: Michael Brückner, Schriesheim/Bergstraße, 1986.
17. p. 95: *Discover,* Time Inc., New York, February 1986.
18. p. 100: *Punch Publications Limited,* London, February 1, 1978.
19. p. 100: *Op. Cit.*
20. p. 105: *World & Press,* July 1, 1986.
21. p. 109: *The New Yorker,* Album of Drawings 1925–1975, The Viking Press, New York 1975.
22. p. 110: *Punch,* February 1, 1978.
23. p. 111: *Time,* February 28, 1983.
24. p. 112: *Business Week,* McGraw-Hill Inc., New York, July 22, 1985.
25. p. 113: *Op. Cit.*
26. p. 114: *South,* The Third World Magazine, South Publications Ltd., London, December 1985.
27. p. 115: *Discover,* July 1986.
28. p. 124: *The International Herald Tribune,* New York, Nov. 6, 1985.
29. p. 125: *Time,* February 1, 1982.
30. p. 126: *Op. Cit.*
31. p. 127: *Mannheimer Morgen,* 1984. Translation of text by the authors.
32. p. 146: *Soldiers,* US Army Magazine, Alexandria, Virginia, April 1983.
33. p. 147: Dick Browne: *Hägar, der Schreckliche,* Der große Hägar Superband, Goldmann Verlag, 1985. Translation by the authors.
34. p. 150: *Time Magazine,* April 1985.
35. p. 153: *Stern Magazin,* Hamburg 1982.
36. p. 161: *US News & World Report,* August 18, 1986.
37. p. 162: *Op. Cit.*
38. p. 163: *Punch,* March 6, 1985.
39. p. 164: *The New Yorker,* Album of Drawings, New York 1975.
40. p. 166: *International Harald Tribune,* January 16, 1986.

41. p. 168: *Spotlight,* Verlag Dr. E. Müller & Co., Herrsching, no. 8, 1986.
42. p. 172: St. Thomas More, *Utopia,* ed. by E. Surtz, Yale University Press, New Haven 1964.
43. p. 178: *The Stars and Stripes,* December 12, 1985.
44. pp. 181/182: *Business Week,* February 18, 1985.
45. p. 190: *Time,* December 23, 1985.
46. p. 198: *The Times,* November 4, 1981.
47. pp. 206/207: *Reader's Digest,* US edition, Pleasantville, New York.
48. p. 208: *World & Press,* 1984.
49. pp. 220/221: *World & Press,* year of edition unknown.
50. p. 239: *Soldiers,* January 1985.
51. p. 247: *Der Spiegel,* Hamburg, Nr. 43, 1982.
52. p. 248: *MAD,* E.C. Publications, Inc., New York, September 1983.
53. p. 249: *Facts about America,* ed. by the Embassy of the USA, Washington.
54. p. 250: *Wirtschaft und Erziehung,* Heckners Verlag, Wolfenbüttel, Dezember 1982.
55. p. 259: *Time,* December 4, 1978.
56. p. 262: *Op. Cit.*
57. p. 274: D. Hughes, *The Star of Bethlehem Mystery,* Dent & Sons Ltd., London 1979.
58. p. 276: *Op. Cit.*
59. p. 277: *Op. Cit.*
60. p. 279: A. S. Hornby, *Oxford Advanced Learner's Dictionary,* London, OUP 1974.
61. p. 280: *Time,* December 16, 1985.
62. p. 281: D. Hughes, *op. cit.*

NOTIZEN

NOTIZEN

NOTIZEN

P. Müller / W. Rumpf

Modern World – Fact and Fiction

Ein Reader für den Englischunterricht der gymnasialen Oberstufe in 3 Bänden

Das Werk enthält Texte aus vielen Wissensgebieten unserer modernen Welt, die vom angloamerikanischen Standpunkt aus einen fundierten Einblick gewähren. Es „lebt" von der Spannung zwischen **fact** und **fiction**, zwischen Sachtext und literarischem Text.

Volume I: Man and Nature – Man and Technology

138 Seiten, DM 15,80, Bestellnummer 535
Lehrerbegleitband: 99 Seiten, DM 9,80, Bestellnummer 536

Volume II: Man and Mate – Man against Man

208 Seiten, DM 15,80, Bestellnummer 537
Lehrerbegleitband: 160 Seiten, DM 12,50, Bestellnummer 538

Volume III: Man and Economy – Man and Humanities – Man and Belief

288 Seiten, DM 17,80, Bestellnummer 539
Lehrerbegleitband: 160 Seiten, DM 12,50, Bestellnummer 540

MANZ VERLAG · Anzinger Str. 1 · 8000 München 80